D0209439

To Margaret, who shared many
of these experiences with me

Contents

Illustrations

Introduction

To many, the idea of American communism seems a paradox. Conventional wisdom tells us that communism is something foreign; one cannot be a Communist and still be a good American. Yet somewhere between five hundred thousand and one million Americans have joined the Communist Party of the United States (CPUSA) since its formation in 1919, and many more have supported its policies and activities at one time or another. At the height of its influence in the mid-1940s, the CPUSA had a membership of nearly eighty thousand, and many of these people were acknowledged leaders in trade unions, fraternal groups, and political and community organizations. As a personal experience, then, American communism has touched the lives of thousands; as a political influence, it has affected the lives of millions.[1]

Many observers have likened the Party to a revolving door through which members passed quickly in and out. During the 1930s, for example, turnover ran over 50 percent of total membership.[2] Some, however, stayed on to become cadres, lifelong revolutionaries making extreme personal sacrifices to advance the goals of socialism. Steve Nelson was one of these.

Steve Nelson's life is virtually a chronicle of class conflict in the twentieth century. His story takes us from the hard-working farmers of a small Croatian village to the unemployed miners of eastern Pennsylvania's anthracite coalfields; from the battlegrounds of civil war Spain to the jails of cold war Pittsburgh; and from a tiny cell of Communist auto workers meeting in the back of a Detroit cooperative restaurant to the upper reaches of Party leadership in New York City.

It is the typicality of Nelson's experience, however, rather than its exceptional qualities, that makes it most significant. In many respects his story is that of the Party's rank and file, and particularly of the immigrant workers who represented the majority of Party members throughout the 1920s and early 1930s.[3] For most of his life, Nelson remained a working-class organizer, reluctantly accepting leadership only after being convinced that the interests of the movement were at stake. When he went to work full-time for the Party in the early 1930s, it was as an organizer of the unemployed, facing the difficult task of converting theory and official policy into successful practice. He was in his element on the streets of Chicago and Detroit or in the anthracite mining towns, but decidedly not in the Party's Manhattan headquarters. Nelson came up from the ranks but remained close to them even as he led. His view of the Party is that of a foot soldier rather than that of a general in the revolutionary movement.

One way of understanding the broader context of Nelson's story is to consider simultaneously three parallel processes: Nelson's own development, that of radical immigrant workers as a group, and that of the Party. The dynamic relationship between individual, class, and Party can help clarify the experience of American communism.

Every immigrant, like Steve Nelson in 1920, faced a confusing array of new impressions and strange conditions. People who had lived in European industrial cities or worked in factories may have been less disoriented than those from farming villages, but all of them looked for ways in which to make sense of their new environment. Each immigrant had to undergo "Americanization," a period of adjustment to life in urban-industrial America. For some, revolutionary socialism offered both an explanation of how American society worked and an organizational structure that could help the newcomer in this difficult period of adjustment.

When Nelson struggled to understand his own experiences and what he saw around him—war, racism, poverty—working-class radicals provided him with answers. The world war, they said, had not been a crusade for democracy but a mindless slaughter of fellow workers in the interests of the rich. Racism was one more tool used by the boss to divide workers from one another. Poverty was not a natural condition but the result of the exploitation of one class at the hands of another, something to be abolished, not endured. Nelson's assimilation into American society came through the Communist Party, which during the 1920s and 1930s offered to thousands of immigrant workers its own version of Americanization.

There were also practical problems, such as the English language. Many immigrants enrolled in English and citizenship classes in public evening schools or at the YMCA. Others picked the language up informally on the job or in the neighborhood or never learned it at all. Still others learned to read and write as Nelson did, through the socialist movement. Their primers were the Marxist texts, Party propaganda, and radical literature handed around by their comrades. Their maiden speeches were delivered not in civics class but on soapboxes on street corners in the slums of America's industrial cities and towns. Their writing exercises were the leaflets and shop papers that they produced to win fellow workers to their views. For those who had never known the opportunity of an education, the Party provided study groups and workers' schools. It encouraged self-confidence, especially among those who, like Nelson, showed potential as working-class leaders. It opened up the world of learning at a time when few others seemed to care.

Nor did the Party ignore the needs of the heart. During the 1920s foreign-born Communists enjoyed a vigorous social life based on the cultures of the Party's foreign language federations. Croatian-American communism, for example, was not all study groups and picket lines; it was also picnics and dances, cruises and plays. While all these activities were infused with the message of class struggle, young immigrants found in them people with whom they had much in common besides politics.

But communism offered immigrant workers more than literacy, culture, comradeship, and the opportunity to develop as leaders, more even than a key to understanding their own situation. It offered them a way out, a solution to the problems they faced. The Party was one means of fighting back. In a world of chronic unemployment, low wages, dangerous work, and discrimination, the Communist Party provided the vision of a more just society and inspired the determination to make this vision a reality. This above all else is what won the loyalty of Steve Nelson and thousands of other immigrant workers and sustained them in the face of overwhelming odds.

The Communist Party moved through its own kind of Americanization, beginning in the late 1920s and reaching a high point in World War II. It evolved from a tiny underground sect, based almost exclusively on foreign-born revolutionaries, into a large, broad-based political movement that brought its members into the mainstream of American life. This evolution was partly the result of conscious policy decisions. In 1928 the foreign language federations were replaced by a structure based on neighborhood and workplace, and during the mid-1930s the popular front strategy freed Communists to work in mass organizations such as the CIO with activists representing a broad spectrum of political views. In the 1940s strong Party support for the American war effort helped it to overcome, at least temporarily, its image as an alien political group. But the Americanization of the Communist Party was also the product of its own expansion and increasingly diverse membership and the interrelationship between this new membership and Communist theory and practice.

Even during the 1920s, Party membership was in itself a step away from the ethnic segregation of the immigrant ghetto. It was at Party gatherings that Nelson first got to know Italian, Jewish, and both black and white native-born workers. The Party's switch to industrial organizing in the late twenties accelerated the breakdown of ethnic barriers among its members and offered an opportunity to recruit more American-born workers.

The Comintern's so-called Third Period (1928–1935), prior to the adoption of a popular front strategy, is often remembered as the most sectarian stage in the CPUSA's history. The Communists attacked Socialists and other leftists as "social fascists," launched dual "revolutionary" unions to compete with those of the American Federation of Labor, and formulated the goal of an independent Negro state in the southern Black Belt. The disabilities that organizers faced in trying to apply such policies emerge in Nelson's description of the Communists' National Miners Union in the early 1930s. But his experiences also suggest that in this period the Party laid the basis for much of its success over the next fifteen years. Here are the roots of what Communists called "mass organizing" among industrial workers, the unemployed, and blacks in the Deep South. Field organizers stressed wages, welfare, and civil rights, not the establishment of a Soviet America. With the beginning of this mass work in the early thirties, particularly organizing of the unemployed, the Party expanded its membership to include many more blacks and second-generation ethnics. By 1936 the CPUSA had more than forty-five thousand members, and for the first time a majority were native-born.[4] The influx of these members, who focused far more on domestic social and economic grievances than on international and theoretical concerns, strengthened the Party's own shift away from the ethnic and political sectarianism of the twenties to a popular front approach.

During the 1930s this younger generation of Communists constituted much of the leadership for the mass organizations that provided popular pressure for New Deal welfare and labor reforms. After building a national network of unemployed councils based in city neighborhoods and industrial towns, Communists worked with Socialists and other radicals to establish in 1935 the Workers' Alliance, the largest organization of unemployed workers in the country. The Party also provided many of the CIO organizers who built industrial unions in the steel, electrical, meat-packing, and other mass production industries by the Second World War. Using its connections in the black and immigrant communities, the Party mobilized fraternal groups that provided invaluable support for the CIO in its early years. In Minnesota, Wisconsin, and elsewhere, Communists worked with liberal Democrats to create progressive electoral coalitions.[5]

As a result of this mass work of the thirties, the Party achieved its largest membership in history by the middle of the Second World War. Its success also left the veterans of these movements committed to a broad-based and flexible organizing strategy. For Nelson, the crucial experiences were organizing the unemployed in Chicago and Pennsylvania and serving as a commissar with the International Brigades during the Spanish Civil War.

This change in direction was accentuated by the Party's policies and the experiences of individual Communists during the war. The alliance between the Soviet Union and the United States allowed Party members to temporarily bridge the seemingly insurmountable gap between being an American and being a Communist. Working through the CIO unions and such black and ethnic organizations as the National Negro Congress and the American Slav Congress, both of which they had helped to create, Party activists mobilized working-class community support for the war. They pushed for greater productivity in the shops, urging workers to forgo their right to strike, and many Party members entered the armed forces. As a result Communists gained important recognition for their efforts and cemented a left-liberal partnership that found its counterpart abroad in the projected postwar cooperation of the Allied powers. These experiences culminated in the liquidation of the CPUSA in May 1944 and its reorganization as the Communist Political Association (CPA), which was designed more as a political pressure group within the New Deal coalition than a revolutionary vanguard.

The disintegration of the Soviet-American alliance in the course of 1945, however, undercut the concept behind the CPA and precipitated a reassertion of Soviet influence over the policies of the American Party. The reemergence of a sectarian position in the CPUSA coincided with the cold war at home and abroad. Increasingly isolated from the mass movements in which they had thrived during the thirties and the war years, Communist activists were vulnerable to attack by the government and right-wing forces. By the mid-fifties government prosecution and cold war hysteria had rendered the American Communist Party impotent.[6]

The significance of the communist experience in the era of the popular front lies both in the ability of the Party to recruit more successfully and in the political impact that the recruits had on the Party. Many who remained as cadres after the thirties led the fight to de-Stalinize the Party and reconstitute it on a more democratic basis following the international crisis of 1956. Khrushchev's disclosure of the Stalinist atrocities in the early part of that year, followed by the Soviet invasion of Hungary in the fall, rocked the international Communist movement. Long repressed doubts about the Hitler-Stalin Pact and the Soviet purges of the thirties now burst to the surface. Calling for a break with the tradition of subservience to the Soviet Party and a fundamental reassessment of the concept of democratic centralism, these reformers sought a new road to socialism based on the cultural and political realities of postwar America.[7] Although their efforts failed, similar movements in Europe and elsewhere have produced more democratic and autonomous Communist parties. Many of the ideas now commonly associated with the term *Eurocommunism* appeared in the program supported by a majority of American Communists during the CPUSA's 1956–1957 crisis. The campaign to transform the Party originated in the isolation endured by this generation of mass leaders in the McCarthy era. This fact has never emerged more clearly than in Nelson's description of his own experiences when on trial and imprisoned for sedition in Pittsburgh.

Until recently, most historians of the CPUSA have conformed to either the "totalitarian" school of interpretation or the "pick-and-choose" school. Those adhering to the former, the prevailing view, have generally seen the Party as a Soviet puppet and its cadres as "malleable objects" of the Party leadership. Practitioners of the pick-and-choose approach, usually political radicals, have rifled through the Party's history looking for failures and successes that will support their own analyses.[8] Perhaps the greatest strength of Nelson's story is that it makes the successes and failures of the Party's history understandable as the product of human agency and individual initiative as well as external political factors. It forces the reader to discard simplification and accept the development of the Communist Party as a complex process. While Nelson substantiates the role of the Soviet Union in influencing the American Party, he offers a counterpoint—that much of the politics of the American Communist movement came not from Moscow but from its involvement in the social struggles of the times.

Work on this book began almost four years ago, but our relations with Steve Nelson go back a decade. In 1970, one of us, Rob Ruck, was living in Pittsburgh awaiting trial on charges growing out of a courtroom melee with police following an antidraft rally. The media, in the convention of the times, had dubbed the defendants the Pittsburgh Five. A friend and fellow activist, Bob Nelson, introduced his father to the defendants as a member of the original Pittsburgh Five, who had been charged with conspiring to overthrow the government under the Smith Act some two decades earlier. The meeting opened a door to the recent past. In the following years, Ruck and Maggie Patterson visited Steve and Margaret Nelson at their home on Cape Cod and on several occasions recorded conversations with Nelson that were edited into radio documentaries.

In 1975 the two of us met while doing graduate work at the University of Pittsburgh. In 1977 Nelson returned to the city for a visit, and we were in the audience when he spoke to a group of graduate students in labor history. His willingness to rethink his own experiences convinced us that Nelson's stories should have a wider audience. We decided to approach him about working with him on his memoirs. Putting his story down on tape and in print was not a new idea to Nelson. Many people had urged him to do so for years, and he had already recorded a good deal about his experiences in the anthracite region of Pennsylvania during the Depression. He agreed to work with us.

That summer we spent a week with him, taping for six hours a day in a little work shed he had built in his backyard. After Jenni Barrett transcribed these sessions, we corresponded with Nelson and asked dozens of follow-up questions that he answered on tape or in letters. During the next year we met twice and continued the taping.

The following summer we wrote the first drafts of nine chapters. Nelson read and criticized these chapters, and at the end of the summer the three of us met to develop another draft. This process continued through three years and involved five drafts, several more sessions, and a great deal of correspondence with Nelson and outside readers.

More than one hundred hours of transcribed interviews along with Nelson's earlier writings and recordings about his experiences in the anthracite region of Pennsylvania, Spain, and Pittsburgh were the main sources used to write this book.[9] In many of our taping sessions, Nelson had given a great deal of thought to what he wanted to say, and we were able to sit and listen, asking an occasional question. Yet there were many times when our questions forced him to think about something or someone he had not considered in years. That is not an easy task, and we were constantly surprised at how well he was able to dig deep and come up with answers to our questions. It is his remembering and rethinking that shape this book. The two of us simply helped put it down in words.

At times we questioned Nelson insistently, often posing alternative interpretations of events. He usually answered thoughtfully and plausibly. We did not always agree with him, and on certain issues we still do not. These divergent interpretations sometimes pertain to national policies, such as the Communists' strong support for the New Deal Democratic Party or their decision to liquidate Party caucuses and cease publication of shop papers during the early CIO era. We differed in our assessment of the potential that the labor party movement and an independent voice within the CIO might have offered American Communists. Two examples on the international scene are the development of Stalinism in the 1920s and the 1956 rebellion in Hungary and the subsequent invasion by the Soviet Union. In our view Nelson's understanding of the roots of Stalinism does not fully acknowledge the impact of seven years of war and revolution in which the Soviet proletariat was virtually destroyed, allowing the Party to substitute itself for the working class as the historic agent of social change. In this context, whoever led the Party led the revolution.[10] Nelson's description of the social basis of the Hungarian revolt also seems oversimplified. He describes it as overwhelmingly reactionary; we believe this underestimates the popular support for the uprising and leaves him with an equivocal position on the Soviet invasion. This contrasts sharply with his adamant opposition to the Soviet invasion of Czechoslovakia.

Some readers will want a fuller treatment of certain problems Nelson raises. Recruitment of blacks, for example, has been a top priority for the Party since the Depression, and in fact the proportion of blacks in the Party rose during the thirties. Nelson was always committed to racial unity, but his direct involvement in organizing blacks was limited, and a reader wishing to pursue the subject would best look elsewhere.[11] This also applies to the Hitler-Stalin Pact and the World War II no-strike pledge. While there was significant opposition to both, Nelson's view is mostly confined to his experiences in the Bay Area, and it may suggest more Party unity on these policies than actually existed.[12] Other issues have spawned even more bitter controversy. Some will question why it took American Communists like Nelson so long to come to grips with Stalinism. Others will examine his discussion of the Spanish Civil War for insights into divisions of the Left. Nelson addresses these questions, but his answers will not satisfy everyone.

A major strength of Nelson's viewpoint is that it reflects the experience of a rank and file organizer; his concern is with the practical problems of mobilizing people to fight around specific issues. But this is a shortcoming in analyzing some questions of national and international policy. Nelson's concern with international struggles, demonstrated most clearly in his discussions of the significance of the Spanish Civil War, is obvious, but his view of the movement itself is primarily one of the local Party in action on a daily basis.

It is possible, of course, that Nelson is correct about these matters. What complicates their discussion is that one can never be entirely objective about such questions. Nelson devoted more than three decades of his life to the Communist Party, and he has a natural tendency to justify the key decisions and actions of those years. His critical reappraisal of his life was a difficult and often painful task, but his basic objectivity is impressive.

For Nelson and many young immigrant workers like him, the Communist Party was the primary means by which they made sense of American society and its host of highly complex economic and political phenomena. It was the prism through which reality passed into ideology. With time, this way of perceiving the world can also act as blinders, hiding from sight things that do not square up with Party policy. We felt that this was more of a problem for Nelson with foreign events than with domestic issues. His judgment of the rise of Stalinism in the twenties, the purge trials of the thirties, and the Hungarian rebellion inevitably depends on outside sources of information.

Anyone using these memoirs as historical documentation should also consider that they were based primarily on oral history. No man's memory is infallible, especially when it covers some seven-odd decades. Wherever possible, we have checked and double-checked Nelson's recollections through follow-up interviews, research in newspapers, HUAC proceedings, court transcripts, Communist Party publications, and secondary literature, and in his voluminous files obtained somewhat grudgingly from the FBI under the Freedom of Information Act. (The FBI material, however, was largely worthless as it was composed of pages ravaged by excision.)[13] A number of people with extensive movement backgrounds, many of them mentioned in the manuscript, were asked to verify the accuracy of Nelson's memoirs. What follows is how one man recalled the history he experienced. For the reader uninitiated in the names and events of twentieth-century radicalism, there are brief explanatory notes located at the end of the book.

Many people helped us on this book. David Montgomery's initial encouragement was compounded by his usual careful reading and penetrating questions of an earlier draft. His tenure at the University of Pittsburgh attracted a number of young labor and social historians who formed our reference group and created a particularly supportive and stimulating environment.

Financing this project has always been a problem: transcriptions of interviews alone ran into thousands of dollars. We were aided in the beginning by a small sum from the Pennsylvania Historical and Museum Commission when John Bodnar hired us to conduct several interviews with Nelson regarding immigration and the Party's activities in Pennsylvania. Robert Colodny, a constant source of intellectual sustenance, then procured a small grant for us from the Provost's Office of Research and Development at the University of Pittsburgh. Later we received a Youthgrant from the National Endowment for the Humanities that allowed us to spend an entire summer working on the book.

Max Gordon, Dorothy Healey, Peggy Renner, David Goldway, Nat Cohen, Stella Petrosky, Robert Colodny, Ben Dobbs, Josie Nelson, Milton Ost, Bob Nelson, Jeremy Brecher, Steve Sapolsky, Pete Rachleff, John McDermott, John Muldowney, Dave Smith, Bill Susman, Morry Calow, Tom Lloyd, and Charley Flato read all or parts of the book and offered their thoughts. Their contributions were innumerable and our thanks deep. Al Richmond was especially sensitive in his suggestions and editorial help. Al Amery, a veteran of the fight in Spain, helped us at a particularly difficult time and typed a large section of an earlier draft for us. Frank Zabrosky of Pitt's Archives of Industrial Society advised us on the NEH grant. Faye Schneider, Marge Yeager, Millie Baer, and Gerri Katz helped us subvert bureaucratic procedures and cut countless corners.

Jenni Barrett, whose historical expertise was particularly important to chapter 5, and Maggie Patterson, who co-produced the early radio documentaries on Nelson, were a part of the project from the beginning and have helped make the book more readable and interesting. Margaret Nelson, Steve Nelson's partner and comrade for over five decades, was the source of much material, and she helped us all maintain perspective and a sense of humor. Finally, Abby Levine, our editor at the University of Pittsburgh Press, found inconsistencies, ambiguities, and problems in the manuscript and then worked with us on clearing them up.

Steve Nelson retains a deep commitment to radicalism, and this is one of the strengths of his memoirs. But even those who disagree with him must consider the links his experiences illustrate between that radical activity and reforms that have changed the character of daily life in this country. For those who share his vision of a changing society and will try to make their own way over some of the paths he has taken, we hope this book makes the going a bit easier.

James R. Barrett and Rob Ruck
December 1980
Pittsburgh, Pennsylvania

STEVE NELSON, AMERICAN RADICAL

ONE

From Subocka to Pittsburgh

Like millions who came before and after me, I brought more to America than my battered luggage. Life as I had known it up to that time revolved around Subocka, a village of fewer than one hundred families in a fertile farming region of Croatia, part of present-day Yugoslavia. It could hardly have contrasted more sharply with life in the industrial cities and mining towns that were to be home for most of my life. The distance between this tiny village in the Austro-Hungarian Empire and Philadelphia or Pittsburgh must be measured in ideas and experiences as well as miles, but it is here that the story begins.

This village, where I was born Stjepan Mesaroš in 1903, nestled in a narrow valley, the hillsides covered with cornfields and the hilltops with forests. Small farmhouses were scattered through the valley, their red tile roofs contrasting with the whitewashed stucco walls. My family's home stood on the banks of the Subocka River.

My family were millers on both sides for generations, and our one stone mill was the focal point of the community. In addition to grinding wheat and corn, we also had a press for sunflower oil and pumpkinseed oil, which were in great demand during Lent. As people waited for their grain, they spoke of local news and what little they'd heard of the world beyond. Because it was one of the few buildings that burned its kerosene lamp late into the night, the mill attracted the local farmers who came to talk or to play cards.

Ours was one of the few stone houses in the town. It had walls of limestone and a red tile roof. Eight of us—my grandparents, parents, three sisters, and I—slept in two bedrooms that were heated by a single stove. The third room was a kitchen in which we cooked and ate. In the attic was a smoking room where meats were hung for curing; below was a brick storage cellar where we stored my grandfather's plum brandy and our winter supply of food. Attached to the

3

house and extending out over the river stood the mill with its huge stone and high-beamed ceiling.

The family was rather well off by Subocka standards. Like most of our neighbors, we raised our own vegetables and farm animals, and the income from the mill was supplemented by the sale of hogs that were fattened on ground corn. The forest had been protected for hundreds of years, and each family was entitled by common right to one tree each year. This provided us with most of the firewood we needed; the rest was gathered by the children from the floor of the woods. We bought our shoes, boots, and coats at the market, but my mother and grandmother made most of our clothing on an ancient sewing machine, one of the few in town.

In many ways it was still a harsh existence. There had originally been five sisters, but two died during a diphtheria epidemic that spared me. If the harvest was a bad one, we felt it along with everyone else in the village. And always there was a lot of hard work.

The mill provided a fairly steady income but demanded constant supervision and repair. Throughout each night a bell attached to a wheel summoned me every time one load of grain was milled and another had to be poured into the bin. The operation required the skills of a blacksmith, wheelwright, and general mechanic. My grandfather was a master of the craft and taught me how to make replacements for the mill's cogs and gears. These had to be very sturdy but also precisely spaced to within one thirty-second of an inch; an irregularly spaced cog would cause the whole building to shake. We had a gasoline motor to drive the mill when the water level was too low in the summer, but it was cheaper to rely on the river to turn the wheel. To ensure an adequate supply of water, the sluices, which regulated the flow, had to be adjusted day and night. Twice a week the stones themselves, which weighed nearly two tons, had to be taken off, turned upside down, and sharpened. They could be removed on a complicated system of rollers, but you had to know what you were doing. One slip meant that the stones would have to be reinstalled by hand, a big job for five or six men. It took a long time to become an expert miller, and for me the process began when I was eight years old.

Much of the work, as difficult as it seemed at the time, was very different from what I came to know in American factories. Even in the mill, work was always mixed with the conversation of the farmers. Often I worked outside in fulfillment of a sort of community ethic that certain kinds of work were to be done in common. In the late summer threshing became the main task, and no family could accomplish this alone. My family had a rather primitive threshing machine, and I traveled with it, working with three or four house-holds at a time until the job was done. Corn-husking was also done collectively. The family picked the corn and brought it into the house where the young people would get together and sit for hours, singing and telling stories while they worked. Money never changed hands. It was always an exchange of labor: you help me raise my barn, and I'll help you cut your hay.

My formal education consisted of five years in a one-room school with 130 other children at different grade levels and stages of devel-opment. Understandably, any learning that took place was almost accidental. In fact, it was the older children who did much of the teaching. One of my tasks in third grade was to drill the younger children on their multiplication tables, and in the process I learned them myself. I must have been out chopping wood for the school stove or teaching arithmetic when most of the reading was taught. By the time I left school, I was able to read only simple Bible stories illus-trated with pictures of God (either an old man or a pyramid with an eye, I was never sure which) and the angels (fat little babies with wings). When I left the old country at the age of seventeen, I was barely able to read, and I could hardly write at all.

My only other educational experience was a brief course at a man-ual training school where I learned about weights and measures. There was some thought given to the idea of having me trained as a beekeeper. I'll never know how much I might have enjoyed this noble profession, for the war intervened to change this and many other aspects of my life.

But as every student knows, some of the best lessons are taught outside of the classroom. Aside from the ancient skills passed on to me from my grandfather, the atmosphere of the mill itself was educa-tional. Here I spoke and listened to as many kinds of people as there existed in our village and occasionally to an outsider.

In spite of how backward life there was in many ways, Subocka was not a stagnant place. The early twentieth century was a period of rapid change, and some of these changes were felt in my region. In a neighboring town, for example, there was a large landowner who reminded one of a feudal baron. He had two or three thousand acres of choice land and dozens of families living on tiny plots in serflike status, but he operated the place on quite a modern basis. He had some of the most advanced farm machinery and was raising crops and breeding cattle for the export market. This kind of mixture of ancient and modern characterized the whole region, as I recall it. There were hundreds of little communities like ours where money was seldom if ever used in the local economy, but there were also larger towns with machine shops, brickworks, and small factories. Our part of the forest was still protected under common right, but in other areas trees were being cut down, processed in large lumber mills, and shipped out for export. A railroad ran through several of the towns close to us, and this was already beginning to affect life and work in Subocka. The younger people especially would walk to the large towns to work in factories or to do the seasonal brickyard work. At the time it would have been difficult for me to visualize a city like Philadelphia or Pittsburgh, but even my little world was no longer the same, and I was aware of this.

Among all my impressions, that of the First World War looms largest, and it might even suggest the only link I can discover between life in Subocka and my later radicalism. I was twelve years old when the war broke out, shattering the daily routine of this little world and changing my own life in a number of ways. The whole experience had a shocking effect. It made me feel that something was wrong in the world, even if I couldn't put my finger on it.

I recall driving five or six neighbors and my father in our wagon to a mobilization center where I saw thousands of men gathered sullenly around tents and field kitchens. All the men seemed worried, not only about the prospect of dying in a war which none of them understood, but also because of the practical problems that arise when a farmer becomes a soldier. One had not finished ploughing; another had not laid in a sufficient supply of wood. Their families would be in rough shape for the winter, with responsibilities falling on the shoulders of wives and older children.

This was all very confusing for a twelve-year-old boy. The farmers used the Serbo-Croatian term *vatru* to describe their fate. I translated the term literally to mean "going into fire" and imagined my father and neighbors marching into a wall of flames. I already hated war without really understanding what it was.

War was like a plague that quickly disrupted our way of life. As the war dragged on, destitute widows and the wives of young soldiers drifted into town half-starving and were taken in by farm families. My cousin returned almost immediately, badly wounded through the stomach and hip. He recovered but limped for the rest of his life. One neighbor came back without a leg, and people wondered, what good will he be on a farm? I surveyed the misery from my vantage point at the center of the community.

The war also broke down some of the barriers between Subocka and the rest of the world. We became aware of death and starvation in

Bosnia, which was less than fifty kilometers away but had never attracted our attention. Russian and Italian prisoners of war arrived to work on some of the larger farms. This business of men from faraway lands with strange languages who left their families and ended up in our little town seemed fantastic.

It was as a result of the war that I first heard of the Russian Revolution, though at the time I couldn't understand what it was all about. One day my mother and I met a neighbor on the road leading into town. He had been a prisoner in Russia, and we were the first familiar faces he had seen. The man immediately asked us about his family. That night he came over to the mill and told us of very strange events that were occurring in Russia. It seemed that there had been something called a Bolshevik Revolution, but he could not explain exactly what this was. We only knew that the czar, a symbol of tremendous power for us, had been dethroned by the people, and this in itself was impressive.

The war also precipitated my disillusionment with the Church. Because I was the first child in the town that the priest had baptized, he maintained a sort of proprietary interest in my soul, though up to this point I too had been conscientious about achieving salvation. I had had some misgivings. At confession the priest was especially persistent on the question of sex, and I could not understand why he kept pressing me on this. Still, I attended confession regularly, and I served as an altar boy for several years. But the Church's attitude toward the war brought many of my doubts regarding religion to the surface.

One Sunday in late August 1914, the priest ascended the stairs leading to the pulpit and spoke down to his congregation about our moral duties with regard to the war. After giving a dramatic description of Franz Ferdinand's assassination by Serbian nationalists at Sarajevo, he exhorted us to rally to the support of the fatherland, the Austro-Hungarian Empire.[1] A few weeks later, when I drove our neighbors to the mobilization center, there he was again, spreading incense and sprinkling the soldiers' rifles with holy water. As I watched him pray that 'our' side would prove to be the better killers, I remembered the words of the Fifth Commandment. I didn't stop going to church completely, but my attitude toward the priest was never the same.

As it turned out, there wasn't much time for church. I had to assume the duties of a grown man at the age of twelve, and with my mother's guidance, I learned how to maintain the mill, keep it going day and night, and hold the family together. In addition to the milling, I had to make parts for the mill and care for the family's small herd of hogs, two cows, and a team of horses.

It was in our little mill under the kerosene lamp that I first heard of life in America from those who had made the journey and returned. Because there were no official guidebooks or other descriptions, my image of America was shaped by these emigrants. One returning family left their seaman's trunk with us until they could relocate, and I was intrigued by what I found inside. Their alarm clock, for example, was a source of great fascination; why should it matter whether one woke up at 7:55 or 8:05? It seemed more natural to be awakened by the first rays of the sun. Most emigrants offered stories of difficult and dangerous work. A young fellow who had worked in a tannery contracted the worst case of arthritis I have ever seen. When he tried to work with a scythe, he looked like some kind of grotesque skeleton. A Serbian who had worked at Standard Plumbing Supply in Pittsburgh described how he had become consumptive from breathing fumes in his shop, while another fellow was called "Nine-fingered Man" because he had lost one finger in a Detroit auto plant. Nor would such dangerous work necessarily bring one a fortune in America. My father let one returned emigrant stay for the winter with us, and when it was discovered that he had stolen the family horse harness and disappeared, no one knew what to make of it. Crime was virtually unheard of in our village, and we concluded that the man had learned to "live by his wits" in the New World.

So when it was my turn to go, I was not expecting any streets of gold. But despite the tales of the returned emigrants, I still looked forward to the trip. It was an adventure that any seventeen-year-old boy would welcome, and even more, it was an escape from a deteriorating home life. His war experience had aggravated my father's drinking problems. He was getting more irresponsible and harder to live with.

Shortly after the war, my uncle came back on a visit from the United States, where he had been living for many years in Philadelphia. When he saw what my mother and the children had to endure, he offered to lend us the money for passage to the United States. My mother sat my sisters and me down and explained the situation, but the ultimate decision was hers. One of our major considerations was that I should avoid the draft. Everything happened so fast that I was stunned at first. There was not even time for me to say good-bye to my sweetheart; we left immediately. Soon, whatever sadness or fear I had was replaced by a sense of excitement as we started the long journey to America.

We made our way to Trieste, where the trip was delayed by a two week seamen's strike, the first strike I had ever seen. I spent the time exploring life in the largest city I'd ever visited. The red-light district depressed and even frightened me a little. I had gone several times to Brod, a fair-sized industrial town on the Sava River, to get gasoline for our motor. I had even seen Zagreb, but none of this prepared me for the size and color of a cosmopolitan port like Trieste. What I remember most is the beautiful crystal blue of the Adriatic Sea and the pungent smell of the waterfront.

The voyage itself was uneventful—boring, in fact. We spent twenty-two days in steerage on the *Argentina,* a rusty old Italian tub. Twenty-two days in the same room with one hundred other people, eating macaroni and dried fish morning and night, vomiting and losing weight. The only part of the voyage that I really enjoyed was the chance to talk with seasoned travelers who answered questions and offered advice. There were brief stops in Naples and Palermo to take on passengers and at Algiers to take on coal.

The *Argentina* arrived in New York Harbor on a steamy day in mid-July 1920. Because Ellis Island was closed for the weekend, we had to sit on board, thinking of what life would be like in this New World. I'd like to present a clear description of my immediate impressions, but I recall instead a series of images: the towering statue; the sky aglow with the lights of a city which had a population larger than that of my entire province; in the city, a maddening crush of horses, wagons, and people; the cavernous interior of the Pennsylvania Railroad Station, where I ate my first banana. What I felt most was a mixture of excitement and confusion. One of the most bewildering sights was what seemed like a wall of billboards stretching from New York City all the way to Philly. Camels, Coca Cola, Chesterfields. A fellow traveler read one that would come to have a special significance for me. It said, "Eat Berk's Frankfurters!"

My uncles, aunts, and cousins met us at the station in Philadelphia, and for the time being we moved in with them. News from home was exchanged for a welcome to the city, but conversation turned quickly to the search for work. My uncle looked me over and assured my mother that I would easily find a job. But there was some learning to be done in the process of job-hunting. At Ellis Island I was asked my trade and exclaimed proudly that I was a miller. And so on my second or third day in Philadelphia, I set out to find the city's flour mill. I would surprise my family and be back in my trade when I returned for dinner. Yes, my neighbors said, there was a flour mill within walking distance, but it might not be what I had in mind. Following

Steve Nelson shortly after arriving in Philadelphia, 1920.

their directions, I came to a building that was a city block long and several stories high. I heard a strange whirring sound coming from inside—electric motors. I looked around, but fortunately I couldn't think of enough English words to ask what seemed to me to be the obvious question: Where was the water? America, it seemed, was truly a different world. Shaken, I returned home and placed my fate in the hands of my uncle, who promised that he would find a good job for me. This was the first English word I and most other immigrants learned—"job."

My new home was an ethnically mixed working-class neighborhood on the North Side of Philadelphia. The immediate area was shared by Germans, Poles, Hungarians, Croatians, and Serbs. There was a Jewish community about two blocks away, and the blacks lived in the most depressed part of the neighborhood, separated from the whites by a railroad viaduct. Athough I soon learned the depth of racial antagonism in the city, there was little overt hostility in the community. It was more a question of two distinct cultures, two separate worlds.

A variety of industrial plants shared the narrow streets with the tiny three-story homes of the workers. Neighbors walked to their work in breweries, tanneries, a cigar factory, a slaughterhouse, or one of several small machine shops, or they took the streetcar to Baldwin Locomotive Works or Cramp's Shipyards. Most homes contained neither showers nor toilets, but there were privies in the courtyards, and the dirt and grease from a hard day's work could be washed away for a nickel in the public baths at the end of our street.

My first job was at Berk's slaughterhouse and packing plant, where my uncle knew a foreman. The place was small by Chicago standards, but then I had never seen Chicago, and it seemed huge to me. I worked with about three hundred others, mostly Hungarians, South Slavs, Poles, and Germans. I doubt if there were more than twenty-five or thirty American-born workers in the plant. The work paid twenty-eight cents an hour for five ten-hour days and eight hours on Saturday. My job was to pick hams and other meats out of the brine in the ice plant, cook them in large vats, load them onto a small truck, and push them into the smokehouse. Constant travel between the two extremes in temperature led inevitably to rheumatism and respiratory ailments, but the greatest hazard came in hanging the meats for smoking. The racks were several stories high and constructed from two-inch pipes that we had to climb in order to hang the meat over a smoldering smoke pit. The trouble was that the pipes collected the fat that dripped from the smoking meat, and they became extremely slippery. The workers took turns climbing the racks, while those below handed the meat up to the climbers. After hanging a few hams you couldn't stand the heat and smoke anymore and had to get down.

After working for a few months, I concluded that I couldn't stay much longer without completely destroying my health. What finally convinced me was the experience of a Croatian immigrant, still in his thirties, who was so crippled with arthritis that it was impossible for him to keep up with the climbing. He was frightened to death, and one day he fell. We made a weekly collection for his family to which all of his workmates contributed. I visited him for weeks in the hospital until I could no longer stand the sight of his wife and kids crying. "Damn it," I vowed, "I'm not going back into that place another day."

I turned once again to my uncle, who talked to his foreman at Baldwin Locomotive Works and got me on the evening shift as his "bucker-up." This was the fellow inside the firebox of the locomotive holding a thirty-pound iron bar up against the rivet. The riveter, in this case my uncle, was on the outside of the firebox with a pneumatic hammer. The job had two major drawbacks. One was the deafening noise caused by dozens of air hammers banging up against rivets. In addition, the hammers spit a constant spray of oil, and there was practically no circulation. By the end of the shift I was covered with oil, and my head was throbbing with the sound of the hammers. I solved part of the problem by installing a sheet-metal tub in my room with a gas burner to heat the water. But the prospect of six days a week, nine and one-half hours a day, at thirty cents an hour really got to me. It looked terrible, and I didn't think I could last. For the first time I asked myself if it was really worth it. "Hell, if this is the only kind of work that I'm going to do, I'm going back. I was better off over there." I lasted about three months at Baldwin.

Next I got a job in a machine shop that had a large forge. During the war the place had been producing artillery and ammunition, but now it was reconverted to machine-building. I was in a work group of ten or twelve men: Czechs, Slovaks, Poles, and one old Irishman. I operated one of three big 350-pound steam hammers. The left hand controlled the steam while the right set the timing. The hot iron hung from an overhead crane, and the men turned it with huge tongs while it was shaped by the hammer blows. Three or four giant men stood about the anvil. One had pockmarks like the face of the moon, and sweat would drip from one pock hole on his face to another and then fall off. We smelled like hell. Every time the hammer hit, steam and sparks spit from the hot metal, splashing all around and looking a little like lightning. The men grimaced. It went on and on. Finally the metal got cold and had to be reheated. This gave everyone a break. They stuck the giant tongs into a barrel of cold water, then took off their goggles and washed their faces in the same water. In spite of the heat and the noise, this was the best job I'd had—thirty-six cents an hour. I also liked operating that big steam hammer. But the business had been falling off since shortly after the war, and the place shut down after I'd been there only a few months.

Around the time I was laid off, I saw an ad in the newspaper: "Carpenters Wanted." I wondered how to get the job, and somebody said, "You have to join the union." I found there were dues and an initiation fee of $50, more than two-weeks' wages on the forge job. But the pay was $1.12 per hour for an eight-hour day and a five and one-half day week. The shorter hours really appealed to me, but it was also a chance to be outside and to be doing work that was really creative, at least compared to hanging hams and bucking up rivets. I borrowed from friends and relatives, paid the initiation fee and dues, and joined the carpenters' union.

I didn't have a toolbox. I bought a hammer and a saw, a ruler and a square, stuck them in a gunnysack, and went to the place where a man was supposed to be hiring carpenters. I had never worked on a construction job and didn't even know the names of the materials and tools. But I got on a job, and the first morning the foreman said, "Steve, jump down into that hole (the foundation) and make a couple of stakes." Steaks? I thought it was a joke, but I took my tools down into the foundation and asked another fellow what he was doing. "I'm making stakes," he replied. I said, "Oh, I see." I just watched him and did whatever he was doing. I had many of the necessary woodworking skills from my milling experience, and I picked up the terminology as I went along. When I heard someone mention a joist or rafter or stud, I went home that evening and looked the term up in a dictionary or carpentry manual.

By the twenties carpentry was so specialized that there were actually skill levels within the trade. I started out as a floor layer. It was said that for this job one needed a strong back and a weak mind. From this level I progressed to shingling and then went on to finishing work of various sorts, door-hanging, and other jobs requiring a little more skill.

For the rest of my time in Philadelphia, from 1921 until late 1923, I worked at carpentry in the good weather and took whatever work I could find during the winter. At one time when my cousin and I were both out of work, we nearly got involved in strikebreaking. An ad in the paper said that men were needed for gang work on the railroad, but when we arrived at an employment agency near Penn Station, workers were distributing leaflets. A man tried to explain the issues. I couldn't understand everything he was saying, but when my cousin wavered, the guy implied that it would be unhealthy to take the job. This I understood; we handed the leaflet back to him and continued our search for work. Rounding a corner, we saw some armed services recruiting stations. My cousin was very interested, and both of us needed work badly. We settled on the Marines, I think, because they had a flashy uniform. My aunt and uncle saved us. My cousin was under age and needed their written approval; fortunately, they refused.

Eventually I was hired at the Bud Wheel auto factory as a hammerman. In those days steel presses were so crude that lumps remained in the metal. I went along the sheet metal with an electric hammer, pounding out the lumps. The blood in your hands stopped circulating because of the rapid shaking, and the edges of the metal were sharp, so you ended up with a lot of little cuts. I also did sheet-metal work at a place called Hale and Kilburn, which made custom auto bodies. For a little while my mother and I worked in the same factory making chairs, and at another time I repaired and replated old milk cans.

But my life wasn't completely consumed by work or the search for it. Through my cousin and a number of other neighborhood contacts, I became part of an informal social club composed of several American-born fellows from different ethnic backgrounds. The experience was important because it improved my English and taught me more about life and customs in the United States and because it made me feel more at ease and provided some relief from the dismal prospect of unending hard work.

We paid dues of 50 cents a week and bought an old sunken boat, sight unseen, for $15. We raised it from the Delaware River, cleaned it off, and named it *Dixie*. I have no idea where we got the name. We went to work, pooling our skills. It took almost a year to get it back in shape. The mechanics picked up an old Packard truck motor in a junkyard, overhauled it, and put it into the boat. Another carpenter and I built the cabin, and from a carpenter's viewpoint it was perfect; from a sailor's it was not. We had no conception of what the winds would be like on the river, so we made it as comfortable as possible. The ceiling was high enough for us to stand up, and the floor was wide enough for dancing. When we took *Dixie* out for our first trip down the Delaware River, we almost capsized. The boat was loaded with people and soda pop, and we had to spend all our time shifting back and forth to save ourselves. Some alterations were made, and *Dixie* remained afloat.

I also tried to get interested in sports, my cousin's main preoccupation. We went to the Bijou Theater where the local kids boxed on Friday nights, but I never really enjoyed it. He seemed satisfied to live his life through sports, but I was restless. I was always searching for ways to understand my own experiences, and this was leading me away from my cousin and the *Dixie* group. The search started one afternoon on a curb out in front of Berk's slaughterhouse.

During my first few weeks at Berk's, part of my mornings were spent driving livestock with a young black laborer who was friendly and helped me out in a number of ways. For the first couple of days, I had to shout at the cattle in Serbo-Croatian until he taught me how to cuss in English. I doubt if the beasts cared what language we shouted, but these were some of the first English words I learned, and I appreciated his efforts, Later in the day, when I joined my gang in the smokehouse, I noticed that he remained in the yards, shoveling manure from the pens and cattle cars. I wondered why he always seemed to get the dirtiest work, but I was a little afraid to ask. One day while we were eating our lunch, this black fellow was playing catch with one of the neighborhood kids. The ball went over his head and landed in a nearby gutter, so I picked it up and threw it back. But one of the white workers snarled, "Let the nigger pick it up himself!" I couldn't understand all the words, but I recognized the hatred in his voice.

The incident made me think about the problem of prejudice, which had been bothering me for some time. In Subocka there had been a certain hostility toward the Turks. I did not understand that it was primarily because of Turkish domination of the area generations earlier; I thought it was because they dressed differently. They were horse traders. On market day they rode through town in a group on horseback, as many as fifteen or twenty men. They were like a little army coming through, dressed in their wide breeches and turbans. The children feared them, and the adults clearly disliked them, though I never did understand why.

Not long after I arrived in Philadelphia, I was walking through the Jewish district with my cousin when he suddenly reached out and pulled an old man's beard. The man must have been over eighty years old, defenseless, and the act revolted me. But when I asked my cousin why he would do such a thing, he simply said, "He's a Jew!" I came home and told my uncle of the incident, but to my amazement he just laughed it off.

This time I was determined to find out what caused this sort of thing. There was a Serbian worker about ten years older than I who seemed to be different from the rest. Any time there was a break in the work, he would be reading a newspaper or pamphlet. I decided to take the chance; he seemed intelligent and might be able to help.

The Serb sat down next to me and explained that both bosses and workers were prejudiced against black people. "You'll soon learn something about this country." he said. "Negroes never get a fair chance." It seemed that once, not that long ago, they had been held in slavery, and now they were looked down upon for this and because of their skin color. This was why the black laborer got the worst jobs even though he'd been there much longer than some of the whites.

The next day the Serb brought a newspaper clipping to lunch that showed the Berk family on its way to vacation in Florida for the winter. The picture showed the young men in white pants and shoes and the young ladies in white summer dresses. The whole family was boarding a Pullman parlor car. The explanation proceeded in Serbo-Croatian.

"What's Florida?" I asked.

"That's a place that's warm in the winter."

"It's that far?"

"A two-day trip by train."

"Who goes there?"

"You can see who goes, only bosses."

"But the boss [the foreman, as I understood the setup] is still here."

"The Berks just hire him to run the factory. They get all the money."

He described the inside of a Pullman parlor car and told me how much some of the biggest industrialists earned and what this kind of money could buy. It was simply fantastic. He asked if I would like to read some things that explained how all this was possible. It turned out that he was a member of the Socialist Labor Party[2] and was interested not only in socialist ideas but also in popular science, temperance, organic foods, and atheism. It was in this way that my discovery of socialism as a way of understanding my own experience became interwoven with a more general thirst for knowledge. He introduced me to *The History of the Proletarian Family,* a series of works by Eugène Sue, the French utopian socialist. For the first time in my life I began to read novels, and these were books where workers were the heroes. He also gave me books on popular astronomy and geography. For a time I read anything I could find on the American

Indians and Eskimos. I still could not read in English, so there was a constant search for books and papers in Serbo-Croatian.

Soon I subscribed to *Radnička borba* (Workers' Struggle), a weekly newspaper put out in Chicago by the South Slavic section of the SLP. Most of the paper was filled with the speeches and articles of Daniel DeLeon, the chief theoretician of the party. Often I couldn't understand these writings, but I did like the reports from "worker correspondents" about labor and the socialist news from around the country. Whatever I had trouble with was more or less explained during lunch breaks or on evening visits to the Serb's rooming house.

He had a single room and a little kitchenette with a two-burner stove where he cooked his organic food. I still remember a picture on the wall. It was a woman standing almost naked with her arms raised. I couldn't understand why that naked woman was there; she didn't seem to fit in with the rest of his personality. He explained that she symbolized Liberty. The place was always jammed with pamphlets. Some inveighed against the evils of smoking, and others were written by Vaso Pelagich, a healer whose name was a household word among Croatian and Serbian nonconformists. Everything could be cured by one herb or another, and going to the doctor was a waste of time and money. My friend would start with this sort of thing and then switch off to explain more about how the capitalists exploited the workers. To him it was all part of the same story. We sat for hours over cups of tea, and I thought he was brilliant.

Eventually I joined the South Slavic branch of the SLP. It was a group of about fifteen workers, mostly articulate Serbians who were much older than I. The group's activities revolved around fund-raising events for the newspaper and an endless round of the dullest debates I've ever heard. We also sponsored a number of plays in Serbo-Croatian. These were crude efforts, but the audiences took them in stride. Because I and most of the other actors worked nine or ten hours a day, there wasn't always time to rehearse properly, and the prompter's whisper could often be heard halfway back into the audience. In retrospect the SLP seems extremely dogmatic and sectarian, but at the time it was my only connection with a vision to which I was becoming increasingly committed.

I listened to my Serbian friend's arguments and joined the movement for a very simple reason: it seemed like a rational response to the situation I faced. What he said explained why I worked so hard while the boss did not and also answered questions that had troubled me for years. In the old country, for example, I had been struck by how pointless the war seemed. It brought only death and destruction, and people did not seem to understand why they were killing one another. And yet it all went on with the support of millions of good people. Surely I must be wrong; there must be some logic to it. The Serb explained that I had been right after all, that poor people did not really have anything at stake in war. But he was also able to show that some people did profit by it, and so it became clearer just how this war had come about. On the question of class, it was not hard for me to understand that I was one of a class of people who must sell their labor in order to live. Everyone I knew—my neighbors, family, and friends—shared the same predicament. That there were others who did not have to work but who lived off the workers—this too became clearer as I looked about me. Socialism offered an explanation of the problems that I and others faced, but it offered more than this. It opened up an alternative to the way that we were living. It showed that we could achieve a decent standard of living for all, that people could live together in peace.

Not long after joining the SLP, I was able to recruit several young Croatian waterfront workers, dredgers and longshoremen who had done similar work on the Dalmatian Coast. Almost immediately we became embroiled in a debate with the rest of the membership on an issue that was dividing the entire Left: the Russian Revolution. The official SLP line damned the Revolution with faint praise; only De-Leon had the answer for everything. At some time during 1922 our branch was invited to attend a benefit concert sponsored by the Russian Famine Relief Committee. Probably because of the Communist Party's involvement in the affair, the older members balked at the idea, while the younger ones insisted that we respond. We argued, "You say that you are for the Revolution, that the workers took over there and the bosses were dispossessed. So how come you don't want to support them now that they're in need?" Even though we didn't fully comprehend its significance, we were ardent supporters of the Revolution, and we continued to insist. Finally they elected me and another young fellow to attend the Relief Committee's conference as delegates. It was at this point that I came into contact with Communists for the first time.[3]

It is not complex theories that attract a young worker to a political movement but rather first impressions of those involved, of their sense of commitment, of the sorts of activities they support. It may have been the stagnancy of the SLP that made the CP seem more dynamic, but I was impressed. Most of the Communists I met were not much older than I, and for the first time I met women activists. In the youth group, there was an even representation of the sexes. There were also ethnic differences between the two parties. The SLPers I knew were nearly all Serbian, while all of the Croatian radicals seemed to have gone with the Communists. Although the Party was an underground group in the early twenties, most CP members were active in trade unions, fraternal lodges, or neighborhood clubs, while SLP members remained isolated. They accused the Communists of being "pork-chop revolutionaries," concerned more with piecemeal reform than with revolution. But it was the CP that was striking roots among immigrant workers. Whereas the SLP spent all of its time *talking* about socialism, the CP seemed to be actively pursuing it. In spite of the strong Eastern European influence in the Party, its members also seemed to be more immersed in American life.

It was probably the CP's emphasis on work within the trade unions that attracted me most. I had become active in the carpenters' union almost as soon as I started work, and I always attended the meetings of my local. One of the first questions I remember raising was why the union couldn't push for an abolition of Saturday work. Most of the younger carpenters supported the idea. I did much of my work in Willow Grove, an hour's ride from home on the streetcar. I used to sit on the streetcar and read *The ABC of Communism* by Bukharin and Preobrazhensky in Serbo-Croatian. It seemed ridiculous to spend all that time taveling for four hours' work. A few supported the idea, but the business agent argued that when you found work, you couldn't be choosy.

I was especially impressed by a Croatian carpenter who was somewhat older than the other CP members, perhaps in his late thirties. He took me under his wing, and we talked about carpentry and union issues. The SLPers had always ridiculed my involvement in the "sellout" carpenters' union, but this Croatian took the matter seriously and told me how he worked in his local. "Why let the reactionaries continue to dominate the ideas?" he said. "Why not go into these conservative unions and sell them your ideas?" I had seen other Communists work on the same principle in my lodge of the Croatian Fraternal Union, and I was struck by their determination.[4]

The situation in the SLP was deteriorating at the same time that I was drawn by what I saw in the CP. With the four other young Croatians I broke away, and during 1923 we started attending a political education class sponsored by the Serbo-Croatian language federation of the Communist Party. This was a fairly large group of about twenty workers, each taking his or her turn in making a presentation. Some of this, of course, was a little too ambitious. When you read Marx's economic formulas to a fellow who is just learning how to read, you're not going to get much of a reaction. But the basic message got through: "The history of all hitherto existing society is the history of class struggles."

I joined the Young Workers League, the Party's youth group, which around 1930 became known as the Young Communist League (YCL). The Party was then divided into a number of language federations, and the league had three branches, one Italian, one Yiddish, and one English-speaking. I joined the English-speaking group, which was composed largely of American-born young people from Eastern European backgrounds.

Although I was not very conscious of this at the time, it now seems that at least part of the YWL's attraction was the opportunity it offered for socializing with people my own age with whom I had something in common. We had all sorts of socials to raise money for the league's paper, the *Young Worker:* dances, picnics, and outings. I met young people from the Italian and Yiddish groups on moonlight cruises on the Delaware River.

At this time the Party in Philadelphia probably had three hundred members, including a large group of recently arrived Jews from Russia who added a real Bolshevik flavor. The various language branches acted as propaganda groups within their respective nationalities, and this limited their influence in broader movements to some extent. But there was also a good deal of industrial organizing going on, especially among the younger comrades. There were YWL branches in the Nabisco cracker factory and another large bakery, and there was also an attempt to organize restaurant and cafeteria workers. During a lockout at Cramp's Shipyard, the Party helped to raise money and publicize the issues by staging parades through my neighborhood, complete with a little band and an American flag. Some of the most important work was going on among the city's hosiery workers, who emerged with a strong Left-led union by the late twenties. The largest occupational groups in the Party were probably the clothing and knit-goods workers and the building trades, where the Communists were quite influential within the carpenters' locals and among painters and bricklayers.

In spite of all the help it had provided me in adjusting to my new life, my political involvement was gradually driving a wedge between me and my family. My uncle, who was a small-time Republican ward heeler, had learned through one of his acquaintances that I subscribed to socialist papers. Because he had helped us to come into the country illegally, he feared that my activities would get him into trouble. At one point he himself reported us to the authorities, but we were given an opportunity to become naturalized in spite of the violation. Life became a continual argument about the government, the economy, the race issue. Sometimes my mother would take his side. Though not nearly as antagonistic as he, she could not understand what she called "your socialism" and thought that I was wasting my time.

Just when I was thinking about leaving home, carpentry was becoming slack in Philly. A Slovenian carpenter friend said he knew of work in Pittsburgh, where he had friends. Pittsburgh was a good labor town, he assured me; we would find a strong union and plenty of work. Rather than face the problem with my family, I chose the easier option of leaving Philly in the fall of 1923. I took transfers from the YWL and my local union and headed for Pittsburgh.

I moved into the East Ohio Street neighborhood near the Party and YWL headquarters on Pittsburgh's North Side. It was the sort of neighborhood that was shaped by the needs of the single immigrant men who made up the bulk of its inhabitants: there were rooming houses, taverns and cheap cafes, stores selling work clothes, and newsstands stacked with the various foreign language papers. There was also a large park where the Party and the radical groups held open air meetings. My carpenter friend and I had a "baching" arrangement, which meant that we shared a couple of rooms and any cooking we might do on our little hot plate. Unfortunately, my friend had a drinking problem, and we soon parted ways. I took a room of my own and was able to pick up some carpentry work on new suburban homes.

It was reasonable to expect Pittsburgh to be a strong labor town, but this was not the case. The steel industry was strictly open shop; any union men were fired and blacklisted, and most other employers followed the example. Workers in the hotel and restaurant and building trades were organized but weak, and the Left was largely ineffectual within the city itself. The Pittsburgh branches of the Party and the YWL had a total of about two hundred members, mostly foreign-born industrial workers. Much of the Party's daily activity involved the ethnic and fraternal organizations, and within these circles the Communists were generally accepted and respected for their work.

The CP's real strength within the region was in the soft-coal towns surrounding the city and among the electrical workers of the East Pittsburgh, Turtle Creek, and Swissvale Westinghouse plants in the Monongahela Valley. In both industries rank and file Communists worked for years to develop a base for progressive industrial unions, and the labor history of the region demonstrates how important this work was for the development of a strong labor movement there.

I joined the YWL branch on the North Side. It was composed largely of recent immigrants, many of whom had arrived since the war. During the week I worked at various carpentry jobs and attended meetings, but the weekend usually brought me to the coalfields. Because I often had to travel to building sites, I bought an old car, and this was requisitioned for the transportation of speakers and literature to the little mining towns along the Allegheny and Monongahela rivers. I listened to the speakers and talked with the miners, many of whom were Croatian immigrants, and what I saw and heard made a deep impression. In the old country families usually sent the biggest son to labor in the Pennsylvania mines, having heard how difficult and dangerous the work was. It was among these single immigrant miners that the Party found its strongest adherents in places like Canonsburg and Uniontown and throughout Washington and Westmoreland counties. Stool pigeons were planted among them, and some men were victimized repeatedly, but it didn't seem to slow them down. The young foreign-born miner didn't own a thing. He put some clothes in a suitcase, stuck the *Manifesto* in his pocket, changed his name, and moved on to another mining town.

The United Mine Workers (UMWA) and especially the leadership of District 5 under Pat Fagan seemed content to trade away everything for the security offered them by the dues check-off system.[5] The Communist miners' slogans were "Clean the union of bureaucracy" and "Fight to enforce the contract." In addition to opposing the Fagan machine and agitating against sellout agreements, our miners worked through the Croatian Fraternal Union, the Slovenian National Benefit Society, and other fraternal lodges and distributed literature about current political issues and the Soviet Union.[6] The Party assumed an important leadership role in the rank and file revolt produced by the union's rapid degeneration.

Some of my mornings and afternoons were spent standing at the entrance of the East Pittsburgh Westinghouse plant distributing shop papers. While the miners fought for control of their union, the electrical workers struggled to build one of their own. The first attempt to organize Westinghouse was launched by a group of Socialists and Wobblies[7] back in 1914 and was led by Fred Merrick, a Socialist who became the Communist Party's district chairman in western Pennsylvania after the war. In 1916 the radicals played an important role in a strike at the East Pittsburgh Westinghouse plant that quickly broadened into a movement embracing unskilled workers from many industries in the area. The radicals led a giant strike parade down the valley from East Pittsburgh, shutting factories as they went, but the march was stopped by force at U.S. Steel's Edgar Thompson Works in Braddock. The strike was eventually broken and the leadership jailed, but many of the activists joined the Party and continued working in the electrical industry. From the early twenties through the 1930s, rank and file Party members and sympathizers carried on agitation for a union, and their efforts laid the foundation for the United Electrical Workers (UE), one of the largest and most dynamic of the CIO unions.[8]

Westinghouse embodied all the characteristics of "progressive" big business in the twenties: the latest in scientific management and piece-rate systems, a pension plan, and, of course, a company union.[9] It was into this atmosphere that the *Westinghouse Worker,* one of the best of the Party's early shop papers, was born.

When I arrived the paper was already in operation. At this point the Party and the YWL had about twenty members in the East Pittsburgh plants and a few more at the plants in Turtle Creek and Swissvale. The groups met at various homes to plan policies to counter those of the employers. One of their accomplishments was dissemination of information on what was happening in various shops. Payment systems were based on individual departments, and this tended to split the workers up. The *Westinghouse Worker* publicized and urged resistance to rate cuts and speedups and attacked various other conditions. There would be articles written by workers in the different departments about what was going on, how rates were being set. On the same page with these shop issues was agitation for socialism. But the trouble was that the agitation took the form of extolling the virtues of the Soviet Union. It was certainly understandable that American Communists would interest themselves in the world's first socialist society, but sometimes news about the Soviet Union was stressed to the detriment of important American developments. We said a lot about the growth of socialism in the USSR but little about what it would look like in the United States.

The Communists were the only ones doing this kind of work, and people responded with considerable support for the *Westinghouse Worker.* Some fraternal organizations permitted collections or lent their halls to raise money needed to keep the paper going. It was judged a great success, not only because it sometimes forced concessions simply by publicizing conditions, but also because it stimulated discussion in the shops and the community around a broad range of issues facing the workers. The paper raised the issues of women's rights and what we now call male chauvinism, for example, when the labor movement and even many radicals ignored the problem. Westinghouse employed a good number of women, and there was constant agitation to upgrade their conditions.

Although production workers provided most of the paper's copy, the *Westinghouse Worker* had to be distributed by people from outside the plant in order to avoid victimization and blacklisting. The company owned the street in front of the plant and would arrest anyone handing out what they deemed to be "subversive" literature. The YWL members got around this problem by boarding streetcars and distributing the paper to men and women on their way to work. Occasionally one of the machinists would actually sneak a stack inside and push the papers off a balcony over the shop floor, scattering hundreds of sheets among the machines below. As supervisors scurried around trying to collect them, some workers were able to shove a copy of the paper into their overalls to be read later.

Another one of our concentrations was at the Heinz plant on the North Side of the city. At Heinz we had several people who had worked there for some time before becoming Party members or contacts. The Party constantly attempted to develop such contacts inside the factories and shops, and here the foreign language publications were important links. Because of the repression at the time, we were extremely careful about getting someone into trouble at work. This often meant that you had to go to the worker's home to discuss union organization or whatever else the issue might be. We would make assignments: "Who knows him? You know him through your lodge, so you might be the best one to talk to him." Then there would be a discussion about how we should approach this person. "You have to watch your step because his wife is a tough one, a strong churchgoer, and the priest is against us." Finally we began to put out leaflets containing information coming from our network of contacts inside the plant, but the production and distribution work was always carried on by outsiders. During the twenties and early thirties, these leaflets, or shop bulletins as they were called, were put out in the name of the Party, but eventually we decided this approach mixed up ultimate aims and immediate issues. In the era of the CIO such bulletins were discontinued or at least not distributed under the Party banner.

The basic labor policy was worked out by the district Trade Union Committee, a group of about eight that met once a month. In Pittsburgh it was led by John Otis, a machinist and a good, practical trade unionist. The committee would call in specific groups from Westinghouse or other plants when it was discussing their problems. It would also represent the district at national trade union conferences. At this time the Party was sending labor delegations to the Soviet Union, and a number of Pittsburgh trade unionists served on these.

One of the things about the Pittsburgh Party that impressed me most was the small group of black Communists there. The most popular figure was William Scarville, a well-known activist in the Pullman Porters Union and a veteran Socialist and IWW organizer.[10] His friend and constant companion was a white worker by the name of Smith, another former Socialist, with whom he shared an apartment. It was the first time I had seen comradeship across racial lines.

Scarville was a striking figure—he was over six feet tall, had shining gray hair, and always wore an immaculate suit, white shirt, tie, and polished shoes. He had a quiet sort of dignity that inspired admiration in you the first time you met him. He was a favorite at Party and YWL educationals not only because he knew how to pepper his presentations with anecdotes about what went on during the night on the train but also because of his remarkable facility for demonstrating complicated concepts with living examples. I still remember his lecture on the social relationship of workers engaged in a production process.

"You take the guys who are working in the mines along the Monongahela River and those barges that bring the coal. You don't know who dug the coal or who transported it or who unloaded it at the Jones and Laughlin mill [turning to a steelworker], but you work at that mill. You are working in the same production process, sometimes even for the same capitalist. So you have a social relationship with those other workers even if you never see them."

It was out of respect for workers like Scarville that young Communists in Pittsburgh developed a fuller understanding of racism.

My role in the YWL work was pretty minor. Mostly I observed, listened, and did as much of the "Jimmy Higgens" sort of work as I could organize around my carpentry jobs.[11] My problem was partly a lack of self-confidence—I felt the reticence that any worker feels in getting up to speak before a crowd. But I also had the special handicap of a recent immigrant worker trying to play some sort of role in the struggle with a five-hundred-word vocabulary. At one point, soon after I arrived, I was asked to deliver a May Day speech for a YWL branch, and I remember my anxiety. The meeting was in the Hill district of Pittsburgh, and the group was quite sophisticated by my standards, consisting of veterans of the YCL in the Soviet Union and American high school graduates. It seemed to me that I just didn't have much to offer people like this. One of my saddest experiences had to do with the first position of any responsibility that I assumed in the movement. The Party and YWL maintained a library in the old Socialist Lyceum, and I was asked to be the librarian. Aware of my inadequacies, I tried to decline but was persuaded by friends to take the job. At some point we discovered that $35 worth of books was missing, and some thought that I had been careless. I was sure that it wasn't my fault, but I still paid the money, an enormous sum at the time.

When I first came to the city, I had hoped to help the movement by doing organizing among steelworkers. I got a job at the Jones and Laughlin Woodlawn plant several miles outside of Pittsburgh, but my career as a steelworker was short-lived. I was with the maintenance crew for the open hearth furnaces. Whenever a furnace was "pulled" in order to reline the inside of it with new brick, it was necessary to erect a platform of asbestos-covered boards. They let the furnace cool down a little before sending you in, but not too long, because this would cost the company too much time. Whatever work was done had to be done on two- or three-minute shifts, because your eyes would fill with sweat the moment you entered, and the heat was unbearable. I had only been on the job about six weeks when I made my mistake. It was a particularly hot day, and as I came out of the furnace, I let out a yell. "Something should be done about this! These things need more time to cool down." The foreman heard me and said, "If you don't like it, you can get the hell out!" He handed me my pink slip, and that was it. It was a costly mistake. I had lost a job I needed and a chance to organize among the steelworkers.

Such experiences strengthened my conviction that I made a better follower than a leader. So I chauffeured visiting celebrities like William Z. Foster and Mother Bloor;[12] I sold the *Daily Worker* and pasted up Communist Party election stickers on the Sixteenth Street Bridge, which crossed the Allegheny near the Heinz plant; and I helped to make up and distribute shop papers at Heinz and other plants. But all of these little jobs helped me to feel that I was an integral part of a movement which had as its goal a world so just, peaceful, and rational that it was hard to understand why more people didn't share our vision.

Maggie shared the vision and was probably the best thing that happened to me in Pittsburgh. Margaret Yaeger was one of the young Communists who helped to distribute the *Westinghouse Worker*. At eleven she was active in the 1916 Westinghouse strike, handing out lemonade to the marchers, and she organized a Marxist study group while still in high school. At nineteen she was a veteran, the product of a classic Steel Valley radical family. After graduating from the *gymnasium* in Germany, her father had emigrated to Braddock. There he worked as a diemaker in small machine shops until unemployment forced him into what he considered the symbol of everything he loathed—the Edgar Thompson Steelworks. He and Margaret's older brother were members of the Socialist Labor Party but left over its position on the Russian Revolution and gravitated toward the CP. After Margaret's father died her mother remained a sympathizer, but her brother became more active and helped to lead much of the agitation at Westinghouse, where he was a skilled machinist.

I met Maggie in the Party office, where she was a typist, and I think we were both surprised at how fast everything happened. Although we had a lot in common politically, there were obvious differences in our backgrounds. She was much better educated and more sophisticated. Once she bought tickets for a concert to be given by Chaliapin, the great Russian opera star, but I wasn't interested, and I think she ended up going with her mother. Though I certainly held my share of male chauvinist ideas, neither Maggie nor her mother ever let me forget what was expected of me in the relationship. She had her own political work and would not accept a passive role. How many young men receive a copy of August Bebel's *Woman Under Socialism* from their mothers-in-law as a wedding gift?

Still, from the moment we were married, Margaret began holding back in order to give me a chance. Although I was politically naive and relatively illiterate, she seemed to sense that I had something to offer the movement. With her personality and intelligence, she might have forged ahead, leaving me in the dust. But time after time she sacrificed in order to give me every opportunity to improve myself. This was partly human kindness, but it was also a measure of her devotion to the movement. If I had the ability to become more effective among immigrant workers, it was essential that I be allowed to develop this ability, even if it meant tailoring her own life to what was required of me. It's possible for people to conclude from our story that Maggie accepted a traditional female role because she shared the accepted view of a "woman's place" at the time. This would be a mistake, for these were not her values. As a revolutionary she consciously gave me all the breaks, feeling that this would be best for the movement.

With Margaret's help I started to read novels, the Marxist classics, and the Party press in English. I would underline things that I could not understand or words that I didn't recognize, and instead of looking them up in the dictionary, a task every worker resents, I asked Maggie. She never seemed to mind her role of "walking dictionary," and she constantly reinforced my political growth. In many ways she was better "plugged into" the local movement than I, and I valued her advice.

Our social life was wrapped up with that of the Party and the YWL. We attended dances and picnics that were arranged to raise money for the Party, the *Westinghouse Worker,* or some strike fund. I especially remember the fraternal lodge picnics, which were great for eating; we would roast whole lambs on open fires and sit down to eat with friends. I think some of the Croatian ladies were disappointed that I had picked this American rather than some nice Croatian girl, but I was very happy.

There were problems in the Party in Pittsburgh, however, and Margaret and I decided to move. Both of us lined up on the "wrong" side in a local factonal dispute. We felt that the sort of friction that was developing might inhibit our own work, especially since she was employed in the Party office. At about this time, Rudy Baker, who had been one of the leaders of the 1916 Westinghouse strike and the socialist agitation during the war period, passed through on his way to Detroit, where he was going to become district organizer. I had met him and his mother among the Croatian Communists in Philadelphia, and he knew Margaret's family well, so he encouraged us to follow him there. Up to this point I had always helped someone else to organize where they worked. Detroit offered me the chance to organize in my own shop and to help build the party's influence and a strong union among the auto workers.

TWO

On the Line

My first sight of Detroit was a factory gate. I never did feel like I got a sense of the whole city, although I eventually got on intimate terms with a half dozen of its auto plants, looming rectangular blocks of concrete with wire and glass windows.

I took my carpenter's transfer from Pittsburgh to the "Jewish local" in Detroit. Although originally set up by Jewish carpenters and cabinetmakers, it was a mixed local by the time I joined. It was engaged in a big strike right then on the Book-Cadillac Hotel. The hotel was one of the earliest skyscrapers, and in the push to complete it, twenty-eight building trades workers were killed on the job. It was a butcher shop. The business agent of the carpenters' local was an American-born worker named Bud Reynolds.[1] He came from an old family of socialists, all of whom were around the movement in one way or another. He was a shrewd-talking, sensible guy and was on the Communist Party's Trade Union and District committees. I got to know Bud quickly and stayed friends with him through the years, hooking up with him when we were both on the West Coast during the war. But neither he nor anyone else could get me steady work in carpentry. That left one thing: working in the auto plants. Automobile bodies were still made like old coaches and wagons, with a lot of woodwork. The bodies were made of wood dressed with tin fastened on with small nails. The tops were wood with a lathed canvas or oilcloth covering. At the hiring hall of a factory, metal polishers and finishers would go to one window and woodworkers to another. I always went for the line that had some woodwork, but I took just about any job they offered.

My first job was at one of the Fisher Body plants. It was the first time I worked on a conveyor. The conveyor is a strange animal because you walk while you work, back and forth between two lines painted on the floor twelve or fifteen feet apart. The parts are there on the side; you grab them and whack them in while trailing along next to the conveyor. Then you run back and pick up some more parts and do it again. The same blasted thing over and over. At that time I was hanging doors. The doors were suspended from an overhead delivery chain, and they'd come to the prearranged spot. I would grab one and shove it into place and drive in a set of pins. Then I'd have to adjust it. If it didn't fit properly, I'd grab a wooden bar and twist and yank till I got it aligned. The whole operation had to be done in two to three minutes.

At LaSalle-Cadillac I assembled body frames on the line. Framing the body didn't require any skill. The line moved quickly, and all I had to do was stay on one side of it and put on four posts while another worker did the same on the other side. In the beginning I couldn't keep up with the damned thing. You had to drive screws in with a pneumatic screwdriver, but sometimes they just wouldn't go in fast enough. I learned to take a hammer and slam them in when the foreman wasn't looking. The assembly line was bad, and it depressed the hell out of me to work on one. A man's shirt would be soaked with sweat and his eyeglasses all fogged up an hour into the shift. You couldn't get off the line for a breath or to take a leak without calling the foreman or pusher over. And they kept a record of how many times you went. If you had weak kidneys, too bad. That's why they didn't hire old guys. Everybody on the line was young—at least when they started working there.

A fellow had work for the production life of a model. When the run of the model was over, he'd be laid off. If he was lucky, he'd get hired on somewhere else. If not, he'd wait till production resumed. I assembled crankcase pans and oil filters at Hupmobile, did wood-framing for car tops at Murray Body and sheet-metal work at Briggs, walked the line at Chrysler and LaSalle, and even hustled a job repairing decorative panels at a Fisher Body plant. Every now and then I fell back on an odd carpentry job when the season in auto was slack.

The constant searching for a job every few months created a terrible atmosphere. There were always so many guys looking for the same thing you were. Once when I was really hard up, I went to the Pontiac plant and saw something I will never forget. There were at least five hundred of us lined up waiting on a cold winter morning, not knowing how many were being taken on. We were stretched out through a zigzagging fence of iron pipes sunk in cement, where we had been standing since before sunrise. We just stood and waited. Once a clerk came out of the employment office and shouted, "You'll have to wait a while. We don't know how many we're hiring today." A trickle of men eventually got in, but around noon the clerk came back out and announced, "No more hiring. You men can break it up and go home now." People couldn't accept that; they'd been there for four or five hours. Guys started grabbing the pipes and rolling them back and forth. They literally lifted them out of the cement, knocking the fence down on top of other men who couldn't get out of the maze. When they finally crawled out of the place, some threw rocks and stones at the plant windows. When I got out of there, I stood across the street and watched. I thought to myself that it was the closest thing to a madhouse that I'd ever been in. The whole hiring routine was humiliating, and yet you had to go through it so often.

There was enough unemployment in Detroit that most men with families hung on to any jobs they could get. You couldn't be choosy; you had to take all kinds of jobs that were beyond human dignity. Management stayed on top of you, and a "pusher," a worker charged with getting the most out of the men, was usually breathing down your neck. It was tough to talk to the guy next to you, much less get away with anything on the job. They'd take your badge and refuse to let you back in.

But we weren't totally defenseless. Some methods of resistance came about almost naturally. Time study men are an example. All workers, no matter how politically backward they were, abhorred the man with the stopwatch. You'd say to yourself, "Here comes the guy who's gonna speed us up again." They would stand there observing you with their stopwatches and mark things down in their notebooks. I had never heard of the Taylor System or scientific management till I got to Detroit, but it didn't take long to catch on. When the time study man started checking you out, you had to go through the motions as if you were busy as hell. You really jumped but you weren't turning it out much faster. If the Taylor man got the better of you, the foreman would be there the next day saying, "Look, you'll have to do it this way from now on. It'll take you less time, and it'll be easier." They always tried to convince you with some malarkey if they thought you'd holler about it. The essence of it was to speed the line up. If they could cut an operation by two seconds and multiply that by all the times the men on the line did it, it added up. When they did speed up the line and you couldn't fight a cut in the rates, you'd have a tendency to let things go right by you. You might forget to put in the screws or just whack them in so they would hold for about as long as it took for the auto to get off the line.

Piece rates gave the men another way to exert some control over production. In this system pay was based on output, so much per "piece." A lot of workers were very careful to set a production norm. They knew that if they worked any harder and beat the rates by much, the rates would be cut. You had to be real careful that neither you nor the fellows next to you got carried away by an incentive system or you'd end up hurting yourselves. Somehow you'd informally determine what production goal to set and make sure no one broke it. When I was doing repair work at Fisher Body, I worked across the bench from a Swedish fellow. The two of us knew how to drag out a job so we wouldn't risk a cut. The foreman was always coming up and saying, "Can't you guys speed it up?" One of us would eye him and respond, "Look, this is delicate work. You can't match that grain of wood just like that. I can do it faster, but what's it gonna look like? You'd reject it, and we'd be working for nothing." We knew how to play the game. Most workers knew. But no matter how solid you can make something like this, it couldn't change the system. Some of us knew that we shouldn't cut each other's throats, but there were limits as to how far this kind of resistance could get us.

I worked in the plants for about four years. I was young, in my twenties, so I could keep up with the pace. After a shift I'd go home, have a meal, and put myself back together in time for a meeting. Sometimes the meetings became boring and I wished I hadn't gone, and other times I fell asleep at home with a book in my lap. But I got out of the plants with all my fingers and toes, and that was an accomplishment.

I didn't come to work planning to be some kind of big organizer. Mine was the life of an everyday worker with problems like paying rent and buying food. The choices for work were limited—you could blow your top and tell the boss to go to hell and leave, like some did. But what was outside? You went to the next place and found the same thing. Your needs compelled you to take anything available, and the company took advantage of this. Nobody stayed on a job long enough to get acquainted with the men next to him and say "Let's do something about this." By the time you got to know these guys, three or four months were up, and you were gone. But even under these conditions, the men would often rebel and win some relief. And although Detroit was an open shop town, there was a skeletal union organization working behind the scenes in the shops trying to organize auto workers.

Not long after I started working in the plants and going to YWL meetings, Phil Raymond, a member of the Party's Trade Union Committee, pulled me aside and talked to me about helping with his auto workers' union. Raymond had been an auto worker for some time but had been blacklisted in Detroit. He was an organizer without pay for the independent United Automobile, Aircraft, and Vehicle Workers of America, a small union that had been suspended from the AFL in 1918 over a dispute about whether auto workers should be organized into different craft unions or one overall industrial union. This union was renamed the Auto Workers Union (AWU) in 1928, and it affiliated with the Trade Union Unity League[2] (TUUL) in 1929. Raymond was a tireless organizer. He'd come to all sorts of meetings to find out who was working where. He was struggling to make some semblance of an organization out of the scattered radical and progressive contacts he had in the industry. That meant Socialists, Wobblies, and anyone else interested in a union—not just Party members. This idea of working together across organizational lines corresponded to the international Communist movement's policies between 1925 and 1928. The Party, though, had its own industrial sections of auto workers where most decisions regarding organizing were made. The union apparatus was too weak to play an independent role, and fear and the blacklist prevented it from organizing openly.

I was a member of a Section Committee which met on East Ferry Street, a working-class neighborhood with a large number of auto workers. Eventually I became the section organizer for this group of seventy-five or eighty, mostly Slavs, Bulgarians, and Poles. Many of these men had never married due to the scarcity of women of their own nationality in Detroit's immigrant communities. They lived in rooming houses or bached together. The East Ferry Street auto workers' section met in the Yugoslav Hall, which was shared by several Slavic fraternal groups. With a dance hall on the second floor and a cooperative restaurant on the first, it served as both a social and political center. Most of the single men in the section belonged to the cooperative and took their meals there. After a meeting at least a dozen or so would hang around till closing time.

Whatever illusions I might have had about how easy it would be to organize auto workers were quickly dashed. The companies were tough customers, and the whole temper of the times made it slow going. Most difficult to combat was the prevailing notion that "You can't build a union in Ford or anywhere else." It was necessary to make people understand that it *was* possible. First the left-wingers themselves had to be convinced that auto could be organized. For proof you had to reach for the unimaginable; that, for example, the czar was in power once, and he was overthrown. I couldn't think of a better argument, especially to persuade the foreign-born Party members who preferred to work within their ethnic organizations or language federations, which at that time formed the basis of the Party. We tried all sorts of ways to get the people who were working around the plants—who would be the spark plugs—to overcome the notion that it couldn't be done. A lot of the talking was first done within the Party itself. We put out bulletins, and whenever a group of workers like the New York needle trades workers won a strike, we publicized the outcome or brought someone to Detroit to talk it up.

The question of how to organize auto workers was just as fundamental as whether it could be done at all. AFL unions periodically made forays into the plants but would concentrate on particular groups of craft workers. One union might try to organize the machinists and another metal polishers, but they ignored the other crafts as well as workers on the conveyor. They weren't concerned with men who fell outside their craft jurisdictions. They excluded assembly line workers completely, leaving them with the impression that the labor movement didn't care about them. Radicals injected into this debate the point that auto workers must be organized on an industrial basis—everybody into one large industrial union.

It was not enough, of course, simply to have the correct policy. While speakers from the Party and other smaller radical groups argued with each other at the House of the Masses, a local labor lyceum, what happened on the shop floor was what ultimately mattered. And there, in sporadic outbursts that no mystic could have foreseen, auto workers were showing that it could be done.

You don't have to belong to a union to object to something on the job, nor do you necessarily need a formal organization to stop production. Small wildcat strikes or work stoppages happened frequently, often catching even the workers who initiated them off guard. I hadn't been at LaSalle-Cadillac very long when I found myself in the middle of one. The Caddie was the fancy car of the day, made with oak bottoms and ash posts. A new model was being introduced that required extra cuts to drain water from inside the body. The ash and oak were tough to work with, and you had to cut a notch from one side and then the other. We were getting the same pay as we had received for the older, easier model. The foremen were hovering around saying, "This is the way the job has to be done" as the change-over was made.

After a period of moving the line fairly slowly while the men caught on to the job, they sped it up. It was impossible to do the job at the old pace of two to three minutes; you needed about five. About two minutes later, someone let a body come through without making the cuts. Then another came by. The pushers were hollering, and men started tossing their tools down. They just stood there, tight-lipped. The fellow next to me said, "Fuck it!" and I got swept into it. Momentum built, and I didn't have to think about it as I found my hand letting my tool slip out of it. In two more minutes, somebody pulled the switch, and the line died. Foremen from all over the plant converged on our part of the line and tried to explain that it had to be done this way, that management couldn't afford it, that unless it was done this way they'd have to stop and revise the model, and we'd be laid off. The line was about two blocks long, and you couldn't even tell how many men were involved. Maybe three or four hundred men were affected, because trouble on one part of the line meant the whole conveyor had to go down. After a while, maybe twenty minutes, when the foremen and supervisors couldn't convince or threaten the men making the cuts to get back to work, a man came down from the main office and said, "We'll let it go on the old basis. Pull the chain and get back to work." People looked at each other and eyed the line to make sure it was at the old speed and slowly, almost deliberately, went back to work. You could see men smiling to themselves and tossing you a wink. They knew they'd been taking a risk, and if they'd lost, they would have been out of a job and likely to end up on a blacklist.

Sometimes a stoppage would evolve into a departmental strike. If you were the one to see or hear about it first, you'd get word to Phil Raymond and give him the dope on it. Phil or any one of a dozen other men would beat it down to the scene and talk with the workers involved as they stood around outside the plant. We saw ourselves as a kind of fire brigade, but our job was to make sure the company didn't snuff out the flames of these little strikes. The first thing you would suggest, if the men seemed to be directionless, was that a street meeting be held right there in front of the plant at lunchtime. You'd try to get the issues laid out in front of everybody and see that a committee was elected to meet with management over the group's demands. Some guys would brave it, knowing that walking into the superintendent's office made them marked men. Sometimes radicals would be on the committees, but most of the fellows were the kind that emerged as natural leaders. They were the ones likely to speak up against the thing before it happened, the ones likely to say, "Damn it, I can't even go take a leak," and say it loud instead of under their breath. You didn't win them all, of course. If the thing was lost, men would have to go to other places and work under different names. Without social security numbers, it was hard for the companies to effectively blacklist everyone. I think I worked under five different names while I was in Detroit.

But if we won, we'd blast the news all over the plants. Even if it was only a small issue, like a penny change in the rates, it was important. Local issues could be won. If you just stood out for the ultimate aim of building a union, people looked at you without much hope. But they thought that we could win some of the smaller issues. This was part of educating the workers about their own potential. You couldn't see a change of attitude very often, but you just had to have the confidence that somewhere along the line the incident would teach others. The cumulative effect of these kinds of stoppages finally wells up to the point where consciousness is greater. Eventually even the fairly backward-thinking workers next to you will drop their tools and walk out. Something you or someone else said at some point penetrated, and when conditions were riper, so were the workers.

Perhaps the Party's most important contribution during these years, and certainly the activity that sustained us, was the publication of almost a dozen shop papers in the auto plants. Called the *Ford Worker,* the *Fisher Body Worker,* and so on, these papers were agitational and educational vehicles for talking about unionism and socialism and making the connections between what was happening on the shop floor and the larger picture. That they informed workers of what occurred in various departments or other plants was vital. How else but by word of mouth would a fellow hear about conditions in the plant or of a successful stoppage? Certainly he wouldn't read about these things in the regular press. The shop papers covered hazards in a certain department or lambasted a particularly unpleasant foreman. They gave detailed accounts of incidents and stressed the overall need for workers to organize. Workers craved to know what was happening in their shops—that the metal polishers had shut down their department and won an increase in the rates, or that a cut had been prevented by shutting down the conveyor on the night shift, or that Sam Phillips, the pusher, had been put in his place when he got on the men's backs.

Sections of Party auto workers put out these bulletins. We'd meet and have a freewheeling discussion about what should go into the paper. Who's going to talk to someone from the finishing department to get the lowdown on their beefs? Who's going to write it up? How about getting it printed and distributed? It was a job organizing these little groups to get the papers out, but we did it for years. We got it down to a system and put out an issue of the *Ford Worker* and other papers every month. We once got out twenty thousand copies of a twelve-page edition of the *Ford Worker* for the River Rouge and Highland Park plants. I fit into this almost unconsciously. I was working on a bulletin, and though I wasn't much of a writer, I knew that we should get a story from this guy and that guy. I passed many an evening in a worker's home, getting the scoop on conditions in his shop for the paper, finding out what he thought of our efforts. I was becoming an organizer without even knowing it. Nobody calls you that, and you're not concerned with recognition. You're doing a job that has to be done. In this way I eventually took over responsibility for organizing the Fisher Body section.

The resources of the entire Party organization, limited as they were, went into the papers. Even Party members who didn't work in the plants helped out. We had a multigraph machine in the office, and every night a crew of young people were there operating it, setting up type, and collating the papers; it was like a little one-room factory. I usually ended up there late at night to meet Maggie, see what was going on, or pick up stuff. Distribution was a touchy matter. To be seen publicly with the paper meant a quick firing. It required a certain amount of courage.

There was an English fellow, Lewis, a veteran of the war and a naturalized citizen. He was a short stocky guy with a barrel chest. I think that he was gassed in the war and had bad lungs, which puffed his chest out. He was a rank and file Party member who became obsessed with one thing, the importance of the Party shop papers. And I don't say that with a sneer. For the years I was in Detroit, he and a woman named Mrs. Victor worked as a team covering the Ford plant. She was a dentist's wife, already about fifty, with three grown children, and she was active in a Jewish women's organization. She and Lewis stood before the gates at Ford selling these papers. Lewis had a peculiar way of doing it. There were all sorts of hucksters standing around during the shift changes, so he had to make an effort to stand out. He had a little soapbox and an Abe Lincoln top hat, a cylinder silk job. He would take the *Ford Worker,* which was about half of a tabloid size, and fasten it to his hat with a rubber band with the masthead on top. He'd stand there and in a circus barker's voice talk to the men on shift changes. He'd say, *"Ford Worker, Ford Worker,* only two cents, only two cents. New issue. Don't be a slave all your life!" and mention some issue covered in the paper. He'd let on that there was a story on, say, the foundry, and the men in that department, even though they might have hated Lewis, couldn't resist. "I'll buy the damned thing," some would growl. But most men would toss some change in the hat and stick the paper deep in their back pockets as they headed home. Lewis knew how to modulate his voice so that he would stick out, but he was not obnoxious. If a man didn't have the two cents, Lewis would just hand him a paper with a smile anyway. Another guy might throw a quarter in. Because he couldn't get a paying job due to his lungs, I believe he got by through selling the paper and collecting a small veteran's pension. He and Mrs. Victor could be counted on for every issue. They were spat at, kicked, and driven off their corners. They were arrested and molested in every possible way. But these two, and others whom I cannot recall by name, stuck it out all the way. They were respected within the organization and would report feedback on the papers. They were the "Jimmy Higgenses" of the movement.

The papers stressed the urgency for unionism and attacked obstacles that prevented workers from believing that unionism was the answer. An important obstacle was the isolation of workers from each other—the work force was split into at least a dozen ethnic and language groups, and men often couldn't even communicate with those next to them. The companies recognized that divisions between workers were to their advantage and used hiring and assignment practices to keep men apart. They buttressed this "personnel policy" with massive surveillance systems. Each plant had a sizable security force, and among them the companies had hundreds of men on the payrolls as informers. The owners targeted Raymond and the Party sections putting out the shop papers and tried to infiltrate them to find out our plans and, most of all, which workers we had contact with. They were successful, firing and blacklisting hundreds of workers. Everyone knew that to belong to the AWU was to put your head into a noose. I myself was fired a number of times. But sometimes we turned the tables on them.

There was a Czech fellow, John Suma, who was always hanging around the Party office. He was about forty years old, a chunky, easy-going kind of guy with a flushed face and perpetually bleary eyes. Usually willing to help out with the dirty work that came up in the course of a day, he was the sort of fellow who could talk simple shop agitation. Apparently he had contracted lead poisoning working for the phone company, and they had given him an easy night job. Illness explained his watering eyes. Every so often he would leave town for a few days to go to Chicago for treatment. Nobody suspected him because he looked like a worker. He said his wife had left him because she was opposed to his radicalism. That, of course, made us feel that he was trustworthy. He found out what I was doing, and I thought he was all right. I never disclosed any names to him because we were very strict on that. We never related names to anyone unless we were on a particular committee together. Suma had been around for about a year when I began to feel a little edgy about him. How could he manage always to be at the office if he was holding down a job, night shift or not? One night after we broke up, I discussed the matter with some other Party leaders. It was decided that I and another men would follow him after he left the office the next night.

The meeting the next evening seemed like it would last forever, and I could barely sit still. It ended about half-past eleven, and Suma made his exit with me and another fellow slipping out a few seconds later. I hadn't read too many detective stories, but I knew enough to stay pretty far back and not draw attention to myself. He started walking in the direction of the phone company and finally arrived at the steps. I thought that maybe I had been wrong when, instead of going into the building, he looked around and headed away. We continued to tail him, and he led us to his hotel. We reported back to the Control Commission, the committee that dealt with security matters. The committee decided to confront him, and I went with Phil Raymond and a couple of others to pay him a house call the next morning. Phil asked if he had been to work last night, and Suma said, "Of course." Raymond produced the two of us, and we explained what we'd seen. Suma got flustered, and when the committee demanded to know who he was working for, he admitted he was an agent and started looking for the door. We never saw him again. We'd print the names and pictures of stoolies in the shop papers, but it was an uphill struggle to drive them out of the plants until after the UAW had become firmly established.[3]

Another big obstacle to unionism came from how the workers saw the world around them. I think a lot of guys believed "I am an individual; I can do what I want," and tried to act accordingly. The Ford idea of individualism held many under its spell.[4] "The hell with the other guy! I'll get somewhere if I work hard. I'm not gonna worry about him." The notion that workers are in a different category from bosses, that sense of class, never occurred to many. The propaganda of the rugged loner was in their mothers' milk, and it hit them in the papers and at the movies. Very often a guy would get angry about conditions and throw his cap down and walk off the job, even though the next day he would have to go somewhere else. The satisfaction of telling the boss off was what counted, especially for the younger workers. It happened to me once at Briggs, when the foreman refused to let me go to the bathroom, and I quit.

Also, the idea of an organized collective approach did not come naturally to many. A large number of the workers came from Appalachia and had no industrial experience to speak of. Here, as elsewhere, the Party was based among the foreign-born and their children, and it had little physical contact with most of the Appalachians. Different cultures and patterns of community life separated foreign and native-born workers, and the Party was unable to bridge the gap. People just had to grow up through this industrial society and learn to deal with it. You could help quicken that process, but you couldn't force it.

We tried to talk about these problems in the shop papers, urging the men to stand together regardless of ethnic differences. The papers helped overcome some of the sense of isolation and helplessness workers felt and allowed radicals to suggest alternatives to the status quo. But they could only accomplish so much.

A continual dispute raged around what we had to say to auto workers in our shop papers. After almost every issue, some leader in the District Office would insist that we didn't put in enough about the Soviet Union. If you objected to it, you wondered if you were right. At the same time, being at the plant, you'd argue at meetings that "those guys won't be interested in that. They're interested in solving some of their immediate problems. It's going to repel them." Pretty soon someone would call you an "economist" for not sufficiently valuing the importance of general political and socialist propaganda. This was a tough problem, and the argument went back and forth.

We projected the Soviet Union as a model of socialism, and that just didn't cut it with a lot of men in the shop. There were districts that were criticized by the National Office for not emphasizing the positive developments within Soviet society. The truth is that some of these leaders would have considered it a sin not to emphasize the virtues of the Soviet Union in a shop paper. Those of us who saw the need to advocate the advantages of socialism ended up arguing with those who wanted to put forth purely trade union matters and those who wanted to feature the Soviet Union on page one of every issue. It was always that sort of tug of war. Sometimes it took a sharp form, and people would quit over it. Those inclined to argue for general socialist propaganda and publicizing the accomplishments of the Soviet Union were more likely to be full-time staffers for the Party with fewer day-to-day connections in the factories. When you work in a Party office all day and never talk to anybody but other highly politicized people, it distorts your view of reality.

There's no way to measure how deeply our ideas penetrated. Joining the union was a tough decision for fellows to make, and I don't blame those who decided to sit it out or keep their support hidden. You can't evaluate our efforts simply in terms of the size of our membership.

Many men we spoke to didn't join the AWU, or stayed active only a short while, but they listened to us. Raymond held noonday meetings in front of the gates, and men stood around with their heads down, smoking cigarettes, taking a break, but listening just the same. They may not have moved into action then, but just a few years later they challenged the industry and won a decisive victory.

We had to chart unknown territory in auto. There was a lot of stumbling and groping for the right path, and a lot of men paid for the blunders. But there's a continuity between our work in the twenties and thirties and the eventual unionization of the industry by the CIO in the middle and late thirties. We kept a certain sense of organization alive, trained ourselves and others in working under difficult conditions, and learned lessons that made the path easier for a later generation of organizers. We learned how to work with people who were backward politically and antiunion. By the time the UAW/CIO came along, the country had changed and was on the side of the unions. The government told workers they had a right to organize, and labor had the money to come in, rent halls, print material, and hire staff. Without the groundwork of the previous ten years, though, nobody can say what would have happened. That groundwork was laid above all by the Communists, in spite of our mistakes, such as stressing issues that had no immediate importance. And even in this case, I think we had an educational impact. There was an epidemic of lynchings in the 1920s, for example, and though there were few blacks in the plants, it was important to raise this problem in the papers. Perhaps our equation of socialism with the Soviet effort was frequently mistaken, but our work for civil liberites and black rights was not.

The shop papers were put out under the Party's name till the organization of the AWU in 1928. After that they came out under the union's name with the exception of the *Ford Worker* and a couple of others that were established papers. Phil Raymond was a known Communist, but the men accepted his paper and often his support. He opened doors and kept a foot in them until the CIO came along. Then the union was liquidated, and people went into the UAW. Raymond deserves tremendous credit for what he did. I know the impression he made on me. He used to get after me all the time. "Can't you get the YWL and Party members at Fisher Body to do something? What about the guys at your lodge?" Phil kept hammering and built a core of people around him. The UAW should not have pushed him aside so quickly.

The Detroit years carried Margaret and me fully into the life and struggles of the party. Margaret was working in the Party office again and active in both the YWL and the International Labor Defense (ILD), the legal arm of the movement. She was a member of the YWL executive board and also helped Rudy Baker and Phil Raymond lay out the shop papers. She helped run them off too, and many a morning found her selling them at one of the plant gates. She continued her work with children as well. While in Pittsburgh Maggie had led a group of Young Pioneers, as the Party's children's division was called. She met with about thirty kids in Makiades's Barber Shop in McKeesport. Makiades was a Greek immigrant whose son was later killed in Spain. The children, anywhere from eight to fourteen years old, learned about the heritage of the working class. The YWL paper had a section for kids and also produced songbooks and coloring books. Maggie taught them songs and directed their plays. In Detroit she met weekly with a Young Pioneers group of over fifty children at the Hamtramck Russian Hall. Mostly children of immigrants, they were sharp kids who performed plays and danced at Party gatherings. While many came to Sacco and Vanzetti defense rallies and joined the YWL as they got a bit older, the emphasis was not on recruitment as much as on offering them something they could not get in the public schools.

We shared an apartment with the Bakers and then with Alfred Goetz and his wife Ruth when Rudy Baker went to the Lenin School in Moscow.[5] Alfred was an auto worker, and Ruth taught public school. We became quite close and lived on sort of a cooperative basis. In the evenings after dinner, Ruth would often play the piano while Alfred sang, and then the four of us would settle back and talk until it was time to turn in. Alfred had been brought to this country from Austria as a child and was eventually deported there during the McCarthy years. He was more experienced than I, a leader in our shop work. But Alfred would often organize a meeting for Sunday, and I'd flip. On Sundays I liked to get out of town. There was a Finnish camp at Loon Lake about ten miles away where we could get a sauna and swim. These outings were a big thing with me. I had to get away from the shop whenever I could. I would tell Alfred, "Look, there are limits to what a guy can do." I thought that sometimes this was not taken into consideration. Some people in the Party wouldn't acknowledge that you had a personal life. Alfred would look at me and say, "What would you do if you were in Germany?" He read German and knew the movement there well. "Do you know what *they* do on a Sunday?" he'd say. "I'll tell you. They get a truck and go into the countryside to sell the *Rote Fahne,* the Party paper. Every Sunday." He was a hard man to argue with, but eventually we got him to schedule meetings on other days.

That sort of attitude made it difficult to keep industrial workers in the Party. You could recruit a man and then lose him suddenly when he was overwhelmed by an intense schedule of meetings on top of a tough work week. It put all kinds of pressure on a worker's family life when he went out and left his wife with the kids, not knowing just what he was up to. I was fully committed, to the point that I would have done whatever was necessary, but this constant pressure to do the thing day and night could become overwhelming.

We spent quite a bit of time with other Party members but never limited ourselves to them. I had friends from the shop who were not members and who didn't know that I was. Two or three guys I hung around with used to come over to the house regularly, and Margaret and I would visit them. Though I wasn't conscious of it at the time in quite these terms, the Party tended to be ingrown. People would only socialize with and meet other Party members. Soon it became clear that this was a detriment. A few members had friends from work or their neighborhoods and were quite as comfortable with them as with anyone else. But some would gravitate toward people they knew and never branch out. I suppose it was natural because we spent so much of our time either on the job or working to build the Party.

Between the Party and the surrounding fraternal organizations, one didn't have to look far for recreation and culture. With cooperative restaurants in the Yugoslav Hall on East Ferry Street and the Russian Hall in Hamtramck, several singing societies, the Finnish camp at Loon Lake, and the Labor Sports Union, there were plenty of opportunities for socializing. The drawback of this was that we rarely reached beyond the immigrant radical community and had little contact with native-born workers.

I was a fairly intense young man. Sports and drinking did not interest me, though when you're organizing you have to talk to guys in bars. Books became more attractive, although I was a slow reader, and it took me a long time to make it through a book. Nobody ever taught me how to get the sense of a passage and whip through it. I didn't know what the word "unwind" meant then, and it never occurred to me that I was overextended. I might have been exhausted from the auto plants or tired from too many meetings, and I liked my relaxation when it came along, but the movement and all that went with it were captivating. My senses were open, and I was soaking in all I could.

Auto workers, especially the foreign-born, stuck to their clubs and fraternal groups. Despite the inroads of a growing mass culture in the cities, these groups were the major form of recreation for most. They offered more than recreation, too; they were the center of a social network that was there when problems occurred. It was the place where you could talk your own tongue, and the dues were the lowest ever invented. There were several Croatian Fraternal Union lodges in Detroit, one around East Ferry Street where I lived and was then working and another near Ford's Highland Park plant, site of the introduction of assembly line techniques to the industry. When I came to Detroit, the progressives in the CFU considered which lodge I ought to transfer to from my lodge in Pittsburgh. I was told that it made most sense to transfer to the Abraham Lincoln Lodge in Highland Park. I went there and after a short while became its president. While it wasn't a paid position, the fact that I was a radical didn't seem to hurt my election. I was able to explain things and translate them into Serbo-Croatian, and I knew English fairly well by then. People saw that I was a pretty serious fellow and elected me on that basis.

Even in the lodge, you couldn't escape the auto factory. Our lodge had about 350 members, and almost all of them worked for Ford. In the first six months that I was president, three of these men died. One was a man of about thirty-six with three kids, an articulate guy who had been the lodge's president before me. He was already thin and consumptive by the time I got to know him, but he must have been very handsome at one time. This fellow had been a skilled worker and had his own home near the Highland Park plant. He died of TB. As head of the lodge, I was involved with his funeral arrangements. The wake went on for three days, and each night after work, I and several members of the executive board went to the house where his body had been laid out. Women came in and knelt and prayed and spent the evening consoling his widow and crying with her. Men did the same but wound up drinking in the kitchen and talking about conditions at Ford. Speeding up the line and the health hazards in the foundry and paint shops were always sore spots with them. This fellow had worked in the paint shop when he first started at Ford, and every man and woman in the room believed he died as a result of the conditions there. Three times in six months I saw this happen, and it struck me why these people belonged to lodges. They took care of funeral expenses and left the woman with something at a time when there were no social security or unemployment benefits. The lodge was vital in all these respects. It bought the cemetery plots, knew the undertakers who wouldn't overcharge, and offered insurance during illness.

It was common for workers to die young; you wore out quickly in the factories. As president of the lodge, I saw what terrible conditions people worked under and that nobody gave a damn. Nobody checked why this man died, and no steps were taken against Ford. You had no claim you could make. More than anything I could have ever read, the moaning and crying that went on during these wakes moved me. It drained every ounce of energy from you if you weren't made of stone. At least the shop papers gave those of us who were pro-union or Communists an outlet. I remember helping write this man's obituary for the *Ford Worker,* putting the blame on Ford and the lack of ventilation in his paint shop.

Communists were able to work openly within the CFU lodges and were often respected as good members of the organization. We were seen not as guys who would just get up and talk, but as men who would recruit for the lodge, attend to the funerals, and help with social functions. We didn't shirk the dirty work necessary to keep the lodge going. After all, we were Croatians and needed the lodge as much as anybody else. At the same time, we were respected for speaking out on issues. One of the first political subjects I ever raised in the lodge was the case of Tom Mooney. Tom Mooney and Warren K. Billings were accused of exploding a bomb that killed nine people at a Preparedness Day Parade in July 1916. They were framed in the midst of the intense prowar hysteria. There was a campaign for Mooney's release underway, and we felt it was important to talk to the members about what it meant. I translated a letter the lodge had received from the ILD into Serbo-Croatian and read it. Sometimes we were challenged by people who would say, "What do we care about Tom Mooney? Why should we help him?" It gave us a chance to explain, and if we did it carefully, we didn't antagonize but educated.

Being a Party member, I was concerned with making the best impression on people in whatever I did. I didn't have to go to all three nights of the wake, but it was the right thing to do since the mentality of the people was religious. There are dozens of people around, and they see you. You're not always agitating for some ultimate aim. You're going through their pains with them. They say, "No matter what the papers say about these Reds, they can't be that bad." And when you spoke, they often listened. You didn't always convince them, but you could talk to them. We would make sure that the ILD sent a letter to the lodges about the various cases. It was read at the board or general meeting. Somebody would snort disagreement and say, "Put it in the wastebasket." And then somebody, not always me, because there were a number of guys with a radical outlook, would start talking about it. It was an educational effort, even in a little lodge where men were concerned chiefly with insurance and death benefits.

Nationality work at this time was usually left to people who were in the lodges. They knew what was right and what was wrong. Common sense told them not to raise things that were meaningless or would get us nowhere. But with something like unionization of the auto plants, nobody called you out of order. We had a lot of autonomy in our work in the lodges, for the main attention of both the district and national leadership of the Party was toward the trade union work.

The foreign-born were generally more receptive to radical politics than native-born workers. There was discrimination on the job as well as a lot of subtle social digs. We were definitely treated as second class. If one cause symbolized the split between native and immigrant America, it was the Sacco and Vanzetti case. Nicola Sacco and Bartolomeo Vanzetti were Italian anarchists accused and convicted for a robbery and murder that took place in April 1920. People felt that the trial was a frameup, and saw it as an attack on themselves. The night Sacco and Vanzetti were executed, August 22, 1927, Detroit was the scene of the biggest demonstration I had ever been at. There were about sixty thousand of us holding vigil in Cadillac Square on the eve of the execution, hoping for a postponement or clemency. Then the information came around midnight that the execution had taken place. There was an area of the square where flowers had been planted and a number of us were sitting there on the curb. When the news came through, people began ripping up flowers and throwing them. Maggie had a funny thing happen to her that night. After news of the deaths, some people were arrested in confrontations with the police. Hearing this, she went to the Defense Committee offices to see if she could help out. She walked right into the arms of the police and was hustled downstairs into a paddy wagon and taken to the city jail. One young woman looked over when Maggie entered her cell and asked why she wasn't taking off her dress to hang it up.

"Why should I do that?" Margaret asked innocently.

"Don't you want to look nice in front of the judge? And how about when you're back on the streets?"

"That's not that important to me," Margaret said.

"Hey, aren't you a hustler?"

"What's that?"

That started Maggie's education on the street scene and how to survive in the Detroit city jail. It seemed that you could talk to anybody in another cell simply by shouting through the toilet. As the hours passed, more and more young women were brought in and charged with prostitution. The police were cleaning the streets, especially in the Italian sections of town, in anticipation of trouble.

Finally, a young raven-haired girl was brought in and placed in the cell directly across from Maggie's. Maggie, leaning against the bars, asked, "What're you in for?" The girl looked back and said, "CP." Maggie was thrilled; at last someone like her was there. But when they started to talk, it was as if they were on two different wave lengths. Finally Maggie asked, "What branch are you in?" The girl looked at her kind of funny and said, "Huh?" Maggie then asked what "CP" stood for. "Common prostitution, what else could it stand for?" The next day the ILD came and got Maggie out.

It was during these Detroit years that I formally joined the Communist Party. It was soon after I became a citizen, which took longer than the normal five years of residence because of a foul-up in my papers. I figured I was old enough and had passed the age of feeling like a Young Communist in the YWL. I was working mostly with men older than myself in the shops and was the youngest one in the nationality group. I figured I could do things better if I were in the Party, so I shifted over naturally. I had already been familiar with most aspects of the Party's principles, and I was growing into it. Raymond, Reynolds, and other guys who knew me, like Goetz, were pushing me to join, and Margaret was already a member.

It did not seem a big step. I simply made application and paid dues. The transition was smooth, and it was now easier for me to connect what I was doing in the auto plants and the CFU lodge with a larger sense of purpose. The explanations of a socialist society made by my old SLP buddy and the Communist carpenter from Philly had stuck with me. It was so clear and simple that I couldn't understand how anybody would want to maintain the capitalist system. I didn't think about how socialism was going to come or consider the details of how the government would be run. No matter when it came, it would be the right thing for the human race. You can't give everybody fifty acres of farmland; you can't give everybody a mine or an auto plant. Social production has to be done in common, and ultimately a socialist society is the solution. I figured that working toward one was as worthwhile a way to spend my time as anything else I had seen around. It never occurred to me to be selfish and just concern myself with making money. I wasn't in that kind of setting anyway; I was surrounded by workers. Even my awful uncle, as reactionary as he was, worked as a boilermaker, and his wife was a dressmaker. One of his kids was a hatmaker and the other a cigarmaker. That was my world. In socialist society there would be no war and relations between people would be fair. All these things made it easy for me to roll with the movement that I saw, the only movement that I knew of. I saw nothing that could compare to it at the time, whatever faults I see now.

In the beginning of 1926, I was working at a small Fisher Body plant where we had a Party branch of six men. As a YWL member, I was active with this older Party group. It was the best job that I ever had in the auto industry. At that time they were making walnut and mahogany dashboard panels with nice inlay work for Cadillac limousines and Olds sedans. I had the task of repairing those which had been damaged but were salvageable. It was piece-rate work. They must have spent $10 on these panels already, so if I could fix them for another four bits it would pay to do it. Otherwise the panels would have been scrapped. I worked across the bench from a Swedish fellow who was a perpetual joke teller. He was nonstop, running through his repertoire whenever the boss wasn't around, and I was the only one who could hear him. I tried to work on him with a little politics, and we'd go back and forth across the bench, trading jokes for political raps till the shift was over.

Even though the plant was fairly small and mostly highly skilled craftsmen worked there, the six of us in the Party unit put out a shop paper. As we worked, we got used to talking with each other over just about anything. During this period the struggle between Stalin and Trotsky was raging in the Soviet Party, and we discussed all the news we could get, both at branch meetings and informally among ourselves. At home, we would read *Inprecor* (International Press Correspondence), a news summary and analysis that came twice a month from the Communist International, tightly printed on onionskin paper. We zealously followed the discussion and polemics. Well, the six of us got a little carried away on one shift. We sat out on the curb during lunchtime and picked up where our discussion at the previous night's meeting had ended. I never thought twice about it, but the next day, all six of us were bounced.

We were captivated by the fight within the Soviet Party and waited breathlessly to see which side was going to win. Many of us, including myself, were convinced that Stalin was more right than Trotsky. The question was which way would the Soviet Union go? Stalin summed it up by arguing that there had been a temporary stabilization of capitalism after the First World War and that the revolutions we expected in Germany and other countries had been smashed. That perspective demanded a change in strategy with a new emphasis on defending and building the Soviet Union. He had a way of convincing us that those who wanted to do the hard work of building socialism in Russia were the true revolutionaries. He called for Russians to tighten their belts. "We will sell butter and eggs—not eat them. And we will buy machines which will make the steel which we must have to make the machines which will make shoes. We will not buy the shoes." I am putting it roughly, but that's the way I understood it at the time. I didn't see a revolution coming in Europe. The movements there had been crushed—driven underground—and fascist currents were already appearing with Mussolini in Italy.

The alternative proposed by Trotsky, as I saw it, was that socialism cannot be built in one country, that revolution had to occur elsewhere or socialism in the Soviet Union was doomed. He stood on the theory that "permanent revolution" was crucial. Stalin attacked this as phrase-mongering, and I thought that it was wishful thinking myself. Never since then have I read Party polemics as intensely as I read those between 1924 and 1928. It was clear to me that Stalin offered the better alternative for the Russian Revolution. We didn't see then the bureaucracy and brutality with which he would act. Nor did we question internal Party democracy in the Soviet Union. We took it for granted that the Party had to be disciplined, that when the majority wins, the minority submits without question. We assumed that the congresses and internal Party processes were essentially democratic. Stalin's line wasn't forced down our throats. Although we did not know what was going on behind the scenes, it was the logic of the argument that convinced us.

By the time of the Sixth Congress of the Communist International in Moscow in July 1928, Trotsky was already in exile. I had some doubts about his being forced out: I thought this was no way to settle the question, even though I strongly disagreed with Trotsky's analysis. The following October about one hundred members of the American Party were expelled on the grounds of being Trotskyists. To us that label meant that they had become "enemies of the Revolution," and I didn't have any personal contact with them that led me to think otherwise.

I really didn't give the Trotskyist point of view serious consideration until I left the Party. I then had to grapple with the question of why things had turned out the way they had in the Soviet Union. It wasn't just that Stalin was crazy. Nor was it simply a matter of the external threats to the survival of the Revolution, although they were

severe and had the effect of fostering a sense of discipline and vigi-
lance in which dissenting views were all too easily dismissed as counterrevolutionary. I think that these problems were compounded by
Lenin's death in 1924 so soon after the civil war and, perhaps more
importantly, the impact of the war itself on the Russian working
class.[6] Seven years of war and revolution had greatly weakened the
working class and left Party ranks badly depleted. After the civil war,
the Party depended increasingly on its own apparatus for all administrative functions. In this context Party rule became centralized and
bureaucratic. But now I think Trotsky should be put with those revolutionaries who fought for social change and that he shoud be treated
objectively by historians.

The Party was stronger in Detroit than it was in other industrial
cities. Chicago was strong too, but it wasn't anything like Detroit in
the late twenties. Detroit was a one-industry town, and it was simpler
to understand. Everybody had a common problem; you saw giant
corporations, and you saw the mass of workers. You didn't make
pickles and ketchup and mayonnaise and a dozen other things. What
you did, if you were male, was hard industrial work. It was all very
clear.

The Party reflected Detroit's particular makeup. There were Slavs,
Jews, and Lithuanians but only a few black members. There weren't
many blacks working in the auto plants yet. They were not accepted
by employers, who felt there was still plenty of "white trash" to exploit. Our main focus was on industrial work, even though that
meant some people who concentrated on nationality work felt a little
slighted. And the largest group of members was composed of auto
workers. Of the four or five hundred members, there was also a sizable group of building trades workers and a sprinkling of housewives,
small businessmen, professionals, and intellectuals. One of the last
was a teacher who offered classes on American history to our members. Some kind of course was going on all the time. We even had a
member who was a violinist and became the business agent for the
musicians' local. During the 1926 miners' "Save the Union" fight, a
few coal miners came to town to speak at various local union
meetings.[7] One played the accordion, and they'd give a talk and pass
the hat to raise money for the support of striking and blacklisted
miners. The accordion player impressed the musicians' local so much
that the Detroit Symphony Orchestra responded with a free concert to
back the miners.

Life within the Party was anything but tranquil. There was always some kind of argument going on, good-natured or otherwise.

Some disputes were simply clashes between people who couldn't get along with each other, but others went to the core of our political practice. The debate over how much material on the Soviet Union to put in the shop papers was central to my leaving Detroit. Jay Lovestone, the Party's secretary, decided to replace Rudy Baker, who was my friend and a supporter of William Z. Foster against Lovestone on internal Party questions.[8] He maneuvered to have Baker sent to Moscow to attend the Lenin School and eventually brought in Albert Weisbord as the new district organizer. Weisbord, a graduate of City College and Harvard, was an aggressive young intellectual who had led the 1926 Passaic textile strike, one of the most important and militant Left-led strikes of the twenties.[9] If I have ever met an egotist in the movement, he was it. When he came to Detroit in the fall of 1927, the *Ford Worker* carried headlines to the effect that Albert Weisbord was now in Detroit to organize the auto workers. I knew we weren't going to get along. He thought that through his own presence and self-confidence he would be able to influence the workers to organize the auto industry.

Weisbord had his own ideas about how to run things, and he disregarded Phil Raymond and others who were a lot closer to the situation. He moved quickly to remold the district organization to his own liking and politics. That led to a division with me on the side of Phil Raymond and Bud Reynolds, men who in my opinion were more able and practical leaders in terms of what was going on in the plants. In my judgment we were stressing building a union, while the opposition's view was based on a more abstract, intellectual understanding of socialism. It was a matter of degree in some cases, but Weisbord pushed it to a point of basic difference. He had less support in the group working in auto but quite a bit from those involved in nationality work. Soon after he arrived, he came to a meeting of our Section Committee on East Ferry Street. He must have found out that I was not thrilled that he'd come here to organize auto—I didn't make a secret of it. Soon after I was removed from my position as head of the section. I wasn't the only one. He couldn't touch Reynolds or Raymond, who were elected by their own constituencies to the District Committee, but those of us on the sectional level were easy enough to replace. He only had to argue that someone else would be better able to carry out policy, and he did have a majority of the District Committee backing him when he first arrived.

About the same time Margaret was fired from her job in the Party office. Weisbord had to get rid of her so he could maneuver more freely. He gave her a hard time from the start, demanding that she be in at eight o'clock in the morning. While he never came in till later, he called every morning to make sure that Margaret was there. One day she showed up for work and found that the locks had been changed. Later that day she went back in and confronted him. "I guess my services are no longer required," she said. Weisbord smiled coolly and replied, "My, but you're a smart girl." And that was that. No one saw it as so unusual. We all agreed that when the majority wins, the minority submits. There was no use hanging around, so we packed our bags and left.

New York: 1928

If it was Weisbord and Party infighting that made me leave Detroit, it was the chance to go to school and learn something that drew me to New York City. There were several of us at that time who gladly got away. We didn't want to fight over what was going on in Detroit. It seemed like it would be a temporary phenomenon; we were sure that Weisbord wouldn't last. In the meantime we felt that we couldn't work very well with him.

When I lived in Pittsburgh, the YWL had sent me to New York City for two weeks at the Workers' School. I saw the possibility of continuing this during the upcoming winter. Besides, we heard that work was available in New York City. The gears on our old Chevy were stripped and needed all sorts of work before we could leave. At that time a fellow could work on his car right on the street, so I jacked it up, changed the gears, and put in the parts I got from the junkyard. Without wasting any time, we put our stuff in, said good-bye to our friends, and went off to New York.

The trip took quite a while, and by the time we hit the city, Margaret wasn't feeling too well. She had broken out in a rash, but we didn't know what it was. We were tired and a bit disoriented as we drove through Manhattan. We went to see a woman who was in charge of miners' relief work. She had stayed at our house in Detroit many evenings and come to us with her friends for various kinds of help. After searching out her office in the Party headquarters, I asked, "Where do you think we can get a place to stay?" She stared at me for a second, replied without hesitation, "Get a newspaper and look!" and went back to her work. Now there was no doubt that she was busy. She was an aggressive, dynamic woman, and work around the miners' strike was demanding. But it hit me like a rock. Get a newspaper and look! We had expected her to say that she had a friend who had a room, or that a woman she knew needed a boarder, or that somebody down in the District Office could tell us where to look. Even with the trouble over Weisbord, the organization in a smaller industrial city like Detroit was more down-to-earth, more personal. We weren't ready for New York City. We got a paper and wound up renting a room from a Mr. Jones, who turned out to be a carpenter. I took my transfer from Detroit and joined a local of cabinetmakers and skilled carpenters, but with winter coming the building trades were depressed, and I couldn't find work. Margaret was still not feeling well and couldn't work either. We didn't have much of a bankroll, but it would last a few weeks. In the meantime I started school.

The New York Workers' School was on Fourteenth Street near Union Square in Manhattan. It was only a flat with four or five rooms that weren't much larger than cubbyholes. The setup was all right in the winter, and when summer came I was already gone—but I imagine that it would have been a steam room.

It was great to be exposed to new ideas, especially if there was a good lecture. Some things, such as political economy, were really over my head at the time. I didn't understand stocks and bonds and the actions of the stock market, but I did get an elementary understanding of the production system—of capitalism—and how it worked. They didn't have to tell me about exploitation. I knew it better than the instructor in some ways. And I knew what goes on in the factory and what happens during unemployment; I'd faced it enough times. I was also learning new things, like the "colonial question." I had heard of it before, but it didn't mean too much. Concepts like "imperialism" were tossed around, and I began to see what people meant by them.

Courses on labor history and political economy alternated with sessions on American history and Marxist theory. Most met one night a week and lasted about six weeks. There were nineteen or twenty students in my classes, many of them from the needle trades, as well as some white-collar workers, a few seamen, and hotel and cafeteria workers. The teachers were usually older men who had been around the radical movement for a time and had mastered many of the weightier political works. Pop Mindel and Alexander Trachtenberg were both immigrants from czarist Russia and spoke their precise and articulate English with strong accents. Mindel, a dentist by day, walked slowly back and forth, patiently explaining Marx's basic theoretical insights. He could converse with his students without embarrassing them and kept his lectures simple, knowing how unprepared we were. Bill Dunne led the course on labor history but missed classes whenever some strike or problem called him out of town. In his place William Z. Foster appeared one night to talk about the 1919 strike in steel. On other nights New York trade unionists came to talk about their own experiences.

I took labor history for one term and then political economy. I couldn't go more than one night a week because you had to prepare for class by reading something. While my English was much better, I was anything but a rapid reader and had to constantly ask Maggie for the meaning of words. The first time I went to class, I sat down in a straight-backed chair and waited somewhat nervously for the hubbub to die away and my education to begin. The instructor handed out an outline for the six sessions, a set of topics with readings listed in the margins. Reports were assigned, and in the following weeks, the session was divided between the instructor's talks and student reports followed by long tough question-and-answer sessions. You might be asked, "What do you mean by surplus value?" or "How do you understand the meaning of the eight-hours strike in Chicago?"[10] The analysis was always handled in such a way as to put the CP or the left wing in the most positive light. While the school, run by the Party, forced us to think critically about society in general, we failed to apply that kind of analysis to our own organization.

A few weeks after school began, I had to give a report on my experiences working in the auto plants. Most of my classmates had never even seen an assembly line, and it was hard for me to figure out how to prepare. When I got to class that night, I just started talking about what it was like to work in the factories, embellishing my descriptions with what I thought were the proper radical phrases. The students, many of whom had read much more than me, started talking about the Taylor System and scientific management as if they had worked a conveyor for years. I mostly sat and listened, absorbing what I could the rest of the evening, marveling at how people who had never been on the line could make such accurate analyses. To be forced to explain some concept to a group like this helped me. But I wasn't becoming an intellectual, although there were many of them in and around the Party in New York. At this time anyone who went to college was an intellectual to me.

After class, the big thing to do was to go down the block to the "Coop," a cooperative restaurant run by some left wingers. We would drink coffee and eat doughnuts and carry on until we couldn't stand it any longer and were falling asleep in our doughnut crumbs. All kinds of nonconformists gathered there and engaged in the wildest conversations. One night, hunched over a cup of coffee, I listened to a guy at the next table say with quiet assurance, "The *Cherry Orchard* was

the best play ever created. Now Chekhov. . . . " I had never heard the
name "Chekhov" before! These young people, many of whom came
from such different backgrounds, helped me to see new things, to
think in different ways. They taught me some of the early radical
songs like "Hold the Fort, For We Are Coming" and answered my
questions.

I wanted to learn as much as I could. I never considered going to
college, though for a while I thought about the Brookwood Labor
College, run by activists and intellectuals from the labor movement
and Socialist Party.[11] But I couldn't take off from work and wasn't
sure that I as a Communist Party member, would be acceptable to the
school.

I think my experience with the Workers' School was fairly typical of
that of a large number of young workers, many of whom were foreign-
born and poorly educated like myself. The radical movement was our
teacher. It was a great step forward to be drawn together in a group to
talk and listen, to be induced to read and study. Where else could we
get that opportunity? Only years later could I see some of the shortcomings of the school: it was rather narrow in subject matter with not
enough attention given to American history and political life. It was
geared toward convincing us of the meaningfulness of communism or
socialism and demonstrating that the 1917 Revolution was the great
historical event of our times. Yet I cherished the chance to attend and
was sorry when another kind of education forced me to stop.

In the twenties an institution like the Workers' School could only
have been so easily sustained in a city like New York, where the
National Office of the Communist Party and a large supportive base
existed. The presence of the national leadership and so many intellectuals and cultural workers created an atmosphere different from
that in Detroit. But it wasn't an atmosphere that I breathed much
of. Margaret had gotten better and begun working in the Party's
National Offices. Her reputation as a reliable comrade and staff
person had stuck with her, and she was recruited to work in the
Organizational Department. After a while she began to work with a
Finnish fellow who then worked for the Comintern. The Comintern
or Communist International was founded in 1919 by Lenin and
served as the ideological and strategic headquarters of the world
wide Communist movement. The man she worked for was named
Valenius, but I think we all called him Smith. He was a very agreeable, low-key person who knew a lot about organization and helped
out during the later factional turmoil.

Because Maggie was at the National office, she would find out about social gatherings, and sometimes we'd be invited. Many of the parties were down in the Village. We met artists and leaders of the left-wing movements and for the first time saw them in a relaxed state, with some of the barriers between leadership and rank and file taken down. It was good for me to see them act like regular people, drinking and talking about things that were not always on the agenda. It was strange but nice to go to a party at the apartment of a middle-class comrade where the rooms were bigger and more comfortable than what I was used to. I was out of my element, but I could still appreciate the scene. A lot of the people who went through City College would be there—young radicals so much more intellectually inclined than my comrades in Detroit. They brought a certain flavor to the New York Party organization.

Much more activity on the cultural level took place in New York. There was a concern about the theater and the arts, and painters, cartoonists, and playwrights like John Howard Lawson and Mike Gold were either in or around the Party. I didn't have much to do with them but would see one of their plays now and then. That was the first time I was exposed to theater, and I loved it. Most of the working-class members of the Party didn't have all that much to do with this sector of the Party either; they had contact in the sense that they too developed a taste for the arts and began to enjoy theater and dance. Ballet and opera didn't mean a damn thing to me; never saw either performed. I'm not proud of it—it's just a fact of life. Either you didn't have the money or you didn't grow up in surroundings that would have exposed you to such things.

But rank and file members and other workers had a chance to meet intellectuals and artists because many of them went into the field, to take part in living movements. Quite a few saw their role as helping labor, and they supported strikes by speaking and raising money, publicizing the struggle, or coming to live and work with the strikers. They had the skills to write leaflets and put together shop papers, and in the course of this work, they began to see "labor" less as an abstraction and more as people. Some of the walls between them and the rest of us melted way. I recall writers coming to the anthracite coalfields of eastern Pennsylvania when I was there in the early thirties. They stayed for a while, soaked up the flavor, and went back home to write about what they learned. An eighteen-year-old artist, Winnie Lubell, came to the anthracite and painted miners going to work and coming home as dirty as chimney sweeps. She painted the monster Pottsville colliery and the railroad hopper cars on the tracks. I never met her then, but she's my neighbor now on the Cape, and that colliery painting of hers hangs on my wall. Most of these men and women were well respected in the Party because they were not cut off from our struggles. Some, of course, went overboard and gave up their art or profession and became what we called "mechanical proletarians." They were much better off and more helpful to us when they recognized what they were and dealt with us from that perspective. In some ways I think that those of us from working-class backgrounds had as much of an impact on them as they had on us.

The base of the Party in New York City extended far beyond the Village, City College, and intellectual circles. While it did not have the heavy industrial base we had in Detroit, the New York Party had strong roots in the needle trades and among seamen, longshoremen, and transport workers. Hundreds of immigrant garment workers and furriers belonged to the Party in both industrial branches and nationality groups. Frequently their elected union leaders were Party members—such as Ben Gold and Irving Potash of the furriers, Sasha Zimmerman and Rose Wortis of the garment workers, and scores of shop stewards.[12] Other labor leaders were close to the Party and consulted with the organization regularly. The militancy of textile workers in the Passaic strike of 1926 and a whole series of clashes in the New York City needle trades still reverberated. These efforts, uphill struggles in what was a relatively quiet, backward period for American labor, spilled over into drives to organize the subway workers, cafeteria and hotel employees, and a number of other trades. And Communists were quite often in the thick of it.

As in Detroit, the Party's ethnic base was overwhelmingly from the massive migrations of the late nineteenth and early twentieth centuries. Many New York members were Jews from Russia, Poland, and the Ukraine, while others came from Southern and Eastern Europe. These ethnic origins and cultures vitalized the radical movements in New York and fed the Socialist Party as well as the Communists. They were the source of an enduring radicalism. Yet in some ways, the Left in New York City was isolated by its very nature. The viability of its radical subculture sometimes prevented it from spreading its wings and leaping out of the old familiar environment. The emphasis on national origins retarded the study of American realities and sometimes led to a tendency to talk revolution instead of getting into the unions and doing the hard day-to-day work. When people came for the first time into the Party, they brought all kinds of ideological and cultural baggage. Some of it was good, and some not so good. The Party was a purifying force to some extent, but it takes a lifetime to cure these things.

School was not the only source of my education in New York. My misadventures taught me a great deal, too. Unable to continue with carpentry during the traditionally slow winter months, I finally found a job in the Chance and Vought airplane factory on Long Island. The island hummed with industrial energy in the late twenties. The Miller Shoe Company employed over three thousand and Nickle's Copper ran a huge smelting complex. A tremendous railroad yard serviced the large companies, and the Long Island Party branch distributed a railroad workers' edition of the *Daily Worker* there every few weeks. Chance and Vought was building planes for the navy (I later learned they were used against Sandino and his liberation forces in Nicaragua).[13] A wooden structure was covered with fabric, then shellacked and varnished. The planes were highly flammable, but they were the best the navy had at the time. I worked on the center section where the wings and fuselage were attached and the engine mounted. The center was a very compact, well-engineered piece made out of seasoned ash reinforced by aluminum castings. The machine gun was placed there, so this section had to be strong but light. I had to make sure the joints were properly bored and precisely machined so that sections could be fitted tightly by hand. While the plant operated on a mass-production basis, with one group of guys making the wings, another castings, and so on, there was still room for skilled work. Working on the crucial center sections, I was getting pretty good pay. Moreover, the Party branch on Long Island was delighted that I was working there.

I had only been there a few months, but I was getting to know some of the other men. Shortly before I started work, Chance and Vought had opened a school for youngsters who wanted to learn how to build planes. You can imagine the attraction for an average kid. Boys between fourteen and eighteen flocked to the company with the dream of becoming aviators or at least mechanics. They worked a regular day shift and went to school in the evening from six to nine. During the day the company put them to work on what they called the "ribs" in the wings. The ribs were balsa sections that formed a stiff plywood. They required a dreadful amount of sanding, and Chance and Vought put as many as a hundred of these kids to work doing that. The boys worked on the ribs for the months that I was there and never got any further. They were paid from one fourth to one third of what most of the unskilled laborers and semiskilled assemblers were making.

At lunch we would run across the street to the lunch wagon. I would sit on the curb not far from these lads and listen to them grumble. They hated sanding, and I couldn't much blame them. It was tedious work. But what really rubbed these kids was that they had thought they were going to go step by step through the process of building a plane. They saw no evidence that the company intended to take them any further and it seemed to me that there was no way it could be done. If you build a plane for the navy, you can't screw around—it has to be done to specifications. So I couldn't see how these kids could get what they wanted, and my political conscience got to me.

A few days later, I was sent to the so-called School Department to show some of the new ones how to sand the wings properly. I asked them a lot of questions, and a number of the fellows I had heard grumbling on the street came by. Pretty soon I wasn't showing them how to sand but was telling them what I thought they ought to do about the company taking advantage of them. I suggested that they should have a committee present their demands to the company in written form and that they should insist they be given a clear indication of what their next steps would be. Well, they never got this indication, because when the committee went to management, its members were fired, and the other boys stopped working. The manager came out of his office and threatened and cajoled, but he couldn't convince them to get back to work. Finally he yelled that they were on strike and would have to leave or be arrested. At that most of the boys started leaving, and I swear many of them had no idea what "being on strike" meant. The next week, when most of the kids failed to show for work, Chance and Vought closed down the school and this aspect of the work was taken over by laborers. Later that week the foreman came over to my work place and told me to collect my pay and clear out.

The company had somehow gotten wind that I had instigated the stoppage, and that was that. Of course, the Section Committee bawled me out for being so careless with these boys and for losing what they saw as a very important spot for a Party member to be in. I had been careless. I thought I was repeating what I had learned from Pittsburgh and the auto plants when I gave advice to the guys. I didn't worry about being fired, only about being arrested or beaten up. But I was fired and had probably cost these kids their jobs, too.

I had a hard time getting a job after that, but then I was hired on a construction job building a subway station at the Queensborough exchange. I was working underground with other carpenters making props, supports for the streets above, and forms for steps. A fellow I knew in the YWL was out of work, and I got him hired as my helper. All the while we worked, we talked about the need to organize, but the carpenters' union wasn't interested in subway construction workers. It was slimy, backbreaking work, and we quit when some timbers gave way and a wall collapsed. That afternoon, after the shift was over, we sat across from each other in a booth at a nearby bar and convinced ourselves that we were doing the prudent thing by getting the hell out while we were still in one piece. This fellow moved on to Pittsburgh soon afterwards, got involved in some business operation, and left the YWL; "got lost," as we used to say. When the panel of jurors was called in my sedition case there many years later, I was flabbergasted when the clerk called his name. He didn't even look at me as he went up to the judge, pleaded sick, and was excused from the jury.

In the meantime the Party was concentrating on industrial workers on Long Island. The TUEL was in operation and had a division that was more or less a catchall for any kind of metal shop where the AFL had no jurisdiction or activity. It put out a leaflet for the workers at Nickle's Copper plant, which was located on the estuary on Long Island near where the barges drew up with its coal, ore, and materials. It was a real slummy kind of industrial establishment. There was a railroad bridge over the channel and a cluster of dirty barges with packs of rats on the waterfront. In the Section Committee I agreed to distribute these leaflets, which were little more than a general call for unionization and an attack on the open shop. I had to come a fair distance, since by that time we had left good carpenter Jones and moved to the lower Bronx, near the Harlem River. Two other people from the section promised to come and meet there in the early morning, about six o'clock, to catch the day shift.

It was still dark when I got there, and I was half asleep. I looked around for my friends as I leaned, shivering, against the fence around the plant. They didn't show, and I knew that I didn't want to have to come back again, so I started handing out my leaflets to the first stream of workers. Before I had handed out more than a dozen, a couple of burly guys came up. One of them stood in front of me and demanded to know what I thought I was doing. I was about to answer when the other guy, who had sidled around in back of me, grabbed my leather jacket and pulled it over my arms, pinning them to my sides. The guy in front laughed and pulled a blackjack out of his back pocket and whack! He operated on me, and cuts opened up on my head and face. I was bleeding like a pig, and the leaflets were blowing into the river. After a few very long moments, a couple of guys coming to work interceded, pushing these two men out of the way and helping me over to the fence where I crouched, holding my head. To add insult to injury, the company goons then had me arrested for disturbing the peace. We went off to court and someone, who must have been sympathetic, managed to contact an ILD lawyer for me. He arrived during my hearing and raised hell. We got off with a fine of twenty-five bucks, which we refused to pay, and they let me go pending appeal. I don't know how it ended up, but I never paid the damn thing. I didn't have to be hospitalized, and they didn't bother to stitch you up in those days. They just pulled the wounds together, bandaged them, and let them heal. But it did take some of the wind out of my sails.

I was in no shape to look for work. When some people we knew who were connected with Camp Unity, a Party camp in Wingdale, New York, suggested I come up there for a week to rest, nobody had to twist my arm. It was March, and there was snow on the ground, but you could tell spring was coming. While I was up there, the people who ran the camp asked if I would do their carpentry work. They were building bungalows and facilities and also had a lot of repair work to do. I discussed it with Margaret, who also was not feeling very well. We decided that I would work up there, and she would rest until she felt better. I worked there through the summer, building campgrounds and serving as the Party organizer for the camp. I was in charge of the personnel who were Party members, not as a manager, but as political adviser. Many of the waiters and counselors were members, and we had quite a good branch. The camp appealed to liberals and left wingers and was cheap enough for working people. It was like any other camp in many ways, except that our cultural activities were geared toward radicalism. I made friends there that I kept for life. My wounds healed, I had time to swim and hike, and I finally learned to play softball. I also got into some hot water. One very muggy night I was sitting around after dinner with a half dozen guys from the kitchen crew. Someone suggested that we go skinny-dipping, and off we went. Unfortunately, we got caught, and the camp administration was enraged. As the Party organizer, I had to make a public apology to the assembled guests.

I had a lot of time to think about what I had learned in New York that winter—not only from classes, but from the fiasco at Chance and Vought and the beating at the copper plant. I vowed that I would think a little more when I was putting myself on the line. I worked, but it was like a vacation in many ways. It was the last one I would have for more than a decade.

Factionalism had clouded the Party's image and disrupted its internal workings continually through the 1920s, and as summer turned to fall in 1928 and we went back to New York City, one last storm burst. Jay Lovestone, the general secretary of the American Party, had supported Stalin over Trotsky during the last major spasm of infighting on the international level. But there was strong opposition, loosely grouped around William Foster, to Lovestone, who had occupied the highest leadership position in the Party since 1927, when Charles Ruthenberg died. While there were differences in personality and style, there were also substantive political disagreements between the two factions.

Before the 1924 election, debate had started over what kind of electoral policy American revolutionaries should follow. Should the Party go into electoral politics strictly on a socialist basis, or should it make a coalition around a more limited program? Efforts were made to build a Farmer-Labor Party (FLP) and involve segments of the labor movement. Foster, who had strong ties to the Chicago labor movement because of his role in the organization of steel and packinghouse workers there, tried to convince his old ally John Fitzpatrick of the Chicago Federation of Labor. But Fitzpatrick had reservations regarding the breadth of support for such a venture and decided against going along with it. Ruthenberg and others in the national leadership nevertheless insisted that a convention be held to nominate a Farmer-Labor candidate. In alliance with the Minnesota FLP, plans were made for such a convention with general agreement that it would nominate Robert M. LaFollette, the progressive senator from Wisconsin, for president. But the Comintern barred support for LaFollette, and the Communist Party was forced to break its alliance with the Minnesota FLP. It then nominated Foster and Benjamin Gitlow to run on the Workers' Party ticket, as the Party was then known. LaFollette received far greater support at the polls than the Workers' Party slate, which garnered only a handful of votes. With the elections over, those around Foster felt that there would be no point going into it again unless there was real support from labor. Lovestone, however, envisioned getting farmer movements and other groups to pursue the labor party idea. The Comintern's intervention in the matter, though, was not an issue.[14]

The other question generating a great deal of tension was the overall estimate of the economic situation in the United States. While we were at Camp Unity, the Comintern had declared in a broad strategy statement that the "temporary stabilization" of capitalism that followed the defeat of the abortive 1919 German revolution had come to an end. The capitalist world system was on the verge of crisis. But Lovestone took the view that American capitalism had a lot of elbow room and could avoid the crisis. He called it an exceptional situation for the American ruling class and foresaw the Keynesian methods of alleviating economic crisis through pump-priming and taxation, although these were hardly talked about at this time. Foster, Earl Browder, and Alexander Bittleman, chief theoretician and economist for the Foster group, argued that the United States was in for the same hard times as the rest of the world system.[15] I didn't believe that there would be revolutionary change, but I could see a lot of economic hardship from my vantage point, and it looked as though things were going to get worse.

There were other points of friction over organizational matters and ways to relate to the trade union movement and carry on "mass work." People were shuffled around for factional reasons and political differences hardened into personal antagonisms. There was a division of opinion in every district. I was young but already identified as an opponent of Lovestone. For a long time the confrontation was brewing, but it was bound to come to the surface. The factionalism was incapacitating the Party, and we were unable to resolve it ourselves. When a stalemate resulted at the CPUSA's Sixth Congress in 1928, the leadership decided to seek counsel from the Comintern.

The Sixth Congress of the Communist International, which met in Moscow in the summer of 1928, developed a new forecast for the world capitalist system and set up a special commission mandated to stop the factionalism within the American Party. While criticizing both sides, the commission came down harder on Lovestone when he refused to accept its analysis. Now Lovestone had taken his case for American exceptionalism before the Comintern and been voted down. His defiance of the Comintern's rulings led it to expel him. A telegram came to the National Office to this effect, and the American Party's Central Comittee soon met and concurred, expelling Lovestone from the American Party as well. By the time he made it back from Moscow, the locks had been changed on the Party offices and his supporters, like Weisbord in Detroit, removed from their positions. Up to this time, Lovestone had had a majority of the Party behind him. This support led him to decide to defy the Comintern. He underestimated, however, the great influence of the Comintern on the U.S. membership and even on many of the leaders of his own faction. There is no doubt that the impetus for his repudiation came from the Comintern. Lovestone maintained a small splinter group for some years after and steadily moved to the right. He eventually became an adviser to George Meany and the right wing within the AFL and to the Central Intelligence Agency on labor matters abroad. His later actions confirmed our belief that anyone who went against the Comintern would likely become a tool of reactionary forces.

Lovestone's expulsion temporarily weakened the party. Fewer than a thousand members went with him, but a fair number of others threw up their hands in despair and took a walk. The Party, never very large in the twenties, was now down to seven or eight thousand members. Several important leaders like Sasha Zimmerman and a few others in the needle trades went with Lovestone. These unions were Yiddish-speaking, and Zimmerman was a spellbinder in Yiddish. People have their likes and stick with them. In the early days Sasha was a good organizer, and people thought, well, he's no worse now than he used to be. But most members, either because they were in disagreement with Lovestone or found bucking the Comintern's decision too difficult, remained in the Party.

I went along with the decision on the grounds that the international leadership was more likely to be right than Lovestone. I respected the leadership of the Comintern. They were the old revolutionary leaders I had read and heard about—Clara Zetkin, Palmiro Togliatti, the Finn Otto Kuusinen, the Frenchman André Marty, Wilhelm Pieck and Ernst Thaelmann from Germany, and the Japanese Sen Katayama. I didn't have too much theoretical and political experience, so whatever they did sounded reasonable to me. I thought, "Who the hell is this peanut Lovestone?" I really didn't like him, either; he was known as a slick artist. You kind of weigh things: could Lovestone actually be better than all these top international leaders, including the Russians? Moreover, I didn't have much respect for a number of the people around Lovestone, especially some of those in the YWL. They seemed too ambitious and ready to talk a good game without having played much. I preferred to work with guys who talked about trade union problems and practical things. I never resented intellectuals—as a matter of fact, I respected them—but I didn't like some of the people in this particular group.

I was swept into the factionalism. I did everything my group did, including some maneuvering like putting our people in some positions in place of theirs. I didn't carry it to extremes, but I certainly was a part of it. What made it difficult was that when it got down to the rank and file level where I was, you'd have friends who took the opposite side. Sometimes you'd lose them over a political question, but not always. Joe Jursak who's been a lifelong friend, actually went along with Lovestone over the question of Bukharin.[16] Bukharin was an idol of young Communists everywhere because he wrote popular understandable pieces like the *ABC of Communism*. He had joined

Stalin against Trotsky in the early twenties, then found himself on the outs with Stalin over the questions of agriculture and how to industrialize. Joe was a young worker who happened to be a delegate to one of the sessions of the Young Communist International, and when he came back, he sided with Lovestone because he believed that Lovestone was aligned with Bukharin.

Joe and his wife Rose both left the Party at this time, and though I hated to see them go, I felt helpless to do anything about it. With some people I destroyed bridges, but not with them. When I was in the anthracite a few years later, the Jursaks came. They were becoming active once again in the Party, and we were happy to have them. When they came to Wilkes-Barre, I made it a point to find out who in the national leadership they had some respect for and saw to it that one or two of these people came to Wilkes-Barre on a social visit. I didn't feel I could convince Joe myself. As a matter of fact, I couldn't discuss our differences for a while. The names of Bukharin and Stalin were not mentioned. But in the course of organizing and getting arrested together almost every Friday night, we found that our differences evaporated. This was partly because we had a little bit of patience and didn't push it. Sometimes people were pushed too hard and couldn't take it, and that was the end.

People cannot always distinguish between what's really at stake politically and what's based on how they feel toward the people involved. The way I see it, you have the formality of a democratic discussion. Two sides are heard, and equal time is given to each. But people don't live in a vacuum, they're often already lined up. Some will choose on the basis of "I don't like that guy," or "He's too flippant" or "I just don't trust him." Others take sides according to how their friends or people they respect line up. Most of the people who held positions of responsibility would be up on the political issues involved, but there were a lot of us who had a hard time sorting things out.

Nevertheless, whatever the issues involved, I don't think expulsions are a solution every time there is a basic difference of opinion. It is important to be able to adhere to a general policy, but people who disagree should not be excluded so long as they are willing to carry out policy. In fact, those who differ on matters of importance must continue to raise questions at the proper place and time. I didn't see that then. We followed the policy of "democratic centralism": if you don't agree, you're out.

The 1920s were a difficult decade for American radicalism. It climbed with the ascent of the Russian Revolution and sailed on the wings of European currents of change. But we flopped to the ground repeatedly. We made plenty of mistakes, and the times were simply not that fertile for the rooting of the Party in American soil. The spirit of the Russian Revolution and the movement abroad carried us through much of this decade. If there weren't any great things happening here, you heard of them building big dams over there, of the modernization of agriculture and the electrification of the countryside. This was a major focus, especially for foreign-born Communists. But by the end of the twenties we were beginning to turn the corner on a period of isolation and weakness. We were ready to enter the mainstream of the American working class and take part in its struggles in what was to be one of the most class-conscious decades of our century.

With the expulsion of the small Trotskyist and Lovestone factions, there was a temporary lull to internal strife. We were now able to turn all of our attention to practical work. The end of factionalism also coincided more or less with some significant reorientations within the Party. One of these was the attempt to "Americanize" the Party. When the Communist Party was first formed, it was based organizationally on the foreign language federations. Up until the late twenties, the language branch was the standard form of Party structure. There might be a Lithuanian branch on the South Side of Chicago, a Jewish branch on the North Side, and a Croation or Greek branch on the West Side. A citywide Central Committee that coordinated activities carried on its business in English. In 1925, at its Fourth Congress, the Party decided to reorganize. Of a membership of some seventeen thousand, fewer than two thousand were involved in English-speaking groups, and it was seen as imperative to get beyond the language barrier. With this effort to Americanize the Party, the language branches were abolished in favor of neighborhood and shop branches. The language papers remained, and work within the fraternal organizations continued, but we were definitely in a better position to sink roots outside our subcultures of immigrant radicalism. We could begin orienting ourselves, a largely foreign-born Party, toward an understanding of American history and the specificity of American conditions. Incidentally, Lovestone carried this reorganization through. He was the mastermind of organizational charts, and I used to think he was some kind of genius to be able to do it. Later on, Browder, who eventually replaced Lovestone as general secretary, added greater substance to this concept of Americanization.

This reorganization cost us a good part of our membership, for the attempt to transform members of language groups into good Bolshevik cadres found many unable to make the transition from the ethnic community to larger struggles. It was at this point that Stjepan Mesaroš became Steve Nelson. As part of the Americanization of the Communist Party, many foreign-born members were taking American-sounding names. There's no complicated explanation for why I chose Nelson, I had worked once with a carpenter by that name, and it seemed as good as any.

This shift away from the security of a foreign-born base dovetailed with a clarification of the significance of trade union work. By the 1930s the membership understood the trade union question much better. That took some doing. There had been some friction between those who worked in unions and those who saw the nationality groups as their focus. We had to convince a lot of people of the need to stress work in the labor movement. We had new members who were not involved in their unions or language-group members who might say, "You go ahead and work in the union. You speak English, I don't. I'll stick to my nationality work."

Every plenum or national meeting would hear exhaustive reports about every union in the country where there was some activity.[17] And even where there wasn't much activity, as in the railroad unions, there was a department concerned with work in that area. A man in Chicago, Otto Wangren, was the head of the Party's railroad commission. He was a human computer. He had it all in his head—every official in every local, every contract, regional situation, and what problems the workers faced. He would stand up and make detailed reports that sometimes meant little to most of us. After Wangren was finished, Foster, an ex-railroad worker himself, would get up. He had a habit of grabbing hold of something, and he would scowl at us and exclaim, "Goddamn it! Every town in the country has a railroad running through it, and by golly, nobody's paying any attention to the railroad workers, who work under rotten conditions for lousy wages!" I remember now as if it were yesterday. But if we weren't making spectacular headway within the railroad brotherhoods, we were beginning to attract numbers of miners, steel and metal workers, and electrical workers and were able to more than hold our own within the garment trades, a continuing base of support.

The idea of industrial unionism was maturing. Moreover, there was no longer any doubt of the need to work within the AFL unions—if we could. Nor was there any doubt of the need to build independent unions where the other unions wouldn't move. Reality called for it. These new directions within labor were not without setbacks, but they signaled a healthy reorientation for the Party.

In many ways the twenties were a radical departure from previous years in terms of everyday life for many working people. When the economy picked up in 1923, and throughout the years of Coolidge prosperity, there was an unprecedented degree of consumption and economic stability. Certainly this "prosperity" did not go much beyond the ranks of native-born white workers who had a degree of skill in their trades, and it did not include blacks or many immigrants at all. But I didn't see it as a harmful thing. Everybody who was able to was getting a car. I had bought a jalopy in 1924, and it didn't change me. It just made it easier for me to function. I was thinking of buying a lot and building a house in Detroit, and other guys I knew were doing the same thing. Some of us were questioning the simplistic interpretation of Marx's theory about the absolute impoverishment of the working class with the growth of capitalism. We didn't challenge its theoretical basis, but we somehow believed that things were different here, that workers in this country wouldn't have to go through the mill where they are ground down to nothing before they rebel.

There were radicals within and without the Party whom I argued with constantly about this question. They'd say, "Things are gonna get worse, and I hope they do. We'll see what happens to these smart alecks when they're laid off." This mood was especially strong among some of the old-timers, what I call "carping radicals," as well as some younger people around the movement. They used to say, "Wait till they starve. Wait till they're fired and their bellies reach their backbones. Then they'll do something." I would say to them, "How come the furriers, who are making $12 a day, are on strike for better conditions, and the workers in this shirt factory over here are working for 35 cents an hour and not doing a thing?" This is where I thought I understood dialectics. The mind does not function mechanistically. Ideas sometimes will influence things ahead of time. They'll give a perspective, and not necessarily because your belly is touching your backbone. An idea can enter the mind first and lead in a direction beyond the stomach. And Communists were there to help germinate those ideas. I didn't worry about the guy having a tin lizzy, and I didn't necessarily believe that the worse things got, the better chances a revolutionary movement would have. I had the idea that the human mind is different from all other kinds of matter. It's not just like a mirror. The mind not only picks up reality but, like the study of history, enables us to reflect on what the picture may be.

And despite all our mistakes, and in many cases because of them, we were learning. We were learning how to build a viable political movement. Most of all, we were learning those everyday lessons of what people wanted and how they see things. We hadn't stopped making mistakes—we were just able to talk to people more directly than before. I think we were heading in the right direction with our approach toward industrial workers. In 1928 we could sense that the numbers of those laid off were increasing and that the foreman was moving the assembly line faster. When the Depression began to hit, we were as ready as anybody to plunge into the fray and offer some leadership.

I read a little history these days, and I see that some historians consider the 1920s one of the most conservative decades in American development. They call the radicals fish fighting the current, decidedly out of the mainstream. At the time I didn't see things that way. I didn't know too much history, and I didn't know the odds. I did know we had a beautiful dream of the future. I saw the logic of socialism, and it held me. I knew I was going to be a worker, and if I was going to be a worker, I wanted to do what was best for workers. What I did get to know about history came later. By that time I was mature, and it didn't matter. But in the twenties, I wasn't frightened.

In some ways, my own life and development were reflecting the changes within the Party. I never had wanted to take any leadership responsibility. There were too many glib people around when it came to something like electing someone to chair a meeting. I'd say, let them do it. When I did get in a position like that, I would stumble my way through it. But with time and the chance to think about things, I saw that I could do it as well as the next guy. My hesitation to take leadership roles probably had something to do with my own class background, but I was maturing and so was the Party in its efforts to reach working people. And just as the Party went increasingly in the direction of trade union work, I too, was leaving my language federation work behind. You might say that my lodge activity in Detroit was my twice-a-month activity. Even when I was a YWL member, my major job was helping out on the shop papers. The more I did that, the more interested I became in the trade union phase of work. I felt that it was a broader field where we ought to be growing.

We might not have been earth shakers then, might not have been making much headway, but I thought we were getting on the right track, doing the right thing. That's what kept people moving on. I was never boisterous about being a Communist, but I was inwardly proud.

THREE

Chicago and the Southern Illinois Coalfields

With the advent of the Depression, I began to work full time for the Party, and as it grew through effective mass organizing, I grew with it. We faced bitter repression in the early thirties, but it was in these years that we first established a firm base in working-class communities.

The struggle against Lovestone and the ensuing factionalism had created a crisis in the Party in Chicago, and this was part of the reason for my going there at the end of 1929. William Kruze, the district organizer, went with Lovestone, taking a small group with him. Some members left, disgusted with all the infighting; many of those who remained were shaken up; and the mass work suffered. The Party asked Clarence Hathaway, who later became editor of the *Daily Worker,* to reorganize the district.

Part of the reorganizing would be a struggle against unemployment, which had hit the city particularly hard. The Party quickly judged the depth of the problem that was developing, and the Trade Union Unity League began putting together a team of people to work on organizing the unemployed. Hathaway had heard of my beating at the Nickle's copper plant and asked me to come to a TUUL meeting. There I met with William Z. Foster, Bill Dunne, Herbert Benjamin, Sam Weisman, and a few others who were discussing the trade union and unemployment situation in various parts of the country. They agreed that in addition to an organizational structure, a clear program was needed, consisting of specific demands around which the movement could fight. Benjamin was chosen to lead the work, and a group of young comrades were to be sent to metropolitan areas around the country in order to get the movement off the ground.

After the meeting Hathaway turned to me and said, "Look, I'm going to Chicago. How about you and Margaret coming too? You're out of a job, aren't you? Maybe you could find a friend to bring along to help with the work." I agreed to talk the matter over with Margaret. Because she had a responsible job in the National Office of the Party, we decided that she should join me later. I hooked up with a young intellectual who was interested in the project. The two of us climbed onto an old Nevin bus for the thirty-hour ride to Chicago.

In my mind Chicago had always been an unofficial capital city for labor radicalism, the home of May Day and the movement for the eight-hour day, the place where the Haymarket martyrs were hung and the Communist Party was born. Chicago was the heart of perhaps the greatest labor struggle in American history, the 1894 Pullman Boycott, which pitted Debs and his American Railway Union against the combined strength of the railroad barons and the federal government.[1] The IWW had started here, and for many years the city was its base of operations. During World War I successful organizing drives were launched in both the steel and meat-packing industries, led by William Z. Foster and Jack Johnstone, who had both since joined the Party. Throughout the early part of the century the Chicago Federation of Labor (CFL) had backed the idea of independent labor politics, and the organization was one of the mainstays of the national labor party movement of the twenties.[2]

But by 1930 the situation had changed drastically. John Fitzpatrick, president of the CFL, who had at one time been on friendly terms with Foster and other Party people, had become staunchly anti-Communist. The footholds that labor had gained in steel, meat-packing and other mass-production industries during the war were completely destroyed in disastrous postwar strikes. The craft unions remained, but many had lost their earlier strength while others, especially some of the building trades, were notoriously crooked. There were a number of reasons for this degeneration, but the point is that Chicago workers approached the problems of the Depression with an extremely weak, conservative, and often corrupt labor movement. Opposing them was a city administration and police force capable of brutal repression.

With these sorts of odds, the Communists had few competitors in the field of organizing the unemployed, at least in the beginning. While the Socialist Party still had some presence in the city, it was not very evident at the time. There were some remnants of the IWW along Halsted Street in the Skid Row area. Most of these men were old-timers and not very active, but the younger ones showed up at meetings. You could always tell the Wobblies by the way they opened their speeches with "Fellow Workers!" We had no animosity toward them, but neither did we have any direct links. They often supported our work but also carried on their own agitation.

The fact that the city had a long radical tradition lent a good deal of color to the local Party in the persons of a number of aging Wobblies, anarchists, and others for whom the Communists were just the latest installment of a very old movement. One of these was Sam Hammersmark or "Sam-Ham," a Party member who ran a bookshop that served as a sort of unofficial hangout for Chicago radicals. In shape and personality he always reminded me of Santa Claus. He could reminisce about the Haymarket martyrs and all the early anarchists and socialists, and his memory was one of the links between our own efforts and the city's rich radical traditions.

One of the first people I met when I came into town and probably the most popular of this older group was "Big John" Holman, a giant Texan close to eighty who was the Party's star soapboxer. His station was in "Bughouse Square." This little park tucked between the "Gold Coast" of the lakefront and the immigrant slums was the city's free speech area. It was also close to the neighborhood of cheap boardinghouses and coffee shops where the hoboes and day laborers congregated. Here the Wobblies and the SLP speakers mounted their soapboxes, the Salvation Army saved souls, and the CP agitated for revolution. There was always a large crowd, and old man Holman was clearly one of their favorites. He had an old Model T, the back of which was fitted with a platform, steps and all. Each night he ascended the steps with a large bundle of *Daily Workers,* and at the end he usually came down empty-handed. The first day I came into town he cornered me.

"What are you doing tonight?" he asked.

"I've just come into town and haven't even found a place to stay."

"I want you to come down to Bughouse Square tonight and as often as you can. I have a big platform, and that is where you talk to the masses."

On this particular night Holman was at his best. "In Texas," he thundered, "I knew a man who, like most Texans, wore a big hat like mine. Now these hats are quite expensive, but they are part of the local costume, you might say. He spent twelve bucks for that hat. So one day I told him, 'Here's a book that only costs a dime. Why not buy it? It may put something *in* your head instead of something *on* your goddamn fat head which is empty like a pumpkin!'" The crowd loved it.

"That leads me to a point," he continued. "Don't be a sucker for the capitalist system. Don't read their press. Give me three cents for a *Daily Worker*. And those of you who have it, give me a nickel, because

I bet that guy next to you doesn't have the three cents but would still like to read the paper. Now, I'm not getting down from here until this stack is gone, and when it is, I have a little surprise for you."

It didn't take me too long to figure out that I was the surprise. I did my best with a little speech about organizing to face the problem of unemployment, but I was no match for Holman.

I reported to work at a building on Lincoln Avenue on the North Side of the city that the unemployed councils shared with the offices of the TUUL and the International Labor Defense (ILD). The Party headquarters was on Division Street in a building that it shared with a part of the mob that was running the North Side. They occupied the loft at the top of the building, and they sometimes used it for target practice. Generally we tried to stay out of their way, but we had a joint bathroom, so we ran into one of them occasionally. Old man Holman was determined to make friends with them and used to tell them, "Well, you don't like the goddam cops and neither do we, so that's one thing we have in common." They seemed to really like him and once even offered us a little muscle in the event of some confrontation. Holman suggested that they might not be bad friends to have, but Clarence Hathaway quickly put a damper on the idea. He was careful not to alienate them; we had enough problems without having the mob after us. He just said, "No thanks, that's not our style." Every once in a while an irate immigrant woman would get the floors mixed up and begin banging on the door of the loft, yelling in Polish about evictions and police brutality. The gangsters had a little peephole that they would slide open, saying, "The Reds are one floor down."

We certainly had no difficulty convincing people that unemployment was a problem in Chicago. My own trade, for example, was one of the worst; virtually all building of any kind was at a standstill. I remember walking into the Chicago Party headquarters for the first time and finding a bunch of fellows, some of them building trades workers, just hanging around. In the course of getting acquainted, one of them asked how I made my living. When I said I was a carpenter, they all laughed. "You might as well store the toolbox away," they said. "Save yourself the trouble of looking around. There's not a job in the city."

The problem was more apparent on Halsted on the near West Side than on any other street. Here a string of employment offices and casual labor agencies stretched for several blocks. Men lined the curbs in front of the offices in oceans of blue shirts and cloth caps. Occasionally a job was posted, and regardless of how menial or poorly paid it was, dozens of men snapped at the chance for work. Bughouse Square was also a popular spot. Often a thousand people or more would be gathered in the small park to hear the speakers and argue among themselves. If you were looking for ideas, you could find a multitude of them here; it was a question of who you were going to believe.

Unemployment hung over the city like a storm cloud, and everywhere you saw its effects. Workers lined up in front of factories and mills in spite of the signs "No Help Wanted." Standing around the lines, you could feel a desperate mood. No one knew where the next dollar for food or rent would come from, and no one could tell them.

Still not everyone in Chicago was suffering. I got a chance to see how the "other half" lived thanks to John Harvey, national secretary for the Young Communist League (YCL), as the YWL was now called. College-educated and New England-bred, John had some rich relations living on Lake Shore Drive, the "Gold Coast." He and I stayed in their apartment for a couple of weeks while they were in Europe. The place was incredible, but what I remember best are the tigerskin rug and the gold bindings on some of the books. The incongruity of the situation used to make us laugh. Every morning we'd come down the elevator, say good morning to the doorman, and hop on a streetcar bound for Party headquarters or some unemployed council. I was especially struck with the contrast between the kind of lifestyle symbolized by Lake Shore Drive and the kind represented by Bughouse Square, which was only a couple of blocks away. On one street the rich lived in splendor while on the next were shabby boarding houses in the shadows of the skyscrapers. One morning John and I had only thirteen cents between us, so we had to borrow a penny from the doorman for carfare. The worst part was that we had to scrounge up a dime in order to pay him back; we couldn't just hand him a penny.

Both the impulse for the unemployed agitation and the plan for organizing it came from the district Trade Union Committee, which was acting in coordination with those in other districts throughout the country. A steering committee was set up, composed of the city's section organizers, a number of trade union activists, and some nationality group leaders. This group included Dora Lifshitz, a garment worker; Nels Kjar, a delegate from a carpenter's local to the Chicago Federation of Labor and head of the Party's Trade Union Committee; Joe Dallet and John Meldon of the TUUL's Steel and Metal Workers Industrial Union; Steve Rubicki of the ILD; an unemployed leader named Bill Holloway; Paul Cline of the YCL; Irving Gersh, a business agent for the Journeymen Tailors Union; and the editors of *Vilnis* and *Radnik,* the Lithuanian and Serbo-Croatian Communist papers.[3]

The Party divided cities into sections each consisting of two or three branches. These organizers knew what was going on in the factories and neighborhoods of their sections. The steering committee contacted Party members and sympathizers throughout the city, and it was around these little groups of two or three that the first unemployed councils were launched. Based in their neighborhoods, the councils mobilized people around demands for relief, resistance to evictions, and other issues facing the unemployed. The steering committee met often to discuss problems and plan the work ahead, but once the movement started to grow, it was replaced by an Executive Committee of the Unemployed Councils of Chicago, which was composed of delegates elected from councils in various neighborhoods. At the steering committee's first meeting I was put in charge of the organizing, and eventually I was elected secretary of the Unemployed Councils of Chicago.

It was this structure that got things going, but then the movement seemed to take on a force of its own. The first council meeting I attended was held at a Greek workers' club on Halsted Street. I remember it well because I made a pretty poor speech to the group. I was extremely nervous and asked Nels Kjar, an old Danish carpenter and Socialist Party veteran, "What the hell am I supposed to say to these people?"

Nels, who was probably the wrong person to ask, said, "You're a Party member; you're smart enough to know what's going on."

Still confused, I asked, "But what can I tell them about what we should do?"

"Tell them that organization is the only answer, that they can't do anything as individuals."

The speech, like the advice, was pretty vague. I pounded the rostrum a little and complained that the bourgeoisie always make the workers pay for depressions. The following speaker was even worse and mentioned Lovestone's expulsion in the course of his speech. The whole approach was sectarian in tone and demonstrated just how isolated we were from most workers.

When the meeting ended, a wonderful Greek comrade, who later fought with me in Spain, took the other speaker to one side. "You know, comrade," he said, "you shouldn't have brought the Lovestone problem into it. These people don't know anything about that, and we have more important things to discuss." I listened to what the old Greek said, knowing that I might have made the same mistake. I had developed in the same sort of sectarian atmosphere. In this case, however, our approach hadn't done much damage. These Greek workers really impressed me. Some were furriers and garment workers, and a few worked in the stockyards, but most were waiters, cooks, and busboys in the city's restaurants. Almost all were single and very militant. Actually, they knew what to do better than I.

"Now, Mr. Chairman," someone called from the floor, "the first thing we have to do is set up a committee that can deal with grievances. Let's have some volunteers." They knew who they wanted on the committee and tried to talk them into it. Many of the early councils were built on existing ethnic and fraternal organizations like this Greek club.

We spent the first few weeks agitating against capitalism and talking about the need for socialism. But even if people listened to our arguments, we couldn't offer them much hope for the immediate future. How were they going to pay the rent, buy food, and survive in the meantime? Answers began to emerge from the actual experience of organizing.

The day-to-day work of the earliest councils focused on the practical grievances brought to them by the people in communities. It was these issues that brought the councils into the mainstream of working-class life and promised the mass base that would be needed if they were to accomplish anything. It was from involvement in the daily struggles that we learned to shift away from a narrow, dogmatic approach to what might be called a grievance approach to the organizing. We began to raise demands for immediate relief by the city and state, immediate federal assistance to the unemployed, and a moratorium on mortgages, and finally we began to talk about the need for national unemployment insurance.

Often councils were formed almost spontaneously, with little Party involvement. If a family faced eviction in a neighborhood that didn't have a council, and they desperately needed help, somebody might tell them to go to the unemployed council office. They might have to travel across the city to our headquarters.

"Come and help us!"

"We can't help from here by ourselves. Get a couple of neighbors together, and we'll send someone over."

The first meeting, a discussion about what could be done, might take place in someone's house. We might ask, "Do you know any politicians around here, maybe an alderman?"

"Sure, so and so. I voted for him. He's a good guy."

"Fine. Get him to go with you on a delegation to see the landlord."

If the alderman came through, that was all right with us. Maybe the eviction would even be postponed. But usually there was an experience that I called "coming to grips with one's own illusions." This guy had confidence in his alderman, but the alderman was likely to say, "Sorry, I'm busy." It might not prevent the guy from voting the machine ticket again at the very next election, but it probably would affect his attitude toward politics to some extent. Or someone would say, "Oh, Father so and so, he's a wonderful man." We would say, "Get him." And sometimes the priests *were* good, militant as hell. They might join the organization, help to win some cases, and wind up dominating it. There were some councils taken away from us for a time in this manner.

Sometimes people who weren't satisfied would start a rival organization with a new name—the Improvement League, or something like that. Then there would be two organizations side by side. Sometimes neighborhood politics would get involved, and you might have bitter fights. It wasn't easy.

When an eviction was about to take place, the neighborhood council would mobilize as many people as it could find. When the deputies came around with a warrant, they would face a crowd at the place.

"How the hell can you do this to someone?" people shouted. "What sort of a job are you doing for a few lousy bucks?"

"I can't ignore the law," the cop would plead. "I can't let you put the furniture back in. I've got orders, and unless they're carried out, I'll lose my job."

The cops reacted in different ways when confronted with what they were doing. Sometimes they just looked around and walked away; other times they roughed people up. I don't think they really knew what to do. Usually Party people were prominent in these confrontations, but if there were articulate local people in the group, it was better to let them speak up and then support what they said. Even if they didn't express themselves as well as Party members might, they were known to the people and would not be looked upon as outsiders. We weren't interested in starting fights. We wanted to establish a lasting organization and to make some ideological headway, to make people think about these problems and who was responsible for them.

We made every effort to make the councils a part of their neighborhoods. For fund-raising we tried to stage events that fit into the cultural life of the community. Most councils relied on bingo, raffles, picnics, and block parties. Since the Catholic church was always sponsoring such affairs, they were part of the natural way of life. We also sponsored dances for the younger people. Sometimes the hall was free, and we could usually dig up an accordian player somewhere.

As secretary of the unemployed councils, my job was to keep things going. I shared this task with many other activists. We spent a lot of time leading local delegations to welfare officials and helping to stop evictions. I told people who to talk to, but often they were reticent. "He'll just tell us to get out, and we're not sure exactly what to say." What can you say? "Nothing to be done?" So, you say, "O.K., I'll go down with you, but you present the case. I'll just back you up." Because I could understand several Slavic languages, I also acted as an interpreter. A Polish worker might come and tell us that his wife was sick and needed a doctor, so I or someone else had to explain the problem to the welfare official. We spent much of our time simply learning the welfare rules in order to be effective. We couldn't just give speeches about the downfall of capitalism, and we couldn't lead from a distance. We had to be with the people.

It was in Chicago that I became a Party functionary for the first time. One did not take this step for the luxurious lifestyle it allowed. I received about $5 a week, and this went mostly for carfare to get around the city. I stayed with a family that was active in the Party, and I tried to be home in time for dinner since this was my only steady source of nourishment. I did carpentry work and other jobs around the house in exchange for room and board. You got through by wearing whatever clothes you had, going out rarely and then usually to an affair in someone's home, and walking to the next meeting if it wasn't too far. If you had a large family, this would be taken into consideration, and you might get $20 or so, but $5 a week was the going rate for most of those active in the movement. I never thought to complain. The attitude was, "Everyone is making sacrifices."

Even though most of the organizing went on in the name of the unemployed councils rather than the Party, many people knew who we were, if only because the newspapers and radio were constantly screaming about the menace that the councils represented. But the red-baiting backfired to some extent. People were faced with immediate problems, and their neighborhood council was often the only place they could turn to. Eventually some people started answering, "So what? Even if they are Communists, they are trying to help us help ourselves and no one else is doing that." Many of the people with whom we worked did not read the newspapers regularly, or read the *Chicago Defender,* the black daily, or some foreign language paper that was more sympathetic. What they knew about us was what they saw us do on a daily basis, and many respected us for our work.

While most of our reputation was based on the day-to-day actions of the neighborhood councils, we also led a number of citywide demonstrations aimed at winning concessions from the municipal government. At the beginning our demands were simple: food, jobs, and no evictions. We knew that the center of local power was in city hall, so that's where we went.

I still remember my first city hall demonstration. Dozens of mounted police with long clubs were already there when we arrived. There was no large square in front of the building, so we urged the crowd of about five thousand to pack the sidewalk and street out in front. For obvious reasons we hadn't announced who would speak, and it was impossible to set up any sort of speaker's platform. Just as I was getting desperate for a spot from which to deliver a speech, I saw a young guy with a motion picture camera who was going to film the action. He was on top of a city salt box, maybe four feet off the ground. The box provided the best vantage point of the crowd, and the cops weren't bothering him. I jumped up next to him and said, "Get down for a minute because I'm going to speak from here." He turned as pale as a ghost. He had found a nice perch from which to do some footage of police violence, but now the clubs might be coming his way. He jumped off, and I started speaking. I hadn't gotten more than a few sentences out when the detectives grabbed me by my legs and dragged me off the box. I pulled away from them, but some mounted cops started riding toward me. The crowd ran in the opposite direction, and I was trapped up against the side of the building. The cops started lashing out with their long nightsticks, and in the background I could hear people screaming, "Cossacks, Cossacks!" and "Shame, Shame!" Fortunately, I remembered some things about horses from my childhood, and they didn't scare me. They're very sensitive on the nose. I pounded them on their snoots, and they reared back, almost knocking the cops off. Finally a couple of detectives got close enough to grab me. They pushed me inside a car, grabbed me by the hair, and pulled my head down between my legs. One of them hit me on the neck with a blackjack, and I passed out. My first address to a large demonstraton had been brief and rather painful.

In this case I don't think I was even booked, just roughed up a little and told to get out of town. Chicago was one of only a few cities in the country at this time to have a special detail, a Red Squad, especially devoted to getting rid of radicals involved in labor-organizing. It shared this dubious distinction with Los Angeles, and it's hard to say which group of cops was worse. They seemed to know all the radicals in town and were particularly vicious with anyone who came from outside. They infiltrated each of the unemployed councils, but often we could smell them. A guy might come around saying, "I'm interested in the *cause*." An unemployed worker doesn't talk like that, and a Communist certainly doesn't, so we could spot him a mile away. Others exposed themselves by behaving badly or advocating provocative tactics when they were put on the grievance committee. Sometimes we guessed that they were just misguided, but in either case we had to try to tame them or get them out of the group. Once you were identified as a troublemaker by the Red Squad, it was pretty hard to stay out of their way, unless you just gave up completely. After this first demonstration, my face was well known, so it was only a matter of time before I had another run-in with them.

There was a very eloquent rank and file Party fellow who often served as a spokesman for our delegations to city hall, but one day he was missing. Instead, I was elected by a mass meeting of several thousand to lead a group of fifty to present our demands to the City Council, which was meeting that evening. We were met by Oscar Nelson, a peg-legged bully who was a leading bureaucrat in the Illinois Federation of Labor and was presiding over the council that day. He had been chosen by the council to "handle" us. He asked me what our demands were, and when I said we were asking the council to formally urge the federal government to enact unemployment insurance, he exploded. *"You mean to tell me,"* he shouted, *"that you want someone to pay you when you're not working!* What kind of lunacy is this! You want to be paid without work! What an idea! Do you think we're crazy? The government would never accept such an idea." I tried to explain how such a system could work, that employers owed this and more to the people who produced their profits, but he had switched tactics.

"How many of you here want jobs? Raise your hands. I'll have a job for you tomorrow morning."

A few people who were desperate and didn't see through the trick started raising their hands. "Yeah, I want a job."

"You! O.K., be out in front of city hall at seven o'clock sharp. You!" He was going all the way around the room.

Finally I interrupted. "Wait a minute. Of course we all want jobs, but we're not here for ourselves. We're a delegation representing organizations from all over the city. We're here in the name of over ten thousand unemployed citizens. We want to go back to them and make a report about what the council is going to do for all of them, not just for the fifty of us."

Nelson tried to ignore me, but by this time most people realized that there was something fishy about his offer and were refusing to go along. Still, a few took the job, which turned out to be one day's work shoveling snow.

Nelson's reaction to our proposal did not seem as unusual then as it might today. In a fundamental sense the unemployed agitation was as much education as direct action. People were flabbergasted by this business of getting paid while you're unemployed. The prevailing attitude was, "I earn my keep and work for whatever I get. I won't take charity." Many held to John L. Lewis's claim that the American worker did not want a dole, but this old individualistic view was of course totally unrealistic. When the engine was finished at Baldwin Locomotive, when the model changed at Ford, when livestock shipments fell off at Union Stock Yards, workers were just laid off, and that was that. Now millions of people were facing this problem at the same time. The country had been in depressions before, but the question of who should assume the responsibility for these periods of unemployment had never hit as hard as it did in 1930. It was the radicals and especially the Communist Party that helped to break down the ideological barriers keeping unemployed workers from what was rightfully due them. This contribution is still not appreciated by most historians.

It was important that people see that unemployment was not the result of their own or someone else's mistake, that it was a worldwide phenomenon and a natural product of the system. March 6, 1930, was the day targeted for an international demonstration of the unemployed for relief. While the national leadership of the movement tried to coordinate the activities in each city, we called a general conference of Chicago activists at the Machinists' Hall about two weeks before the big march. The meeting was very successful, with over six hundred neighborhood council leaders, union activists, and Party people responding to the call. As the session was about to break up, a dozen paddy wagons pulled up to the entrance, and the hall was surrounded by uniformed police. All doors were shut, and we were all questioned and searched as we walked out, in single file, between a double row of cops. One hundred thirteen of us were separated from the rest and jammed into the wagons. This group was questioned by members of the Red Squad, who identified the "real agitators" on sight, and all but fourteen were released.

These "masterminds" of the Red Conspiracy were a rather motley group and included Nels Kjar, the old carpenter and leader of the Party Trade Union Comittee; Andy Newhoff, who worked with the ILD; Gene Rodman, an unemployed painter; Joe Dallet, who led the

Steel and Metal Workers Industrial Union; two black Party activists from out of town, B. D. Amos and Harold Williams; Fred Fine, a fourteen-year-old boy whom we called "the Kid"; myself; and a few others. Dora Lifshitz, the only woman arrested, was separated from the rest.

We sat for five hours, wondering what would happen to us, while Nels tried to prepare us for the inevitable. "This is a setup for a beating. Just don't give in. If they divide us, it will be tougher for each one."

Eight detectives came in, all big guys, and sat on a platform facing our bench. "Jesus," someone said, "they don't look alike, but you couldn't tell them apart." The biggest of the bunch, Sergeant Barker, motioned for two other dicks to join him as he walked over to the bench. Without a word they grabbed two of our men, shoved them out into the corridor, and closed the door. Soon we heard screams, and the twelve remaining men stiffened. Barker and the two detectives came back smiling crookedly and elaborately wiping their hands with handkerchiefs. "You," Barker yelled, pointing a finger at the Kid, "you little monkey."

"Who, me?" The Kid stood up.

"Yeah, you—you little bastard—come up here."

The Kid, ninety pounds and five feet four, walked up to meet Detective Barker. Barker stood towering over the boy, and his face was redder than usual. After a pause the detective put one big hand on the youngster's thin shoulder and slapped him hard across the face. The Kid stood hunched silently with the spotlight glaring in his eyes, staring the detective square in the face. The second slap, fast and chopping from the other side, was harder.

"Now you talk, you little bastard! Look me in the eyes, you little punk—come on, look me in the eyes! You'll go home to mama and stay there, won't you? You'll have enough of these Reds before I'm through with you." Another slap. As if blinded momentarily, the Kid started to sway. Then another hard slap turned him half around, and his knees began to fold. The men on the bench shifted nervously.

"Comrades, keep your heads," Nels whispered, not forgetting the seven other detectives, who sat fingering their revolvers. "You see their game. They'll shoot the first one of us that takes a step. They'll say we started a fight, and they'll have an excuse to attack and arrest more of our people." Joe Dallet was losing his temper. "How the hell can we sit here and do nothing?" he demanded. "He'll kill the Kid."

"Sit down, Joe. Don't be a fool," the old man said. "You see how happy they are. They think their game is working." Gradually Joe calmed down.

Detective Barker turned back to the Kid, dramatically throwing open his coat to reveal the holstered revolver on his hip. The kid's eyes were riveted on the gun.

"What are you looking at that gun for?" Barker asked slowly.

The Kid stood motionless, not saying anything.

"What are you looking at that gun for!" shouted the dick. The Kid remained silent.

"What would you do with it, you dirty little Jew bastard, if you did have it? You'd shoot me with it! You'd kill me, that's what you'd do! Wouldn't you? Wouldn't you!"

The Kid's eyes were steady, and blood dripped down his chin. Hesitating, he suddenly shouted, "Yes, I would!"

Barker was struck with each word as if it were a bullet. Jumping off the platform, he screamed, "I knew you would! I knew it! But you ain't gonna have it!" The men on the bench broke into loud laughs. Joe pounded me on the back, saying, "What a kid, what a kid!"

But the ordeal was far from over. I was sitting next to the last man when two detectives pushed me through a door into another room. They forced me into something that looked like a dentist's chair and strapped me in it. Detective Miller, whose five brothers ran the gangs on the West Side, came into the room. He turned, slowly removing his glasses and wristwatch, and unbuckled his holster, laying it on a small table near the door, which he locked. Then he put on a pair of canvas gloves and pulled out a blackjack with a mother-of-pearl handle. "So you're a big shot agitator. So you won't leave town, eh? You'll get out all right, even if I have to send you in a nice wooden box!"

The blackjack clipped me across the head, and then he carefully worked me over. After some fifteen blows, I gave a twisting jerk with all my strength, tore the chair loose, and fell flat on the floor, pretending to be unconscious. I heard Miller's assistant say, "Maybe you'd better lay off the son-of-a-bitch. He'll leave town now. He's had enough."

Miller unstrapped me, pulled me clear of the chair, and kicked me in the ribs as hard as he could. I went out like a light. When I regained consciousness, I cleaned my bloody face in the washroom and wandered over to an open window for some air. Still dazed, I stared out of the window at the city. Consciousness came suddenly when I saw Detective Miller standing at my side. As the cop smiled in hatred, I knew I wasn't dreaming. I looked out at the lights of the city through the large doorlike window. "What are you looking out the window for?" Were you going to jump? I'll open it for you, go ahead. You got no reason to live." He shoved me. "Go on, jump. What are you waiting for?" Realizing that the bastard meant business, I braced myself against another shove and edged away from the window.

An hour later I found my friends sitting on a cement floor in front of the elevator. Harold Williams was stretched out, his torn pants revealing an enormous rupture, and B. D. Amos had had his front teeth knocked out. Joe Dallet was bleeding from the mouth and had a gash on his cheek. Andy had a big lump on his cheek, and Rodman's thick black hair was caked with blood. The Kid stood there, his eyes all bloodshot. Only two men in the group, Kjar and Paul Cline, had not been beaten. This, we figured, was done deliberately so as to throw suspicion onto their integrity.

On March sixth, two weeks after our arrest, I marched along with seventy-five thousand other workers to demand relief and unemployment insurance. The thirteen of us marched together with our families, but Harold Williams, who had received the worst beating, was still recovering in the hospital. Over one million unemployed workers marched throughout the United States, and millions more took to the streets in Europe. In Chicago the demonstration was a big success, and the trial resulting from our arrests turned out to be a big victory as well. The beatings had generated a lot of publicity. The *Labor Defender,* the ILD publication, devoted an issue to the case, and even the *Chicago Tribune* questioned the police tactics. A committee of prominent liberals, including a number of black ministers, issued a statement deploring the brutality.

We were brought to trial on charges of sedition and organizing for an armed revolution. The prosecution presented a very flamboyant case designed to show how dangerous we were. Fortunately for us, we had a jury trial and we had the International Labor Defense in our corner. We also had two wonderful ILD lawyers, Benthal and Goldman. Benthal, an old Socialist and labor lawyer, went way back. Not only did Goldman make a brilliant defense; he even dressed me up in one of his suits because I had none of my own. Both were red-baited in the press and by the city authorities, and neither received a fee for his work on the case. They were the sort of lawyers that made the ILD such a great organization.

Anyone who has been clubbed over the head and tossed into jail without any idea of when he might emerge can appreciate the importance of the ILD. Its lawyers traveled the country, from big cities like

Chicago to isolated little textile and mining towns, to defend Communists and other labor organizers when no lawyer would have taken the cases. But formal legal defense was not the organization's only responsibility. So far as the Party was concerned, every worker on trial for radical or labor activity was a political prisoner, and cases were fought for what they could teach the public as well as to preserve our valuable organizers. For such defense work to be successful, local defense committees had to be established to publicize the trials and raise money. In Chicago this work was done by Steve Rubicki.

Steve was a skilled machinist and a genius at organization. Everyone in the Party loved him. In a three-piece suit and gold cufflinks with a stickpin in his tie, Rubicki cut quite a figure. But the fancy clothes clashed with his speech and mannerisms, which were strictly South Side Chicago. His grammar was atrocious, and everyone winced at the sound of his sentences. After listening to him, you might think, "Would someone translate that?" But he was extremely sincere and always managed to make himself understood. He would come up to some prominent liberal and say, "Listen, you're a good liberal man and here is this terrible travesty of justice happening right here in your city of Chicago. What are you going to do about it? Can you influence someone or at least make a contribution to the defense?" It was obvious that he believed his was a very righteous cause, and he was just aggressive enough that it was almost impossible to turn him down.

The trial lasted about a week. The jury, comprised mostly of workers, a number of whom were unemployed, voted for acquittal. The case made the government look bad, and it slowed the repression down a little.

Our arrest and beating were only part of a more general attack on the unemployed organizing. In an effort to stop a movement that was growing with lightening speed, the police had raided the headquarters of the Party and of *Radnik,* the South Slav CP paper, and had arrested street-corner speakers. By the beginning of March about 150 activists were in jail, but the trial victory helped to turn this situation around. Apparently it convinced the city government that such cases could not be won in Chicago during the Depression, so the struggle would have to take place outside of the courtroom. This was the last big prosecution for quite a while, but the beatings in the streets continued.

Some young radicals now charge that in our pursuit of everyday grievances, the leaders of the unemployed movement lost track of the primary goal—building a movement for socialism. This simply is not true. The word "socialism" may rarely have appeared on the meeting agenda of a local council, but there was constant face-to-face discussion. There was always Party and other progressive literature around the councils. You would go to a key person and say, "Look, I want you to read this." The movement's papers, *Unemployed Worker* and, later, *Fight Hunger,* pressed people to consider the root causes of the Depression and unemployment. It's true that we didn't have a blueprint for revolution in 1930. We were so busy in the daily struggle to improve conditions and educate people about the need for socialism that we didn't have time to sit around and philosophize. We felt that by getting a young person to join the YCL or just by broadening his or her horizons a little, we were contributing to a mass movement for socialism. We saw the councils as vehicles through which we would win immediate struggles and advance our political point of view.

Recruitment went on constantly. You would say to someone, "Look, you probably know that many of us in this movement are Communists. The capitalist press has made the word taboo, but let me tell you what it really means." So you had the job of telling interested people what socialism was. If they seemed responsive, you might invite them to a branch meeting or some other affair. The recruitment that went on in the councils was extremely important to the Party in the long run. It transformed the social base of the Party in the course of the decade, bringing in younger and more Americanized people and giving us a firm base in the black community for the first time.

While there were few black members when I arrived, the situation changed quickly during the six months or so that I remained in the city. The work of the councils allowed for the breakthrough. The South Side black neighborhoods probably had higher levels of unemployment than any area in the country at that time, and the people were very receptive. There was no need to rent a hall. You just turned over a soapbox in front of a poolroom or bar or on a street corner, and a crowd would gather.

Black ministers were especially responsive, often appearing on delegations or lending their names in support of local councils. The little storefront churches were best, but a couple of the large Baptist congregations in Chicago helped too. In New York the most prominent religious supporter was Adam Clayton Powell, but the one I remember best was Father Divine in Philadelphia. I met him later while working with the unemployed in the anthracite. I came to a conference in Philly, and he opened his doors to us. His congregation provided a free lunch, and later some of us slept in the shelter that they provided for the unemployed in the black community. Father Divine preached on social problems as well as salvation, and he appeared at and even led large demonstratons. The Party sought out these religious leaders, recognizing their influence within their own communities. It was another situation in which a broad approach to mass work allowed us to be more effective.

The twin problems of fighting racism and attracting blacks through the unemployed movement were constant topics for discussion at both the Party District Committee and unemployed councils Executive Committee meetings. The Party sponsored a nationwide drive for black membership in 1930, and the results were impressive. It was remarkable to see the reactions of white workers at citywide meetings and demonstrations. There was more brotherhood in these organizations than I had ever seen before, and some white workers were genuinely moved by the problems facing blacks. It was especially tough to break down barriers in a place like Chicago, where bigotry had been nurtured over the years in race riots and countless minor confrontations. Our educational efforts bore fruit within a couple of years, when Chicago came to have one of the strongest unemployed movements in the country and one of the largest black memberships in the Party. Much of this was the product of hard work by others in the years after I left, but with the successful March sixth demonstration and with councils established in neighborhoods throughout the city, the groundwork had been laid by the time I left in the spring of 1930.

Chicago had become a hard place for me to work. The Party felt that the Red Squad was determined to get me out of town one way or another, and the fact that the legal route had failed made my situation more dangerous. This and the need for an organizer in southern Illinois led to the decision that I should go down there with Andy Newhoff, the new Party organizer, and assume the position of organizer for the National Miners Union (NMU).

The NMU is usually remembered as the Communist dual union in coal, set up to compete with John L. Lewis's United Mine Workers (UMWA).[4] It was a product of the Comintern's shift toward the ultrasectarian "class against class" line, but the origins of the union lay as much in the American coalfields as in the Kremlin. Beginning in 1926, the Communists had joined with Powers Hapgood, John Brophy and various other progressive elements in the UMWA to form the Save the Union movement.[5] The movement called for an aggressive organizing drive to rebuild the union's crumbling membership; a labor party; nationalization of the mines; and reinstatement of all those whom Lewis had expelled. (By this time these miners constituted a sizable proportion of the membership in some regions.) Today most Americans think of Lewis as the father of the CIO and progressive labor politics, but at the time many workers viewed him as the most conservative and autocratic of the AFL leaders. He was both feared and hated, and his name was a swear word in every miner's vocabulary, spoken under one's breath, of course. He was a labor dictator if ever there was one in the United States.

The source of much of the dissatisfaction lay in the so-called Jacksonville Agreement. Signed by Lewis in 1924, the agreement ignored many long-standing grievances but was supposed to maintain wages at the 1924 level until 1927. The wage provision was never respected by the employers, however, because the union had grown so weak. Thus miners throughout the country faced one wage cut after another. In 1927–1928 the miners of western Pennsylvania struck, and the strike quickly spread to eastern Ohio. Communists and other militants organized a Pennsylvania-Ohio Relief Committee to collect food and clothing for the miners' families, who were living in tent colonies and facing constant attacks from the state police. Lewis used the revolt as an excuse for wholesale expulsions of the strike leaders. When he ordered the men back to work and joined with the owners and the state police to smash the strike, it seemed there was no choice but to create an honest and militant alternative to the UMWA. Although most of the new union's leaders were Party members like Pat Toohey, Frank Borich, Vince Kemenovich, Paul Bohus, Tom Myerscough, and Fred Siders, it actually had a strong following in some parts of the central bituminous fields. But eventually the strike was smashed, and the NMU never really recovered.

Lewis's autocracy led to the formation of the NMU, but Comintern influence elevated sheer expediency to the level of a formal policy of dual unionism. At the urging of the Soviet Party leaders and against the better judgment of several experienced Americans, including Foster, the NMU launched an organizing drive and challenged the UMWA for leaderhip of the miners. The decision to form the new union alienated Hapgood, Brophy, and many other former allies. In the fall of 1929, the NMU affiliated with the TUUL, which was a member of the Red International of Labor Unions (RILU), a Communist-led international labor federation. This cut the Communist miners off from the mainstream of the labor movement. The NMU was born weak, and it grew continually weaker under attacks from the employers, the UMWA, and the police. Nowhere was the situation worse than in the southern Illinois coalfields, where the Party was in disarray when I arrived in the late spring of 1930. The local organizer had taken up with a miner's wife and had to beat it out of town. This led to bitter feelings among some members, and the level of activity dropped accordingly. A local strike was smashed, followed by the usual blacklisting, and some of our people had scattered to Detroit and any other places they thought they might find work.

Our life in the Illinois coalfields was fairly typical of what Party organizers faced out in the field. Margaret joined me, and she and I and Andy lived with a Finnish-American miner and his family in West Frankfort. They had a fairly large house and only two children, so Margaret and I had a couple of unheated rooms to ourselves. We cooked and ate with the family, sharing all the food we could scrape together. Occasionally we had some hamburger, but otherwise the only meat we ever had was the rabbits we shot in winter. We bought a lot of potatoes and our hosts, like most miners, raised their own vegetables, which they shared with us. On one special occasion the miner's wife bought a piece of beef and baked some potatoes in with it. Unfortunately, the meat came out so tough that it was pretty hard to chew. She was ready to cry because the meal was a failure, but none of us said a word. We all dutifully chewed it, and that was the biggest party we had in West Frankfort.

Food was hardly the most depressing thing about the coalfields. The whole landscape was stark and dominated by the industry. The mines themselves were very large and efficient with as many as eight hundred or a thousand men in one mine, working with the most modern equipment. The coal seams were high as well, though sometimes only eight or ten feet thick. Operators here were able to take out three times as much coal each day as in other bituminous fields. The business structure of the region had always been tied in with the large power and railroad corporations, but by contrast, many of the little towns were the most primitive places imaginable. I still remember a town called Westville where one of the local NMU leaders lived. Right next to his house was a giant slate pile where kids played. There was one concrete road running through the center of the town, which consisted of a company store, a post office, and a string of twenty-five little company houses, each looking exactly like the one next to it.

But the worst aspect of life in the Illinois fields—and a reality that the men of the NMU had to face daily was repression, and this was the main reason why the NMU finally had to be dissolved. It was virtually impossible for our men to carry on any kind of organizing, especially in the smaller towns, where anyone who passed through was spotted. The attacks on Communists and other militants were staggering. By the beginning of 1930, the ILD had dozens of cases pending in the Illinois fields.

At the time I went down to southern Illinois, there had been no ironclad decison made to liquidate the NMU, though the TUUL leadership certainly believed that this would be necessary. I was supposed to probe the question with the union's rank and file. But Newhoff and I understood that the union was no longer viable and that we were really supposed to convince the remaining membership, perhaps two hundred men scattered throughout the region, to go back into the UMWA. Wherever we met them we had a difficult job because they would say, "I'm not going back into that goddamn mine with Lewis's henchmen." Emotionally we were with them, but we tried to shake them back to reality. We'd say, "Look, you're not in the mines. There are six hundred men working in your mine, and how many of you are out? Only twenty-five. You've got to get back into the mines where the workers are if there is still time." Some were able to get their jobs back. Blacklisting all the NMU men would have caused too much trouble for the UMWA leaders, who were helping the owners to separate the Reds from the other miners. Many of the NMU people were respected, so aside from the top leadership in the area, the UMWA bureaucracy relented and let some of our men go back into the mines.

But many of our most dedicated members knew their leaders were still not prepared to dissolve the NMU, and this was what made our job so hard. Here I was, a young stranger, a carpenter telling miners what to do. Neither Newhoff nor I could hold a candle to the men who led the NMU in Illinois. These were among the finest men I'd ever met and also perhaps the toughest. They were different from most of the people I'd known in the Party in the cities. Most were firmly rooted in their regions, from families that went back for generations in the United States.

Freeman Thompson, president of the district, was a tall and impressive-looking man in his early fifties. He seemed to have some IWW experience in his background and was a "down home" sort of radical and a great speaker. Another fellow by the name of Voyze may have been the toughest of the lot. There were many stories about him. One was that he had served as a bodyguard at a national convention of the NMU in Pittsburgh, where UMWA thugs attacked the NMU men. Fifty UMWA men surrounded the hall where our guys were meeting, and Voyze was at the door with a baseball bat. The first one that showed his head, whammo! The legend says that he knocked half a dozen men cold before they retreated. But he feared they would still try to get in because they were regrouping at the back of the building. While he guarded the door, he sent two men up on the third floor where they tore a radiator off and started teetering it on the window ledge over the UMWA gang. Then there was a group of Kentucky-bred miners, and the one I remember best was a wonderful guy by the name of John Sloan. He lived in a tiny coal town, isolated from the main mining region, and he was constantly harassed. But he hung on with the Party throughout the Depression and at one point opposed Lewis for the presidency of the UMWA.

These were the sorts of men who kept the militant labor movement alive in the twenties and early thirties. In the tradition of "Big Bill" Haywood, they were extremely articulate orators and tough fighters for the working class.[6] To them organization meant more than life itself. It's a tragedy that every one of these men was hounded out of the coalfields after giving so much to the workers they represented.

At one point even I, who was sent down to liquidate the union, caught the hope that maybe the NMU could be revived. The miners around the town of Ziegler went out on a wildcat strike and staged a mass meeting. Some of us from the local leadership were at a conference in Chicago when we got the news, and we decided to go straight to Ziegler. Steve Rubicki drove us down in his big eight-cylinder Nash; we used to say it was two blocks long. Steve was sent because it was assumed that someone would be arrested and would need legal help. We stopped in Springfield to pick up Freeman Thompson who noticed, as we pulled away, that two carloads of guys whom he recognized as UMWA goons were following us. As the two cars began to pick up speed, Thompson yelled, "Steve, give her the gas!" It was a little dirt road, and I swear Rubicki was doing sixty miles an hour, but the UMWA men had Hudsons and were slowly catching up. Finally we came to a place where the road was under repair and you could only drive on one side. There was a temporary plank bridge over a little creek, and Steve hit that little bridge so hard that the planks flew up into the air behind us. The guys following us had lost their bridge, and they almost ended up in the creek. "They shall never kill the Revolution!" Steve yelled, as if it were all planned. "We'll outwit them every time!"

But the meeting in Ziegler was anticlimactic. There was a fairly large gathering, but a part of the crowd consisted of vigilantes who stood around the edge, waiting for a chance to pounce. One of the leaders was arrested when he tried to speak, and the others had to slip off in order to avoid the same fate. Newhoff and I were able to escape because we weren't known as well as the others, but it was clear that the NMU was through. This strike was smashed, and more of the local people victimized. We had to give it up.

While the union was dissolved, the struggle against the owners and the UMWA bureaucracy was not. At least two other insurgent groups had been established, each with a firmer base of support than the remnants of the NMU. In the area around Ziegler and West Frankfort, there was a militant rank and file movement within the UMWA led by some popular young men, and around Belleville a rival union, the Progressive Miners of America, had gained a strong foothold.[7] We urged our members to go on fighting by supporting these groups.

The hardest part was going back to the little Party groups in places like El Dorado, Harrisburg, or Oriente and saying, "That's it! It's over." It's impossible to describe the feelings of the men. In many cases we were asking them to go back into a union which for them was the incarnation of decadence and corruption. Some even feared that the corruption had spread to the Party. They said things such as "This sounds like a sellout. We're not saying that you're on the payroll, but someone might be."

I still remember one of the most stubborn men, an old fellow we called "the Boxer" because he had actually been a boxer in his younger days and even claimed to have fought the great John L. Sullivan. He was the classic old-fashioned coal miner: high-starched collar, bow tie, and derby hat at all meetings. He strolled about the town like a real gentleman, cane and all. He hated Lewis so much that he would get up in the public square in front of the courthouse and blast the UMWA officials to their faces: "Which of you goddamn sons-of-bitches is ready to come up and take your goddamn glasses off?" He was in his seventies but still ready for a fight. He had been the president of his local at one time, and he wasn't going to let "that goddamn Lewis" take it over. The other obstacle was a Lithuanian miner about thirty-five years old by the name of Cateracus, a man with a huge family of about eight kids. He had been a soldier at some point and retained his military bearing. I stayed with his family often as I traveled, and whenever I came, at any time of the day or night, he would say, "Steve, you must be hungry. Let's have something to eat. Tell us again about the Revolution." The kids would sit around like little mice, listening to the stranger from the big city. He was the Boxer's main support. The bitterness about the decision to liquidate lasted a long time, especially among men like these two, but eventually everyone came to realize that the change must be made if we were to live to fight again.

My stay in southern Illinois was short, not more than about six months, because the National Office chose me to go to the Lenin School in Moscow. At the time the Party was still small and badly in need of trained people. I was thrilled with the prospect of seeing the Soviet Union and even more with the chance of going to school.

FOUR

The People of the Anthracite

I didn't make it to Moscow that fall. By the time I had untangled myself from the problems in southern Illinois, the academic term had already begun at the Lenin School. Instead I was assigned as subdistrict organizer for the anthracite mining region of eastern Pennsylvania. Margaret and I spent the last $15 of our savings on an old Model T, loaded it with books, clothes, and my toolbox, and started out from Chicago at the end of 1930.

Driving up the Susquehanna River Valley near Wilkes-Barre, we saw giant coal breakers and what appeared at first to be burning mountains. As we got closer, these turned out to be huge slag heaps that gave the area around them a smoky, sulfurous atmosphere. The mining towns themselves tended to be larger than those in Illinois. There were few one-mine towns here. The northern anthracite region was dominated by two fairly large industrial cities: Wilkes-Barre, with around eighty thousand people, and Scranton, with over one hundred thousand. The central and southern areas each had a few towns of ten thousand or more, as well as many smaller ones. Roads were bad, though, so smaller towns were often isolated from one another.

Behind the very real beauty of the region lay a bitter poverty. The depression had started here in the twenties, and by the time it reached other areas, the eastern Pennsylvania mining towns were already devastated. The change in home heating to oil and gas caused a sharp drop in the demand for hard coal, and the number of miners in the industry fell from 140,000 in 1928 to less than 80,000 in 1930. The political repression was as bad as anywhere in Illinois, and the economic situation was much worse. At the time my new assignment was considered to be one of the roughest outside of the South.

It didn't surprise us to find a weak local Party organization. There was virtually a rule of terror by the coal companies, who controlled the police and local officials in most towns. Political agitation all but assured arrest. The NMU, which never had much of a foothold in the region, was smashed and retained only a small group of CP members and sympathizers. The Party was based largely on older immigrant miners who were often carrying the sectarianism of the twenties into the new decade. As a result the organization was small, with perhaps fifty members scattered around, isolated, and pretty ineffectual.

But the low state of Party morale wasn't simply a product of the region's depressed economics, repression, or the character of the membership. Since the early twenties this subdistrict had gone through a long string of organizers, mostly young people from Philadelphia or New York City who were used to a different kind of life. They missed the theater, the movies, and the other amenities of a big city. The Party office, a tiny room tucked away on the second floor of an old building on Public Square, was filled with signs of their disillusionment. When we opened the door we were greeted with the sight of fifteen or twenty bundles of the *Daily Worker,* one hundred papers to a bundle. It showed a lack of concern on the part of the person who'd preceded us. If he knew he was leaving and couldn't distribute the paper, he should have stopped the order. In the desk drawers we found copies of telegrams: "Release me," "I can't stay in this hell-hole." It seemed that some past organizers had not only failed to fit in but had actually given up. As we met the rank and file members, it became clear that they understood all this and deeply resented the constant shifting of Party functionaries. At first I was probably seen as just one more replacement, and it took a little while to win the confidence of the people.

We arrived at "Carry's Patch," a group of shacks in the town of Ashley, on New Year's Eve. It was just past midnight when Margaret and I knocked on the door of Tom and Stella Petrosky, young Polish immigrants with a family of eight children. With the ten of them jammed into three rooms and an attic, there was no room for us, but they made hasty visits to the neighbors and soon found us places.

The next morning Stella made breakfast for everyone. It was a pretty luxurious meal for the anthracite coalfields: French toast and her own syrup—sugar water with a little jelly mixed in. We met over coffee with the handful of people who made up the core of our first unemployed council. Mike Mitelsky knew the Petroskys from the old country and immediately promised to help. The others included Ivanoff, the nearest neighbor, and a young Irishman by the name of Tom Bradey and his wife.

But it was Stella who provided the real spirit for the group, and she made arrangements for the first public meeting. After the parish priest refused to let us use the church hall, she went with a couple of the men to a local poolhall owned by a disabled miner. None of the tables were in use because nobody had the nickel to play a game. The younger fellows hung around, hoping that someone who still had a job would come in, plunk down a quarter, and treat the whole group to a game. Tom Bradey explained what kind of a meeting this would be and that it would probably only last an hour. The old miner agreed, and that little poolhall became the unofficial headquarters of the unemployed council of the town of Ashley.

The room was nearly filled when I arrived, and Tom Bradey rose to open the meeting. Men continued to come in, and a group of women peered in through the windows. Stella went out to them and said, "Come in and hear what this man has to say. You're as good as anybody else here." The two local cops wandered in to see what was going on. I sensed an atmosphere of excitement; something was finally happening.

I looked out at the people. I could see the gnarled hands and blue scars that were the lifelong miner's trademarks. When a miner is injured, coal dust settles into the wound immediately, and the scar remains black and blue for the rest of his life. People sat clothed in their poverty, the men wearing patched overalls and broken boots, the women wrapped up in scarves, shawls, and heavy sweaters with holes in them. As I started to speak, I realized that the words were coming much more easily than they normally did. I was speaking from my heart. "What is a miner to do?" I said. "You're out of a job, and you're not the only ones. Workers throughout the country are out of work through no fault of their own. Has the industry no responsibility for the workers who are unemployed because of overproduction or some other reason? They brought the miner here and promised him a job. He worked until he got too old or until they didn't need him any more, and then they just threw him away.

"Coming into town, I saw the mules that pull the coal cars. What do the owners do with *them* when unemployment sets in? Well, they put the mules out to pasture. In fact, they feed them well and fatten them until work starts up again. They feel a responsibility to those mules because they represent an investment, but they refuse to accept any responsibility for the miner and his family. What can we do? I say we must fight for unemployment insurance.

"What's unemployment insurance? A simple proposition. Out of the profits of the coal mine, a certain share should be put into a fund so that when a miner is out of work he would get some sort of compensation."

I realized that most of those in the room had probably never heard of the term because the concept had been either ignored or attacked by the unions and the local politicians. In order to demonstrate the practical importance of organizing ourselves around this demand, I raised the everyday sort of problems that were on everybody's mind. "What are you going to do when you can't pay your rent? Should you be thrown out of your home, your family and furniture tossed into the street? This must not happen, but what can you do about it? The government must provide for rent until you get back to work. But it will be a long fight to win unemployment insurance. What can we do about the situation in the meantime? Let's go down to see the legislature and the governor in Harrisburg. Let's go see the county commissioner and ask for immediate relief in the form of food and some basic staples for those families in need. We can't depend on the local poor board alone. It's an outmoded institution set up two hundred years ago in England, and it can't do the job that's required in our modern industrial society.

"Where do we begin? Let's not wait for any miracles; we can do things right here. Let's organize an unemployed council that will take up local grievances. If some cold-blooded landlord decides to kick a family out, the council can go down and reason with him, if possible. Let's get this council organized and start helping those who are really in need."

As I looked out over the group, not a person was moving. People sat silently, some with tears in their eyes. Gradually they started raising specific grievances, and there was some discussion. Finally Tom Bradey rose again, "Any worker who's willing to help can join the council," he said. "How many are willing?" To my amazement everyone in the room raised his or her hand, even one of the two cops who were standing at the rear of the hall. Bradey and Stella asked a few of the more articulate people to stay after and establish a committee, which the audience empowered to work out plans for the next meeting. The movement of the unemployed had come to the anthracite.

Even more people came to the next meeting—seventy people crowded into the little poolroom. Just being together with others facing similar problems made people more willing to voice their grievances. One woman was suffering from diabetes and had no money for medicine. Others had little or no food, and right in the middle of the anthracite coalfields, people were often short of heating fuel. The neighborhood kids walked the railroad tracks searching for stray lumps of coal, and they often boarded the freight cars to push a few lumps off. But this was only a stopgap approach, and the authorities and railroad dicks were beginning to crack down on the kids.

After some discussion of these and other problems, it was agreed that a grievance committee should meet with the county welfare officials. I was asked to accompany the first delegation. I knew from my experiences in Chicago that this would lead to red-baiting and charges that as an outsider, my only reason for coming to the region was to cause trouble. On the other hand, I had encouraged these people to hold the meeting, establish the council, and take some kind of action. I felt that I had no choice but to go along.

The delegation consisted of the grievance committee and those who had raised grievances. We did not overstate our case or shout. We simply explained the problems and asked the officials what they could do about them. The answer was, essentially, nothing. They denied having funds for this kind of aid and asked us to clear the office. When we refused to leave without some kind of promise, Bradey, Mitelsky, and I were arrested. The incident was reported in the local papers, which emphasized that among those arrested was a certain Steve Nelson, a Communist who had come to stir up trouble in Luzerne County. The local politicians became concerned and started to discuss some ways in which the movement might be defused, including the possibility of establishing a more "dependable" organization for the unemployed.

Fortunately the smear campaign backfired, as it had in Chicago. People seemed glad that there was an organization trying to do something for the unemployed, and they were not particularly interested in the fact that some of those active in it were Communists. The news spread throughout the county, and we began to receive calls from Plymouth, Kingston, Pittston, Hanover, Nanticoke, and other towns.

The committee in Ashley couldn't cope with the number of requests for help, so we announced that there would be a meeting on Sunday afternoon for all those interested in the unemployed problem in the county. A local businessman agreed to rent to us the Crystal Ballroom, a large hall over a hardware store on North Market Street in Wilkes-Barre. He made the rent low and didn't bother us much when we were behind in paying it. The hall was large enough to hold four hundred people, and it became the headquarters of the Luzerne County Unemployed Council and the center of its activities over the next five years.

People from all the neighboring towns flocked to our first county meeting. The audience broke into groups from the various towns, and someone from the Ashley council met with each group to explain how to go about setting up a council, holding a meeting, and taking up grievances. The meeting produced a core of people who remained active organizers throughout my stay in the anthracite area. One of the most outstanding of these was a young Irishman by the name of John Muldowney. He had a wonderful way about him, neither overbearing nor shy. He sang a series of beautiful Irish ballads and said that he would have brought his violin but thought that might be inappropriate at the first meeting. Muldowney was one of a large group of young miners who came forward as organizers in the new movement and also joined the Party. Others were Bruno Zelinsky, Joe Salonas, Jimmy Hanlin, Eddie Cook, George Haggerty, and Pat Devers, a Polish miner who had assumed an Irish name. There was also a group of Italians from Swoyersville, including John and Joe Drago and Jimmy Cacciatore. Some of the older miners who took part were Fred Feshenko, Joe and Tony Raguscas, and a large number of others whose faces I remember better than their names. Some of these were local Party people whom the new movement attracted, but many had had no contact with the Party or joined only after working for some time with the councils.

At this point a lively discussion developed among the Party people in the region over whether we should devote our attention and meager resources to building the Party organization, and rely upon its members to take the initiative in various areas of mass activity, or concentrate more on the unemployed councils. We could not recruit without effective mass activity. We would have no means through which to approach the miners, and we'd wind up simply regrouping the older immigrant workers, who still saw the Party as some sort of underground organization. Many of these older radicals were isolated from their neighbors, largely because they tended to be sectarian. Only mass organizing and struggles could break through this isolation. Yet it seemed impossible to keep the councils going without an effective Party organization, a core of activists to do much of the day-to-day work and spread the movement to more towns. We agreed that there was no easy answer; it was essential to do both. We would have to concentrate as much of our time and energy as possible on building the councils and working in the unions, but we would have to link this work with the effort to build the Party in the area.

The next step was to develop contacts in the four other counties of the region—Carbon, Schuylkill, Northumberland, and Lackawanna—in order to spread the movement there. People who were mostly either Party members or sympathizers were invited to a conference that laid plans for building councils throughout the region. Wilkes-Barre, Scranton, Nanticoke, Shamokin, Minersville, Shenandoah, Mt. Carmel, and a number of other towns were represented at this meeting.

Joe Dougher represented Scranton. He was a personification of the militant anthracite miner. Starting out in the mines at the ripe old age of twelve as a "breaker boy," he wound up heading an insurgent rank and file movement in the UMWA during the late twenties. A total of twenty-nine locals that had been affiliated with this McGarry movement were expelled from the union, and Joe was blacklisted in every mine in the region. He then threw himself into organizing the unemployed, leading the movement in the northern anthracite along with Helen Dorrio, a young schoolteacher, one of the few professionals among our core group of organizers. In 1937 he went with me to Spain, returning to the United States the following year. Dougher eventually ended up in Cleveland, where he was one of two Smith Act defendants freed by the jury. After leaving the Party, he went through the whole gamut of New Left groupings before he died. I'm sure that toward the end he considered me some kind of revisionist. But I saw him in the film *Harlan County,* and in many ways he seemed the same old Joe Dougher, tough and militant as hell, always ready for a fight with the "coal barons." No one can take away from him the credit for the organizing he did with us in the anthracite coalfields.

Once the movement began to grow, it seemed that nothing could stop it. It spread from one town to another, and within three years there were fifteen or twenty thousand people organized into unemployed councils in the anthracite counties. As in most mass movements of the thirties, there was a high degree of turnover in membership, but the councils became a significant force in the power relations of these communities.

Local authorities responded to all this organizing in various ways. In Minersville, Pottsville, Mahanoy City, and a few other towns, it was possible to function more or less with their consent. In both Scranton and Wilkes-Barre, the police were pretty vicious, but the situation was complicated in Wilkes-Barre by the fact that Mayor Loveland was a liberal Unitarian whose wife was a member of the Women's International League for Peace and Freedom.[1] Margaret was always working on him through his wife. He shared some of her views, and she was generally sympathetic with the plight of the unemployed.

We tried whenever possible to hold meetings and rallies on weekends because we wanted to attract as many employed people as possible. But Wilkes-Barre Chief of Police Taylor, in cooperation with the state police, developed a system of tracking down and arresting our core group of organizers on Friday night and jailing them until Monday morning. This became almost a ritual, and for a while it was pretty difficult for us to operate effectively. The problem was how to avoid being arrested but still be able to attend meetings. We solved it by rather devious means. Sometimes we advertised one speaker, so that the police would be looking for him or her, and then sent someone else. But this ceased to work as more of our people became well known to the police. The most successful strategy was to have the speaker hide somewhere in the hall hours before the scheduled meeting and only come out when the hall was packed. The police hesitated to make an arrest in the presence of such a large crowd. After a couple of years, none of this made much difference, because there were competent organizers in most towns, and those of us leading the organization were not as important as we had been at the beginning.

We faced one of the most serious threats to our organizing in Shamokin, a fairly large town at the southern edge of the region. Coal had been mined here for over a hundred years, and the Philadelphia and Reading Coal Company had controlled its production for much of this time. The company had spent a fortune framing the twenty-four "Molly Maguires," Irish immigrant miners who were executed in the late 1870s for the crime of trying to organize a union, and the same company continued to rule the area around Shamokin with an iron hand in the 1930s.[2] Since there was no other work in the town aside from the mines, the decline of the industry meant that the Depression had hit hard. There was plenty of potential for an unemployed council, but several efforts to organize one had been disrupted and broken up by the police.

The local Party people, hoping that the police might deal more carefully with a woman, asked Margaret to come down and make another try. They asked for a permit to hold a meeting and, of course, were refused. They talked the situation over with Margaret and decided to go ahead. Margaret climbed up on a platform, and a large group of miners gathered closely around her. The police hesitated. She spoke briefly, and plans were announced for a meeting to establish a council. As the crowd dispersed, the police arrested her. Margaret protested loud and long as only she could. But the judge, without much of a hearing, sentenced her to ten days or a ten-dollar fine. Margaret refused to pay the fine, claiming that she had violated no law and would rather spend ten days in jail. But Mike Demchak, a local miner and key Socialist Party activist who assumed an important role in the organizing that followed, said he would pay the fine in order to get her out. She put up an argument, but Mike persuaded her by saying that she could do a lot more good on the outside.

These continual attacks by the police were taken up at the next regional meeting, held in Wilkes-Barre. Two carloads of miners came up from Shamokin and asked those at the meeting to help them in a free speech fight there. A big campaign was launched. Councils throughout the region sent protests to the Shamokin officials, demanding that the right to free speech be respected. The regional committee worked with the leaders of the local council to assure a successful meeting. Business and community leaders were asked to petition the town officials in support of our request for a permit. This time a permit was granted, and a large group turned up for the meeting. The free speech fights went on in Shamokin and other towns throughout the early thirties, and through these struggles and the changing political climate of the New Deal era, our right to organize was won by the middle of the decade.

Issues like the right of free speech allowed us to reach out to professionals in the community. There were not many such people in a town like Wilkes-Barre, which was populated largely by those who worked in the mines and those who owned and ran them. But any large town has a few ministers, teachers, social workers, and lawyers. As interest in the unemployed developed, some professionals started turning up at police court hearings, and others wrote letters to the newspapers protesting the role of the police and insisting that the right of free speech be guaranteed to all.

Mrs. Muller, who taught social work at Bucknell University and was especially interested in the distribution of relief, was quite moved by our struggles. She wanted to learn more about those of us who were active, so she invited Margaret and me and a few others to her home for dinner with some of her liberal friends. The other people at the dinner included three ministers, two professors, a social worker, and a librarian. Mrs. Muller lived in one of the better sections of town along the river in a community where the unemployed seldom appeared.

The dinner was a bit out of the ordinary for unemployed workers. The food itself was wonderful, but I had never faced such a bewildering array of knives, forks, spoons, and plates. I followed my usual routine in such situations: I watched what everyone else did and then just imitated them. In noting how the ministers and professors used their utensils, I found that Maggie and my other comrades were also watching.

The evening went off beautifully as far as the meal was concerned, and the small talk ended with a more serious discussion about the issues facing the unemployed and about the Depression in general. Finally this discussion led to questions of socialism and Marxism. The economics professor, a middle-aged man with heavy glasses and nervous mannerisms, turned to me and asked, "Why are you so interested in the everyday problems of the unemployed and in getting relief? Aren't you defeating your own purpose by feeding the unemployed and making them so satisfied with the status quo? As they continue to live under the system called capitalism, how will they see the point that socialism is the system they should support?"

I answered that there was no contradiction between the struggle for existence today and advocacy of socialism for the future. We couldn't sit on the sidelines and let the unemployed starve. Even the most optimistic of us knew that socialism, like prosperity, was not just around the corner; in the meantime people had to exist. This included us personally, for we were in the same boat as the rest of the unemployed and preferred not to starve to death. There was also some danger that people could be attracted by demagogues like Father Coughlin, who advocated tolerance for the German and Italian fascists, and politicians like Huey Long, who stood for a fascistlike state capitalism.[3] There was talk in Washington that certain people were looking for "a man on a white horse" to take over the government. Retired Marine Corps General Smedley Butler, who had led occupation troops in Nicaragua, said he was invited by certain business interests to be that man but had refused. Such ideas emanated from the conservative forces in the country: the Liberty League, the Hearst newspapers, and others who thought that a type of fascist rule would solve many of our problems, including unemployment, and avoid the danger of socialism.[4] This right-wing threat was difficult for any progressive person to ignore.

But misery does not lead to socialism by itself, I argued. People have to fight against the evils in the present system in order to learn what is wrong with it. If they are ever convinced that a socialist system is better, they will accept the argument from those of us who are active in fighting for their immediate demands more readily than from those who like to preach from the sidelines. I explained that as we reached many people around immediate issues, they came to know us better and asked questions about socialism. Many among the unemployed responded well to the discussions and conversations that developed naturally from the struggle at hand. We invited those whom we thought were ready to go more deeply into these questions to the Party's political discussions and educational meetings. Here we would discuss with a limited group of people what socialism would mean for the working people in particular. We'd point out that it would provide a rational system as opposed to the anarchy of capitalism. I added that the fourfold increase in Party membership in Luzerne County in two years argued strongly in favor of mass work as a means of political education and recruitment.

Midway through my explanation, I realized that I was sounding a bit like a professor myself, but we needed to carefully explain why we worked the way we did. There was so much misunderstanding regarding the Party's policies that I jumped at the chance to set the record straight. I was also trying to tailor my explanations to the audience. You wouldn't speak this way before a group of unemployed miners, but these people were of a different breed.

The professor of philosophy, a soft-spoken young man who'd been listening intently, posed the next question. Everything he had read in Marxist literature claimed that development came through contradictions, but if you have a society in which the contradictions are overcome or eliminated, what will be the motivating or driving force to further progress? I explained that the motivating force would be a national plan designed to meet the basic needs of all citizens. When we have planned what amounts of various goods are needed, it will not be difficult to adjust the hours of work from eight to six per day, and then from six to four in order to avoid overproduction and allow time for leisure. But wages would not be cut. The money that formerly went into private hands to earn more profits for individuals would instead be used for all the people. There would also be greater care for natural resources. For example, the coal companies around Pittston or Scranton washed the coal in the big breakers in our rivers without the slightest concern that they were polluting the water so that those who lived downstream could not use it. This water is a natural resource, and under socialism it would be protected.

This discussion went on all evening until finally it was time to break up. It was a Friday night, and Harold Spencer, our editor and publicity man who was at the dinner, suggested that perhaps he and I should not go directly home because we might be picked up on the way by the police. Dr. Frane, a local minister, wanted to know what Spencer meant by this. So we explained that this had been a problem in Wilkes-Barre for the past year—almost every Friday night, we were picked up and taken to jail. He wanted to know why. When I said we were locked up to keep us from organizing the unemployed, he was astonished. "They have no right to do that," he declared. "The

Bill of Rights and the Constitution guarantee you your rights." I said, "Yes, Dr. Frane, we know that, but what exists on paper apparently does not apply to some of us in the coal region. What rules here is 'might' and not the question of 'right.' " He became quite concerned about it and wanted to take us home in his car. We told him that his assistance would not change the situation, for after he left we would still be picked up and have to spend the weekend in jail. "That is preposterous!" he exclaimed. He could not believe that this was happening in his country. We insisted that we could manage ourselves and let him go home. Actually we did not want to get him involved, since we were concerned that he would be red-baited if he were ever caught with us in his car.

Dr. Frane's congregation included a member of a large coal-operating family. The family had owned the land from colonial times, and when coal was discovered, they acquired the rights. They owned the railroad that hauled the coal as well as many important businesses in town. They and their friends also controlled local politics. On Monday, Mrs. Muller called. She told me that on Sunday she had been to church where Dr. Frane had delivered a wonderful sermon in which he told his congregation that they were not living like real Christians. Many of them were satisfied with their own situations and knew very little about the plight of the unemployed. He said there were people they condemned as radicals who were doing more for the unemployed than those in the congregation. "Last Friday," he said, "I met with some of these radicals, right in Wilkes-Barre, and I must say that I got the impression that they were better Christians than some of the people in this congregation. In fact, I can tell you that this man Steve Nelson who is known as the local Red is more like a saint than many around us—for he is concerned with the plight of the unemployed."

"Why did he do that?" I yelled into the receiver. Surprised, Mrs. Muller replied, "Why not? I thought you would be happy to know this." I explained that Frane was finished as a minister in Wilkes-Barre. Indeed, two weeks later this liberal minister was given his notice of dismissal. He left town without a murmur.

Fortunately the others who had attended the dinner were not frightened by this incident. A few weeks later they invited us to another gathering at which we discussed Dr. Frane's case. Most of those present felt that he did the right thing and saw him as a man of great honesty and courage. We expressed a different view. We said that while his sentiments were admirable, he cut himself off from activity in the area, and that we hoped the others would see the need for a long pull in the struggle instead of losing their effectiveness as

Dr. Frane had done. The upshot was that the liberals found their voices and began to speak out for civil and constitutional rights and for the rights of the unemployed. A number of people became very vocal and took part in many of the activities that followed. They spoke out against deportations of the foreign-born and protested attacks on strikers and the arrests of Communists and radicals. They fought for the Bill of Rights and the Constitution, and to this day that remains a credit to them.

The structure of our organization in the anthracite region was theoretically the same as that in a big city like Chicago. The town unemployed councils were comparable to the neighborhood councils, and our regional committee in Wilkes-Barre served the same coordinating function as a city executive committee. But in some very practical ways the organizing itself was different. Most of our initiative had to come from the local level because we were relatively isolated from the national leadership of both the Party and the unemployed movement. Technically we were under the Philadelphia district, which had some very good organizers over the years. The district leadership could send the literature we needed, supply us with teachers for some of our more ambitious educationals, and give advice on especially difficult problems. But it was impossible for anyone to get around to all the little towns, at least not on a regular basis. This meant that the local leadership was much more autonomous than it might have been in a big city like Chicago.

The isolation of the mining towns also produced a greater intimacy among those active in the movement. The activists who traveled through the region speaking and organizing were extremely close. Any contributions or revenue went into one kitty, and anyone who worked full time at organizing was welcome to share in it. There was usually enough money to keep us going. I had never worked in an area where the activists had a higher degree of morale or enjoyed their work more than in the anthracite.

Widespread unemployment was more a precondition than an explanation for the success of the unemployed movement. The key to the quality of our councils, I believe, was in the kind of people we found among the activists. A movement like that of the unemployed councils is based on the strength and dedication of hundreds of rank and file activists, workers who built the movement within their own communities.

A crowd of characters springs to mind. Carl Herman, elder statesman among the radical Lithuanian miners, managed to be active in everything that happened in the coalfields while he was dying of "miner's asthma," what we now call black lung. A younger Lithuanian miner, Peter Paul, came up from the ranks to become Party organizer for the Schuylkill County area, but he died at thirty-eight from the same disease. Joe Barr was the first environmentalist I'd ever met and a real working-class intellectual. He explained how coal could be treated in other ways in order to avoid pollution of the rivers and air, and he built up a large collection of fossilized rocks that he'd discovered while working in the pits. He passed some of these on to the Museum of Natural History, but others were kept in a potato sack under his bed. He pulled the sack out at every opportunity and used the fossils to explain the mysteries of evolution and the origins of life to any miner who would listen. His little shack was a mass of science books and rocks. Many others have their own stories, which deserve to be told, but here I can only offer a few that are more or less representative of the others.

John Sutherland was a young miner who lived in a town called Freeland, an odd misnomer for this little patch of shacks stacked along the railroad tracks. The only railroad cars that passed through the town were those hauling coal from the nearby mines, and there was no other sign of civilization—no grocery, no school, no drugstore or official building, not even a policeman—just the row of shacks constructed from rough pine lumber. The insides of the houses, which were owned by the coal company, had neither plaster nor insulation, and the outsides and roofs were covered with tar paper. Cracks in the inside walls were filled with newspapers and pages from an old Sears Roebuck catalog. Sutherland and his family lived in one of these.

Things were rough in the Kentucky coalfields in the twenties, and the young miner and his wife had moved to the anthracite only to learn that the Depression had preceded them. They became active in the local council, and when I came to the area for a meeting, they invited me over for dinner. This hospitality came as a matter of course. The people realized that we worked full time for the movement and really had no way to support ourselves. Most had little to offer. Our diet usually consisted of a lot of starch and a hot dog or hamburger now and then. They shared with us whatever they had. In the five years we spent in the region, I don't think we ate in restaurants more than twice.

I came to Freeland early for dinner and was welcomed to their little shack. The place was warm, cheerful, and clean in spite of the evident poverty. Their children, a three-year-old and a baby of about a year, were crawling around the freshly scrubbed floor, playing while their parents were busy around the stove with our dinner.

Mr. Sutherland said sheepishly, "Well, we've got a chicken and some sweet potatoes roasting in the oven, but we haven't got any flour to make white gravy. We can't have our chicken without the gravy and maybe a few biscuits."

I said, "Maybe I can scrape up something," and reached into my pocket. There I found thirty-eight cents, all I had to my name but not enough for flour. Sutherland thought they might be able to borrow some flour from a neighbor, and his wife went out and came back with a plate packed with flour. This was the customary way that miners' families borrowed from one another. A plate was filled with flour, and it was expected that it would be returned in the same manner.

It seemed strange that they had a chicken but no flour. Sutherland guessed my thoughts. "I guess you're wondering about the chicken. Well, you don't have to worry about that—I got it this way—" and he tapped his holster, which was hanging on the side of his belt under his jacket. There was no gun in it, but he obviously had a pistol somewhere. "I got down along the woods by that big farm and there was a chicken straying in. I figured the fox would get her if I didn't, so I shot her right through the head. I had to lay low because I was afraid that the report of the pistol would be heard, but they were running machinery and didn't hear anything. In Kentucky we pray to the Lord and thank him for the meal before us. But this time pray for the farmer who raised her and for my lucky shot."

The kids were put up to the table, and they stuffed themselves with the sweet potatoes, chicken, and gravy. You could tell that it was not a common meal in this house; it was more like Christmas or Thanksgiving. After the meal Sutherland called in a couple of his neighbors and without batting an eye, told them what we had for supper and how he got it. And then he asked me to explain what had to be done in our society so that people did not have to eke out an existence in this manner, so they could forthrightly get their meals by earnestly working, and not just working for somebody else, but for themselves.

Sutherland had already been exposed to some degree of socialist thinking. He was anxious for me to tell the neighbors the embarrassing situation he had to face in not knowing where the next meal was coming from. So he primed me, and I answered the questions as best I knew how. We went to the unemployed council meeting thinking how nice it might be to have a chicken for dinner any time you wanted to.

People like Sutherland, common workers with a socialist vision, made up the backbone of the movement, but we also needed men and women like Harold Spencer, the "resident intellectual" of our little

Working for the unemployed in the anthracite, early 1930s. From left to right, standing: Lucy, a young woman activist; Steve Nelson; Harold Spencer. Seated: Margaret Nelson; B. D. Amos.

anthracite group. Harold and his brother Charlie left North Adams, Massachusetts, to go to the University of Wisconsin where they both became radicals. After graduation Charlie went to Allentown, Pennsylvania, where he was quite good on trade union matters, while Harold went to the anthracite. Harold had been a history and journalism major at Wisconsin, and we were glad to get a professional, someone who could write a good leaflet or a little news story for the *Daily Worker*.

Around 1936 we had a circulation campaign for the *Sunday Worker,* which at the time was at a high point under the editorship of Clarence Hathaway. Weekly circulation in the anthracite was around two thousand, and we had quite an operation, with a distribution network that included a car and newsboys assigned to each unemployed council. We decided to keep circulation up by having a radio hour every Sunday. We found a few sympathizers who were willing to subsidize the venture, and Harold became commentator for the *Sunday Worker Radio Hour*. In addition to increasing interest in the paper, the program was an organizing tool. Harold announced the time and place of local meetings, government rulings on matters affecting the unemployed, and labor news. He also commented on the key stories in the paper. Since Harold had a great sense of humor, he always managed to get a few wisecracks in amongst the news stories. He loved the work because it was just the sort of thing that he did well. I'm sure that Harold would be the first to admit that he was not always the most efficient person in the world—he never made a newspaper deadline—but I'll be damned if he didn't always have that program ready.

Harold was also responsible for getting out the *Anthracite Unemployed Worker,* the organ of the Luzerne County Unemployed Councils, which began to appear some time in 1935. It was a nicely printed sheet with a circulation of about five thousand, and it carried news about what was going on in Congress, the legislature, and the unions. He traveled around getting information on meetings and delegations from the chairmen of the various councils. Here's an example of an intellectual who did excellent work for the movement, was well-liked, and fit in with an overwhelmingly working-class organization. I remained close with Harold after he left the region to work in Philadelphia, and he gave me a lot of support during my trials in the fifties. He left the Party around 1956 but remained active. Today he and his wife Alfreda Mahler, a modern dance teacher, live in Cuba.

In the little town of Swoyersville, the local council revolved around a group of related Italian families. These four families shared a common experience in the Old World, and they stayed together in the New, helping each other and making a very fine impression on their neighbors. They were resourceful in many ways. They had the best vegetable gardens, and with the leftover scraps they fed rabbits, which became their source of meat. Later on the government began to issue such things as dried milk and something that we called "bully beef," a canned beef that would probably now be sold for dog food. It didn't taste like much and was mostly gristle and mush. This together with oatmeal was given out by the relief administration after about two years of struggle. With this surplus from the government, the Italian families decided to get young ducks, and they fed them what they could not eat themselves. Thus instead of eating bully beef, at times they had duck, which was considered to be pretty elegant dining for unemployed miners. In this way they kept their families going while other less resourceful people could not meet the situation as well.

I recall one neighbor of theirs in particular. Mr. Thompson had worked in the mines and by this time was past fifty-five, but looked more like eighty. He had had a broken arm that had been improperly set, and it stuck out as if he were wearing a splint. Thompson used to visit these Italian people, and they liked him. He had a house full of children but did not know what to do about the most elementary things. On more than one occasion, I saw one or the other of the Italians show him how to prepare the ground to raise vegetables.

In many ways these Italian families were advanced and progressive, but in other respects they retained certain backward attitudes, particularly regarding women. Their women's place was in the kitchen. Once my friend Joe Jursak, his wife Rose, and Margaret and I almost caused a revolution when we went to one of their famous duck dinners. We suggested that the women, who usually sat in the kitchen and ate by themselves, should all eat with us. This was an extremely difficult thing for these Italian men to accept, and I don't think the women ever did make it into the front room. But we learned later that they had been following all the arguments from the kitchen, and it's hard to believe that they didn't continue the attack on their own after we left.

I was also impressed with the level of culture that these families maintained. They could hum all the famous Italian operas and taught me what little I know about the Renaissance. Jimmy Cacciatore told the story of Giordano Bruno, standing as if he himself were to be burned at the stake. "I could say that the world is flat to save my own life," he recited, "but it would go on turning just the same." Unlike many of their Slavic neighbors, the Italians were strongly anticlerical and had no connection with the Church, viewing it as a reactionary institution that had opposed all progress for hundreds of years.

Our legal specialist was a lawyer named Sheprovich who had come to Wilkes-Barre from New York City. I found him almost by accident the first time we got into serious trouble. One day we went to Swoyersville to give the Italians and a few of the other local council people a hand in stopping an eviction. We put the furniture back into the house, but the state police arrested both Joe Jursak and me. The Italian women brought their umbrellas to the demonstration that day even though there was no sign of rain, and they put up such a fight when their husbands were about to be arrested that the police let them alone. They settled instead for us, figuring that it would be easier to prosecute outsiders than local people. The fight that the Italian women put up became the talk of the county movement, and their men were especially proud.

Joe and I spent a long weekend in jail before being bailed out. Someone had heard of Sheprovich and suggested that we see him about the case. There was no particular reason that he should have been interested. In fact, he specialized in real estate, but whoever made the suggestion said he seemed like a nice guy.

I went to his office and explained who I was and why we needed a lawyer. He seemed glad to help, and when I asked about the fee, he said we could talk about that later. Something under the glass top of his desk caught my eye. I looked closer but couldn't believe what I saw. There, staring back at me from the top of this real estate lawyer's desk, was Rosa Luxemburg.[5] I recognized the picture as the outside cover of a New York City YCL membership card. Sheprovich had apparently belonged to the youth organization while in college, and though no longer connected with the Party, he kept the picture as a memento, figuring that none of his real estate friends would ever recognize who it was. But to me it suggested that he might have an attitude toward social problems rarely found in any lawyer outside the ILD.

Sheprovich provided invaluable service to us throughout the thirties, risking his reputation and sometimes his own neck in the process. This Swoyersville trial was held in the local real estate office, owned by the justice of the peace, who sat there under a large portrait of Herbert Hoover. The court was packed with local vigilantes and police, and our supporters had to stand outside. A state policeman described our crime. We had addressed a mass gathering, he said, urging them to "demand this and demand that," and had caused a disturbance on the town's main street. Sheprovich asked what we had done besides giving speeches, but the justice wasn't interested and sentenced us to pay a ten-dollar fine or spend ten days in jail. We paid the fine, but as we filed out we noticed a long line of cars packed with men. Sheprovich guessed they would follow us. He said he would lead, and we should stay as close to his car as possible. He advised us to be prepared to duck flying stones and to keep our windows down to avoid shattering glass. The lawyer knew what he was talking about. As soon as we pulled away, stones started flying. But rocks also began to fly at the vigilante cars, and they quickly retreated.

While Sheprovich was hardly a typical unemployed council activist, the movement's acceptance of any person willing to work hard is best illustrated by the story of Gus. I met him in Hazelton, a beautiful town perched atop the highest point in that part of Pennsylvania. The large settlement of Montenegrin miners there wanted to start a council.[6] One of them came to Wilkes-Barre asking for help, and I offered to go down to hold a meeting. We met in an abandoned store, and the meeting itself was successful but uneventful. I explained what the councils were trying to do and how this could be accomplished in Hazelton. A grievance committee was established, and a collection was made to cover expenses such as gas for the trip to the county welfare office and paper for leaflets. When the hat made its way back up to the front and we turned it over on the table, a ten-dollar bill lay among the pennies and nickels.

I spotted someone at the back of the room whom I had pegged for a detective. He was a short guy with jet-black hair and a thin mustache. He was extremely well dressed in a white suit and Panama hat, and he leaned back in his chair, occasionally saying something to the man next to him. After the meeting was over he solved the mystery of the ten-dollar bill by coming up to say he had dropped it in. His name was Gus, he said, and he was concerned with the problem of unemployment, even though he wasn't a worker. I had already guessed that by looking at his hands and face as well as the clothes. But he was a little reticent about discussing exactly how he did make his living.

He invited me to his house for coffee and a chat. I was more than a little suspicious, but there was an air of sincerity about him that was hard to dismiss. Besides, the local people all seemed to know him. His home looked like that of a successful professional though his speech and mannerisms suggested working-class origins. He introduced me to his wife who made coffee and gave us something to eat.

Gus admitted that he had never done a day's work in all his life.

"You may not approve of that," he said, "but it's the truth. I'm close to forty years old now, and all I've ever done is gamble. I came to this country from Greece and quickly became a professional gambler. I know that you and your people will probably not want to have anything to do with me, but I really respect what you're doing. I just wanted to talk with you."

He discussed his trade freely. There had been a big game in the local hotel several weeks ago, and he had cleaned the local newspaper owner out for about $3,000 in one night. Since then he had had some trouble getting a game going. There were some miners in the town who'd gamble with him every payday. When he didn't clean them out completely, it was only because doing that made him feel too guilty; he decided they should take something home with them.

In the same hotel where all this gaming went on was a Greek dishwasher who had left New York City because of some labor organizing trouble there. He watched Gus gamble for a while and then introduced himself. It turned out that they had come from the same town in the old country, and the dishwasher had even worked for Gus's father. They embraced, but then the little dishwasher stepped back and lashed into Gus. "You're a disgrace to our people for what you're doing around here. You're a disgrace to your father and your family. You make your living by taking advantage of these hard-working miners, and you don't seem to realize that you're taking bread out of their children's mouths. This is no decent way to live."

Startled by all this, Gus became defensive. "What do you want me to do? This is the only life I know."

The dishwasher continued to speak harshly. "Don't you know that gamblers don't contribute anything to society? They're leeches. They live by taking away from others through trickery. Why can't you take any kind of job? Wash dishes like me if you have to." He was a radical and tried to explain that life could be different. "You could never make your living this way in the Soviet Union. You would have to work or you would not eat."

Gus was confused. "What kind of society is it there? How is it any different than ours?"

"It's a socialist society. It may not be perfect, because it was one of the most backward in Europe when the Communists seized power. It took a long time to rebuild the country after the First World War and the Civil War, but they're trying to achieve something for the common people. The coal mines there are owned by all the people and not by a few companies. Here the miner produces three times as much for the owner as he gets in his pay envelope."

As Gus reproduced the conversation, he explained how new all this was to him. He was astounded. "How did you learn all this?" he asked. "You were nothing when you worked for my father. You didn't even go to school, but you seem to have changed since then."

"I have been reading books, my friend," the dishwasher said, "good books by a man named Karl Marx."

"Who's he?" Gus asked.

"Well, here you are forty years old, and you've never heard of the world's greatest thinker! He's known better now, all over the world, than he was when he still lived."

The little dishwasher had made a tremendous impression on Gus. They talked more about the books, and Gus made a trip to the library. The dishwasher gave him Greek editions of some of the books, and Gus read them in both English and Greek. For the next few weeks he could do nothing else. But still he could not fully understand the ideas they sought to explain. He decided that he needed to talk to someone who knew the books well, and he had settled on me.

I explained that I myself had been an illiterate immigrant worker and had labored for years to understand Marxism. I was not a philosopher, but I would be glad to answer any questions he had. We spent the afternoon discussing what socialism was, how it would work, and how to help in the struggle to achieve it in the United States. Every individual who supported the ideal, I emphasized, must work hard to bring it about.

"Well," he said, "I'm ready. What can I do to help?" I knew I had to find out more about what kind of man this was. It was not the policy of the CPUSA to recruit professional gamblers. What kind of impression would it make on workers if the local Communist made his living as a card shark or pool hustler? Also, years of experience had made me just a little skeptical about such rapid conversions. I was still worried that he might be a police agent of some kind.

I said he would have to look around for some other way to make his living. This suggestion hit him like a ton of bricks. "I'm forty years old," he said. "What can I do now?" I tried to reassure him but couldn't suggest anything concrete. He remembered a cousin who owned a diner outside of town and said he would ask him for work.

"But how am I going to keep up this house?" he asked. "I've got a wife and three kids."

"Well," I said. "You'll finally learn how the working class lives."

Gus was well-known throughout the lower anthracite and agreed to introduce me to people in Pottsville, Mt. Carmel, Shamokin, and other towns. He had fleeced people in each place but still had many friends. The miners maintained a kind of respect for him somehow, even if they knew better now than to get into a card game with him.

The first place he took me was Mahanoy City, tucked away in the hills between Hazelton and Shenandoah. It was a typical anthracite town composed largely of second-generation immigrant miners. Gus headed straight for the poolhall, where we found about thirty young miners loafing. Out of seven or eight tables, one was occupied, and the owner sat in the corner waiting for customers. Gus greeted him by name and slipped him a five-dollar bill. Then he turned to address the young men around the tables. "I'd like to ask you two guys who are playing to stop for an hour, while this fellow speaks. After he gets through with his message, I'll set everyone up. This is Steve Nelson. He's from Luzerne County, and he's an organizer for the unemployed councils. He'd like to talk with you for a little while about a problem you're all facing—unemployment."

In all the situations I'd come across in my organizing, I'd never been in one like this, and I was flabbergasted. I usually came to a place where the meeting had already been arranged by a local Party person or a friend, and the people who came were there to talk about unemployment and to organize a council. These guys had come to shoot pool. Usually I had at least one comrade at hand in case the police took a notion to break up the meeting, but this time I was walking into unknown territory with a notorious professional gambler as my partner.

There were no chairs, so the young miners squatted down, as was customary in their trade. Since miners spent most of their working lives sitting on their heels digging coal, it was nothing to squat down for half an hour or so for a talk. Hoping for the best, I opened with the "retired mule" talk. I explained that both the government and the employers had a responsibility to them that they would never assume unless the people organized themselves and demanded what was rightfully theirs.

The response was wonderful. These miners not only organized one of the best councils in the region, but they also established a little labor library in an empty store. It was in their library that I heard radical folk music for the first time. They collected working-class literature and books on Marxism, and the place became a center for many of the young miners in town. Eventually some of these men joined the Party.

From Mahanoy City Gus took me to Mt. Carmel, Shamokin, and other towns, where we repeated the process. It was a rather unorthodox method for organizing unemployed councils, but it seemed to work. We reached the young miners who were sitting around the poolrooms with nothing to do, and the most active among them joined the councils. Gus followed through on his promise to switch jobs and went to work in the diner. The Second World War took him out of the kitchen and into a Schenectady, New York, General Electric plant where he worked with his wife and kids. He became active in the Party and the United Electrical Workers and, as far as I know, never went back to gambling.

My relationship and work with Gus did not go unnoticed in the councils and the Party organization. Many were dubious about having anything to do with a man like him. But I had a hunch that a good idea can penetrate the minds of people who don't work with picks and shovels, and that even someone like Gus might recognize the value of socialism as a way of reorganizing society. Admittedly I was taking a chance, but he seemed to prove my point in the end.

As Party organizer in the region, it was not unusual for me to become involved in the personal problems of individual Party members. When you live in a community for five or six years and work with people on a daily basis, you come to know and love them. When they're faced with problems, you try to help. This was especially so with the women of the anthracite.

In the course of our efforts, many women became active in the councils. They perhaps understood what unemployment meant to the family better than the men could. For generations women had assumed a special role in the struggles of the anthracite miners. During strikes they were always involved in picketing and demonstrations and were often much harder on scabs than the men. But the people of the anthracite, even some of our radicals, were often quite backward in their attitudes. The stories of Stella and Carol show some of the problems faced by these anthracite women and the different directions in which their problems could lead them.

Out of the hundreds of fine people you meet and work with in the course of organizing, every once in a while there's one who stands out as a symbol of everything good about workers as a class in society, as a symbol of the struggle of workers for a better life. Stella was one of these. She was not a sophisticated revolutionary; I doubt that she had ever sat down and read many Marxist works. Stella was an everyday sort of heroine, a typical working-class housewife who'd decided that she had had enough and was prepared to fight. People respected her for the tremendous strength she showed in holding her family together. Faced with the seemingly impossible situation of trying to raise eight children without a husband in the middle of the area hit hardest by the Depression, she refused to give in. She insisted that her poverty was not her fault but the system's.

During our stay in the region the family lived in a shack that was built literally on the side of a smoking slag heap. When the Depression hit and Tom became unemployed, he started to drink. Stella knew that Tom's problems were not of his own making, so she tried to be sympathetic. But soon Tom started abusing the children and then Stella herself. With this she threw him out of the house and decided to make her own way.

Stella and the kids were singled out for a bit of advertising by the poor board. One of the papers ran a picture of the whole family and beneath a caption to the effect that "This family will never want for food thanks to the efficiency of their local poor board." Less than a year after the picture appeared, the family was on the verge of starvation. Stella organized. When the poor board said that it couldn't make welfare grants of milk for the children, Stella not only confronted it but also rallied many other women and children facing the same situation. One of my most vivid memories is of her heading a long line of women and children (with her own eight in the lead) holding empty milk bottles and yelling, "We demand milk!" Stella spent so much time down at the poor board representing herself or others that the officials would wince when they saw her coming.

As crowded as it was, Stella's house became a sort of center for the radicals in the area. Harold Spencer, John Muldowney, Margaret and I, and many of the unemployed miners active in the councils and the Party would come by for a cup of coffee and to talk over the most recent problems in the area. The Petrosky kids grew up in a radical environment, and in this way too Stella made her presence felt. Each of the kids supported the movement, at least in spirit. Jenny, the oldest, shared the burden of holding the family together with her mother, and she grew up to be a wonderful woman, a militant leather worker. She married John Muldowney and remains active to this day.

Stella aspired only to be an "honorable daughter of the working class." She was proud of her background and opted to fight where she was. Her friend Carol, however, was a different case. Carol and her husband Stan were active in the unemployed council in the town of Wyoming.[7] Both worked a short shift in one of the few textile mills still operating in the area, Stan as a loom fixer and Carol as a weaver. Stan was big and powerfully built and always pleasant and cheerful, while Carol seemed to carry the burdens of the world on her shoulders. She was always squinting, as if to make out what the next problem was going to be.

Working different shifts, they shared child-rearing and other duties during the week. On Sunday Carol went to church while Stan took care of the chores at home. He had been a sympathizer for years and joined the Party once it had been rebuilt in the region. Carol was just coming around politically through her involvement in the local council. When it came to a Party meeting or some other important event, Stan would usually stay with the kids in order to let Carol attend. Margaret and I got to know both of them well and often spent hours on weekends with them and their children. In spite of their busy schedule and all the problems they faced raising a family during the Depression, they always managed to remain politically active.

When work picked up a little in the mill, the company introduced a "stretch-out" system designed to speed up production. Without any union organization, the three hundred workers launched a wildcat strike, and soon United Textile Workers organizers arrived to help direct the struggle. Both Stan and Carol became active on the strike committee, but as the weeks dragged by, Carol became despondent. "We can't continue like this," she said. "I'm going back to work."

Stan had sensed that something was deeply troubling her, but he was still shocked. Every Sunday she had sought the advice of her priest, who strongly opposed the strike, and apparently he had influenced her decision. She said that she would not abandon her children and that it was hopeless to continue. Claiming that the strike was against God's will, she urged Stan to come back to work with her. At this point Stan realized that although they had both become radicals, Carol's continued association with the priest had made her a scab. He became bitter toward the priest, and this resulted in a fight. She said she would walk past Stan and the other union workers on the picket line and go back to work. It became impossible for them to live together, and Stan left.

The strike was lost, and Stan was fired. Carol advanced on the job because the company believed she had sparked a "back to work" movement. The matter was brought before the Party's Subdistrict Committee, and we had to tell Carol that she was wrong. This decision crushed her. She thought that because she was a close friend of Margaret, myself, and others on the committee, we would side with her. Recognizing how confused and depressed she was, we weren't bitter about what she had done, but we couldn't condone her actions. We were forced to expel her. It was the only expulsion I can remember during my time in the district. Stan also tried to be understanding, but her decision to return to work had erected a barrier between them. He concluded that the only thing he could do was to leave town, and he set out for Minnesota.

At this point relations with Carol took another turn for the worse. Stella was arrested by the Immigration Department and threatened with deportation, a tactic routinely used by the government since the 1919–1920 Red Scare. When the case came to trial, everyone wondered who the prosecution witness would be. To our amazement Carol appeared on the stand. When she was asked the question, "Is Stella a Communist?" Carol answered that she had seen her at meetings. Even though she knew that our meetings were open to nearly anyone with a sincere interest and that we encouraged non-Party unemployed council activists to attend, she implied that anyone who attended the meetings must be a Party member.

During the lunch break Stella cornered Carol in the hall. Over the years Stella had been through a lot. Her husband Tom had started to drink and had degenerated before her eyes, finally turning on her and the eight children. Her oldest son had been sent to the reformatory for a petty crime that he really had no part in, and she never knew where the next dollar to feed her family was coming from. Through all of this her work in the councils and the ideal of socialism had sustained her. She was a remarkably strong woman, but the thought of her friend betraying her, helping in the effort to deport her, was too much. She broke into tears and lashed out at Carol. "Why are you doing this to me? Why do you want to separate me from my children? You sold out for that lousy textile job! You're probably getting paid to testify against me today!" We put our arms around Stella and tried to comfort her.

Carol's performance was a foreshadowing of what I myself would face in the fifties. The prosecution asked, "Were you taught about the need to overthrow the government at these meetings that you and Stella attended?"

"Oh yes," Carol parroted, "they taught us that."

Obviously Carol knew what she was supposed to say. "Well, what did they say?" the prosecutor coaxed.

"They said that we should overthrow the government by force and violence."

"But how was that going to be done?"

"They said it had to be done by force."

"What books did they use?"

"Oh, they used all kinds of books—Lenin, Marx, and other books like that."

"And what did Stella say when she heard these things being said?"

" 'Oh,' she said, 'that's the way. I agree that's the only way it can be done!' "

Stella screamed back, "Carol, you're a dirty liar!" The judge admonished her to keep silent.

Stella was represented by Attorney Schwab of the Committee for the Protection of the Foreign-Born. He argued that this woman couldn't possibly have made the statements attributed to her. Stella was not in the least familiar with terminology like "the dictatorship of the proletariat" because such terms were not used at Party meetings. "Furthermore," he said, "people have a right to advocate new ideas under the Constitution of the United States, if they so desire." He quoted Lincoln to the effect that "when the people tire of this form of government they have not only the right but the duty to overthrow it."

Of course the prosecution and the judge had already decided that Stella should be deported. The case went through a series of appeals, and finally, many years later, after tremendous protests from all kinds of people, it was dropped. Carol became a "professional witness" in the fifties and was used by the government in a number of cases.

The situation forced us to discuss how we could guard against people like Carol getting into the movement. Some of the old-timers insisted that we must exclude anyone who retained some tie with the Church, for this was a good indication that beneath all that person's radicalism lurked the mind of a reactionary. But most of us argued that almost every younger person connected with the movement, and some of the best people we had, kept up some kind of religious contact. We couldn't use that as a criterion for judging commitment. We concluded that we would have to work more closely with new people and see how they behaved in daily work. If a person was so backward as to go back to a job while others were on strike, we should cut him or her loose immediately. We would have to be more careful about who was coming to our meetings, or good people like Stella would end up getting hurt.

All the people of the anthracite faced poverty, repression, and a daily struggle for existence, but the plight of the old miners was a living symbol that things were apt to get even worse. And for those who tried to put the symbol out of their minds, there were frequent funerals of relatively young men who had died of miner's asthma. I can still clearly recall standing at the door of the unemployed council's headquarters and looking down the flight of stairs as several middle-aged miners, looking old far beyond their years, climbed slowly, gasping for air.

Paul Nelson, a Lithuanian miner who had spent most of his life down in the pits, was one of these. He was a Party member and, though in very bad shape, never missed our county meetings. As sick as he was, he spent all of his time on Party and unemployed council activities. His devotion made a deep impression on the younger people in the movement. He had been a "hard-rock miner," drilling holes through rock in order to reach the coal seams. Because there was no ventilation or even a spray of water from the drill, years' worth of rock dust had settled in his lungs. Paul had taken a liking to me from the time I arrived, and when he died at only forty-five years of age it was a heavy blow.

A large crowd of Paul's friends—miners and their families and people from the Party, the councils, the fraternal lodge, and the unions—crowded around the coffin on a hillside in front of the Nelson shack. Even Stella's children, who could usually instill life into the most somber situations, stood quietly with their heads bowed. Many people cried with grief over the loss of a good friend and comrade and in frustration over conditions that would one day claim many of them or their loved ones. The banners of the union locals and unemployed councils hung limp and silent. Everyone stared at the ground, waiting for someone to express what all of us were feeling.

The miner's wife, son, and daughter-in-law were crushed with the loss and bitter over the fact that nothing was being done about the conditions that had killed Paul. They had watched him die slowly and knew that many more would follow. The coal companies didn't care, and there would be no help from the state or federal governments.

Although I'd been to many funerals in the region, this was the first time I'd been asked to speak. The crowd drew in as I began. I explained that this man had died much too young because of the greed of the coal company. There were no safety regulations, no proper ventilation, and no adequate inspection of the mines. The companies were interested only in how much coal they could get out of the ground; and a miner could always be replaced. Because of unemployment people were begging for jobs. Now they had hired this man's son, and in another fifteen years he too would be spent and gone. There would always be more where he came from.

People were enraged by this industrial mass murder. They might have marched down to the mine and destroyed the whole thing, but that wouldn't have solved the problem. Instead they gathered about the widow, sharing her grief and offering to do what they could to help. But her strength amazed me. "No one needed to tell me what I heard today," she said. "I knew it ever since my father died from the same miner's asthma. This will continue to happen. I tried to get Paul to move away, to take work in some other industry, but he said, 'Where are we going to go? Here we have a home and good friends. There are no jobs in the city, so we have no choice.' We stayed until death found us."

At least Paul had his family until the end. Throughout the anthracite old single miners lived alone. When they were younger they had lived in boardinghouses with fellow miners of their own nationalities. During the Depression the older ones were among the first to be laid off. When boarders could no longer pay rent, the head of the household had to move into a smaller house, and the old miners were left without homes.

In Wilkes-Barre many of these old men came to unemployed council meetings early and slept in the headquarters after the meeting had ended. The councils raised the issue with the county officials, who eventually set aside land on which the men could build their own shacks. The county also agreed to provide cheap building materials, a stove for each shack, a common water faucet, and one outhouse for every eight or ten men.

Every shack was eight by eight, a single room where one and often a couple of miners cooked, ate, and slept. The shacks all faced the same way, with smoking coal piles for a backdrop. There were no women, no children, no trees; just the old miners. Although there were no street names or numbers in the little shantytown, the occupants often painted flowers or humorous names on their doors to distinguish one shack from another. If you went up to see one of the old boys, you might be looking for "Big Jim's Retreat" or "Prosperity Is Just Around the Corner." But the signs did more than identify the shacks; they signified that the human spirit remained alive amidst all this poverty and decay. With nothing to occupy their time, these men welcomed the work of the councils. The men who lived on this human scrap heap became the strongest supporters of our demand for social security. They understood what it meant to be discarded after a lifetime of hard work.

And yet for all of its ugliness and poverty, Margaret and I loved the anthracite. It was the first place where we actually felt at home. Even though we seldom had a nickel between us, we could feel that we were sharing what we had with others and we counted on them to share theirs with us. Margaret spent a lot of her time bailing me out of jail, but we never felt defeated or isolated. I could always rely on the support of a group of comrades who were as dedicated to one another as to the movement itself.

Many of our positive memories can probably be explained in terms of our organizing success, but it's impossible to separate this from our personal relations with the people of the region. If we had come to them with "the word," an explanation of "how to do it," they would have been turned off. But if you were willing to listen, to see how you could work with and help them, then they would accept you. They'd already been through a long series of struggles. The history of the region was one of bitter class warfare, and they understood which side they were on. You had to make them feel that you were one of them. If you did, it was a wonderful place to be.

FIVE

Two Years Abroad: 1931–1933

When word came through that I could leave for the Lenin School in Moscow in late summer 1931, I anticipated the trip mostly in terms of another crack at school. I was particularly interested in learning more labor history and in leavening what I was learning in the field with a little theory. I had never seen the inside of a college or university; only the cubbyholes of the Workers' School in New York. While I didn't have any formal expectations, I was as excited about the opportunity to continue my haphazard education as any college freshman. The idea of adventure was far from my thoughts, and I had never been irresistibly attracted by the lure of the only socialist country. A lot of people wanted to go to the Soviet Union in the worst way, to live, work, and see for themselves, but I never had that desire. I felt that the Russian people had made their revolution, and they had a right to benefit by it. It was not for me to go there and enjoy it. But I felt lucky to have the chance, and my curiosity began to grow as my departure neared.

It was probably Rudy Baker, who had wound up as the Party's organizational secretary after Lovestone's ouster, who suggested I attend the Lenin School. The Party was attempting to develop as many leaders as possible. We needed people with the skills that did not often come naturally to a coal miner or steelworker, and this training could take place at the Lenin School. Ours, the third group from the States to attend, was composed of fifteen workers and union activists, most of them young. There was a steelworker from Youngstown, a shipyard worker from Baltimore, and several women from the Cleveland and New York needle trades. Bill Lawrence, an old friend from Philly whom I would meet again in Spain, was also along. The Party was then especially concerned with advancing blacks to leadership, and almost half of our group was black. I was a little surprised at how inexperienced some of them were. They lacked the practical knowledge you pick up from a few years of organizing. One fellow had been a bootblack in New York City and another a sharecropper in the Deep South. The latter, Mack Coad, was forty-two and had had almost no formal education. We often studied together, going over the readings and comparing notes after class. Mack Coad also went to Spain and later became an organizer among Southern sharecroppers.

I tied up some of the loose ends in the anthracite, said good-bye to Margaret, and boarded ship in New York in the fall of 1931. The plan was that she would join me soon in Moscow as her skills could easily be put to use there.

It had been a little more than a decade since I had last crossed the Atlantic, and it struck me how differently I now at the age of twenty-eight saw the world. It was as if everything was reflected through the prism of class. Sensitive to how larger forces affected them, I could now see something beyond the ship and the seamen. We were instructed, however, to act as tourists and not attract any attention to ourselves, so I kept most of this philosophizing to myself. Instead I played shuffleboard and talked about fishing and sports with my fellow passengers.

But it wasn't easy to be inconspicuous. If we had acted like everybody else, our black comrades would have been pretty well ostracized, because none of the other whites on board would have had anything to do with them. Things came to a head one night at a dance. One of the blacks approached a woman in our group and asked her to dance. She whispered, "You know what the rule is!" and tried to back away. He didn't think the rule was that important, and a few of the other women agreed, so they danced. Although a bartender came over and butted in and one of the guys told him to kiss off, there wasn't too much of a commotion. But that night and for the rest of the voyage, we rehashed the incident and tried to discuss it self-critically.

The ones who refused to dance argued that we had to live up to the decision made by the Party in New York. For them it was a question of Party discipline. But those who danced felt we had to bend a little or we would be letting our comrades down. I saw it that way too, as a matter of common sense. Some of the black comrades, however, believed that the first viewpoint displayed white chauvinism. Our inability to resolve the incident created certain tensions that were never totally soothed the entire time we were in Moscow. Before long the story spread throughout the school and was hotly debated as a conflict of Party discipline vs. the Negro question in America. Even the Comintern tried to step in and resolve the matter, but nobody could really settle it, either politically or in terms of personal relationships. You can't unscramble scrambled eggs.

But if the dance precipitated some lingering friction, our stop in Hamburg made us realize just how much we had in common. In London we had changed ships and boarded a Soviet freighter transporting livestock for breeding purposes in the USSR. We were just about the only passengers beside the hogs and bulls, and the animals took precedence over us. They had the run of the deck to get some exercise, and it was hard to miss their stench. In Hamburg we docked to load copper bars for the electrification of the Russian countryside and laid over for two days.

In Hamburg, a working-class city known as a "Red Center," the waterfront workers were led by the left wing and could be counted on to vote for either the Social Democrats or Communists. But the Nazis were visible, and you could sense from their fairly brash posturing that they were gaining strength. While we saw left-wing workers distributing literature, squads of Nazis in paramilitary dress also roamed the city. A few of us took a ferry ride across the harbor and found ourselves smack in the middle of a depot where scores of Nazis, some with sidearms, had gathered. I felt that I was in some sort of madhouse. You could tell that a confrontation was coming. The longshoremen we talked with seemed confident that they would defeat the Nazis, but it was unsettling to see armed gangs and the constant skirmishing in front of the headquarters of the various left-wing groups.

I didn't realize how great the rift between Social Democrats and Communists was. I saw only the menace from the Right. The damage done by the Social Democratic Party's (SPD) compromise with the kaiser during the First World War had not been forgotten, nor had the SPD's lack of support for the Russian Revolution been forgiven.[1] Moreover, when war-wracked and defeated Germany was on the brink of a revolution in early 1919, the SPD had worked openly to put down the insurrection. Unfortunately, it was not evident to the Communists then, as it is in retrospect today, that by 1931 a new generation of Social Democrats had come on the scene. Perhaps a strong antifascist coalition could have been formed. At any rate, the threat of fascism was clearly underestimated.

When Mack Coad, the black sharecropper, and I walked through town, we found ourselves the target of Nazi taunts. A handful of them at a corner cafe jeered "Monkey" and "Go back to Africa" at us from their table, and when we walked off they followed. We couldn't afford to get into a fight and dodged into the lobby of a hotel. That threw them off track.

Our fears were somewhat assuaged as we picked up steam heading out of Hamburg harbor on our way to Leningrad. Aboard ship was an old Russian revolutionary returning from a European trade mission. He spoke English and attached himself to our group. As we were approaching Leningrad, its factory stacks belched smoke. This fellow was overjoyed, saying that when he had left three years ago, not many had been smoking at all. The contrast was clear. This country was working while the States and most of the industrial world were falling deeper into depression. It was heady stuff to be considering as I set foot in the first, and, at that time, the only socialist society.

On a hurried excursion through the city, I felt like I was walking through the pages of John Reed's *Ten Days That Shook the World.*[2] Here was Leningrad, the city of revolution, where the sailors of the *Aurora* had rebelled, hoisting a red flag and storming the Winter Palace. I was flushed with awe and also experienced a sense of relief. In the anthracite someone was frequently following me, and jail was almost a weekly ritual, but here I felt at ease because I didn't have to keep looking over my shoulder. We caught the train that evening for Moscow.

We were met at the station by a committee from the school and caught only glimpses of the city as we sped over cobblestone streets. I could sense the contrast between Moscow and the cities of the West but had little time to reflect about it as we plunged into the fairly well-insulated environment of the school.

The Lenin School was near Sun Yat-sen University, which had been set up specifically for students from colonial countries. The instruction there was in the appropriate native languages and dealt more closely with the problems of colonial and agrarian societies. A few of our guys wanted to study there, but the language barrier stopped them. There were about five hundred students from dozens of countries at our school, which was divided into language sections of German, English, French, Italian, and Spanish and a catchall section in Russian for those who couldn't manage in any other tongue. The bulk of these students were rank and file activists whom their respective parties wanted to develop for leadership. The school was supported by an international fund maintained from Party members' dues, with the deficit made up by the Soviet Party.

The director of the school was a dynamic Russian historian, Krisanova, whose revolutionary roots went back to the 1905 rebellion. She was assisted by a score of intellectuals from a number of countries and an advisory committee representing the different nationality groups. I served on the committee during one term, but I could hardly follow the translator. With all the different languages going on at the same time, it was like meeting in a Tower of Babel.

There were two programs, one for just a year and the other a more in-depth three-year course. Most of us were there for the shorter one. The curriculum was geared toward the students' respective nationalities. For example, although we Americans had sessions on the world trade union movement, we concentrated on the labor movement in America. Most courses ran about five or six sessions; they were intended to give the students a general view of the topic. We were responsible for presenting certain questions in class and for supplementing lectures with what seemed to me an almost impossible reading load. We studied political economy, the origins of capitalism, and Lenin's writings on the colonial question and revolution. Often we listened to men and women who had taken part in these revolutionary movements. We were treated to a brief talk from a man past eighty who had been a drummer boy in the Paris Commune of 1871. Another time participants from the 1919 Hungarian Revolution and the Canton uprising of 1924 spoke to us and answered questions.

These people added an extra depth to the readings and discussions. In addition to these sessions there were series of lectures on dialectical materialism and Marxist methodology. They would have been difficult enough in English, but it was next to impossible to follow our translator, who interspersed heavy doses of Russian whenever he couldn't figure out the English equivalents. The workload was intense, with most of the day taken up by classes and the evenings a mix of lectures, meetings, and reading. On Saturdays we sometimes participated in *subotniks* (voluntary labor sessions) and at one point helped to lay the foundations for Moscow University.

Some students rebelled against the strict discipline and regimentation, but only a handful. We were by and large a serious group, and though we all resented certain rules and sensed that some aspects of our lives were too highly structured, we considered ourselves quite fortunate to have this opportunity. In that short year I could sense dramatic changes in my capacity to handle charts, graphs, percentages, and statistical information—material that had until then puzzled me. I learned how to structure reports and presentations and read more systematically. The school gave me more self-assurance and, most of all, prompted me to think in terms of a broader framework.

We lived in dormitories with four to eight beds in a room. It wasn't fancy, but it was more than adequate for me. There was a cafeteria with very simple fare: mostly potatoes, cabbage, fish, and black bread. In the morning you could run downstairs in your slippers for tea and bread; you didn't even have to go across the street. You didn't have to pay for your meals; you didn't have to buy a damned thing. In this respect I had never had it so good in my life.

Margaret, who arrived a few months later, was living at the Hotel Luxe, which housed most of the foreigners working in Moscow. She worked in the press department of the Comintern, which was head-quartered in Moscow. She alternated between clerical work and activities cloaked in a certain sensitivity, and at the time neither of us felt we should discuss them. She shared a room with a young woman who was a vegetarian and had one hell of a time trying to find enough food to eat. These were lean years, and people got in the habit of queuing up anytime they saw a line on the street. They'd line up first, then try to find out what was for sale. I was pretty well protected from these difficulties, but Margaret had little choice but to accept them as part of her daily life.

Once in a while we would go to the movies or attend a cultural event together, but a night with each other would have been easier to arrange at an exclusive girls' school. When I visited Margaret's quarters, I had to leave my pass downstairs at the desk. If I hadn't picked it up by ten-thirty, the phone rang, and I was ordered out. A key to an available room was a hot item because space was in high demand. We spent most of our time together in long rambling walks through the city, often ending up in the Park of Culture alongside the river.

The mixing of people from different countries was an education in itself. I had a friend from India who at fifty was one of the oldest students there. A lifelong revolutionary nationalist, he managed to make it to Moscow only after escaping from a British prison in his homeland. One morning, waking up early and glancing in a corner, I saw a head on the floor and a bunch of teeth grinning at me under a pair of twisted legs. He was crouching there doing yoga, which until then had been a complete mystery to me. Another roommate was an activist in the railwaymen's union in New South Wales, Australia. I regret I never found out his real name. He was a working-class intellectual of the sort you seem to find mainly around radical movements. Many of the students from the British Commonwealth were like that; they were able to discuss Shakespeare almost as easily as piece rates. The Australian, our Indian friend, some Scottish and Cockney roommates, and I passed many an evening sprawled on our beds exchanging stories and arguing politics. I learned as much from them as I did from my classes. More important, they really made me feel part of a movement in which solidarity on a global scale was more than an abstraction. I met some of them again on the battlefields of Spain. George Brown, a tall handsome Irishman from England, was killed there in July 1937. The sight of his body stretched out on the road to Brunete is something I've never forgotten.

On summer mornings the whole student body would go outside for fifteen minutes of what we called "physical jerks" and a few laps around the block. In the evenings our Russian hosts generously gave us access to movies and other events. I saw my first Shakespearean play there; it was *King Lear*. What really amazed me was that it was delivered in Yiddish. I was with a friend from New York City who sat next to me giving a line-by-line translation, hardly missing a phrase. The Yiddish theater played to packed houses night after night. After a while you even got used to the strong undercurrent of whispering from the dozens of translators. In the early years of the Revolution, full cultural recognition and rights were given to the Jews and other minority groups. During Stalin's campaigns against "Cosmopolitanism" and the influence of foreign ideas, however, anti-Semitism once again took root. The demise of this theater during Stalin's Russification program in later years was a tragedy.

One incident occurred, however, that troubled me. As the American delegate to the school advisory committee, I was meeting with the faculty to establish procedures for the second term. Walking into the meeting room, I could see that there was a bustle about something. Big stacks of outlines were in front of the German and English sections, and the professors were scribbling changes in what looked to me like the core curriculum. I wandered over to one, and when I saw that he was hacking out sections of the outline, I asked what was going on. After all, classes for the new term started in the morning, and the curriculum had already been discussed and adopted. He stiffened a bit but offered no explanation. Whoever was chairing the meeting called it to order and then dissolved it almost immediately, saying only that certain major revisions in the curriculum were to be made that night.

Mimeograph machines hummed through the night, and the outlines for the term were ready and waiting the next morning, but not in the form previously discussed. Later I got an explanation. The Russian Revolution, a key topic for historians in the Soviet Union, was a touchy subject to discuss then because of the internal Party fights that had flourished in Bolshevik ranks since the 1920s. A historian had apparently published a piece in some historical magazine in which he dealt with a particular incident in the 1917 struggles. Part of his article concerned the activities of Trotsky and some of his adherents; he acknowledged that they were present at a certain meeting. This Stalin could not tolerate. He made an address criticizing Soviet historians who did not know how to present history from a "revolutionary Marxist" point of view. That this piece ascribed a positive role to Trotsky was considered counterrevolutionary. Stalin dubbed it "rotten liberalism."

Then I understood what the professors were doing; they were eliminating anything that could possibly entangle them or the school in the toleration of rotten liberalism. Stalin's speech was like a big whip cracking through the universities and institutions. No one discussed whether this was the way to write history. It disturbed me, but I accepted the explanation that people who played detrimental roles didn't deserve to be mentioned in history. I simply justified the Party's action.

Although we lived more or less within the shadow of the school, we broke loose from time to time. Trips to state farms or factories, quite extensively organized, were regarded as practical work. In small groups we would question the trade union head or Party organizer to find out how the factory was run. At an airbrake manufacturing plant in Moscow, similar to Westinghouse Airbrake in the Turtle Creek Valley near Pittsburgh, we were asked to come back at the evening shift change. Our guide explained that there was going to be what they called a "comradely trial" of one of the workers. At half-past five we showed up at the gates and joined the thousand or so workers coming off their shift as they streamed across the street to a meeting hall. A teamster who operated a team of draft horses between the plant and the railroad yards was brought up on the charge that he had made an anti-Semitic remark. He had told another worker that the other man was "just like a Jew." He had used the expression *zhid* rather than *yevrey,* the equivalent of saying "kike" instead of "Jew." When a Party member who had overheard tried to talk to him about why this was the wrong thing to say, the teamster balked. He replied, "What the hell, we all say it. You know how it is in the village where I come from. It is not considered anything. Besides, aren't they that way?"

It seemed as if the whole shift had come over after work, and that surprised me because I tried to get out of the shop as soon as I could after work. I think they were genuinely interested in the issue. They weren't compelled to be there as far as I could tell, and while some seemed to lose interest in the proceedings and wandered out, most stayed.

Someone from the shop committee holding the court nominated as chairman a young guy who had just returned to the plant after a two-and-one-half-year stint in the Red Army. He had been active in the YCL before he went and was elected by acclamation. He got up on the platform with the teamster, a prosecutor, and a defender.

The worker serving as prosecutor spoke briefly, arguing that statements about Jews such as had been made came from the czarist days and had to be rooted out. "I think that he should be severely reprimanded as a lesson to others," he said. The defender then spoke and, to my amazement, was more critical of the teamster than the prosecutor. But after criticizing the man, he took another tack. "Look, we know about the village that Ivanov comes from. There's no Party organization there even now. The only thing Ivanov ever had contact with was the Church; there was not even a school there in the old days. Czarist poisons penetrated deeply. Ivanov is a product of that old society. While his crime is against morality and Soviet law, I believe we should take his background into consideration and be lenient." It was then Ivanov's turn. A chunky man in his late thirties wearing a *rubashka* (heavy, belted work shirt), he resisted the idea that what he had said was wrong. That was when the argument really began, with guys from the floor insisting that he explain what he meant when he said, "Besides, aren't they that way?" That hung things up for over an hour until a proposal was made to assign two comrades he knew and respected to work with him on this question. In addition, he would go to night school to learn something about the national question. Only a few held out for the tougher position, that he be fired, and the proposal carried easily. I was tremendously impressed with how they were combating anti-Semitism and backwardness. It was not with a hammer, but with education.

Methods of production and the role of workers in the process of running a factory were outlined to us in detail. Although I never sat in on one, I know there were departmental meetings where workers discussed conditions, raising beefs and complaining as well as suggesting alternative ways of doing the work. But the ultimate defense, to be able to show your fist and strike, was ruled out in the Soviet system. That didn't concern me very much at the time. "How can you strike against yourself?" was how we looked at it, not realizing that even in a socialist society you can stretch things too far. A worker should be able to say, "This is not fair; the pace is too fast." I can see in retrospect that even in a socialist nation, unions ought to be independent, and that even if the factories are owned collectively, one group of workers shouldn't have to make sacrifices for everybody without the opportunity to adjust grievances. And the only way you can adjust them is to let off steam by saying "Strike! We are going to stop until this is corrected." The administration of a factory could be made up of good people who had worked in the plant, but such people can become bureaucratic. You have to be able to shake them up, and only the strike ensures that you can.

On one excursion we floated down the Volga on a paddle steamer to Stalingrad, then undergoing major industrial development. Near there we visited a collective farm. We were very skeptical about what we saw in this place. It was a newly organized collective, and the Party group that joined it was struggling to get the thing going. You could see the strain. The civilian leaders packed pistols. "There are still White Guards and counterrevolutionaries around," they cautioned.[3] "A number of undesirable elements have already been weeded out." Their lack of support was unsettling, as was the evident shakiness of their agricultural knowledge.

We journeyed next to a state farm which, in contrast to the collective farm, was government-owned and operated. A totally socialized venture, it employed people who worked in shifts, and the produce went to the state. In terms of farming techniques it was further ahead than the collective farm. Large posters graphically warned against vermin, and the farm's organizers, serious about developing a sound agricultural base, questioned us at length on how to properly build a silo (about which we knew very little) and care for livestock. The day we visited was a big day for the farm because the first shipment of tractors was due to arrive. A group of young women had been trained as drivers and mechanics from manuals previously shipped to them. They had pictures of the tractors and were eager to impress us with their mechanical knowledge. They smiled and repeated the English terms they had learned: "carburetor," "piston," "fuel pump." Apparently a package of summer shorts was delivered in the same crates as the instruction manuals. The women naturally assumed that this was the way you were supposed to dress when you drove a tractor. That would have been fine in spring, but they cut quite a picture shivering in late fall winds as the farm awaited its tractors. We could see a jump from the old to the new society, but the backwardness of a primarily agrarian peasant country is not easily overcome.

That first flush of being in the Soviet Union, of feeling as if I was treading on holy ground, dissolved as I began to sense the awesome tasks the Revolution still faced. Seven years of war and revolution, of invasion from abroad and civil division within, had devastated an already underdeveloped country. Now, just a decade later, the country still showed the wounds. The problems on the road to socialism could not be easily ignored. The crudely constructed *troikas* (vehicles drawn by three horses) driven in the city by people who still lived as peasants and the use of wood for heating instead of coal were signs of tremendous underdevelopment. Yet what impressed us the most were the steps away from this backwardness—the ever-present excavations for sewage and water systems that made walking around Moscow an adventure in itself; the criss-crossed pylons for electrification, still green and awaiting electric cables; the sense that this country was working while back home in the anthracite coalfields, most of the people were not.

Striking contradictions arose from the efforts to build an industrialized socialist society out of an underdeveloped agrarian country. Some friends Margaret made aboard ship on her way to Leningrad reinforced the sense that the jump to the future would not be made overnight. On arrival one young fellow took her to meet his uncle, the director of a shoe factory in Leningrad. When introduced, the director took hold of Maggie's hand, kissed it, and started to sweet-talk her in French. As she told me, "He went through all this French crap, and I was about to fall through the floor. What the hell kind of socialism is this, I'm thinking." It turned out that the director had managed the factory before the Revolution and was still holding down his job. A new group of people capable of running the factories had yet to develop. In the meantime this fellow, while an efficient enough director and clearly not an active opponent of the Revolution, was by no means undergoing a transformation into the new socialist man. And he was not an isolated holdover. Nor could production make a corresponding leap to a new plateau of socialist values and relations; there were still many barriers that could not be jumped.

Another acquaintance from Maggie's ship worked in the Caucasus, a mountain range between the Black Sea and the Caspian. When he was in Moscow, he had tea with us in Margaret's room at the Luxe and wryly illustrated the difficulties of collectivizing agriculture. One evening he told a peasant working on the farm to make sure he filled his tractor's radiator with water before he knocked off work. The next morning he found the tractor half-submerged in the river. When he found the peasant and asked him what happened, the man responded, "I drove it into the river to fill the radiator. It got stuck. The horse drinks this way. I can't understand why this damn tractor won't!" Our friend said he spent hours trying to figure out whether the peasant did it deliberately, as an act of sabotage, or whether he just didn't know any better.

I saw this inefficiency—you couldn't help but see it—but side by side with it I saw an effort to do something great. The Revolution unleashed tremendous forces that remade an entire country. There was a creativity and energy in the Soviet Union then that I have rarely witnessed since. To me, this outweighed the negative and contradictory aspects involved in the process of development. Naturally I now can see the brutality and arbitrariness that displaced millions in the forced collectivization of agriculture and the essentially undemocratic process by which decisions were made and carried out. I didn't see these things then. I accepted Stalin's argument that the class struggle continues under socialism and that "class enemies" must be decisively confronted and eliminated. The idea of converting people who disagreed was lost in the shuffle. We allowed ourselves to take this concept of "class struggle" and pervert its meaning until we reached the point where anyone who disagreed with the position of the Party could be labeled an enemy of socialism. The concept of democratic centralism, forged in the underground, war, and counterrevolution, allowed for little flexibility or dissent. How could you seriously suggest alternatives, much less pursue them, when to do so could expose you to the charge of being counterrevolutionary? These mistakes had tragic consequences. But I didn't see this when I was in the Soviet Union in the early 1930s. Then I felt that I was in the midst of a vast, almost noble undertaking that required total effort, total support.

During the latter part of my stay, I received a message that Dr. Karlov from the English Commission of the Comintern wanted to see me.[4] This didn't surprise me very much. The Comintern at that time was trying to help the European parties, forced underground by the rise of fascism, get back on their feet as well as service the needs of the growing national liberation movements in Asia and Africa. Every now and then some person would disappear from school for a few weeks, and it wasn't hard to figure out what he or she had been doing. This time it was me.

Once I was seated across from Karlov in his office at the Comintern, he came right to the point. "The Nazi rise to power in Germany has forced the German Party to reestablish itself on an underground basis. We cannot continue to communicate with them through the usual channels, so we have to have people go there to deliver and bring back information. We would like to have you go. Someone with an American passport would be less likely to arouse suspicion."

I really didn't have to give it much consideration. If the Comintern wanted me for the job, I would do it. To carry on the fight against fascism, I was prepared to go to any length. I had gotten a firsthand taste in Hamburg of what the Nazis were about, and if there was anything that was worth putting yourself in jeopardy to fight, they were it.

Karlov knew how to outfit people for these trips, and after checking out my shabby wardrobe, he suggested my first mission would be to secure the services of a tailor. Within a few days, I had promoted myself a suit, and with the dark leather bag Karlov entrusted to me, I climbed aboard a train for Germany. At the border with Germany, my passport was taken and my luggage searched. The customs agent literally tore apart a novel I was carrying, but he found nothing, and my passport was returned when I detrained in Berlin. After checking into a hotel suggested by Karlov and registering as a tourist, I searched out the restaurant where I was supposed to make contact.

I had fairly precise instructions, and at the proper time the next day I entered the restaurant and sat at the designated table. I had a hard time focusing on the menu, and my waiter was impatient with my indecision. Finally a German man of about my age eased himself into the chair across from me. He smiled and extended a hand. "How are you doing this evening? Your cousin sends regards." That's what I had been waiting for, and I responded with the proper countersign. I felt a little better having made contact and was even able to enjoy the meal. When he suggested we take a walk after dinner, I was glad to get out of the restaurant. A number of uniformed Nazis had entered and were strolling from table to table as if they knew everybody in the house. I had been warned to expect this and act nonchalantly, but I couldn't quite get over the thought that at any moment I might be trapped. The fact that my contact appeared a little nervous didn't ease my edginess.

We strolled in the park across the street from the restaurant, and even though it was quite cold, we finally sat on a bench by the pond. My contact broached no subject more serious than that he had always marveled at how ducks could stay outside in the winter, and I reciprocated with similar small talk. After a few minutes of this he said, "I will leave shortly. I will take your suitcase with me. Tomorrow, dine at the restaurant on the other side of the park in the early evening." And he casually walked away with my leather bag, which held a few second-hand novels, some shirts, and certain well-concealed documents and information. I felt a little naked without it but was glad to be through with the first contact. I waited a few minutes and took the long way back to my hotel.

I slept in late the next morning and passed most of the day on a shopping tour, trying to build up my credentials as a tourist. Finally it was time for dinner, and I wandered into the small restaurant suggested by my contact. The proprietor seemed to expect me. He took me to a small table for two near the back and brought me some rolls and a salad. A few minutes later, an older fellow came over and asked if he might join me. He too suggested we stroll after dinner and guided me through the park. At a fairly secluded spot, he identified himself as head of the Party for part of Berlin. Then he proceeded to brief me. "When the first arrests began to take place—they were wholesale—many people scattered, and it was very difficult to maintain communications. Even now, as I talk to you, we are having trouble reestablishing connections, although we had an underground setup established before the Nazis came to power."

I leaned back against a railing, alert for anybody watching us, and tried to absorb every word he said. I knew I would be called upon to make a precise report.

He continued quietly. "Many loopholes have occurred because people sometimes betray their comrades out of ignorance or fear. This is especially a problem with some of the former elected officials in city and town governments. People are frightened because they and their families are known. We have to use our judgment when we attempt to reestablish relations and get people involved." He went on to discuss the trade union situation and indicated that the Nazis were merging the different labor federations into a Nazi Labor Front. Nevertheless, Party members would try to work from within them.

After painting what seemed to me an awfully bleak picture, he suggested that things would likely improve. He told me that a Nazi picked up by the police had been found with a button of the Red Front, a Communist paramilitary organization, under his lapel; no doubt there were many more like him. I didn't know whether to believe him or not. When I left, however, I had my suitcase back. I returned to the hotel and pondered how I was going to kill three more days waiting in Berlin before I could return. I had been told to spend a few days roaming the city so as not to arouse suspicion. For three days I walked around feeling terribly uncomfortable. I couldn't wait to get the hell out of there. When my waiting time was up, I flew back to Moscow without any trouble.

I was met at the airport and driven to the Luxe where Karlov awaited me. He told me to go back to my room and return the next day to meet with members of the German Commission and report on my trip. "But would you leave your suitcase here, please."

At this meeting they pumped me for every word my contact had said and asked questions about the behavior of the Nazis, the train ride, if I had been frisked, and so on. I felt like I was on the hot seat because I didn't want to mislead them. As I reported my contact's generally upbeat analysis, one old German I knew from photographs as Wilhelm Pieck, a prominent Party leader who had escaped the Nazis, sat there shaking his head slowly. My report didn't square up with his sense of things.

Afterward I sought out Margaret for a few minutes to tell her I was all right and would meet her later that evening. Even though I wanted to tell her where I had been, I didn't. We were under discipline to keep absolutely quiet about these activities. It had after all been a risky venture. A breach in security could endanger the lives of the men and women in the German underground. So without so much as an explanation, I settled back into the routine of my final weeks of school.

A few weeks later Karlov asked me to go to Switzerland on a far less dangerous mission. I was to deliver funds and information to the editor of *INPRECOR* (International Press Correspondence), a news organ of the Comintern. The trip almost turned into a fiasco. In Vienna, I had to change trains and buy another ticket. For some reason, nervousness perhaps, I forgot whether I was to go to Zurich or Basel for the rest of the journey. I sat there shaking with a map unfolded on my knees and finally remembered it was Zurich. After finding a hotel, I went to the rathskeller near the train station where the editor, an old Hungarian revolutionary, was to meet me.

The rathskeller looked like a miniature Grand Central Station with hundreds of tables and a blue haze of tobacco smoke rising toward the vaulted ceiling. It was packed with people chattering away in different languages and consuming enormous quantities of beer. I sat in a corner nursing a beer and waiting for the editor. A fellow about forty-five years old came over and introduced himself, but I had no idea who he was. The editor was supposed to be much older, and this fellow was Czech, not Hungarian. I told him that he must be mistaken, I wasn't waiting for anybody. He bent over and whispered in my ear that the old man was sick. "I have been instructed to meet with you."

I mumbled something and got to my feet, making my way through the crowd in front of the door. Glancing over my shoulder, I could see the Czech following me. When I got outside I walked rapidly away and lost him. I wasn't sure what I should do. Who was that guy? I thought that if I stayed in Zurich, I might be arrested, and the funds and message confiscated. On the other hand, if I returned prematurely, *INPRECOR* would be left in the lurch. Besides, if this Czech fellow were an agent, would he have let me slip away so easily? I decided I would stay one more day on the chance that I would make contact.

The next morning I went to the park and sat in the grass, gazing at a hiking trail that wound its way up a nearby mountain. Just about the time I decided to give it a try, a woman in her fifties sat down on a nearby bench and started speaking to me in slightly accented English. She said that she too was a tourist with time to kill and began to talk about Zurich. Grasping my arm, she very earnestly informed me, "You know, there are some extremely interesting things to see around here. Why, not far from where we're sitting, there's a plaque on the wall of a house where Vladimir Ilyich Lenin stayed before he returned to Russia to lead the Revolution! You know, Lenin, the Bolshevik."

My heart felt as if it would pop out of my mouth. I muttered, "Oh, is that right?" and excused myself. By the time I reached the trail, I was almost running, but I decided it was just a coincidence. Still, I had so much adrenalin pumping through me that I took the trail by storm.

That evening I went back to the rathskeller and ordered my mug of beer. I hadn't been there long enough to imagine more than two or three agents in the crowd when the Czech fellow entered—this time with an older man in tow. The Czech pointed me out to the older fellow, who came over and immediately began scolding me for getting him out of his sickbed. Then he slowed down and laughed, commending me for my caution. We took a walk and transacted our business, and I gratefully left Zurich the next morning.

About a month later, as my session at the Lenin School was drawing to an end, I was summoned once again to Dr. Karlov's office. He pulled his chair alongside mine and, smiling slightly, asked, "How would you like to take the long way home?" I didn't know what the hell that meant, so I replied, "Well, so long as I get there sooner or later." Karlov grinned and confided, "The comrades in charge of this work will explain. This is a different arrangement than the one you had before. It's out of my area of responsibility." That set me wondering, but not for long. Karlov excused himself, and a few minutes later two men entered his office. One was a young Chinese man of about twenty-eight or thirty and the other an older Russian. I thought the Chinese man was Wang Ming, a high-ranking member of the Chinese Commission. The Russian, who introduced himself as Petroff, was a member of the English Commission and seemed present mainly to ensure that I understood Wang Ming.

Petroff spoke first, telling me that they would like me to take a trip by way of Europe and the Indian Ocean, stopping in Bombay and Ceylon and winding up in China. "We want you to make certain stops and talk with certain people. Are you in agreement?" I told them that certainly I would be interested in seeing those places and was willing to do what was necessary. Petroff responded, "Good, we will discuss the political things with you. Others will talk to you about another matter." I wasn't sure what that meant either, but I had already committed myself. Petroff went on, "As far as we are concerned, this will be partly an education for you and partly the opportunity to perform the service of elaborating certain thoughts that we are trying to transmit to our Chinese comrades. The Comintern has been apprised of the situation in the soviet regions of China—especially that of Kiangsi province.[5] There the difficulties are very great, and the comrades are asking for our opinions on their problems."

The situation in Kiangsi was indeed desperate. Chiang Kai-shek had launched four campaigns against the Communists, and the soviet they had established was completely blockaded.[6] Five million people under Communist government were trapped. Salt supplies had run out and Chiang was beheading any salt smugglers he caught. "But the worst thing," emphasized Wang Ming, "is that Chiang Kai-shek is now contemplating using gas to exterminate the whole population in a fifth offensive." It was chilling to hear this. What defense could be used against gas? Wang Ming explained that there were certain recommendations I would deliver to the Chinese comrades, but that "they will have to make the ultimate decision, because we don't know what's possible."

After pausing to let that sink in, he told me, "You will listen to some discussions there. If you get the chance to come back, then you will give us the information. If not, we'll have to live with the decision that they make." By then the magnitude of the job was starting to shake me up. Wang Ming concluded, "This is a big assignment. Do what you can to see that you get there and stay as long as necessary." I was too startled to ask any questions, especially about the significance of his last remarks. The two shook my hand gravely and walked out.

Another fellow soon came in and explained that part of my assignment was to transmit funds to the Chinese Party, with the hope that the money could be used to buy gas masks. "For money anything can be brought," he explained. "Our Chinese comrades will know better than we. We cannot send them anything from here, but if they are facing a gas attack, we will do what we can to provide the economic means to help them protect themselves." I couldn't think of any questions for him either, and he too departed after first telling me he would be in touch before I left.

I attended several briefings with Wang Ming and Petroff over the next few days. I received a list of contacts for Paris, Bombay, and China (which I had to commit to memory), some letters, and a set of train tickets that would get me to Paris. There was no way to say good-bye to Margaret. She had suddenly dropped out of the picture a few weeks before, and I had concluded that she too was doing the same sort of work. Without ceremony or a firm sense of what was ahead, I boarded a train for the long trip to Paris.

In Paris my connection was the owner of a little garment factory. After I identified myself with the appropriate code word, he suggested I return in two hours. When I came back, he ushered me into his office and over a little wine and cheese gave me the name of an agency through which I could make my travel arrangements. He then gave me some photographs, money for travel expenses, and a chunk of currency for delivery in Shanghai. The next day I was on my way to Venice, where I picked up the ship.

My cover was that I was a student of architecture. I said I had inherited a little money and wanted to circle the globe. I let on that I had some trouble in my family, inferring that I had been divorced. It wasn't an ironclad cover because I couldn't have carried a discussion about architecture too far. But it wouldn't have jibed to say I was a carpenter seeing the world; nobody would have bought that. The tramping journeyman on tour was a thing of the past.

There was a group of about twenty Russian Jews on board. They had fled to Germany during the Revolution and were now fleeing once again because of Hitler. Most of them were doctors or professionals on the way to Shanghai, where they hoped to reestablish themselves. They played cards all day and tried to draw me into conversations that rarely got beyond hunting or fishing, about which they knew very little. There was of course no way I would admit to them that I had been in Russia. Another passenger was an Indian returning from a Chicago dental school. By talking to him I incurred the contempt of the Britishers aboard; they couldn't understand why an American would pal around with a Hindu.

Another passenger, a young Austrian girl on her way to marry one of Chiang's government officials, decided I looked like a good listener and came over to my deck chair every morning to fill me in on her life. She told me about the man she was going to marry, and I had a hard time restraining myself. She seemed hurt by my coldness, ·so I tried to explain. I didn't want her to conclude that I objected because he was Chinese. That forced me to start talking politics and say what I thought about Chiang Kai-shek. I tried to avoid her after that because I thought it best to stay out of political discussions. It was a long journey, and I had little choice but to try to make friends with some of the White Russians, whom I inwardly detested.[7]

You soon get used to the routines aboard ship; morning walks, afternoon card games, and evenings at the dinner table. I even got used to my seersucker suit, which the Comintern bought for me before I left. These threads were the most expensive I had ever owned. Our first stop was Port Said. We then proceeded to Alexandria at the head of the Nile. I didn't get off ship there because I didn't want to risk being searched and questioned. But even from the ship you could see squalor. Some of the British went ashore, and when they came back, they insisted on regaling all males aboard with tales of people having intercourse with animals at a brothel. A few passengers went on a side trip to the pyramids, but I didn't want to shell out the money to go there. I was trying to figure out how I could save a few dollars so that when I got home to the anthracite, I could buy a car.

Between Alexandria and Bombay I settled in, playing chess, which I had learned to appreciate in Moscow, and reading books I had picked up on the Left Bank before I left Paris. I didn't, for obvious reasons, want to bring any political works along, so I had bought a number of novels you couldn't get in the States. That I could be seen reading *Lady Chatterley's Lover* as we steamed through the Red Sea didn't do my young-architect-on-tour image any harm.

Eventually we reached Bombay. Misery just oozed out of everything there; people were lying in the streets; beggars were on every corner. British cops patrolled the streets protecting foreigners from being nagged by the poor. I couldn't get over the spectacle of all these people lying on reed mats in the scorched streets and alleys. Their arms and legs were as thin as sticks. I saw the century-old British textile factories, two blocks long and four stories high with iron grillwork on the windows, and heard the whirring of power looms. If there was a fire no one could escape. I remembered my Indian roommate, and I understood better his bitterness toward British imperialism.

My contact in Bombay was a postal clerk. I destroyed my photograph of him before we docked and went to his window in the post office at mid-morning. I bought a few stamps and arranged to meet him at lunchtime. Everything went smoothly, and I delivered a letter that contained a list of contacts throughout India. The letter itself appeared harmless enough, but the application of heat would bring out the names and addresses between the lines. The clerk filled me in on what was going on in the party organization in Bombay and answered my questions about how people managed to survive such poverty. You couldn't learn as much about imperialism by reading about it for a month as you could in one day's walk through Bombay. I was glad when we left the next morning for Columbo, where we picked up some supplies and made deliveries.

Columbo looked like the closest thing to paradise I had ever seen. As we steamed closer you could make out lush vegetation and a beautiful natural harbor. The people walked around without much need of clothes, and I idly thought about what kind of life I could have living there. But Columbo was a British colony, and that brought me back down. Watching tourists throw coins into the water where young boys would dive for them left me half disgusted, half enraged.

From Ceylon we headed due west through the Bay of Bengal to the Straits of Malacca and Singapore. We then curved northward through the South China Sea to Hong Kong. Hong Kong was a most impressive city, but our stopover was only a day as we slowly wound our way up the China coast. Along with most of the passengers, I disembarked in Shanghai and headed for the International Settlement. Dating from the intervention of Western powers in the nineteenth century, the settlement was an autonomous part of Shanghai under foreign control. Each major imperialist power maintained its own protected territory in the settlement. Here foreigners were immune from Chinese law. Within this enclave all sorts of fast and shady deals took place. Ironically, I, who was there to aid in the overthrow of imperialism, was to be shielded by the very institutions and rules imposed by imperialism.

I checked in at the Palace Hotel, a pretty fancy place overlooking the Huang-p'u River. The river itself was jammed with sampans and the thousands of people who lived on them. I was to wait at the hotel until contact was made, and for the next two days I rotated between my room, the hotel restaurant, and short excursions through the settlement. The doorman, after finding out that I was alone, offered to procure a woman for me. I said no thanks. Besides him, nobody paid me much attention.

On the third day, I heard a knock on the door. When I opened it, a young Chinese boy who worked as a bellhop informed me that a man named John was waiting for me in the hotel bar. A bit cautious, I asked the boy to tell him that I'd be right down. As soon as I saw him, however, I knew that he was the right man. He was about forty-five, a German, and he matched the photo I had been given in Paris. We shook hands, and over a drink we chatted about my voyage. When he found out that I didn't have an appointment for dinner, he insisted that I dine with him and his friend.

That evening he met me in the lobby and took me to the home of another German, who introduced himself as Hans. They were both lower-echelon people within the Comintern's operation in Shanghai, responsible for setting up communications and transportation arrangements. We spent the evening discussing the Soviet Union and the latest news about Germany, but neither mentioned my report. Hans told me that a meeting would be held three or four nights hence, when certain key people were back in town. They would pick me up at the hotel at the right time but until then would have no contact with me.

I had three or four days to kill. The brothels didn't interest me, and I didn't like hanging around the bar all day, so I spent most of my time exploring Shanghai. In the Chapei district to the north of the settlement, where the Japanese had invaded in 1932, there were mounds fifteen feet high that I was told contained caskets from those killed in the fighting. They hadn't been permanently buried yet. It had rained fairly hard recently, and much of the dirt had been washed away. You could see stuff seeping out of the mounds into the open sewers.

One day I took a ferryboat ride across the river. I walked for hours through the fields, stopping to watch how the Chinese worked their land. Back in the city I observed people living in sampans. I saw a woman with a baby teetering as she crossed from sampan to sampan. A man was pissing over the side of another boat, and not far away a woman was dipping into the river for water. Most foreigners strolled through this as if it weren't really happening. To pay for a rickshaw ride, they'd throw the coins on the sidewalk so their hands wouldn't touch the hands of a Chinese man. The rickshaw men, skinny but with big developed legs, were treated as if they were horses.

I saw a bunch of building trades workers erecting a steel frame for a building about four or five stories high. It was being constructed without the benefit of cranes. Instead a bamboo scaffolding about twenty feet wide had been built on an incline around the building. Large I-beams were unloaded from a boat onto the sidewalk where two dozen men in pairs put on yokes chained to gripping tongs. The tongs grabbed tightly to the I-beam, and the twenty-four men stood in place. You could see them straining to lift, but the beam wasn't budging. The headman began a chant, and pretty soon I saw the beam rising, barely moving. Finally they were able to straighten up, and, continuing the chant, they started up the incline, shuffling slowly with tiny steps. It took them a quarter of an hour to make one side of the building and turn the corner. What I saw these four days helped me understand why a revolution was needed in China.

On the evening of the fourth day, I was sitting in the lobby reading a two-month-old magazine and deciding what to do about dinner when a stranger approached and asked me to come along. It was already dark as we took a rickshaw for several blocks and got off. On the corner was Hans. The stranger walked away as Hans and I took different rickshaws and headed for a distant section of the International Settlement. We wound up at the well-furnished home of an impressive-looking older Russian who ran a photography shop. There were a number of servants present, and I had a little difficulty understanding why the Russian would employ them. Later I found out that all the servants were members of the Chinese Party and were keeping up appearances.

The Russian ushered us into a dining room, and we sat down to a fabulous meal of a dozen courses. My only regret was that not knowing the Chinese custom of only eating a little of each course, I filled up on the first few and had to sadly watch Hans and the Russian tackle the remainder with me on the sidelines.

When dinner was cleared away, three men joined us. One was a stocky Russian about fifty-five years old with salt-and-pepper hair and a military bearing. The second was a German who clearly had an important connection to the Comintern. I knew him as Ebert, but when I compared notes with others in later years, I found out they knew him by other names. He was shorter than I but a bit heavier, and he wore glasses. The third was a slightly built Chinese of about forty who represented the Party in Shanghai. It was of course operating underground. During these years eight successive Shanghai committees had been arrested and executed by Chiang's government. After introductions the Russian host turned to me and asked, "What's the reaction of the comrades over there? Are there any suggestions from them as to what should be done regarding Kiangsi?"

I produced a letter given to me by my contact in Paris. The letter, written in Russian with accompanying French and Chinese translations, was sealed but carried substantially the same message I was to deliver orally. The essence of it was that while the Comintern would do what it could to help, the decision was theirs to make because Moscow was too removed from the latest events. While they looked a little disappointed that I had not brought more definitive advice, they weren't too surprised. The discussion turned to the question of Chiang's expected offensive against the soviet zone. The threat of massive gas attacks was raised, and I spoke up, indicating that I had brought some money from the Comintern to help procure gas masks if necessary. At that I pulled $50,000 out of the money belt and handed it over to the Chinese man. It was a tremendous relief not to be carrying that much cash around any longer. But after thanking me, my host asked me if I would continue to serve as the financial middleman. Money would be wired to a local bank in my name. I was to handle these transactions during the next few days and then join them for a second meeting. Seeing that I had been more or less dismissed for the night, I left with Hans and returned to my hotel.

Sure enough, a telegram from Paris arrived at the hotel the next day, instructing me that a sum of money had been deposited in my account at a bank in the French section. The amount of money was not that great, but after it was exchanged for Chinese currency, which was undergoing astronomical inflation, the sheer volume of the bills was astonishing. It took four boxes about the size of orange crates to haul them off. I felt ludicrous as the Sikhs guarding the bank opened the doors for me. Standing outside the bank waiting for a rickshaw, I was convinced I would be robbed. How would I explain that? I took a rickshaw for several blocks and then got off to switch to another, as per instructions. As I stood on the street waiting for another rickshaw, the first rickshaw man couldn't understand why he couldn't take me where I was going. I had to admit to myself that the whole operation was pretty crude. If someone was following me, I wouldn't lose him by switching rickshaws! By the time I arrived at my destination, I was about to blow. It was crazy. I had stuck out like a sore thumb. I handed the boxes over and walked off, my shirt soaked with perspiration. I shook my head, muttering at the stupidity of those responsible for the arrangements.

When I had to repeat this process a few days later, I told myself I would speak up and demand that a safer method be found. I swear the Sikh guards were laughing at me as I again made my exit with two cartons under each arm. When I dropped the money off this time, I was told that Hans would pick me up for dinner that evening.

After going through the by-now familiar operation of switching rickshaws, we wound up at the old Russian's home. I was hoping for a repeat of his earlier hospitality, but he served only a fairly light meal. The same three men arrived together after dinner. Over tea and cigarettes, the discussion began. It was considered too difficult to secure an adequate supply of gas masks. You could buy them for the soldiers, but how do you buy gas masks for all five million people in Kiangsi? Furthermore, gas would wipe out all the livestock. The more they discussed the possibility of protecting themselves from gas, the clearer it became that it just couldn't be done. The discussion turned back to the question of what should be done.

Ebert argued that the Communists must remain in Kiangsi and defend it against another attack. He dismissed the gas campaign as a device to intimidate the populace. He feared that the loss of this base would be a setback for the other soviet zones and lead to the liquidation of Communist influence throughout China. When he was through, the Chinese comrade responded that despite these potentially serious implications, Party leaders in Kiangsi had just advised him that they had to break out, even at maximum sacrifice. It was fruitless to continue in their position.

The argument got more than a little heated after that, and I found myself torn between both positions. Finally, Hans turned to the Russian, who except for an occasional question had remained silent during the argument. "What do you think of the possibility of breaking out?" he asked.

You could see him going over the major points of the debate in his head before he answered. Finally he said, "From what I can see, judging from the forces that the enemy can bring to bear on Kiangsi and from what our people seem to have down there, if you want to define this strictly in a military sense, it's impossible. But," he continued, holding up a finger, "it's really a political question as much as a military one. If it is the opinion down there that it can be done, it must be tried. I can see no other alternative."

That took some of the sting out of Ebert's arguments but by no means resolved the dilemma. Gas masks were not a real alternative, and it was not feasible to remain blockaded in Kiangsi without salt or adequate supplies. I left the meeting feeling that the Chinese would try to break out. About a year later, when I was back in the anthracite, I read that there had been a breakout from Kiangsi by the Communists, but at a tremendous cost. The main forces of the Red Army had managed to escape, however, and were marching away from Kiangsi with Chiang's armies in pursuit. Their flight turned into the historic Long March.[8]

I didn't have a word to say during the discussion, not even to ask a question. I was awed by the magnitude of the problem. Five million lives and the fate of the Chinese revolutionary movement were hanging in the balance. I just sat there sipping tea and listening.

I thought I would leave Shanghai soon after this meeting because we had agreed I wouldn't make further contact. There was too much of a chance that my bank withdrawals had aroused someone's suspicions. But an early departure wasn't in the cards. I stayed another five or six weeks, making two more discreet transfers of funds and waiting for my ship, the *Empress of Asia*. By this time word of my financial doings generated rumors that I was a gambler. I encouraged that the best I could, inquiring where the action was and even making my way a few times to the gambling houses, only to quietly slip out the back door. I don't know if I was able to fool anyone.

Because I couldn't carry on like the other tourists in Shanghai, whoring and drinking, I ended up, of all places, in a library. I dug a number of biographies out of the stacks and passed hours reading about Grant and Sandburg's Lincoln. Frankly, after a week or two, I was bored to death. I saw every English movie that passed through town (that's where I saw *King Kong*) and got to know virtually every block of the International Settlement. If I could have spoken the language, I would have made excursions into the countryside, but I felt helpless without knowing Chinese. I spent many evenings with Hans, who had some small business in the settlement as his cover, but I was wary of making any new acquaintances. I was afraid of running into my fellow passengers, especially that pesky young Austrian woman.

The *Empress of Asia* finally departed Shanghai in October bound for Nagasaki, Yokohama, and across the Pacific. I felt more like a real tourist on this passage, relieved of my tasks as a courier. I chatted with whoever wished to pass the time and was glad to take on anybody at chess. One American mining engineer who specialized in oil-drilling bragged about the life of ease he maintained in Java as he sat across the board from me. He lived with a beautiful Eurasian woman. These women, he explained, "are so cheap to keep! They cook for you, sleep with you, and clean for you—and all with no responsibility!" He justified the American oil companies' activities in Asia as readily as he defended "keeping" this woman. On one level he appeared to be a very strait-laced moral guy as he headed back to the States and his wife and family. On another level the man was imperialism in a nutshell—use the women and rip off the natural resources. The whole trip brought home to me how widespread and vicious the set of relations and domination I called imperialism actually was. I had a sense of it that was more profound than what could be picked up in books. I felt that I had seen its impact in the faces of people from Alexandria to Shanghai. They weren't faces I could easily forget.

There was another face I couldn't forget. As we sailed back across the Pacific, I kept thinking of Margaret. I didn't know if she would be waiting for me in Wilkes-Barre or whether she was still in Moscow.

Although I realized she was heavily involved in the Comintern's courier service, I had absolutely no idea that she too had been sent to Shanghai. She arrived there, it seems, within a few weeks of my departure. While working at the Comintern, she had attracted someone's attention as a reliable comrade. They asked her to make a trip to Berlin, and when she returned, they put her to work on a fairly steady basis. In a little more than a year, Maggie made several of these trips. Their purpose was to assist the parties in Germany and Eastern Europe survive conditions of fascism.

There was of course an element of risk. As she now puts it, "You could imagine that you were going on a great big James Bond mission if you wanted to, but if you were smart enough, you'd play it down." We didn't see our missions as glamorous, the way they're portrayed in the movie *Julia* that was made from Lillian Hellman's book. It's easier to romanticize these kinds of things after the passage of time, although that's not to say that there weren't moments of excitement.

As Maggie recounts, "In one case, I was waiting in Germany for a few days until an answer to the message I had transmitted could be formulated. When I met my contact for our evening stroll, she told me to go to Prague. I hopped a train to Prague, and when I got there was told to continue on through Bulgaria to Sofia. Before I got there I could sense something shaky. I didn't know what had happened, but you could tell by the way people acted on the train. Too many border guards were getting on, and conversations sounded off-key. I arrived at night and went right to my hotel, still suspicious but unable to put my finger on what was wrong. The next morning I walked through the streets and could tell immediately that there were too many cops around. When I got back to the hotel dining room and had breakfast, I struck up a conversation with my waiter. 'You know, this is a very nice city. I was just up to the Rose Garden. But it seemed there are an awful lot of police around.' His answer was, 'Of course; we just had a *putsch*. The government was overthrown.'

"I spent the rest of the day trying to sort out what happened from the rumors. I had to decide what to do. Should I go and make the contact or skip it? I waited a couple of days to see if I could get a better sense of what was happening, and on the second day I decided that I might as well try. I went to the small shop that my contact ran. I made the correct purchase and the appropriate greeting, and I thought this guy was going to fall over. He took one look at me and whispered, 'Come back at seven o'clock.'

"When I got back there that evening, the place was closed up with an iron gate pulled down in front of the windows. I went around to a side door and tried it. It opened, so I went inside and up a flight of stairs. It was pitch dark, and when I sensed I was at the top of the flight of stairs, I said, 'I just came from Prague. I know something's happened here, but I'm not sure what.'

"I could sense that there were at least two people there, and I waited for a response, hoping somebody would turn on a light. A voice I recognized as that of the shopkeeper replied, 'Have you got anything?' At this point I didn't know what to do. I figured it might be a setup—if I gave it to them I was caught, and if I didn't I'd probably be busted anyway. What choice did I have? I thought about it a few seconds and turned it over to them. 'When you get back,' the voice instructed, 'just tell them that the apparatus has remained intact here. We have not been interfered with at all, and everything is stable. You are the first person to get through.'

"I didn't know just what it was that I had handed over, nor did I really care. It's really not safe to know what you're transmitting because if you did know, it would be liable to scare the pants off you. I just wanted to get the hell out of Sofia, and I caught a train back to Prague the next morning. In Prague they looked a little surprised that I made it back at all, and when I returned to Moscow the Bulgarian representative to the Comintern came to see me to verify for himself that the organization there had not been disrupted."

After returning from one of these trips, Margaret started making inquiries about me and found that I had gone home. She didn't realize that my journey was via Shanghai. Not long after that, they asked her if she would catch a Mediterranean steamer to China and serve as a conduit for funds to the Chinese Party. Thus she followed my path a few weeks behind me.

A woman traveling alone in those days was something of an exception, but Margaret successfully used a number of covers. The empire of the Swedish financier Stavitsky had just toppled, and parts of his fortune were surfacing all over the world. Being German, she let on that relatives of hers, possibly connected to Stavitsky, were interested in finding safe places for investments. She played the role of the sharp young woman looking at investment possibilities in this and that. It was as plausible an explanation as working undercover for the Comintern, and most people accepted it at face value.

She stayed in Shanghai for five months, relaying money to the underground Party network and residing at a hotel in the French section. Eventually she got a tip from a friendly hotel manager that Chiang's police had been asking questions about her. That was her cue to exit. On the steamship back to Naples, everything appeared normal. In Naples she picked up another boat for Odessa. Among the passengers accompanying her was a young American agent. He was a persistent cuss. As she recalled, "I was standing in the stern of the boat watching the waves, daydreaming, when a voice from behind me asked, 'Kotory chas?' which means, 'What time is it' in Russian. I had seen that movie before, so I turned around and said, 'Did you say something?' He mumbled something but didn't go away. He began asking me questions: What did I want in Odessa? Did I know that I looked very much like Louise Bryan (the wife of the American ambassador to the Soviet Union)?

" 'You don't say? Who's she?' I responded. He was trying to decide whether to have me grabbed, and I was told my passport had been picked up at the previous port of call and inadvertently left behind. As we neared Odessa, I thought I was in trouble. But for some reason, they decided not to arrest me, and my passport mysteriously reappeared by the time we docked in Odessa."

It wasn't until we were together again in the anthracite that we felt secure talking about these trips. Even then we kept our stories to ourselves. Most of the people we had come in contact with in the German and Czechoslovak undergrounds were eventually caught up with. They couldn't consistently carry on those activities and not have their numbers come up. By our silence we felt we were helping to protect them.

Knowing that my mission had helped, even if just in a small way, those who sought to overturn the system of imperialism made me feel good as I steamed homeward. At a time when it was difficult for anticolonial struggles to find aid, the Comintern played a positive role. For all my later doubts and criticisms, I wouldn't want to take that away from them. That, by the way, terminated my relations with Dr. Karlov and the Comintern. I had no debriefing; I didn't report to anybody. I came home with whatever rubbed off on me in the way of experience and nothing else—except for the $70 I managed to save out of my slim travel money. That went toward an old Model T that I found in a Scranton junkyard. We needed a car for the unemployed council work.

I landed in Seattle on November 7, 1933, and grabbed a cross-country train for Chicago. I picked up every newspaper I could find along the way and tried to get a sense of what was happening. It had been two very long and intense years, and I was glad to be back. I couldn't wait to get to the anthracite and my comrades.

SIX

The Struggle
of the Unemployed
in the Anthracite

The transition back to life in the anthracite fields was less difficult than I had expected. I welcomed the sight of eastern Pennsylvania's rolling hills, and even the coal breakers looked good. I think I was just glad to be coming home and anxious to get back into our work.

By the time I got back to the United States in late 1933, the whole political climate of the country was changing. The councils had struck roots in dozens of towns throughout the anthracite, and nationally the movement was beginning to exert considerable political pressure on FDR's New Deal administration. Along with activists from other parts of the state, the leaders of the anthracite unemployed movement started to discuss a mass mobilization to put some pressure of our own on Governor Pinchot's administration. We wanted to force the politicians to confront their responsibilities to their unemployed constituents.

At the end of the year, a meeting of local leaders from Pittsburgh, Philadelphia, Reading, Allentown, Easton, and the anthracite took place in Harrisburg. There we developed plans for the first Hunger March on the state capital. We decided to present a petition to the state legislature demanding immediate relief in the form of food; provision of coal or other heating fuel; maintenance of electricity or gas used for heating and lights; postponement of home and farm mortgage payments; abolition of sheriff sales of farms; and cancellation of all mortgage auctions.

One of the most influential people at this state meeting was a man from Philadelphia, a transplanted Southerner by the name of John Parks who was later killed at the battle of Jarama during the Spanish Civil War. At the time he was chairman of the Unemployed Councils of Pennsylvania. He had a way of lifting his face to the sky with his eyes shut as he made his points. A tall, wiry sort of guy, he was the personification of the small farmer from the hills of Tennessee or the backwoods of Kentucky. His arguments carried a lot of weight. He pleaded for a coalition of the unemployed in the state, including any group willing to work with us on the march, and he argued against attacking labor leaders for their failure to participate. We should simply ignore them, he said, and go straight to the rank and file, asking local unions to send representatives to Harrisburg, and to support the unemployment insurance bill in Congress introduced by Rep. Lundeen from Minnesota.

After we'd agreed upon the demands, we discussed how to deal with the legislators. "Don't count on seeing them when you come to Harrisburg," Parks warned, "unless you do a lot of homework. Go and see them when they come home on the weekends. Send in neighbors and people who have voted for them in the past, and corner the two-bit politicians who deliver their votes. Buttonhole them and talk to them about our demands." In the meantime, he said, we should try to find some of the more receptive men in the legislature now and talk to them about endorsing our demands by writing them up in a bill. Since we were not lawyers, we couldn't draft the legislation ourselves. They could write it up in a form that could be presented to their colleagues as long as it incorporated the ideas that we had discussed. We hoped that some legislators would be sympathetic. One who did help was Darlington Hoopes, a Socialist from Reading.

We went back to our respective towns and for several weeks held council meetings to prepare for the Hunger March. Committees were set up to ask local businessmen for the use of their trucks in order to take as many people as we could to Harrisburg. Those businessmen who did not have trucks were asked to provide canned goods and other food, primarily coffee, bread, hot dogs, cheese, and sugar. We provided each of the open-bed trucks with chairs and makeshift benches, and everyone was assigned to a truck and driver.

We worked out a detailed plan so that each contingent took off from a particular point at the right time. Every local group chose a leader and an organizing committee. In the center of town or in a public square, a crowd would gather to see their local contingent off. As we passed through the various communities, impromptu meetings were held, and the march grew as the various contingents joined us. There were several routes. One was from the lower anthracite—Pottsville, Shamokin, and Minersville; another from the upper anthracite—Carbondale, Scranton, and Wilkes-Barre; and the third from Nanticoke and Berwick.

On the day of the march I was with the group in the forward car.

We arrived in the public squares before the rest of the caravan, and people like Muldowney, Dougher, Spencer, and myself addressed the crowds. We spoke from eight in the morning till four o'clock, when we reached the lower part of the Susquehanna River near the town of Northumberland where the east and west branches of the Susquehanna meet. Because we were not trained in using our voices effectively, we spoke with everything we had in us. Our throats were hoarse by the time we reached the point where all the groups had agreed to meet.

It was amazing how well this rudimentary organization worked. There was no hollering or complaining. When we reached the bare field along the riverbank that was our gathering point, we saw the Minersville Lithuanians. They already had big vats of coffee brewing over campfires and were handing it out to nearly a thousand people who had come in the various contingents. All who stopped had coffee and sandwiches and an hour of rest before pushing on. We were aiming to reach Harrisburg before nightfall.

We came to the Harrisburg city limits about half an hour before sunset and, to our amazement, were met by the state police on motorcycles and horses. They told us that we were not allowed into the city by order of Governor Pinchot. Each contingent was stopped in its tracks as it approached the city. The word was, "You cannot get into the city, period."

We stopped and tried to figure what to do. We'd previously arranged for the steering committees of each contingent to meet at a garage lent to us by a local council activist. In a short while everyone who was involved in organizing the march was present, except for John Parks. He had been arrested in Philadelphia and was still in jail.

Another fellow, an English seaman by the name of Colman, was spokesman for the Philadelphia contingent. He was short but powerfully built and wore a cloth cap and an old leather jacket. In a strong Cockney accent, he proposed in the name of the giant Philadelphia group that we had only one choice, and that was to force our way into the city, irrespective of the governor's orders.

This struck me and some of the others as totally unrealistic. Even if we did get into the center of the city, where would we go, and what would we do? But the real question was, who was going to face the cops with their clubs and guns, and what would the consequences be? I argued that this proposal would lead us into a trap and that we had to find another way. Several people agreed, but none of us knew what to do. One of those who supported my idea was Si Gerson, a YCL activist who was covering the March as a cub reporter for the *Daily Worker*. Undaunted, Colman replied, "Well, if you're not going to do that, let's take it to a vote."

The majority voted against his idea, but the question of what to do still remained. Gerson and I proposed that we send out cars to various areas outside the city to see if we could find some empty lots, fields, or barns in which to put people up for the night. It was early spring, and the nights were fairly warm; people could get by somehow. We would reconvene in the morning.

Colman sat scowling on a bench in front. He said, "Well, you go out and find a place where all these people can be put up. There must be at least three thousand here, maybe more. We came from Philly with about fifteen hundred, Pittsburgh came with twelve hundred, and the anthracite brought down almost a thousand. Where are you going to put all these people?" We had no answer for him, but Gerson agreed that we should go out, take the initiative, and see what we could find.

We drove eight or ten miles out of town, followed by the state police on motorcycles. Every chance they had, every light we hit, they came up and wanted to know where we were going and why. "You carried out the governor's orders," we told them. "You wouldn't let us into the city, so we're looking for a place to stay for the night."

About eight-thirty or nine in the evening, we saw three huge barns and a farmhouse on the left-hand side of the road. The unusual symbols tacked on the barns and the house told us it was the home of a Pennsylvania Dutch farmer. Gerson said, "Well, this is it. We might as well try." We jumped out of our little Ford and walked up to the house. Just then the light in the living room went out, but we knocked on the door anyway, and a man and woman opened it. They were standing in the vestibule, the woman carrying a lantern, and they looked as if they were going upstairs to bed. This was a little farmhouse with the living room and parlor on one side and the kitchen and dining room on the other. In the middle were stairs without bannisters going straight up to the bedrooms.

The man spoke up. "What can we possibly do for you folks?"

Gerson and I looked at each other, and we didn't know where to start. One of us said, "We have here in the city a delegation of the unemployed that has come from all over the state, and the governor didn't permit us to get into town this evening, claiming there was no space for us." (We made it easy on the governor because we weren't sure about the farmer's politics.) "We were sent here by the delegation to see if we could possibly stay on your land and put as many people in the barn as we can for the night."

He looked at his wife, and they began a conversation. They approached the problem in the truest Christian spirit, using religious terminology. "The Lord sent them here, and perhaps it's up to us to do something to help them."

At that point I put in that while our demands were for the unemployed, they were for poor farmers too. We were asking for a moratorium on mortgages. It seems that this, as much as religious considerations, opened the door to their hearts.

The man turned to his wife and said, "What do you think, Mother?" And she said, "The Lord will never forgive us if we turn people down who are in such desperate need." Turning to us, he asked, "Well, how many are you?"

We didn't dare say that we had more than three thousand people. In fact, we really didn't know how many there were now. So we said, "Oh, there are pretty many in trucks; we couldn't really count them all! But there are quite a few." He said, "Well, how many? Five hundred or so?" We said there were a good many more than that, but that he didn't have to worry because they could sleep in the trucks.

The farmer turned to his wife and told her, "Well, Mother, I think you're right." Looking at us, he said, "Get your folks down here, but whatever you do, be careful of fires. If anything burns down here, my insurance won't cover it. I don't want to lose the barns and my cattle." We assured him that everything would be well taken care of.

When they said good night and walked up the stairs, I was shaking with excitement. I don't think that I had ever shaken like that before. Gerson hugged me and said, "Well, we did it. Now we're gonna tell those guys that if they had gone out, they might have been able to get a place, too." But I said, "Oh, let's forget it. We'll just go back and tell them what we found."

It was close to ten o'clock when we walked into the small garage that was serving as unofficial headquarters for the march. The members who remained were settled down and sleeping. With cheerful looks on our faces, we proudly announced, "We found a place to stay!"

"What do you mean 'found a place'? For all of us?"

"Yes—we found a place for everyone."

"Where?"

"Just tell each of the columns to line up on the highway within the next hour. They should follow a Ford coupé with Illinois license plates in which Si and I will be riding."

When we finally told the people that they had some place to go, you could sense their relief. Some trucks were broken down and never made it—they just stayed right on the road. But 90 percent of the marchers were able to line up and follow us to the farmer's place.

The police motorcycles tore off after the strange caravan, trying to figure out where we were heading. We made sure that they didn't know because we feared that they would go down ahead of us and scare the farmer. When we came to the place where we had to make a left turn onto the farm, we waited until the column was solidly in place. Then we began to turn into a huge hayfield. There must have been at least two hundred vehicles—mostly battered jalopies and small trucks. Since it was early spring, we didn't hurt the grass.

Spontaneously, a committee was set up that lined up the trucks and told each driver where to go. In no time at all, some miners rounded up big barrels and stood at the barns telling everyone, "Put your matches here. No matches in the barn." Every miner in those days, and workers in general, used long wooden matches that they struck on the side of their pants to light their pipes and cigarettes. When I passed by in the morning, I found a barrel full of matches at each barn door.

The women were told to go into one barn, the men into another. I was so tired that I don't know what happened the rest of the night. I woke up in the morning to the sound of pots and pans and the smell of coffee. There were the Minersville Lithuanians again, making coffee. The Philadelphia crowd, which had close connections with the middle-class Jewish community there, had brought goods that we could not get in the coalfields. We devoured bagels, salami, kosher hot dogs, corned beef, rolls, and coffee for breakfast. It seemed there was enough to feed an army.

When everybody was full of food, we started off the day with a meeting from the back of a flatbed truck. As the people gathered around with the farmer standing by, someone said, "The governor of the state did not have the heart to let us into the city of Harrisburg, but this poor farmer and his wife, mortgaged up to their ears, did not hesitate to permit us to come on their property to spend the night." The farmer was then given a chance to speak. He climbed onto the back of the truck, cleared his throat, and started speaking very slowly. He explained how his religious ethics taught him to be decent to all who deserved to be respected. "And since you people are going there for a noble cause, I couldn't do any less than to let you stay here."

Somebody found a blanket, and the farmer was lifted onto it and thrown into the air, a customary show of respect in England and other countries. I was afraid that the old blanket would rip and he would hit the ground, but it worked out all right. Afterward, the farmer stood on the platform with his wife joining him, both of them trying not to cry. I saw more than one person in tears. People were touched that this man would put us up for the night when the authorities of our government met us with an army of policemen.

The trucks were turned around, and we proceeded to the city limits. There, as agreed upon at the farm, we dismounted and took our signs out and started to march. The state police were there, but their clubs were not drawn. Apparently our persistence had persuaded Pinchot to abandon his idea of forcibly restricting our access to the capital. The motorcycles were on the sides of the road, but they didn't block our way. We lined up twenty abreast. Eight entire blocks were jammed with unshaven men and bedraggled women carrying signs and walking straight down to the state capital. The banners read, "We Demand Unemployment Insurance!" "We Demand Relief!" "We Demand Assistance to the Needy!" "Moratorium for Farmers!"

Quite a few local people, many of whom were out of work themselves because of short work weeks at the steel mills and on the railroads, joined the march to the capital. A considerable number of them were black. There we held impromptu meetings right on the capitol grounds, and state legislators came down to mingle with us, looking for people from their own districts. "Oh, I'm with you, I'm with you. We'll have to do something about this question," they assured us. There was a collection taken for gasoline and other expenses, and I saw a legislator drop the first ten-dollar bill into the hat.

A special committee was elected to see the governor immediately and ask him to provide us with a place to stay. He agreed that we could stay on the state fairgrounds for as long as it took to present our demands to the legislature. The crowd was determined that we were not going to go back until we got some guarantees, and the legislators understood this.

A big holler went up when it was announced that we got the state fairgrounds for our headquarters. It was our first victory. The Red Cross was going to provide cots, blankets, and food. Committees from all areas met to select the speakers who would address the legislature. But then we were told that we could only send one person to speak, and that we would be confined to the gallery.

We didn't like that. We had asked for four speakers—someone from the coalfields, another from the steel mills, and at least two speakers from the big cities of Philadelphia and Pittsburgh, one black and one white. Each was to develop one point in our proposal. Our main demand was that the Pennsylvania legislature go on record as encouraging the U.S. Congress to act on Congressman Lundeen's unemployment insurance bill. This bill became the rallying point around which people mobilized nationally for unemployment insurance.

While we were prepared to make some concessions, we insisted upon the four speakers. We also wanted to have as many people as possible on the floor near their representatives. We were willing to negotiate about the number of people that were allowed in, but it seemed that the administration's supporters, without consulting the rest of the legislators, acted arbitrarily to restrict us to one speaker and confine everyone else to the gallery.

We could not accept the ruling, so we tied some ropes to the gallery bannisters. When our one official spokesperson went to the podium, the three speakers who were not allowed to talk slid down onto the floor and also went up to the podium to be heard. When the confusion died down, they asked the legislature to take a vote on the matter of whether or not they could speak.

The plan worked. A single representative asked that the others be allowed to speak. With the galleries packed, this irregular motion carried, and the other three were allowed to proceed. Well, the ropes were still dangling, and many of the younger people slid down and went over in an orderly manner to their own legislators and sat next to them—to be sure that they remembered that the local people were watching them, not from a distance, but right from the floor of the legislature.

We remained in Harrisburg for two more days. While we were there, people back home heard that we had obtained the state fairgrounds, and more trucks began to arrive. Soon the fairgrounds were packed, and we were facing a dangerous health hazard. We had to beg the people who had already seen their legislators to go home.

In the meantime the legislature passed several of the motions that we were after, including the demand for direct relief. We decided we had completed our mission to Harrisburg and dispersed to our different towns and cities.

The march to Harrisburg was part of a nationwide unemployed movement that helped to win the welfare structure most Americans now take for granted. During the early thirties hundreds of thousands of signatures were collected on petitions demanding unemployment compensation. In February 1931, 400,000 workers demonstrated on National Unemployed Insurance Day and half a million joined a similar protest a year later. In December 1931, December 1932, and at FDR's inauguration in March 1933, the National Unemployed Council led workers from throughout the country in hunger marches on Washington, D.C. and helped to draft legislation, as we did in Pennsylvania, and the leaders of the national organizations appeared before congressional committees. Within a year of our Harrisburg march, the federal government expanded its relief programs and funded giant projects under the Works Progress Administration (WPA). In the summer of 1935, Congress passed the Social Security Act. This bill incorporated our main goal of unemployment compensation as well as a pension system.[1]

Margaret didn't return from Moscow for almost six months after I got back. She was surprised at how much things had changed. Shortly after her arrival, we held a big demonstration in Wilkes-Barre around some local issue, and she actually cried at the sight of the big turnout. The movement had still been fairly small when we left, so she was thrilled to see so many spirited people. But even more important was the fact that we had won the free speech fight, with which she had been intimately involved. When she left it was almost impossible to hold a meeting, even in a closed hall; organizers were constantly arrested and held without charges in order to disrupt the plans. Now she saw people marching down the main street of the town with their banners and flags. The Harrisburg march had given us valuable organizing experience and had also brought many new people into the movement.

Our steady growth in the region led to the establishment of the Unemployed League, a "loyal" group organized by Democratic politicians to undermine the success of the more militant unemployed councils. The league made every effort to put on a patriotic front. Meetings were opened with the pledge of allegiance, and the flag was displayed prominently. Although the organization may have attracted some people genuinely interested in the problem of unemployment, it was primarily a vehicle through which small-time politicians could be assured of getting on the gravy train once the New Deal programs started coming in. Since they had the political connections, they were favored. The pitch was, "If you stick with the Unemployed League, you're more likely to get a WPA job than if you go with the Reds." They did provide a certain amount of competition, and we had to trim our sails a little to suit the wind. We never pledged allegiance at meetings, but we always had the flag out front at demonstrations.

At its high point, the league's following was perhaps one-fourth the size of ours, and the explanation for this is simple. They were not as effective in handling grievances because they weren't prepared to push, to use militant tactics if necessary. They compromised without a struggle. When the official said, "No, you can't have it," that was it

A meeting of the unemployed in Wilkes-Barre, 1933.

for them. They tried to use whatever political influence they had, but when that didn't work, they were at a loss. We learned the rules and where they might be bent; then we applied pressure: "We're not leaving this office until you act on this." After a while some of those who had been attracted by the league came around saying, "I took my problem to those politicians in the league, and they just ignored me." We would take up the case and try to show that it could be won with a struggle.

The league also tended to be less democratic than the councils in its structure and composition. It had fewer delegate meetings than we had, so it tended to be run from the top down. It was dominated by Anglo-Saxon types and generally failed to attract many immigrants. When it did attract support from an unemployed miner, he was apt to be a local union official. The American Legion spirit dominated, and many anthracite people found the atmosphere inhospitable.

When the league first came into existence, our speakers spent a lot of time blasting it, but we came to the conclusion that this approach was no good. It would be better to work with it if possible. We usually couldn't reach the leaders on the question of united action, so we addressed our leaflets to the rank and file membership. We didn't have a lot of success, but at least we neutralized some of the opposition by showing that we were anxious to work together.

The crisis of the thirties pushed people to the limits of capitalist ideology and sometimes a bit beyond in their daily struggle to exist. People occupied unused company land in order to plant gardens, and they often worked collectively on community projects, if only because the situation demanded it. Although the unemployed movement was the most important part of the struggle for me, it was just one aspect of people's attempts to survive and maintain some dignity in the midst of a social catastrophe.

Several other movements paralleled that of the unemployed, among them "bootleg" mining, the Anthracite Mine Workers of Pennsylvania, and the Luzerne County Labor Party. It's wrong to think of these as isolated developments because they were related to one another through individuals, ideas, and events. Nor is it accurate to see any of them as the "creation" of the Communist Party; each was a strategy developed by the region's workers to meet particular problems, and each was shaped by daily life in the community. Communists played important roles in each, but the Party in the thirties generally, and especially in the hard coal region, was strong because it was really part of a broader struggle for change.

It didn't take miners long to realize that there was only a few feet of earth between them and the region's coal seams. They believed that God or nature put the coal there as much for them as for the owners, and there was nothing that could keep them from digging it out. These bootleg miners dug into the sides of the mountains or sunk shallow shafts straight into the earth. The operators, concentrating on the richer seams down below, never went after this coal. A bootleg operation consisted of a miner, his son, and a few others, perhaps men with whom he had worked before being laid off. They would get an old auto motor and attach one end of a cable to this and the other to an oil drum or a large old wooden tub that was filled and then hoisted out of the shallow shaft called a "doghole."

When I arrived in the anthracite in 1931, there were only a few bootleggers in operation, but the industry mushroomed over the next few years. Although this may be an exaggeration, it was claimed that at the height of the digging, probably 1934, there were over twenty thousand miners involved.[2] The heart of the industry was in the lower anthracite where there was more outcropping of the seams than in the wider valleys of the upper end.

The first bootleggers mined the coal for their own fuel and to exchange for goods and services, but a market developed quickly, and the little operations expanded. Pickup trucks brought the coal to Reading, Easton, and even Philadelphia, where it was sold door-to-door—"Coal, pea coal, anthracite coal!" Some men got larger trucks with chutes so that the coal could be unloaded into basements more easily. Others pooled their tools and labor to open larger shafts and increase production. It's estimated that by 1933 bootlegging was a $30- to $35-million industry in northeastern Pennsylvania.[3] The bootleggers were mining on coal company property and then undercutting the companies with their own coal in the local market.

The companies were enraged at this wholesale violation of private property, even though they had paid no attention to this coal in the past, and they complained to the governor. State police poured into the region, but the situation was already out of hand. The private police of one company were said to have dynamited a thousand holes in one year—while the bootleggers opened several thousand new ones. Local officials were often afraid to tell a miner that he couldn't take coal out of the hills because this was the only means of support for him and his family. When outright suppression of the digging seemed out of the question, some companies decided to try surface mining themselves. Large steam shovels were put into operation scraping off huge scoops of surface coal. The first of these shovels came to Minersville, a bad place to start. The big shovel began to dig, and soon whistles were blowing all over the place. Hundreds of miners gathered with shotguns and got into an argument with the state police. In the meantime someone put a stick of dynamite under the shovel and blew it to pieces. So much for the origins of strip mining.

The bootleggers established themselves as the Bootleg Miners Union for protection against the companies and also to regulate themselves. The heart of the new organization was around Shamokin, and the leaders were Joe Rauwa, John Kuchinski, and Fred Pfeiffer. Many non-Party miners were involved, but Party people were chiefly responsible for conceiving of and establishing the union. They set out to minimize competition and ensure safety. I helped to write the constitution, which included safety guidelines, pledged members to support one another in legal problems, and established the going rate for coal. Eventually this rate was accepted throughout the area.

The organization soon expanded to include delegates from all over the region. I never saw greater unity among a group of workers than existed among these bootleggers. Call a meeting, and by word of mouth the whole region would turn out and act together.

Some bootlegging continued right up to the Second World War, but the industry had begun to die of its own internal contradictions long before that. It was virtually impossible to ensure safety under such primitive conditions, and the number of accidents grew with the industry. A bootleg miner of course could not get any kind of insurance, so whoever got hurt was just out of luck. When the operations reached a certain stage, they required larger amounts of capital. Then the big companies who controlled banks and equipment firms in the region were able to strangle the bootleggers financially.

Naturally the political significance of the bootlegging was discussed at Party meetings, and we took it as a positive sign. Instead of lying down next to the coal piles and freezing, the bootleggers took the coal to build fires for their families and sold it to buy them food. Their acts affirmed the concept that human life comes first and private property second. To this extent the experience represented a political advance by thousands of miners, but we didn't overestimate the meaning of bootlegging. We saw it primarily as an immediate response to a problem and not as a major step on the road to socialism. For me the significance of the phenomenon was overshadowed by other events, especially those surrounding the rank and file revolt in the UMWA.

The roots of the revolt went back several years. When I came to the anthracite fields in 1931, I found the same sort of little pockets of NMU membership as I had found in Illinois. In the anthracite the

Party was largely concentrated in three areas: Scranton and vicinity, Wilkes-Barre and vicinity, and the Shamokin-Minersville area in the lower end of the region. The regular NMU organizer had already been withdrawn, and at the very first Section Committee meeting in the lower region, the question of the NMU arose. We were confronted with all the same problems we had faced in Illinois: hatred for Lewis and his "scab" union, dedication to rank and file democracy, and resistance to the UMWA's program of dues checkoff and its bureaucracy. Arrangements were made for a meeting of all Party miners and other NMU members. I had to admit that I couldn't do the job. Phone calls were considered prohibitive at the time, but it was an emergency. I called the National Office of the Party and asked that they send someone knowledgeable to explain the situation. Jack Stachel, who was directing the Party's trade union work at the time, addressed the meeting. Most of the fifty or so miners who attended were impressed with his argument. He said the NMU's isolation was a signal that the Party's trade union policy must change, not only in the anthracite but throughout the country and the economy. Although there was some dissension, I was glad that I had made the call. He was able to place the problem in a broader perspective than I might have done, and the fact that he represented the national leadership helped.

It was right around this time that we had to face another obstacle between our people and the rank and file miners, a pamphlet by Pat Toohey called *Coal Miners in Soviet America*. Pat was one of the leaders of the bitter and unsuccessful 1927–1928 strike in the western Pennsylvania bituminous fields and became secretary of the NMU.[4] He was a great organizer, but the pamphlet was the very incarnation of the Party's 1920s sectarianism, full of revolutionary jargon. It tried to project a Soviet model for socialism in the United States, and though many of the older miners considered it to be a fine piece of propaganda, we were sure that it was hurting us. We needed literature that was geared more to the values and problems of American miners. Eventually this and a second pamphlet, *The Name is Lewis, John L.*, by Tom Myerscough, another western Pennsylvania militant, were withdrawn.

I agreed in principle with these men that Lewis was a dictator and that the UMWA's policies were reactionary. There was no doubt about that; it was just a question of what was the best way to reach the working and unemployed miners. Dissolution of the NMU and withdrawal of these pamphlets did not mean that we gave up the fight against the UMWA bureaucracy. As in Illinois, Communist and other progressive miners entered insurgent movements and struck to enforce contract provisions.

The heart of the trouble in the anthracite was the 1931 contract, which was rammed through personally by Lewis. I saw the spectacle, and I'll never forget it. The miners had made numerous demands regarding safety, better ventilation, and a shorter workday. The leadership produced nothing; the contract under consideration was essentially the same as the last one. It took all of Lewis's bravado to get it through. The regional convention to consider the contract was held in Hazelton, so I got a press card and attended. Around noon the negotiating committee made its report, which was badly received. They promised the miners that Lewis would be arriving promptly at one o'clock to argue for acceptance of the new contract.

The delegates went out for lunch and beer and were all back by one o'clock. They stood at the front of the union hall, watching a railroad siding that ran right up alongside the building. About one-thirty a locomotive pushed a single Pullman car down the siding to the front of the union hall. I couldn't understand what was happening. The car stopped, the door opened, and a Pullman porter put a stool under it. Lewis stepped out of the car dressed like a Wall Street banker, a large gold watch chain strung across his formidable belly, a big white fedora perched on his head, and a thick freshly lit cigar sticking out of his mouth. The anthracite miners, many of whom had never seen the "great man" in the flesh, stared in awe. I myself was struck by the sight.

Without a word to anyone Lewis stepped down and crossed the street in front of the hall. Some local UMWA officials tried to get his attention with "Hi, Chief!" "Hi, Mr. Prsident!" but Lewis ignored them. He walked straight ahead, wearing his usual scowl. He mounted the platform and stood waiting for everyone to settle down.

Without taking a piece of paper from his briefcase or asking anyone a question, he told the people to be seated. He scanned the faces, then opened his speech without a word of salutation. While I don't remember his exact words, the exchange went something like this. In a booming voice he said, "I'm told that there are some in this hall who are opposed to the contract negotiated with the coal operators by your negotiating committee. Did I hear right?"

There was silence in the hall. Finally a voice rose from the back. It was Mike Demchak, a militant young miner from Mt. Carmel whom Lewis recognized. "Brother Lewis," he said, "this contract is no different from the one we've been working under for the last five years. The conditions of the miners were deplorable under it in the past, so why did our committee see fit to sign the contract again? Why didn't they discuss the issues we raised in local meetings?"

Lewis interjected, "Get to the point, Mike."

"Well, I think I've made my point."

"All right then," Lewis said, "sit down. Anyone else?"

"Brother Lewis," another miner called out, "I have the same question."

Lewis replied, "If you haven't got another question, then sit down. I'll get to that one."

There was dead silence in the hall. Nobody dared to ask another question. Anyone who spoke would have been identified as a trouble-maker and singled out for punishment. Lewis's officials, whom the miners often referred to as goons, were circulating in the hall, walking up and down the aisles. They were hard to miss: big, burly fellows, some with huge diamond rings that had the appearance of brass knuckles.

Lewis cleared his throat, looked around, and said something like, "Before I hear the next question from the floor, I want to ask all of you one. Are you aware of the economic situation of American industry at the present time? Do you know that over ten million people are out of work?" he bellowed. "Do you want to join them? Some may not be aware of this situation, but your negotiating committee was. We want to save the United Mine Workers, and those who are not reckoning with this truth are blind and would lead our organization to destruction."

Absolute silence. No more questions. The air was thick, and a mist of fear settled over the miners. I sat there speechless, wondering how a single individual could so arbitrarily rule the people who paid him to be their president. At the time Lewis's salary was comparable to that of most corporate executives or of the president of the United States.

"I hear no more questions," Lewis said. This was the cue for one of his lieutenants to call for a vote. "There's a motion on the floor to endorse the contract negotiated by the United Mine Workers negotiating committee and the anthracite coal operators.

"You've heard the question," Lewis said. "All those in favor, signify by saying 'Aye.'"

I don't think that half of the people voted for the motion, but when Lewis asked for all those opposed, the voices were faint and few. There was no question about it; Lewis had had his day. He had put over the contract. He concluded by stating, "The ayes have it, and so order the contract signed."

Lewis adjourned the session, saying that the meeting would continue after three o'clock. He had an important press conference, he said, and had to get back to Washington for some urgent national business. His whole bearing was calculated to impress the audience with his importance, to make them thankful that such a big man should take time out from his busy schedule to concern himself with their little problems.

The contract was signed, and the working conditions remained the same. More miners were blacklisted for speaking out against the contract locally, and the companies were emboldened by this sellout, becoming even more arrogant than before. They knew that those still working would fear losing their jobs, so they pushed production and ignored safety rules.

Even the problems that were addressed in the contract persisted because local officials made little attempt to back the piece of paper with action. One of the most serious grievances was the issue of payment for "dead work." A miner was paid by the ton of coal. When a seam is undercut and then dynamited, a lot of rock comes down on top of the coal, and this rock or slate had to be loaded into cars before a man could even begin to load coal. The rock would be thrown into a separate car, and the miner was paid nothing for this tonnage. A miner also spent a lot of his time extending track into his chamber so that the cars could be pushed further in to be loaded, and this too was dead work. The miner had to go out and get track, ties, and spikes and then lay the track himself. According to the contract, he was supposed to be paid so much per yard, but the owners ignored this.

The worst aspect of the degeneration of working conditions, however, was the system of subcontracting carried on by many of the miners themselves. Owners allowed certain miners to hire laborers. It was common for one miner to have two laborers working for him; in effect he assumed the position of a boss for the little chamber where the three worked. The miner himself made a pretty low tonnage rate, but the laborer received only a fraction of this for his efforts. The miner was actually making his living from the sweat of the laborer. Often these subcontractors were leaders in the union local, and the union itself began to assume a "boss mentality." Laborers were in the same local, but they were often reluctant to speak up for fear of reprisals from the men for whom they worked.

The miners fought back. During 1933 wildcat strikes broke out across the region. By special order from Lewis, any local president who entertained a strike motion was to be immediately suspended and tried for disobeying rules laid down by the executive. As usual the ingenious miners found a way around a rule. They packed the halls, but no one stood at the podium. Someone who remained anonymous made a strike motion from the floor and it was passed unanimously. The president could not be held responsible. The trick spread throughout the anthracite, and soon many locals were on strike. Of the eighty-five thousand miners in the entire region, twenty-five thousand were out at the peak of the strike.

A group of local officers who had been friendly with the NMU but were not party people emerged as the leaders of the strike and the union that grew out of it. Maloney, Shuster, and Cappellini had a long history of trouble with Lewis and his henchmen, but they were so strongly supported by their rank and file that he was never able to get rid of them. At first the backbone of the movement was a series of insurgent locals within the UMWA, and it might have remained that way if the rebels had not been viciously attacked by the UMWA officials, who actively sought to smash the strike. The union bureaucrats put pressure on local officials who supported the strike and urged individual miners to cross the picket lines.

The strikers, like those in the 1927–1928 strike in the central bituminous fields, thought they had no choice but to establish an independent organization. Every mine shut down by the strike became a local of the breakaway union. The informal leaders of the strike were elected as officers of the new union, the Anthracite Mine Workers of Pennsylvania. They set up their own organizational machinery, collected dues, and launched a variety of strike-support activities. .

With the UMWA officials actively encouraging unemployed miners to go into the struck mines, the new union saw the support of the unemployed movement, now quite strong, as absolutely essential. For our part the Party people and others in the councils strongly supported the new union because it had the mass of miners behind it wherever it set up locals. Like any new union, it had strong spots and weak ones. Its greatest strength was in the Wilkes-Barre/Scranton area, while in the lower end, Minersville, Shamokin, and Pottsville, it never really broke through. This district of the UMWA, District 9, was led by Marty Brennan, one of the better officials in the union. He ran the district more democratically than others and, as a consequence, the new union was correspondingly weak there.

The councils supported the new union and the strike in a number of ways. I was invited to speak before locals where I assured members that the councils pledged themselves to keep unemployed miners from scabbing. Leaflets were distributed among the unemployed, and many of those active in the councils became local leaders of the strike.

The success of coal-mining strikes has always depended on the degree to which the entire community could be mobilized to support the strikers, and this wildcat strike against both the operators and the union bureaucracy was no different. The councils' support was only one element in a broad mobilization of people and resources. One of the most unusual developments in this case was the appearance of a "children's strike," in which the school children of Wilkes-Barre and the surrounding towns "struck" their schools and actually picketed them in support of their fathers' cause. The women also played a major role, helping to maintain morale and holding families together. Everyone was well versed in the issues of the strike, and it was the constant topic of conversation wherever you went. As in all coal strikes, the people held a deep hatred for those who returned to work.

Six or eight weeks into the strike, things began to come apart. Some miners drifted back to work, and those still out made reprisals. Strikers drove through coal towns throwing small sticks of dynamite onto the porches of those known to have gone back to work. Although some people were hurt, the attacks occurred at night when no one was on the porches, and fortunately there were no deaths. The Party people condemned such tactics and worked to secure broad support for the strike locally. But the operators secured an injunction to halt picketing, and when the strikers violated it, thirty local leaders were arrested and kept in jail. This accelerated the collapse of the strike.

The story ends in tragedy. Just before the new union's regional conference in Wilkes-Barre, bombs were sent to some members of the coal operators' executive board, several public officials, the sheriff, leaders of the union, and some judges. Out of a dozen bombs mailed in cigar boxes, only the one sent to the president of the new union, Thomas Maloney, exploded, killing him instantly. After an investigation, the sheriff arrested no one from the coal companies, no one from the United Mine Workers, no one from the strikebreakers, but a man from the union's executive board, a German anarchist by the name of Fugman.

I knew Fugman well and worked with him during the strike. He had been a skilled miner in the Ruhr and was respected by his fellow miners. The case against him was so weak that the prosecution had to cook up a story totally unrelated to the union and the events of the strike. Maloney was accused of having relations with Fugman's wife, a lie according to all who knew the two men. Allegedly he killed Maloney out of jealousy. The old German never knew what hit him. A close personal friend of Maloney, he was shaken by the man's death and yet had to defend himself against the charge of murdering him.

In every poolhall and saloon and on every street corner, miners asked one another the same question. How was it that out of all the bombs sent to officials, coal operators, the sheriff, and the judges, the only one to explode was that sent to Maloney, the miners' leader? Nevertheless, the incident generated such fear that it diverted attention from the main problems of winning the strike and determining who was really responsible for the murder.

This poor immigrant miner pleaded innocent and called for support. It was obviously a frame-up, but the only people who came to his aid were the left wingers in the area. One other who helped was a fine liberal by the name of Jennings who owned a small printing shop in Wilkes-Barre. He printed everything free of charge for the union during the strike and invested a lot of money in Fugman's defense. But soon he himself was arrested on some trumped-up charge, and people had to organize a defense committee for him.

We did the best we could to build a defense for these two men, but neither had much of a chance. Jennings spent some time in prison, and poor Fugman was sent to the electric chair. We were sick over the outcome and felt terrible that we couldn't do more. Throughout the trial the defense committee feared that the prosecutor would somehow try to make politics the issue, and it would have been easy. For this reason the defense committee discouraged ILD involvement. The coal companies got away with murder in Fugman's case, and the implication was that they could do the same to others.

When the strike was smashed and the new union with it, the spirit that brought the rebellion to life did not die but fed directly into a new venture, the Luzerne County Labor Party. Several who had led the strike and held positions in the Anthracite Miners of Pennsylvania were convinced by the experience of the strike and the frame-up that there was no hope of working with Democratic or Republican politicians and that it was essential for the miners to have an independent political voice.

The Luzerne County Committee of the Party and the leadership of the councils worked with the new Labor Party from the beginning. We made up a slate of people who had been active in the new union and put them up for the positions of sheriff and county commissioners in the 1934 election. None of us expected to seize control of the local government. The defeated strikers took a practical view of politics: if they could win those offices, maybe they could keep the police off their backs.

In the course of the strike, injunctions had been issued, strikers had been jailed for picketing, the president of the union had been murdered, and then his friend and union brother was framed for the deed. It was reasonable to expect that the rank and file miners would lose faith in the system and try to win some degree of control so that the same thing wouldn't happen again. But history doesn't always move as fast as we might like. In extraordinary moments of social upheaval we can sometimes break through traditional views and strike out in a new direction, but generally the process takes a long time. Most anthracite miners and their families were not prepared to make the break. We suffered a landslide defeat, garnering only about 5 percent of the vote.

To some extent our failure can be explained in terms of the usual problems facing a new political party. It was practically impossible, for example, to get any kind of publicity, since all the local papers were tied in with one party or the other. Finally Heffernan of the *Wilkes-Barre Independent* ran a picture of our slate in his Sunday edition, but most people remained pretty ignorant of the new party's program.

Beyond such practical problems, however, there was a serious tactical mistake. Some of the local union leaders who were close to the CP came to us with the idea of a new party, and we jumped at the chance to be part of a labor party movement. We failed to investigate how much support there really was for such a move. Would other unions and organizations come out for it? Should we call some sort of regional conference first to test the water?

The Party organization itself was not badly hurt by the experience. In fact, some of the union people who'd been active in the campaign joined the Party, while others continued to work with us. But the message was well taken. As the character of the local Democratic organization began to change with the coming of the New Deal, we made every effort to work with the more progressive politicians.

The fact that the Party continued to run its own candidates during the early New Deal may give the wrong impression of our attitude toward the Democratic Party. We supported pro–New Deal candidates and ran our own people largely for propaganda purposes. In 1936 I ran for the Pennsylvania state legislature on the Communist ticket and didn't get more than two hundred votes, although I was a vice-president of the state Workers' Alliance, a national union for public works employees.[5] As a result, I was well-known throughout the region for my work with local councils. We had more than two hundred Party members, and we had hundreds of sympathizers in the five hard-coal counties, but people went with the Democratic swing. I can't say that I blamed them. Luzerne County had long been controlled by the Republicans. The Democrats never adequately represented the interests of workers, but they offered a chance for change at that time.

My campaign gave me an opportunity to explain what a socialist government could do about the problem of unemployment, but it also allowed us to raise other issues, particularly the need to support the young CIO unions and to join the struggle against fascism. While our presence in the campaign may not have offered us any hope of sharing in political power, it did allow us to bring socialist ideas before workers.

Earl Browder's campaign that same year demonstrates how we ran our own candidates but still supported the New Deal. His motto and the whole tone of his campaign was "Defeat Landon at All Costs." In this way he sought to give critical support to FDR. We wanted to work with the liberal wing of the Democratic Party and to achieve a certain amount of legitimacy as a party of the Left. We held a rally for Browder in the Wilkes-Barre armory, which held over three thousand people, and the place was jammed. Many in the audience were rank and file Democrats. We didn't get their votes on election day, but that's not what counted to us. They were coming to recognize us as friends.

For years there had been essentially no difference between Democrats and Republicans: both had represented the interests of the coal companies. Now there was a feeling that Roosevelt was doing something to relieve the problem of unemployment, and that signified a real change. People identified with the government as basically pro-labor. We had no illusions. The Democrats were still a capitalist party, but they were an alternative to the Republicans and were delivering the Wagner Act, Social Security, unemployment insurance, public works, and other badly needed reforms.[6]

The Party was successful in the anthracite fields during the thirties. The organization itself expanded from perhaps fifty members to more than two hundred between 1931 and 1937; and even more impressive were the mass organizations it played an important role in building, particularly the Bootleg Miners Union and the unemployed councils. We led a great demonstration to Harrisburg in 1934 and trained dozens of organizers in little and big towns throughout the region. Nor were such successes isolated events. In New York, Wisconsin, Minnesota, and elsewhere, the Party was building coalitions with New Deal Democrats and Farmer-Labor types. Communists were vital to the organization of the CIO, the most active and successful labor federation the nation had seen since the old Knights of Labor.[7] The importance of our position in the struggle against fascism was broadly acknowledged, even by those who disagreed with us on other issues. How had the Party grown from a small isolated sect in the twenties to a significant political force in the thirties?

Part of the answer, of course, can be found in the peculiar characteristics of the decade. It's hard to appreciate the depth of the crisis that the capitalist system faced in the thirties. With fifteen to eighteen million people unemployed, the Communists' claim that the system was collapsing and should be replaced was a lot harder to dismiss than it had been in the twenties. But these economic conditions only provided an opportunity for the Party to grow and enter the mainstream of working-class life. Specific changes in the character of the Party itself from the beginning of the Depression explain why we were able to take advantage of this opportunity. The real key, I believe, was a greater flexibility in our mass work that was inseparable from the vital question of recruitment.

Through our contacts in the unemployed councils, trade unions, and other mass organizations, we gradually came to recognize that the old sectarian approach, with its emphasis on abstract theory and rhetoric, constant adulation of the Soviet Union, and a hostility toward all radicals outside the Party, would not work. We concentrated instead on issues of vital concern to working people. This new approach brought us into contact with many more people, and we recruited vigorously. As people began to enter the Party through their experiences in mass organizations like the councils, thousands who had not shared the sectarian experiences of the previous decade constantly reinforced the voices of those of us within the Party who argued for a broader and more flexible approach.

In this sense the changes in the Party during the thirties reflected more than a change in tactics; there was a change in attitudes, especially among those most active in mass work. Once this new broader view was infused into the organization, it was never quite the same. It was no coincidence that in the crisis of 1956–1957, when there was a call for changes in the Party's whole approach to the struggle in the United States, it was people with such experience who responded.

The policy known as the Popular Front was officially formulated by Georgi Dimitrov, president of the Communist International, at its Seventh Congress in 1935.[8] It proposed a worldwide alliance of all progressive political forces to protect democracy against the danger of fascism. But as a tactical response to the problems facing Communist organizers throughout the world, a kind of "popular front" concept had certainly been growing for some time before this. The key to our successes was the idea of organizing around the most serious problems facing workers by taking the broadest possible approach and making an effort to work with any individual or group in the struggle. Such an approach provided a chance to break down racial, ethnic, political, and other barriers that divided workers from one another. By uniting in a struggle around a specific shared concern, people with little else in common came to appreciate the crucial importance of working together.

One of the most moving examples of this kind of breakthrough concerned two old miners in the little town of Plymouth. Both were Lithuanians nearing sixty, and they worked in the same mine, but here the similarities ended. The first was a staunch Party member in the old mold, dedicated but also extremely sectarian, especially on the question of religion. The other was a pillar of the local church and a leader in the fraternal lodge. Each was articulate and righteous in his own way, but the issue of religion caused them to see one another as the very incarnation of all that was evil.

When the local council was formed in Plymouth, the first meeting took place in the Catholic miner's basement. He had a son who went away to study for the priesthood but changed his mind and returned to go into the pits with his father. The seminary had given him an education far superior to that of the average anthracite miner, and he developed as a natural leader in the unemployed movement. Father and son threw themselves into the organizing with a vengeance, and because of their ties they were able to involve a larger group from the church than might otherwise have been the case. Council meetings were opened with Hail Marys and Our Fathers, but the Plymouth council was one of the most militant and effective in the region.

The Communist miner was disoriented for a time: all his preconceptions were crumbling. But he soon recognized the importance of what was happening. I talked with him a few months after the council was organized, and he told the story with tears in his eyes. "He was always a good union man," he said. "We were members of the same local and worked together in the mine. Our kids grew up and went to school together. I divided myself from him all these years by making religion and the Soviet Union the most important issues rather than working with him on problems we had in common." It was the reality of the struggle against unemployment that brought these men together.

There were even deeper divisions in the anthracite than those existing between these two old Lithuanians. Minersville and Higgins are both mining towns in Schuylkill County, and they shared many of the problems characteristic of such communities. Unemployment had devastated both. But it would be hard to imagine two towns more different in terms of ethnic and religious composition and political climate.

Minersville was inhabited largely by foreign-born workers—Lithuanians, Ukrainians, Russians, and Germans. The Lithuanians were the most organized; they had cultural and literary groups and a number of fraternal organizations and they exerted a progressive influence in the town. It was a situation in which the natural social and cultural atmosphere of a town reinforced class consciousness and political radicalism. It was almost as if a man was not a good Lithuanian or Russian unless he was also a militant union member. Even those who were neither Party members nor sympathizers respected the Lithuanian Communists, for they knew the role they played in the community. The immigrants' radicalism was also reinforced by the town's older traditions. Minersville's reputation for militancy went back to the days of the Molly Maguires in the 1870s, and before the First World War the town had been the scene of a number of bitter textile strikes led by Socialists. The older workers could still remember the visits of Eugene Debs, Elizabeth Gurley Flynn, and other radicals.[9]

During the thirties Minersville produced more than its share of Party activists and organizers for the unemployed movement. Carl Herman, Paul Rauch, and Peter Paul were all miners who had been active in the Left opposition within the UMWA and had become leaders in the local unemployed council when they lost their jobs. Minersville always seemed to organize more rallies, raise more money, and send more people on marches to Harrisburg and Washington than any other town. The activists there arranged picnics, bingo and baseball games, and other events that became the focal points of social life in the community.

In the course of planning for the 1934 Hunger March on Harrisburg, we held a meeting of activists at the Minersville Lithuanian Workers Hall to discuss how we could attract the largest number of people from the towns in the immediate area. Minersville itself was no problem; even the local business people would support the march by providing food and trucks. People also had ideas for approaching those in some of the other towns, but when someone mentioned going over to talk to the miners in Higgins, a dozen protests were heard. I asked what was wrong with the idea.

People explained that although the only mine in Higgins had shut down and the workers there were in very bad shape, they had remained aloof from the unemployed movement because of prejudice against the foreign-born. Families in Higgins went back to Revolutionary War days. Some people were descendants of the Hessian mercenaries who had come to fight for the king of England, and they still spoke a dialect that was a cross between German and English. Extremely clannish, they did not welcome outsiders in their town. The Ku Klux Klan had organized in Higgins, and only two years ago a group had come to Minersville and paraded with sheets over their heads, carrying signs that said, "Foreigners, go back to where you came from!" The Higgins miners were also the last in the area to join the UMWA and had only come in under extreme pressure. When the mine there shut down, many people in Minersville felt that these conservative native-born workers had it coming to them.

In spite of all this, some in the audience felt that we should make an attempt. A meeting was being held that same night in the Higgins High School to discuss the unemployment problem, and after a long debate it was agreed that a delegation should be sent to the meeting. About a dozen people agreed to go.

The people of Higgins had gone several times to the Philadelphia and Reading Coal Company and pleaded with it to reopen the mine on the grounds that there was no other way for them to make a living. The company remained unmoved. We arrived at the meeting just in time to hear the latest delegation to the company report its failure. I passed my little card, identifying me as a member of the Luzerne County Unemployed Councils, up to the chairman of the meeting and asked for permission to speak. The chairman called me to the front of the hall, and I looked out over the crowd of young and old, men and women. In the front rows was a group of older miners showing the familiar blue scars on their hands and faces. They might have been the Minersville Lithuanians or a group from any of the other mining towns. I started by trying to explain that the Depression was a natural product of the system and not their fault. Then I went into a modified version of my "retired mule" speech. I said that we were going to Harrisburg to present our problems to the governor and legislature and to demand that they allocate funds for immediate relief and public works projects. I closed by saying that one would never get anywhere by begging for what was rightfully his.

It was a pretty moderate talk, but it must have seemed radical by Higgins standards. Yet the audience surprised me and my friends from Minersville by bursting into loud applause. There were questions from the floor about how unemployment insurance would work. In the course of answering these, I mentioned that we were also in favor of a pension for the elderly, and this was met with great enthusiasm by the old miners in the first few rows. At the conclusion of the meeting, the minister who had led the delegation to the company said that "the Lord Himself must have sent these people into our midst when we had no other place to turn."

When the gathering for the march on Harrisburg finally took place, it was a thrill to see a truck from Higgins with its banners and the local minister leading the group. They met with the Minersville group, who had arrived first. I like to think that some of those who sat over coffee with their Lithuanian brothers and sisters and discussed common problems with them were the same people who had marched with sheets over their heads two years before. Perhaps as a result of the process begun that night at the high school, each side overcame some of its prejudices and recognized the importance of working together.

But if things were so ripe for change in the thirties, why didn't the Communists lead the working class to revolution? I can hear younger radicals asking, why did you choose reformism? In the first place, there was no such choice to be made. As a Marxist I believed then and still believe that there are stages in social evolution and that revolution occurs when the capitalist system reaches a certain stage of crisis. One should not apply this principle rigidly. There are exceptional situations, especially now in the Third World, where the old neocolonial regimes are so corrupt and the people's oppression so severe that a revolution flares up at a relatively early stage in capitalist development. Cuba, I think, would be a good example of this.

But no one was throwing up barricades in America in the 1930s. Working people were bewildered by the capitalist crisis but not thoroughly disillusioned with the system. What if the isolated little groups in Union Square in New York or Bughouse Square in Chicago decided one day to declare the revolution? In the unlikely event that they won a broad following in such cities, how would they bring the word to the farmers in Tennessee and Alabama, to the ranch hands in Texas? Opposed by the combined might of the military and the state and without the support of the masses, how was this miraculous event to have occurred? It's a utopian notion. The Communists of the thirties didn't plan for a revolution because there was no possibility of one. It was not because they'd been lulled to sleep by New Deal reformism. We concentrated instead on building a mass movement that could one day accomplish such a revolution. And this brings me to the second part of my answer to the young radicals' question.

Some might read this account of organizing in the thirties and picture a Party totally dominated by day-to-day activities aimed at achieving specific reforms, a socialist movement without socialist ideas. Such a view is very misleading and misses the most important aspect of what communism in the thirties was all about.

The Communist Party accomplished an important process of political education in the thirties. I saw it occur on a local level through the lives of dozens of working people in the anthracite fields. Many came into the unemployed councils apolitical, never having been a member of any kind of mass organization. Some responded to the Party's educational efforts and became effective organizers and speakers with a broad socialist conception of society.

It was not as mechanical as it sounds, of course. For everyone who went the whole route, there were countless others who came in and out or just came once, never to be seen again. The Party had a turnover rate of more than one half its membership even in the best of times. A number of authors have emphasized international events in explaining why people left, but I think it had more to do with the nature of our recruitment. Many people joined through an interest in a particular problem. Shamokin was a long way from Moscow, and people in the anthracite were primarily focused on the problem of unemployment, not the Comintern line. This meant that many who joined were not prepared to devote a lifetime to revolutionary activity. Yet their involvement in the unemployed movement brought them into contact with the Party's political education work.

The anthracite was an area where new militants had little education and might have some very backward attitudes. We had to deal with some serious problems of male chauvinism, for example, and I don't simply mean that women were expected to do the dishes. It was not unusual in the region for a man to verbally abuse or beat his wife, and charges were sometimes brought up at Party committee meetings. Although some good Party people resented this intervention, feeling that it was personal business, we took action on such cases. But we didn't immediately expel people either. How far can you bend the stick before it breaks? Do you really want to break it, or are you trying to shape it? We took a similar attitude toward racial and ethnic prejudice. The Communists may be proud that in an era when bigotry was widespread, it was never tolerated in the Party. But the goal was always to reeducate, especially if the offenders were otherwise solid. If they persisted in their prejudices, they were cut loose from the movement. There was an endless stream of educational meetings, Party schools, and other functions designed to educate the recruits in the basic principles of Marxism and give them a socialist vision of society.

We also had professionals and intellectual Party people come from Philadelphia and New York to give special classes. One series of lectures might deal with the economics of capitalism—the causes of unemployment and depression—and another with the problem of imperialism. We constantly raised issues of national and international importance that otherwise might never have reached the anthracite fields. Margaret was especially active speaking before church and fraternal groups about the implications of the Scottsboro Boys case.[10] Blacks were a tiny, almost invisible minority in the region, and the Communists were the only ones to bring what we then called the Negro question before the anthracite miners and their families. I saw unemployed miners, immigrant housewives like Stella, even people like Gus go through the same explosions of political and intellectual awakening that I had experienced. It was a beautiful thing.

Sometimes we would gather young people, mostly YCL members, from all the little towns for a two-week course in Wilkes-Barre. They stayed in peoples' homes, and we supplied beans, potatoes, rice, and whatever other food we could find. Then some of them would be sent to the national school in New York.

It did not always work. We kept the Crystal Ballroom clean and decorated so that when it wasn't being used for meetings it could revert to its original function. But there were a lot of young people around, and some of them were attracted to the YCL. Around 1935, we decided to hold classes with about fifteen of them, but most turned out to be more interested in the YCL's dances than its politics. Each had played some role in the councils, but they just weren't ready for long discussions of Marxism. They made humorous cracks, and sometimes the classes were bedlam. We decided that the size of the class was part of the problem and picked out the five or six most serious kids. They came to classes with the regular Party members, and three or four stuck with it and became active.

To the extent that a broad, flexible approach to mass work can be seen as part of a Popular Front atmosphere, much of our work in the anthracite fields was guided by this concept long before the front was formally declared in 1935. But it's important to remember that Dimitrov meant something more specific when he used the term in addressing the Comintern's Seventh Congress. He was referring to those broad Left political coalitions that were already forming in France and Spain in the face of a growing fascist threat, and he was suggesting them as a model for all Communists and progressives throughout the world. In this sense the theory represented a shift of emphasis from the everyday struggles of industrial workers and the unemployed to a focus on the one great struggle that came to dominate the world scene from the late 1930s through the Second World War: the conflict between fascism and democracy. As I watched events unfold in Europe, I found myself making the same shift. I was about to enter this conflict on its first great battlefield.

SEVEN

Civil War in Spain: 1937–1938

During the thirties, we tried to sink roots and stimulate action on the immediate issues confronting the American people. Two years abroad had gotten the wanderlust out of my system, and I was content to settle back into the mountains and coal patches of eastern Pennsylvania. Our daily activities there revolved around matters of survival—evictions, relief, bootleg coal, and the unemployed councils. Our focus rarely went beyond Harrisburg, the state capital, or Washington, D.C. Yet that is not to say our sense of the globe had shrunk.

Once made aware of the tragedies unfolding in Europe, I could not ignore them. Those of us around the movement followed the ascent of fascism in Italy and Germany with a mixture of horror and resolve; horror at the rapid and thorough destruction of the trade unions, civil rights, and the Italian and German radical movements; resolve that we would be more than idle spectators.[1] As the picture appeared to me, there were two rivals on the world scene. There was an increasingly menacing fascist bloc and the countering force of the Soviet Union. The intensity and scope of the crisis suggested that the Western nations would be unable to sit this one out. They would have to go one way or the other. While the Soviet Union called for collective security agreements with the West and the Balkans to isolate fascism on the international scene, we raised these questions in the anthracite. At meetings, in our paper, and on our radio show, we urged a boycott of German goods, condemned Germany's racial theories, and tried to explain what was going on there.

It was not easy to develop a movement around European events. People were preoccupied with making it through the week and felt they had enough to worry about already. The First World War had left a bitter taste in many people's mouths, and the sense that we were secure behind our Atlantic and Pacific walls was strong. Moreover, there were forces in this country, loosely grouped around the Hearst newspapers and the Liberty League, which argued that we could do business with Hitler. We countered with a "Don't Buy Nazi Goods" campaign and urged Congress to join with the Soviet Union and Western Europe in a pact of collective security. We called attention to the fate of imprisoned German unionists and political prisoners like Ernst Thaelmann, leader of the German Communist Party. But being thousands of miles away, mostly we watched.

I read about it in the papers each day. As a matter of fact, I would read about what was going on in Europe before I looked at what was happening in Washington or Wilkes-Barre—even though my everyday work was locally oriented nitty-gritty organizing. It wasn't always possible to make the links between the two. There wasn't what you could call a really concrete fascist presence in the anthracite coalfields. Legalities were now observed, if in a peculiar way at times. This made the task of educating people to the significance of European developments that much harder.

Spain edged closer to center stage in the drama of the 1930s. On the one hand, forces patterned after the fascism of Mussolini and Hitler grew in strength. On the other, the politicization of both peasants and industrial workers there spawned flourishing anarchist, socialist, and communist movements. The impulse for social and political change welled up out of the miners of Asturias, the dockworkers and cafe waiters of Seville, and from thousands in and around Saragossa, Barcelona, and elsewhere. In the middle teetered the Monarchists, renounced at the polls and unable to retain a grip on power. Electoral struggles alternated with armed uprisings and attempted coups. In this cauldron a unity of antifascist forces emerged, bringing together in coalition for the 1936 elections not only the Communists, Socialists, and anarchists but the bourgeois democratic Republicans as well.

The capacity of these different and historically antagonistic groups to cooperate and weld themselves into a potent political movement had a significance that went beyond Spain. It was both a stimulus and a reflection of changes the Communist movement was undergoing worldwide. The Seventh Congress of the Communist International, the first since 1928, evaluated the experiences of the last seven years. They had been disastrous. A skeptical attitude toward bourgeois democracy and contempt for social democrats and socialists had contributed to the frighteningly easy consolidation of fascism in Germany. In his speech at the Congress, the influential Bulgarian Communist Georgi Dimitrov, emerging from a Nazi prison after being framed for the Reichstag fire of 1933, had argued for changing our attitude toward both bourgeois democracy and social democrats. Communists must place a new emphasis on building the broadest possible alliance of forces to stop fascism and hold on to "every inch of democratic gains made by the working class," he stressed. Continuing hostility among leftists would be suicidal, as it had been in Germany. The actions of the Left in Spain preceded this Comintern reevaluation. There the threat of a fascist takeover was as real as it had been in Germany and Italy and the rethinking of communist strategy had come earlier.

We watched with joy the victory of this Popular Front in Spain at the polls in 1936. The people had once again opted for a democratic Republic. And then months later in France, another popular front brought an alliance of left forces to political power there. It seemed as if the fasicst tide had begun to recede.

Suddenly, on July 18, 1936, newspaper dispatches brought word of a rebellion by rightist armed forces in Spain. For eight days we hung on every bit of information we could obtain, following the almost spontaneous defense of the Republic as people rallied to its aid in Madrid and Valencia, Bilbao and Santander, taking over barracks and weapons to form a civilian army. In savage fighting throughout Spain, the coup was beaten back. At least two thirds of Spain was in Loyalist hands, and the fascist-backed military rebellion seemed doomed. Armed units of anarchists, trade unionists, Socialists, and Communists were mobilized along with small units of the armed forces that had remained loyal to the Republic. But as time passed, the rebels gained increasing support from Hitler and Mussolini, and soon Spanish skies were filled with German and Italian warplanes. Intervention from the fascist bloc renewed the threat to the survival of the Republic. Francisco Franco, head of the revolt, counted on not only German and Italian military supplies and logistical aid but the very presence of their troops on Spanish soil.

When Franco, Hitler, and Mussolini attacked Spain, the die was cast. No longer could our campaigns be confined to agitation. The tragedy of the Spanish struggle strained the nerves of every conscientious man and woman, much in the way that Vietnam was the focal point of more recent times. In July we had been swept away by the heroism of the populace. By the fall we were warned that the menace was again serious. Fascist forces were moving on to Madrid, and their leader, General Mola, announced he would have tea there at the Puerto del Sol on October 12. It was hard to see what could stop him. But somehow, despite the odds, the cry "No pasarán!" was raised in Madrid, and the defenses steadied and repulsed the fascist attack.

Republican Spain issued an appeal for aid, but the Western countries, fearful of antagonizing Hitler and skeptical about the Left's participation in the Popular Front, held back their support. France, despite a treaty with Spain and the presence of the Popular Front government headed by the Socialist Léon Blum, bowed to internal pressures and British threats and opted for a policy of nonintervention. Thus Spain was cut off from its logical source of military supplies. The United States followed suit as Congress, by passing the so-called Neutrality Act, voted in January 1937 to ban shipments of war materials to Spain. Only Minnesota Farmer-Labor Party Congressman John Bernard voted against it. These diplomatic measures equated the legally elected Republican government with the fascist rebels. Even this attitude of noninvolvement was a sham, for while the United States pressured Mexico not to allow the resale of planes it bought to Spain, our country permitted the sale of arms to Germany and Italy that were then shipped directly to Franco. Consequently Republican Spain was virtually isolated internationally, its biggest source of aid the Soviet Union, while Franco could count on full backing from his German and Italian cohorts. But if the Western governments idly watched the spread of fascism, many of their citizens did not.

We began to read that groups of emigré Germans and Italians, antifascists living in exile, were arriving in Madrid to serve in the defense of the city. Volunteers from France and battalions of Czechs, Yugoslavs, Poles, Hungarians, and British soon joined them. Many of them died defending Madrid in the fall of 1936, but they bought precious breathing space for the embattled Republic.

Many of us in the United States knew we had to move beyond passing resolutions that urged our government to aid Spain, and the example of the European volunteers was part of the answer. The Party set up a Committee for Technical Aid for Democratic Spain in New York to organize people who were willing to go to Spain. From Wilkes-Barre we took carloads of people to Philadelphia to hear André Malraux, the French writer, and John Strachey, the British political theorist, appeal for support. On the ride back we discussed when we were going to do something ourselves.

Soon we got a message from New York that volunteers were being solicited and that I should survey who was willing to go from the anthracite. They thought it best to send only men under a certain age and, if at all possible, those with some military experience. Most of our World War vets were already pretty old, but we were willing nonetheless. Eight men decided to volunteer from the Wilkes-Barre area. I was among them: I felt that I couldn't ask anyone to do things that I wasn't prepared to do myself. Most of the eight were either coal miners or unemployed miners, and all were active in either the unemployed councils, the Young Communist League, or the Party. At thirty-four I was one of the older men going.

But when the time came to go, the District Committee in Philly rejected my application, arguing that I was needed in the anthracite. Three or four weeks later, however, I got a phone call saying that if I was still prepared to go, the road was open. The committee indicated that recent events in Spain had changed the situation drastically. In February and March 1937, the American volunteers had suffered heavy casualties on the battlefields of Jarama. A minor crisis resulted due to the number of leaders wounded and killed or simply unable to stand up to it. The American Party thought that I might be able to help fill the gap. I discussed the matter with Margaret, and she was of the same mind as I. "You know what's right as well as I do," she said, "but the choice is yours to make." Without telling too many people goodbye, I left Wilkes-Barre and headed for Philadelphia and then New York City. We were set to sail on the *Queen Mary* in March 1937.

I want to be very clear when I say that the struggle in Spain was to defeat the fascist attempt to destroy the democratic Republic. Our purpose throughout three years of civil war was not to set up some sort of workers' republic, be it socialist, anarchist, or what have you. That was not the aim of the Popular Front government elected in 1936 nor was it how we understood the demands of the times. Certainly I have always wanted to see Spain ultimately develop into a socialist society, but we fought there for more limited but no less vital objectives— Spain's survival as a democracy and the defeat of fascism.

The Popular Front did not pit class against class. Instead it brought petty bourgeois and bourgeois elements together with liberals, peasants, workers of various political persuasions, and Left organizations that united basically to save the democratic Republic. There was clearly a progressive content to the political program of the Popular Front that would have extended civil liberties, strengthened the bargaining power of workers, and spurred land reform. And there were openly revolutionary currents within it. Yet the goal of the Popular Front was not a socialist republic. Large segments of the front, a majority I believe, would not have gone along with more revolutionary aims. The front's unity, was based on antifascism and a commitment to democracy and a republican form of government.

On the *Queen Mary* there were about one hundred men bound for

Spain. Nearly every one of them had a friend or two on board. I had known Joe Dallet from Chicago, and Joe Dougher was a buddy from the anthracite. They were all "tourists," although some had hands calloused from pick and shovel, some had necks burned red by the sun, and some carried in the lines of their hands the black grime of the assembly line, of mines and steel mills and shipyards. On board we hardly ever talked about Spain and avoided political discussion. We just tried to look like we were tourists on the way across.

At my table were a Boston merchant and his wife and a middle-aged fur buyer for a New York department store, a Mr. Berg. They discussed many topics, including the war in Spain, but when Spain was mentioned I clammed up. I was proud of my circumspection and was more than a little startled when, on debarking, Mr. Berg slipped an envelope into my hand and whispered, "Good luck where you're going." The envelope contained a ten-dollar bill.

We docked at Le Havre and took the train to Paris. I went to see Arnold Reid, who handled arrangements for getting volunteers into Spain. "Here's how we stand," he said. "They're shipping out as fast as possible, but we have to be careful. We can't risk a collision with the French government; we can't give them an excuse to shut us down. The borders are sealed, and if a volunteer's caught, it's jail and deportation. This damned nonintervention is making it difficult to get men across. Some of the boys have to wait a long time—too long. The Volunteers' Committee has them scattered around under cover. Ever hear of the Red Belt? Most villages around Paris—working-class districts on the outskirts—have Communist or Socialist mayors and councils. They're taking care of most of our fellows. I think I can get you and Joe in soon, but don't count on it."

There were twenty-five men leaving in our group, of which Joe Dallet, who spoke French, was the leader. I had seen some of them on the boat coming over. The rest were strangers, but you could spot them. We were scattered throughout the railroad station in clusters of fives—American tourists, most of us in our early twenties, wearing berets, and carrying no luggage. Fine tourists. We stood around, conspicuously trying to be inconspicuous, eyeing each other and watching Joe. I was glad to be going with Joe and glad to be moving toward the frontier after only four days' delay in Paris.

The train announcer called our departure for Arles, and at Joe's signal, we rushed on board. Obeying earlier instructions, we spread out through the cars, two or three to a compartment. Joe and I found a place together near the middle of the train. He was full of excitement and responsibility. The men too were excited, and no one slept much that night. We kept telling each other we ought to sleep so as to be fresh for our hike over the mountains—for we all believed we would cross the Pyrenees into Spain the following night. Instead, we played pinochle and talked.

At dawn Joe noticed a peasant woman selling milk on the platform of a station where the train had halted. He bargained with her and returned triumphantly to the compartment carrying her whole supply, a two-gallon earthenware jar more than half full. All at once a horrified look came to his face. "Steve, everybody'll know I can't use this much milk myself! My God, I'll give the whole show away." But a brown-bearded man—already dubbed "the Professor"—had noticed some bottles in another compartment. The bottles were rinsed and filled with milk and passed around to the tourists. Within a half hour the milk was gone.

After an all-night ride we left the train at Arles, where a man in a yellow sweater stood on the platform, as Arnold had foretold. Joe stared at the man and gripped the right lapel of his coat. At this signal the man nodded and beckoned carelessly and walked away. Joe followed him. I followed Joe, the Professor followed me, and so on. Twenty-five men were strung out in single file, each one scared of losing sight of the man in front. It was an odd sight for the streets of a quiet little French town. Presently we realized we were making a show of ourselves, and we formed little groups of two or three, strolling carelessly. The man in the yellow sweater led us to the other side of town, where an ancient stone building stood beside a little stream.

It was the former poorhouse and had been fixed up for us. Joe learned that the mayor was one of us and that the little town of Arles was already taking care of seventy-five Spanish refugees besides all the volunteers that came through, all out of the people's own pockets. In addition to us, there were fifty other Americans awaiting their trip into Spain.

We were dismayed to find we had to stay overnight and that the others had been waiting for four days. Joe reassured us that if we had to stay a day or two, it was because it was necessary. There was no point in complaining.

We crossed the alley to an enormous building, stone below and clapboard on the second floor, where we were to sleep. The lower floor had been a stable. We climbed wide rickety stairs to the loft, and Lew Secundi, who was later to become transport officer for the International Brigades, came to greet us in his fluent Brooklynese. "Hiya, gang! Welcome to the Hotel des Antifascistes."

The "old-timers" gathered around to welcome us and show off the establishment. A potbellied stove stood on either side of the loft, and bales of straw were stacked against the walls. We were warned to be careful of fire. There were blankets in a corner, and the straw was to be our mattresses. There was not a light in the place, and everyone went to bed at dusk.

The first arrivals had established a routine of living, and Lew explained the rules at a joint meeting called immediately. "Now, guys, we got to make the best of this. After all, we're in for tougher things than this. I hope there'll be no complaining. You'll find there's an awful lot of work living in a place like this. In order to make things go smoother, we elected a house committee of three men. I suggest you fellows also elect three to that committee." We did that and settled in and waited.

Two days later our contingent moved out. We were taken by auto to another little town, nearer the Spanish border. Joe, I, and three others were quartered in the home of a French carpenter, a Party member, whose wife greeted us like her own sons. All of us appreciated their kindness, but we wanted to get out of France.

Joe and some others were playing cards and the French woman was cooking lunch when a young man wearing leather puttees came in hurriedly and demanded to know who was in charge. Joe stood up. "I am," The man said, "All right, have your gang meet at the park right away. There'll be cars to pick you up. You're moving out."

"Wait a minute," Joe said. "Who are you? How do I know this is on the level?"

"It's all right," the man said. "I'm handling this district. I was going to Spain, but I got stuck here because I can speak French. I'm from Quebec. It's okay, man. Just get down to the park."

We loafed nervously around the park, trying to look like tourists. After a long anxious time, a taxi stopped, and its driver came quickly across the grass. He gave a signal with his right hand, and Joe answered the gesture. The man spoke in French, saying, "Five of you come with me." We got into the taxi and he banged the gears, just about lifting the car off the ground. Looking back, we saw another group of the boys piling into an old touring car.

One of the guys had never ridden in a taxi before. "Boy, this is good! Imagine going to Spain in a taxicab."

"Don't be a sap. How can we be going to Spain when we're bound east?" Joe pointed off to the right, where the Mediterranean lay.

But it was all right. We had come too close to the border and were being taken back to a little port where a boat would pick us up. Still,

I didn't like going back the way we had come, with the border getting farther away instead of closer.

After an hour or so, the taxi stopped beside a long stretch of beach. There were a few little houses like summer cottages, with the windows boarded up, and a small stone pier stretching out into the water. We could see a village a mile or so away, and that was all. One by one other cars rolled up and stopped, until all twenty-five of us had been deposited on the beach. Each group as they arrived said the same things: "What the hell is this? Where are we? Where's the boat?" And to each group Joe answered, "It'll be here. Take it easy." But Joe did not look easy. He was worried and glanced often out to sea. We were so conspicuous on the barren beach that anyone who saw us would know why we were there.

One. One-thirty. Two in the morning. We had been there since five the previous evening. Joe came over and whispered, "Maybe they can't find the place. Maybe they overshot us in the dark. If we're still here in the morning, all the gendarmes in France will be down on us." I said nothing, but Joe went on. "I got to do something," he said. But there was really nothing we could do.

Finally the boat came. The sleepers on the cottage verandas were kicked awake, and everyone ran for the pier, stumbling and falling in the soft sand and swearing excitedly. The boat was about thirty feet long, pointed at bow and stern, with a single mast and a one-cylinder engine. It was manned by two French fishermen. Joe, who had stood on the pier counting noses, was the last man aboard, and finally the boat began to move.

France was behind us. We were on a boat, and the boat was taking us to Spain. Some of the men shook hands solemnly, and others capered on the deck and cheered quietly. They stood around the deck trying to keep out of the way of the second boatman, who was setting the sail. They were anxious for him to get through with his work because Joe had told them that he would bring out food as soon as the boat was under way.

Joe was talking French to the man who stood at the tiller. From time to time he paused to translate hastily. The French comrades had been laboring over their engine since earliest morning. Moreover, the mayor of their village, a man unfriendly to the cause, had sent gendarmes to observe them, and it had been necessary to satisfy the gendarmes. They apologized for their lateness and brought greetings to the Americans from the comrades of their village. They wished us to know that this boat had been purchased with money raised by the Party branch of their village—the gift of the French comrades to the

Spanish people in their struggle. The men nearest the helmsman patted him on the back when they heard that. The boat represented a lot of money measured by the incomes of a handful of fishermen, railroad workers, teachers, and dock workers, and we knew that.

A dim glow came from the forward hatchway. Down in the hold, the second sailor had lit a lantern and was pulling out loaves of bread, long cylinders of sausage, round cheeses, strings of onions, and flasks of thin red wine. He arranged them on the floor of the hold, laying them on the gunnysacks in which they had been packed. He grinned up at the circle of heads peering hungrily over the hatch and motioned to us to come and eat. With the knife from his belt the sailor cut off chunks of bread, cheese, and salami; picked up a small, flat wine flask with a long spout projecting from it; and sprang up the ladder to the deck.

The helmsman said that they usually made the trip in six hours, but with the wind turning against us, they wouldn't be able to use the sail, and it would take longer. It would be light before we approached the Spanish town of Port-Bou.

I sat in the bow, straining my eyes to the right, trying to believe I could glimpse the looming mass of the Pyrenees. A streak of light showed in the east, and Joe called, "It's getting light. We'll have to go down in the hold pretty soon." The streak of light grew broader, and without orders from anyone, we went below. By common consent, in a common weariness, talking ceased, and some fell asleep.

Sunlight filtered through the cracks in the side of the boat and poured through the open hatchway. The air in the hold was thick with gasoline fumes from the engine and the smell of tar and old fish, onions, stale tobacco, and sweaty bodies. Some of the guys were bleary-eyed and others a bit cranky. Shorty Friedman yelled, "Hey! I can see the Pyrenees! *I can see Spain!*" He had his eyes glued to a crack in the planking. The others clustered around him, begging for a look, but he clung to his place. "Go find a peephole of your own. This is mine!"

At the knowledge that they were actually within sight of Spain, the men racketed around the cramped hold, talking and laughing. On deck one of the French sailors had spread fishing nets on frames. Occasionally he grinned down at the roistering Americans. Suddenly he called out to Joe in a sharp voice. Joe immediately commanded, "Something's happened. Everybody quiet."

We were still instantly. The hatch cover slid into place, leaving the hold in semidarkness. From somewhere outside we could hear the rapid throbbing of a diesel.

"Relax," I said. "It's probably a nonintervention patrol. The worst that can happen is we go to jail a while."

We heard a roar of chain slipping through a hawser hole. Joe groaned. "Oh God, they're anchoring! Quiet, everybody. Give me a chance to hear what's being said."

The French comrade, seated casually on the hatch cover, answered questions shouted at him from the patrol boat. Joe whispered translations. "They're asking him for his papers. The other comrade's getting them." Silence. The engines of both vessels were stopped. There was no sound but the lapping of the water against the side, and the heavy breathing of the men crowded in the hold. Then we heard a voice from the patrol boat. "What's he saying, Joe? What's he saying?"

"They want to know what cargo's being carried," Joe whispered. "Furniture, he says, furniture." Joe listened intently. "He's alongside now," he said. "Quick, scram over to the other side! Hurry!"

We crowded against the sides up into the bow, pressing away from the hatchway. We watched the hatchway and tried not to breathe. A streak of light appeared, and we could see the face of a French naval officer. The hatch cover slid back into place. "We're busted!" Joe said. He was still whispering, and none of us moved. "He's giving it to our comrade. 'Furniture!' he says. 'You're lying, Red; that's a fine kind of furniture. Here, catch this rope,' he says. They're going to tow us. Tear up everything you have; all the papers. I've got a list of some of the men who've gone to Spain. Grab some of the sheets—we'll have to eat this list, and do it fast."

Joe shouted in French toward the deck: "Comrade! Can we throw anything in the water?" He listened. "They say to stay down and not move. They're having to stand up there with their hands up. We're being towed to a French port. All you guys! Don't forget, we're American tourists! Everybody stick to that when they question us."

Tourists! Remarkable tourists, ragged, filthy, caught at dawn crammed into the hold of a fishing boat. I whispered to Joe, "We've got to change that story. We can't tell anybody we're tourists now. It's ridiculous."

"I know it's ridiculous. But we can't take it on ourselves to change the decision." Joe spoke aloud, and instantly the others were listening, their eyes intent on the two of us, to whom they looked for leadership.

"Circumstances have changed the decision for us. That cover was never meant for a thing like this. We must tell them we're volunteers for Spain," I insisted.

The men argued back and forth, but the roar of diesels had ceased. I cursed myself for not having foreseen the situation. We had thought of capture, worried about capture, ever since we got into the boat— and now, at the last narrow moment, we debated what to do in the face of capture. But there was not time. The boat was barely moving. "Listen. The French will support us," I argued. "It's our only chance. How can they organize a defense for a bunch of tourists?" I knew I had spoken badly, but some were nodding agreement. Joe, however, was still dubious.

The hatch opened, and we were ordered up on deck. I moved quickly to be first up the ladder. I was now convinced that we had to adopt new tactics.

A voice said, "Well, god almighty, what are we going to say?"

"Tell them the truth!" I answered over my shoulder as I climbed to the deck.

People were gathering on the pier and on the street near by. They had seen the patrol boat coming in with the other vessel in tow and were curious. The crowd, composed mostly of men, kept growing. Nearly all of them wore blue shirts and dungarees, and many had baling hoods stuck under their wide leather belts. I figured they were longshoremen, fishermen, and teamsters. They looked all right to me.

The French officer motioned us toward the gangplank, and the crowd moved closer, trying to get a better look at us. Near the gangplank I halted, snatched the beret from my head, and flung up my clenched fist. "Viva la República Española!" The men in blue shirts and dungarees roared back an answer: "Viva!" Their fists shot up, scores of them. Joe and the others behind me had their fists up too and were yelling. Joe bellowed, "Vive le Front Populaire!" and the crowd's answer shook the air. A gendarme ran up the gangplank and tugged at my arm, shouting. I followed him down the gangway through the ranks of the men in blue shirts and dungarees.

We marched through the cobblestone streets of the ancient town on our way to jail. Children ran into the streets, and women leaned from the windows or came hurrying from stores, shops, and little factories. We marched with our heads and fists up, and we grinned at them and shouted, "Long live the Spanish Republic! Long live the Popular Front!"

After a day in a crowded little jail in Port Vendres, where our boat had been impounded, the French police took us to the prison in Perpignan. The newspapers had headlined our arrests, accusing us of inciting the longshoremen of the port to riot and of defying the police and even the magistrate of the district. For three days we were kept with about fifty other prisoners in a small room pierced only by two tiny windows high up in the vaulted roof.

The American consul arrived on the fourth day, and Joe and I talked with him in the warden's office. He had little interest in our conditions and declined to inspect our cell. What he wanted was our passports, which we refused to give up.

After several days of confinement, I was feeling pretty helpless. On the fifth day, I was sitting on the floor, leaning back against the wall, idly watching Joe converse with a French prisoner on the other side of the room. They were crouching over a man lying next to the rusty coal stove that heated the cell. Joe suddenly beckoned for me to come over. "Look at this guy!"

The man on the floor, thin, dressed in ragged clothes, was scratching his left arm with a contrivance of pins. The arm was raw and bleeding. His shirt was unbuttoned, and his chest was a mess of festering sores. Joe called our guys together and said, "That guy by the stove's got syphilis or leprosy or something—I don't know. But if we get whatever's eating him, we're done for. No Spain. No nothing. Whatever it is, we've got to get him out of here."

We talked it over for a few minutes, and Joe translated our sense of urgency to the other prisoners. We then started banging on the iron doors to the bullpen, screaming for the warden. Within a half hour we had him in the cell looking at the sick man. The sight of the man's chest made the warden nauseous, and he had him taken to the infirmary.

Forcing the warden's hand was a real shot in the arm and won us the respect of the other prisoners, who were now willing to follow our lead. It was only the beginning. After listening to the warden berate us in both French and English, Joe and I presented a set of demands the men had agreed on. Flustered and unfamiliar with an organized presence in his prison, the warden relented. We secured an additional half hour in the yard each day and the right to empty the cans of filth from our cell twice daily and to disinfect them with lime and carbolic acid. Finally we won a transfer for half of the men to another, unoccupied bullpen. It was much like the other one but it felt almost roomy after we had been jammed together for a week.

All the Americans had been transferred, and as soon as we were together, Joe called a meeting. "We've got lots of space now," he said, "and plenty of time. It looks like we'll be here for another two weeks, maybe longer. We can't just sit around. Anybody got any suggestions?"

I didn't, and it didn't seem as if anyone else did, but finally Shorty

Friedman suggested that we organize classes with talks and discussions. The idea caught hold immediately, and before the day was out, the Professor, Shorty, and Tiny Sundstrom, a Finnish-American auto worker, our "school committee," had organized a set of lectures and classes. We set up a daily schedule of physical exercise, classes, free time, and chores and stuck to it more or less for the next two weeks. It was the only thing that made our confinement bearable.

After two weeks Joe and I were called out of the cell and told we were going to Ceret, about twenty kilometers southwest of Perpignan at the foot of the Pyrenees. The court sat there and we would be able to meet with a lawyer from the Popular Front Committee. We were handcuffed and chained together and were marched from the prison to the railroad station. Unshaven and dirty, we looked like pretty rough customers, but more than a few men and women in the streets saluted us with clenched fists and shouted encouragement in French. As we rode toward Ceret, I could see the mountains. I wondered how much of a job it would be to get over them—and if we'd get the chance to try.

We arrived at the courthouse, where small groups of townspeople were gathered. Because the magistrate had not yet arrived, the gendarme permitted us to walk up and down the sidewalk in the sun. Next to the courthouse was a house with a huge bay window facing the street. The window was open, and inside the room a woman was dusting a grand piano. She glanced at us and smiled, and Joe remarked that the piano was beautiful. She asked Joe if he played. He said he did; and at once the woman spoke to the gendarme, telling him to bring us into the house and take off our handcuffs. He saluted respectfully and obeyed; it turned out she was the wife of the local inspector of police.

Joe took off his coat, rolled up his sleeves, filled and lit his pipe, and sat down at the piano. He played some Chopin, a little ragtime, and finished off with the Marseillaise.

A crowd including gendarmes, passers-by, the assistant prosecutor, and other officials, gathered outside the open windows. When Joe finished playing, they applauded enthusiastically. A newspaper photograher came running up and begged Joe to sit at the piano again while he took his picture. Joe was pretty embarrassed about it, but it turned out well. The next day the local papers, even the reactionary ones, had editorials to the effect that the Americans, who at first appeared to be hardened criminals, proved to be men of culture, and they described the concert Joe had given in the police inspector's house. They couldn't figure it out. I couldn't figure it out either. I had known Joe for a long time, but I had not known that he was a talented pianist. I said as much to him on the train back to Perpignan.

He looked away uncomfortably and replied that there were things a lot more important than playing a piano.

"You've been holding out on me," I said.

Joe said, "Nuts! You think I want to go around impressing the comrades with what a hell of a superior guy I am, like a lot of these bloody bourgeois intellectuals? Make them think I'm better than anybody else because I had a chance to learn music—that they never did?"

I didn't answer. A lot of things about Joe became clearer. His "hard" manner. His way of speaking that was deliberately profane and deliberately ungrammatical. A rudeness that in another would have passed unnoticed, but on Joe's lips had a faintly studied air. I had supposed this odd effect flowed from Joe's intensity, his earnestness of character, but I realized now that Joe's manner was a screen that I had never penetrated.

Joe was leaning forward, gazing out the window. There was a lot about him I didn't know, he said, a lot he never talked about. His father was rich, and he had grown up with all the advantages wealth could secure. He stared out at the mountains and started to describe his tour of Europe in 1928.

I could hardly believe what he told me. He had really done it in style—the best hotels, the finest restaurants, and fancy wine. In those days, he explained, he had just one idea in his head; a good time. "I traveled all over Europe, and I saw exactly nothing at all. I didn't know people existed. That brakeman, for instance—to me, he was just a part of the train, like the engine or the doors or the seats. Waiters were just flunkeys. Think of all the millions of lives that I passed by without ever knowing they were there! It was like living inside a soap bubble. I tell you, when I think of those days I just crawl all over!"

I promised Joe I wouldn't mention this to the other men, although we talked about it a number of times. The movement is entitled to the best in its people, and I think Joe realized that just being himself was his way to give it. Besides, most people like Joe who came into the movement and put on a blue shirt and a dese-dem-and-dose accent, speaking out of the sides of their mouths like they thought a worker would, just didn't cut it. It was better when they didn't pretend to be someone other than who they were.

On the seventeenth day after we were jailed, our entire group was taken to Ceret for the trial. Remembering the experience in the port, we were set for a demonstration as we marched through Perpignan en route to the station. But the police too had learned. Buses were drawn up before the jail; the Americans were hustled into them and driven to the train. Nevertheless a crowd had gathered at the station, and the train pulled out to the accompaniment of cheers and singing from the platform.

In Ceret the Popular Front Committee had mobilized the townspeople to greet us. They were lining the main street, crowding the sidewalks. The gendarmes directed the column into narrow back alleys where only dogs and stray cats would witness our passing. But to reach the courthouse it was necessary to enter the main street, and the crowds were waiting. They burst into a roar as we appeared: "Vive l'Espagne! Vive les Brigades Internationales!"

Three hundred people were crowded into the little courtroom, and through the windows I could see more people gathering outside. The judges, three bewigged gentlemen, were also aware of the gathering. They cast nervous glances over the courtroom, out the windows, and at the prisoners who sat before them. They were anxious to begin.

The judges agreed readily to counsel's request that Joe be allowed to speak for the entire group. Joe was asked two questions:

"You are Americans?"

"Americans and Canadians, yes."

"Why did you come to France?"

"In order to reach Spain, to fight in the Loyalist army against fascism."

The last words of his answer were lost in a storm of applause that swept the courtroom. The judges waved their hands for silence, the prosecutor frowned, and the gendarmes threatened to clear the courtroom.

There was no dispute on facts or on the law. The trial consisted of speeches by the prosecution and the defense. The Americans listened intently to the address given by Monsieur Gregory, their French attorney. They did not understand a word he said, but it was perfectly obvious that he was putting his whole heart into his argument. For the moment, he was the front line.

At the close of his address, we were removed to an anteroom while the judges considered their verdict. We crowded around our attorney, pounded his back, and exclaimed, "Bon! Bon! Very bon! Great going kid!" He smiled back at us, delighted by our praise. Within ten minutes Joe and the attorney were called back to the courtroom. Ordinarily all prisoners would have been brought back to hear the sentence, but the judges evidently feared a demonstration.

It was an agonizing wait till the door flew open and Joe rushed in, grinning from ear to ear. In a solemn voice he intoned, "For violating French laws and an international agreement to which France is a signatory, bumble, bumble, bumble, you are sentenced to twenty-one days in prison. Four more days to go, gang! And then eight days to get your fannies out of France."

Six days later, after finishing the sentence and spending a night in a hotel bathtub and a day hidden in a farmhouse outside of town, I was riding on the back of a motorcycle down dark bumpy side roads towards the Pyrenees. The Popular Front Committee had broken up our group, thinking it would be harder for the police to keep track of us. I had no idea where I was when my French cyclist eased to a halt and motioned for me to duck into the woods by the side of the road. I stumbled over something soft, and a Cockney voice cursed heavily.

"I'm sorry, man," I muttered and lay down on the ground and panted for a few minutes. I ventured quietly, "Any Americans here?"

"Steve!" A figure rose out of the darkness and pulled me down.

"Lewis!" Lewis from Chicago. We lay side by side, laughing and calling each other bad names because we were so glad to see each other.

Out of the darkness a voice called softly, "Vámonos, camaradas!" All around us shadows were rising out of the earth. I was amazed at the number, and Lewis told me there were thirty men in our party. They were mostly English and Canadians, with a sprinkling of Americans and others.

We walked through darkness, each man following the steps and heavy breathing of the man in front. We moved through fields, through what appeared to be a vineyard, and through another field to a river. A voice called softly, "Ici! Ici!" and the guide turned toward the voice. My eyes were growing used to the darkness; I could distinguish vague shapes now. The guide and the man who waited by the riverbank took up a long plank, a two-by-twelve, thrust it out over the water. The guide trotted down it. I followed, not happily, teetering above the racing water.

The end of the plank rested on a rock midway across the stream, and a second plank was thrust out from the opposite shore. I made the crossing safely. The guide took me by both arms and pressed down as if fixing me to the earth—indicating that I was to stay there and wait until everyone was across.

We walked for half an hour, then halted, and the guide went down the line with Lewis as interpreter, speaking to each man separately.

We were to keep contact at all times with the man in front. We were not to smoke or cough or make any sound. Whenever a halt was made, each man was to be in touch with the man behind him, and let him know when the line started.

Ten minutes later we stopped again, and the guide spoke quickly to Lewis. Lewis translated, "Pass the word back. We're going to go along between a canal and the river canyon. Hug the left. If you fall off the cliff, you could be killed."

I had heard in prison of a French youth bound for Spain who fell off a cliff and was injured in the fall to the river below. This must have been the place. I dropped willingly to my hands and knees and proceeded with the utmost caution. Beyond a sluice the guide waited anxiously. He seemed vastly relieved to have us safely past that spot.

The ground had tilted up sharply; we were really climbing now, climbing into the black wall of the mountains. The ground was soft and wet. The guide seemed to be leaping from rock to rock, and I tried to copy him, but I immediately missed my footing and sprawled full length in the mud. I seemed to be slipping much more than the others. The trouble, I decided, was with my shoes. They were good shoes, but they had rubber soles, and rubber soles were not good for wet climbing. All the others had been given *alpargatas*—rope-soled sandals that tied around the ankles and were strictly nonskid.

We shuffled cautiously along a ledge on the sheer side of the mountain. Word came up from the rear to stop, and the guide edged past us toward the end of the line. Lewis and I turned and looked down. The lights of Ceret were directly below; it was as if we had climbed a ladder out of the town.

The guide returned, cursing. Two men had missed a turn, and he was furious at their clumsiness. He set a stiff pace. We reached the end of the ledge and started climbing again. The hillside did not look so terribly steep to the eye, but it was steep to the legs and lungs.

We stopped to rest, and a fat little Dutch comrade sank down near me, groaning and panting. He was an older man of forty-five. He stretched his short legs before him and shook his fist at his feet. Lewis and I watched the Dutchman. When the time came to start, he had to struggle to stand up. Within ten yards other men began passing him. A tall Canadian whispered, "We got to go slower. The old boy can't keep up."

Lewis spoke to the guide, and they both went back to the Dutchman. I followed them. Lewis said, "Look, Comrade. We got to get across before morning. It's one o'clock now—ein Uhr. Only four hours.

Must hurry. Mach schnell, ja? Wir mussen schnell machen or something. Versteh?"

The Dutchman looked from Lewis to the guide. "Go ahead," he said. "Go ahead, I try."

We climbed through another heartbreaking hour. The trees were smaller here, and fewer. We crossed patches of soft snow, and then snow that was less slushy, and then we were walking on snow that was dry and frozen and there were no trees at all, only bushes, and the rocks were covered with deep moss. At the crest of a ridge, the guide halted us. "He says we can rest for ten minutes," Lewis said. "We've got to skin along another ledge."

The ledge widened and tipped steeply, and conversation stopped. Lewis called back encouragingly to the Dutchman, and the guide hissed sharply for silence. The ledge ended, and the ground fell away on either side; we had reached the top of the ridge. As soon as the guide stopped, we turned back to the Dutchman. He stood for a moment, staring straight before him. Then his knees buckled, and he toppled and fell forward.

The guide knelt beside the Dutch comrade for a moment and then sprang up. He whipped a long Catalonian knife from the sheath on his belt and with it cut and trimmed two saplings growing nearby. He laid the two poles side by side and spoke to Lewis. "He wants belts," Lewis said. "He's making a stretcher."

Five belts were offered. The guide chose the three strongest and swiftly looped them between the poles, at each end and in the center. He jerked his long black serape over his head, and threw it over the belts. The stretcher was ready. A sweater came flying out of the darkness and fell at the guide's feet; he grinned and pulled it on. I rubbed the Dutchman's face with snow. He stirred and his eyes opened, and we rolled him onto the stretcher. Lewis and I and a Canadian and a Londoner each took a corner. Feeling himself lifted, the Dutchman groaned in protest, and tried to sit up; the guide thrust him down, and he lay back weakly and began to cry, pleading with the men to put him down, to leave him. "I no good," he kept repeating.

The weight of the stretcher pole on my shoulder was less than I expected. I looked up at the sky; it was blue-gray now, and the stars were fading. The guide waited for us and warned us to be silent. There was a patrol station close by. We went on, placing our feet down cautiously, trying not to breathe too loudly. The pole was now cutting into my shoulder. A hand touched my arm, pushing me aside. Without a word, four fresh bearers took over the stretcher.

The guide called softly, "Camaradas! Adelante!" His voice was worried, and his anxiety affected the group. In the east the sky was perceptibly lighter, and I prayed that the sun would stay down just a little longer.

The guide rounded a great boulder, and the path suddenly became a narrow ledge. A tall Canadian, carrying one corner of the stretcher, cried out suddenly and disappeared over the bank. The Dutchman clutched the neck of the man on the other side to keep from falling. We thought the Canadian was killed; but in a moment he came scrambling up the ledge, swearing and raking snow out of his collar. But the Dutchman would not be carried any more. He went forward on his own short legs, supported between two other comrades.

It was not possible for us to run, but we jogged along, our breathing like that of hard-pressed horses. And still the guide danced before us, beckoning us on—faster—faster! He called out something, and Lewis sobbed, "Just five hundred meters, boys!"

Then we sprinted. The muscles in my thighs burned, and there was a sour taste in my mouth. Even the Dutchman, who had torn himself away from the men who supported him, was running. The sky was growing lighter.

The guide had stopped beside a heap of stones and was patting them, grinning. "España! España!" he called.

We halted by the pile of rocks and stared down the slope into the valley before us. It looked like the valley on the other side, the French side, but it was not like that valley because it was Spain. We stared down into the valley for a while, and the only sound was the gasping of exhausted men.

When we could breathe again, and before any man spoke, a big Welshman stepped forward. A blood-soaked bandage was wrapped around his ankle, where he had cut it on a rock, and his face and hands carried the blue marks of a coal miner. "Now, lads, this is a good time for a song, and I know a good song for this time." In a clear tenor voice he began to sing the "Internationale."

By foot, truck, and finally train we made our way to Albacete, one hundred miles from the front and base camp for the International Brigades. Albacete was crowded with men from the front, from the hospitals, from the States and Europe. They lounged on the streets, basking in the sun, flirting with the girls, with whom they enjoyed singularly little success. But Albacete was also where many of the volunteers got their first taste of military training. From there, on November 5, 1936, the first brigades had moved to the defense of Madrid and a few months later to the key battles at Jarama. There were for the thirty months of the war perhaps forty thousand men and a small number of women who passed through the International Brigades, although there were never much more than a third that number in Spain at any one time. There were five brigades: the all-German Eleventh, the Thaelmann Brigade; the Italian, German, and French Twelfth, the Garibaldi Brigade; the Slavic-speaking Thirteenth, the Dombrowski Brigade; the French and Belgian Fourteenth; and the mostly English-speaking Fifteenth, in which the Americans formed two battalions, the Lincoln and Washington, and the Canadians one, the Mackenzie-Papineau Battalion.

While the International Brigades were only a small portion of the total Republican armed forces, they played a crucial role, especially at this early stage of the war. Our value went beyond our numbers because our presence showed that the Spanish people had many supporters, even though the Western nations refused to help the Republic. We were a volunteer army inspired by conviction and became a powerful symbolic force.

The brigades had sustained heavy casualties in the defense of Madrid and then at Jarama. The Lincoln Battalion had been especially hard hit at Jarama, losing over a hundred men. In Albacete the brigade staff committee evaluated the Lincolns' needs and assigned me as the battalion's new political commissar, contingent on their approval.

Blind discipline to authority might work in some armies, but it was out of the question in the International Brigades. A volunteer army fighting because of its beliefs had to be reassured that the aims for which it fought were clear and justified. The men had to have confidence in their leaders. The idea of political commissars had been around as far back as the Paris Commune,[2] but when I was assigned to serve as one, I didn't have a good conception of what that meant. I asked around and got nebulous answers. I was told a commissar must be one who is trusted by his men, that he must be able to explain every situation, to see that military decisions and objectives are understood, and that the mens' needs, physical and personal, are taken care of. The fellow who had been the Lincoln's commissar at Jarama had been removed. He didn't do anything wrong—he just didn't measure up to the situation. I asked if I could meet someone who had served as a commissar and was taken to a hospital to talk to a man who had been the commissar for a French battalion until he was wounded at Jarama. His head was completely bandaged, leaving only slits for his eyes, mouth, and nostrils. Through my translator, he told me what the others had said: the commissar must be the most devoted and respected man in the unit. I had come to Spain with the recommendations of the American Party, but I knew that I still had to prove myself to the men with whom I would serve.

It was the end of April when I joined the Lincolns in Alcalá de Henares. They had just been pulled off the lines at Jarama where they had suffered heavy losses, and they were looking forward to some time to recuperate. They didn't get it. There was new trouble at the front, and after a May Day review the Lincolns were called back to Jarama.

I had to go to Madrid that day for a briefing with the International Brigade, so I did not accompany the Lincolns to the place that they called home. I have never forgotten my impressions of this city under siege. As we drove into Madrid, we heard what sounded like machine gun and rifle fire, and now and then larger explosions that I knew must have been artillery. It was just after sunrise, and the street-lights were painted blue so that they cast little light. The streetcars were also running with blue lights. The motormen and motorwomen kept clanging the bells as if to say, "Get out of the way! I'm in a hurry!" Going in one direction were trucks full of soldiers. Ambulances went back and forth, some with their sirens blowing. People scurried in and out of the subways. It was an organized bustle—all seemed to know where they were going. A siren blew, and everyone disappeared, including my driver and companions. We left our car on the spot and got into a building doorway.

Early the next morning, I picked up a ride on a truck that took me as far as the village of Morata. Morata lay in the shallow valley of the Jarama River, a valley some ten miles wide with a long ridge on its far side. The truck driver pointed to the ridge. "There she is," he said. "The fascists are on the other side. They can't see into the valley here. Our lines are on this side, just at the crest. All you do is just follow this road two miles. You can't miss." I started walking, excited to be finally coming up to the front.

I overtook a Spanish soldier, strolling comfortably down the road with two chickens, tied by their legs, slung over the barrel of his rifle. We smiled at each other and walked together; and I learned by dint of many gestures that the chickens were not destined for the stew pot. The hens were to live at the front and supply eggs to their soldier-owner.

In the fields by the road, peasants were at work tending their crops, and this sight too gave the war an oddly domestic flavor. They seemed indifferent to the faint intermittent sound of gunfire from the crest of the ridge. This was reasonable enough; the fascists couldn't see over the ridge to fire directly on the peasants, so if once in a while a person was hit, it was only by accident, so to speak. And meanwhile the crops must be tended.

I met two Americans carrying a corrugated iron can between them and asked directions to the Lincoln Battalion headquarters. "Right over there," they told me, "where those three guys are standing. The dugout below those trees is headquarters."

The dugout had a corrugated iron roof covered with branches to hide it from air observers, and nothing outside revealed that anything went on there. But inside the air was cool and damp, and the atmosphere was full of activity. I was reminded of a bootleg coal hole at home—lots of business going on inside, and nothing to show outside.

Oliver Law sat against the wall, his feet sticking out into the room; he was filling out a report. Oliver was commander of the Lincoln Battalion's Tom Mooney Machine Gun Company and later battalion commander. He pushed out of the dugout and greeted me. Marty Hurahan, the battalion's commander, was out inspecting positions. We stood looking up the valley toward the village of Morata, a huddle of white houses on the hillside. Oliver glanced at his watch; it was just short of nine o'clock. When the long hand stood straight up, three muffled explosions sounded from beyond the ridge, and three smoke columns shot up from the village of Morata. You saw the shell bursts before you heard the explosions. Another round, boom-boom-boom. Between rounds you heard rifle bullets crack past overhead. At nine-fifteen the artillery fire stopped, and the smoke puffs ceased blossoming in the village.

Every day a fascist battery shelled Morata, always from nine to nine-fifteen. At eight-fifty-five the villagers moved out; trucks en route through the village stopped on the road; and the shelling began, continued, and stopped. The trucks then moved again, and the villagers returned and resumed their living, immune from war for another twenty-three hours and forty-five minutes. Of course the adobe houses were knocked about a little. Some livestock and occasionally a person were killed, and then it was back to normal. The Americans were certain a German battery did the shelling; only German officers could be capable of so intensely methodical a routine.

"That's our alarm clock," Oliver said. "You can set your watch by it. We can go tour the lines now."

A bunch of men were digging a trench that was to be our communicating trench between the line and battalion headquarters. The trench zigzagged for about three hundred and fifty yards. It was wide enough to carry a stretcher through and was largely out of danger in case of bombardment and attack.

We entered an olive grove. Close to each tree, a hole six feet deep had been dug, large enough to hold one or two men. The holes were roofed with branches, grass, and leaves. "The men off duty sleep here at night. They're safe from anything but a direct hit," Oliver explained. "They're pretty good now, but in wet weather they fill up with water. The boys dug them close to the trees so the roots would keep the ground from caving in."

A trench began as a trace, deepened into a ditch, grew deeper and deeper still until the walls were higher than the head of a tall man, intersected another trench at right angles to it—and we were in the firing line. Directly in front of us, a man stood on a step dug into the trench wall, peering through a crack between two sandbags into no-man's land. His rifle lay in the crack against his cheek. I yearned for a look at the fascist lines and the space between, but I hesitated to ask the soldier to step aside. I wished I could get over feeling like a tourist.

Every ten yards along the trench a man kept watch—the fascist lines were only five hundred yards away—and others lay in the little dugouts they had scraped out of the rear wall, loafing, sleeping, reading, writing letters, cleaning equipment, and talking. Save for the occasional sound of rifle or machine-gun fire, the atmosphere was peaceful, almost sleepy. But the whistle and crack of bullets came more frequently here, varied by sharp thuds against the sandbags. Oliver smiled at me. "The ones you hear won't get you," he said. "The thing that gives us the worst time is their damned minethrowers. They use a spring action, so there's no explosion, no warning."

When night came I was still dissatisfied. I had been in the trenches all day long, but I had not lost the tourist feeling. I said to Oliver, "I think I'll take a walk through the trenches. I'll find my way back all right."

"The password," said Oliver, "is *nuestra victoria*."

I spent some time chatting with the first guard I met, Ruby Ryant. He had been busted as sergeant of the Mooney Company for overstaying a leave in Madrid and was now a "demoralized element." Ryant had strong complaints about the food. It appeared that Jackie Shirai, an excellent cook, had gotten mad and quit. Since then the cooks had been men who had gotten into trouble and were given the job as punishment. The results of this policy were evident in the food. I wandered for an hour or two in the trenches, and the men talked freely to me. The feeling of strangeness began to fall away.

The next day I tackled my first problem as political commissar. I got a few men together and raised the subject of the chow. I began reasonably, "But can't you persuade Shirai to take over the cook's job again?"

"We talked ourselves dry!" Ruby exclaimed. He pitched his voice to imitate Jackie's arguments. " 'No work in the kitchen for me. I got a good Russian rifle; I came here to shoot fascists.' Bull-headed little fellow. He's bent on shooting fascists with his goddamn Russian rifle, and nothing will change his mind." I proposed a way to trap our comrade, and we agreed to put the plan into effect that evening.

Jackie was the first man of the machine-gun crew in the chow line. He dipped into the stew kettle, held his plate to his nose, and made retching noises. "It stinks!" he yelled. The man behind him dipped a piece of bread in the kettle, tasted, and walked away in disgust.

"What do you expect?" Ruby said. "Nobody could make anything out of the rotten meat they send us."

"Jackie could!" another answered hotly. "Here we got the best goddamn chef in the world in our outfit and we eat this muck!"

Jackie heard. He filled his plate and went over by himself and sat down, pretending not to hear. Jackie's eyes were fixed on his plate, and his face was woeful. The talk continued and grew louder. It wasn't an act any more; the boys were warmed up. How could they fight fascists when their stomachs were poisoned by the chow sent up from the kitchen?

I stood up. "We're making a complete cleanup in the kitchen. It won't be a punishment place anymore. We'll put the best comrades we've got down there; it'll be an honor to work there. After all, the health and the lives of our men depend on a good kitchen. Now, who will it be?"

A chorus of voices yelled, "Jackie! I nominate Shirai!"

"No kitchen," Jackie said. "I'll fight fascists, but no more kitchen."

The guys started to argue why it had to be Jackie, and he began to bend. "I can't work in a kitchen with a crew like they gave me. Everybody's screwy! Or lazy! They don't want to work."

"You can pick your own men," I told him.

Jackie hesitated. "But when there's a fight I'm leaving the kitchen! I got a damn good rifle, and I'm going to use it!" Everybody knew he meant it.

Pretty soon Jackie said, "I'll take Dempsey; he's a good cook. Tony's a good coffee man, and Big Joe can cut meat. That's all." He glared at the cheering group but soon broke into a grin. Pivoting sharply, he saluted the men and went back to the kitchen, his rifle slung over his shoulder. But Jackie always kept his rifle constantly propped next to the stove, and he would grab it whenever things didn't suit him in the kitchen and announce he was through, he was going to shoot fascists.

This was one problem settled, but there were a thousand others, and some of them could be handled and some could not. I did what I could. I learned. Fortunately for me, the fascists' offensive was stopped at that point. There was no immediate action, so I was able to feel out the situation. Where beefs were legitimate, I tried to do something; where they were not, I lowered the boom. Wherever possible I encouraged the men to help themselves—as in the case of persuading Jackie to take over the kitchen. In such instances the job was to suggest, to stimulate, to cut through red tape and release the men's own intiative.

Meanwhile, the war had to be fought, and the fighting was more than a matter of cooks and political discussions. It was also a matter of pick-and-shovel work, for "what is captured by the gun must be held by the spade." The problem was to get the men who wielded guns and shovels to believe this and act on it. They had captured this ground by their guns, all right, but the ground was hard and dry and often rocky. Their answer to the slogan was, "We can't dig through the whole of Spain!" It wasn't a question of lining them up and ordering them to dig trenches. I knew that they would dig if ordered, but if they understood why digging trenches was necessary, it would be better. The battalion command went into a huddle and considered the problem in detail.

Along the ridge the opposing lines ran roughly parallel, and at most points the slight crest of the ridge was between us, so the Lincolns could get no clear view of the enemy trenches. This was a dangerous situation in itself; it made surprise attacks or raids possible. The object, then, was to get a better view of the ground between the lines. Barring an offensive, this could only be done by pushing the Lincolns' lines forward, bringing them nearer to the fascists. To accomplish this we would have to dig a series of trenches straight toward the hill crest from the front line for a distance of about ten yards. We would then make a new front-line trench at right angles to these trenches. In other words, we would dig a series of T's and join the crossbars. This meant an unholy lot of work, and it could only be done at night to avoid drawing enemy fire.

Marty Hurahan, the commander, and I got the men together a group at a time and scratched diagrams in the dirt. "Here we are, and here they are, and here's the ridge. You know that ridge is the key to the whole position, the key to Madrid. If they can advance just fifty yards to the crest, they've got the whole valley under observation and the road and the railroad as well. Fifty yards means ten miles in this case—right?"

There was a murmur of agreement. On that basis we explained the plan for the T's, emphasizing the advantage of having two lines of trenches, one of which would serve as a support trench in case the first line should be captured. We bore down on the importance of getting rid of blind spots between the lines. They understood that all right; they had stood guard.

For weeks we dug the T's out. It was hard work, but everyone understood what it was for. The morale of the outfit improved when the men were occupied with useful work, and there was less grumbling about petty things.

Night patrols were sent out. Their job was to go as close as possible to the fascist barbed wire. The fascists had lots of barbed wire and steel posts, and we had none, but they put their barbed wire too close to their trenches—within ten or fifteen yards. The patrols lay near the wire and watched and listened, and when a machine gun let go a burst, they took careful bearings. Sometimes they ran across a fascist patrol or working party, and there would be a dustup, a sudden fury of bursting grenades. It was sometimes a problem to get back to their own lines. Word had been passed, "Patrol out—don't fire," but some guard was always getting jumpy, thinking it was a fascist attack and and shooting into the air to give the alarm. Thus there was always plenty of excitement, and that was good for morale, too.

I made my headquarters in the "library," a hole dug into hard yellow clay and covered with canvas. It served as library, clubhouse, and recreation center. Here the scanty store of books and newspapers was kept and the checker games and ping-pong balls and paddles. The man in charge had health too frail to permit heavy duty, but he would not leave the lines. "I'll be okay in a fight," he insisted. "I'm no good with a pick and shovel, but I can handle a rifle all right." He was conscientious in his library duties, seeing to it that the books and papers were kept in circulation. He let me use a bundle of *Daily Workers* for a pillow the first night I was there.

Not too long after I arrived, I was informed that an attack would occur before long. This time we'd be the ones on the offensive. Before the attack, however, the Lincolns got the leave they had been waiting for. It was to be in the ancient village of Ibáñez.

The people of Ibáñez were gathered in the plaza to honor the foreign soldiers who had come to rest in their village after three months in the trenches. There were not many inhabitants, and these were mostly women and children, young boys, and old men. There were no young men at all. When the Americans appeared in the plaza, the people stirred and murmured, and the women held their children up to see.

The representative of the village, a lame man, nervously began to speak. "Ours," he said, "is a small and old village. We have done all we could. We have sent thirty-one men to the army, our teacher among them; he is now a commissar. For the past year our school has been closed, and the church likewise—our priest left us for the fascists on the very day they began their war against us.

"You have come to us from far away, and we accept you as our sons, our brothers and comrades. We know how badly you need rest, and we are honored that you come here. We have cleared out a section of the flour mill for you, and all last night our women worked making mattresses of flour sacks and filling them with straw. We hope they will be comfortable for you, for they are the best we could do. You are welcome here.

"Viva los americanos!" the townspeople shouted.

"Viva la República Española!" came the Lincolns' reply.

The shower truck was waiting, and clean clothes, but right away there was a minor crisis. Sergeant Hayes and some men had dropped in at a little wine shop run by an old lady. The old lady was overwhelmed with delight, but all she had was anise; there was nothing else in the shop to drink. They looked at the anise doubtfully and sipped. But they were feeling good; they were clean, they had money, and for the first time in months they were out of sound of gunfire. They opened the hatches and began heaving down the anise.

A mine thrower works on spring action, and the shell sneaks up on you. The fellows knew about mine throwers, but they'd never met anise before. It went down easy—a sissy drink. Their eyes got glassy, and somebody made a remark somebody else didn't like. A bottle sailed through the air, and the war was on.

It took some time to stop the ruckus and haul the reeling men out of the wrecked shop. The battalion staff gathered, ashamed and angry. The battalion had been disgraced. The Spanish people must not think of the Internationals as roaring, carousing mercenaries.

The guilty nine were lined up on the plaza facing the battalion and the watching townspeople. We finally reached a decision. This was my job, and I didn't like it, but it had to be done. Sergeant Hayes was an old-timer, a veteran of many labor struggles. His legs were unsteady, but he understood what was happening, and tears ran down his cheeks as he listened to me tell his comrades of his disgrace. "So we recommend," I concluded, "that these men be sentenced to five days in the brig." I looked up and down the ranks. "Do you approve?" There was some grumbling, but no one dissented. The nine were marched off to the "jail," hastily improvised from an old toolhouse facing the plaza.

I told myself that the battalion had approved the sentence, but I was uneasy. I had a feeling we had been too severe. When I heard some talk that evening, my uneasiness grew.

At dawn the next day the officers of the staff were awakened by a knock at the door. Outside stood five men carrying their tools, a delegation from the village. They apologized for waking us and begged us not to punish men who had been so long in the trenches and had done no real harm. The staff looked at one another unbelievingly. For the first time, we were divided on an issue. The discussion was hot. Some argued the decision was made and must be carried out; otherwise the men would have no respect for the military decisions of the command. But Oliver carried the ball for the group inclined to reverse its former position. "Since when," he demanded, "can't we admit a mistake? The men will respect us all the more for it! And I know about this anise; it fools everybody. Besides, it's silly to expect men not to drink after all they've been through. The decision has served its purpose—to show how seriously we regard such conduct. I move it now be withdrawn." The motion carried, and we drew up a statement explaining the action.

It wasn't easy to face the battalion. "Comrades," I said, "we made a hasty decision yesterday. We failed to take into consideration that this was the first day after such a long strain. We've decided to withdraw the sentence. However, we want to use this case as an example of how serious we consider any action that will hurt our relations with the people here."

The men cheered, and I grinned back at them. The uneasy feeling was gone. I watched them scattering to the river and the threshing field, which was soon turned into a baseball diamond.

The problems, I found, were least among those men who made friends with the people of Ibáñez and greatest with those who let themselves be cut off by the language difficulty from the life of the country. The latter group, once swimming and games had palled, had nothing to fall back on but gossip and liquor. They were bored and restless. The majority of the men, however, showed an amazing ability to make friends with the villagers despite the language barrier. They were not merely friendly visitors; many of them made themselves part of the community and took part in its work and its problems. Almost the whole battalion turned out to help harvest the barley and in one day grew extremely lame and blistered with the unaccustomed labor of using sickles. They wasted so much barley that the farmers, with the utmost tact and delicacy, asked them not to trouble themselves further in the matter.

We staged a picnic for the children in the grove by the river. There were prizes of food and strange new games for the children. At the end little Maria, a charmer with long curls and enormous eyes, was elected sweetheart of the battalion.

Julius, who had left a teaching career to come to Spain, reopened the school, and soon thirty children were attending. But no one did more than Dr. Magid, a Canadian attached to our battalion, and his staff. Within three days they had a medical practice going that kept them on the jump day and night. The first patient, hesitant and afraid, was brought by his father. He had gotten a piece of something embedded in his eye weeks before. Dr. Magid operated successfully. The next morning there was a lineup of villagers outside the door, and each morning thereafter the line was longer. The first-aid men were put to doctoring; overworked in the trenches, they worked doubly hard here. They had their reward in the gratitude of the people; never before had there been a doctor in Ibáñez.

The medical staff and those favored by them dined on eggs, milk, cheese, and butter—priceless commodities that were the gifts of grateful patients. They were seldom offered directly but were left in strange places by donors too shy to bring their gifts openly.

In Ibáñez there were pretty girls, and each pretty girl soon had a soldier suitor. Courtship was not easy, for each girl had also a mother or grandmother, and wherever the girl went, her chaperone went also. This cramped the style of the Americans, but they persevered.

By all these means and more, the men of the battalion put down roots among the people of Ibáñez. But while we were becoming a part of the village, our June days ran away. Our brigade was soon to take part in the Brunete offensive, the biggest action yet undertaken by the Republic.

The fascist lines lay like a half-closed hand thrust from the southeast about the throat of Madrid, closing from two sides on the city. The hand lay across all roads and rail lines save one; over this one road passed all supplies to the beleaguered city. At a meeting of brigade commissars and commanders, the divisional commissar, Carlos Torro, sketched the hand with charcoal on the white wall of the farmhouse and held a candle closer to light the sketch. "Here on the wrist, below the thumb, is Brunete," he said, "and beyond it, the heights of Romanillos. Those heights command the fascist supply lines. If they are taken and held, the hand will be cut off at the wrist and the fascists compelled to withdraw twenty miles. Madrid will no longer be under artillery shelling."

Torro explained that one purpose of our attack was to relieve pressure on Madrid by cutting off this salient. The second, perhaps greater, purpose was to relieve pressure on the north by compelling Franco to draw planes, tanks, and guns away from there. If our plans worked out, we would be able to give our Asturian and Basque comrades the first tangible assistance of the war.[3] Franco would have to pull out his Italian columns and his German planes and tanks to meet our attack. We gathered fifty thousand of our best men for this action: the Lister division, the Modesto division, and all five International Brigades. It was to be the first offensive the Republic had attempted. We all understood that much of the future of Spain depended upon how well we carried out this operation.

Torro went on to more detailed matters. There must be absolute secrecy until the forces were in position for the attack, and no movement, except at night. It was essential that every man understand the plan of attack and its purpose. Commanders and commissars were to work closely together, and if the commander were disabled, the commissar was to take over. Each commissar, in turn, had to prepare his substitute immediately, and detailed orders for each brigade would come later.

The Lincolns left Ibáñez on July 2, on short notice; the church bells rang, and the village people came running to see us off. We departed amid cheers and tears and clenched-fist salutes. We rode in trucks a while, and then we marched. For two days we marched, making a wide sweep around Madrid, to the north, following a devious route over roads some of which seemed newly built just for the purpose. The roads were crowded with men, trucks, and tanks, all moving up at night.

On the night of July 4, shortly before midnight, the order came through. Oliver showed it to me. The brigade was to move up at two in the morning and be in place by six-thirty, when the attack was to begin. There was a feeling of vast forces moving, unlike anything I had felt in Spain before. I also experienced mounting anxiety that we might be late arriving. Everybody was on edge.

Our artillery let go at six-thirty, just as the haze was lifting from the valley of the Guadarrama, a broad and rolling plain spread out below us. The Lincolns were still a mile away. We were late. But the gunfire ended the suspense. The men hurried forward breathlessly, as if fearing the battle might be over before they arrived.

The valley was like a huge map, and scattered over it were villages, toylike in the distance. Toward each village a column was advancing, fanning from the base of the ridge. Overhead planes flew, *nuestros,* snub-nosed Chatos. Columns of tanks rolled down the hill, vanished into an olive field, and reappeared beyond, moving swiftly.

Major Nathan, the imperturbable and extremely British brigade chief of operations, stood below the crest of the ridge. He identified the villages in the distance. Quijorna was the one farthest to the right, and Brunete was next, three miles out. Villanueva de la Cañada lay straight before us, and the heights beyond it, across the river, were Romanillos. Once those heights were taken, we would have the Madrid road under fire, and the fascists before Madrid would be in a pocket.

The villages were vanishing in the mushroom clouds of dust and smoke kicked up by the shells. All across the plain, pockets of fire and smoke were blossoming. The planes were over Quijorna, and a vast column of flames and smoke shot up suddenly. The air shook. They had probably hit a gasoline pump.

The Lincolns lay on the hill and watched and wondered. Somewhere in the dust and flame around La Cañada was the Washington Battalion, and with the Washingtons were most of the gang I had known in the Perpignan prison. Finally a runner came up. We were to advance to fill in a gap between the Washingtons and the British battalion in the rear of La Cañada.

We moved down the hill toward the valley. As we descended the steep incline, stretcher bearers with the first wounded began to pass us coming back up. The blood seeping through the canvas chilled me.

The ground had looked smooth from up above, but it was laced with gullies and depressions. Once on the plain, we followed these depressions, seeking cover from the bullets that now began to crack overhead. The village was set on a hill with the ground all around sloping up to it; and the fascists were well protected by the thick brick walls of the houses. They had machine guns in the church tower sweeping the ground all around the village. Other machine guns, well emplaced, were at the outer rim of the village.

The Lincolns crawled forward into position. We were about four hundred yards outside the town when we were ordered to dig ourselves in—no easy task with the ground so hard. We scratched and dug and sweated while the sun beat down on us and bullets whipped overhead. Not all the bullets went overhead; some of them struck.

By the time we got into position and dug in, it was late in the day. We were tired, hungry, and thirsty. Oliver and I set up a command post

Lt. Edo Yardash, Lincoln Battalion, and Steve Nelson in
Brunete, Spain, summer 1937.

close to the infantry line, and I went back to look over the machine-gun positions. They were set up and well placed. Rae Steele had found a well-protected spot below the crown of a road, and he and Ruby were firing alternate bursts. The rest of the machine-gun company was spaced to the right of Ruby's gun. Between them they pinned the fascists down, holding them without overheating their guns.

I stopped beside each gunner, checking the target in the fascist lines. When I returned to the command post, Oliver wasn't there. Oliver and I were to have remained at the post while the adjutant went forward. Later I learned that the adjutant had disappeared, so Oliver went forward instead, and got himself into a spot beyond a ridge where he couldn't get out until nightfall. At the same time Hurahan was seriously wounded. That left me in command.

It felt strange to be responsible for the Lincoln's part in the fight, but I decided that things were in pretty good shape. We were well established in a good position, and it was near sunset. The stretcher bearers were taking the wounded back; and food would be coming up presently. Everything was all right. A feeling took shape that we were through for the day; we would sit tight through the night and clean up the town in the morning. It wasn't a conscious thought, just a feeling; I wasn't really aware of it until the runner brought me the order.

I read the order and passed it over to Dennis Jordan, my assistant. He was bewildered and angry. "What the hell!" he said. "We're doing all right. We'll get into a mess if we try anything. The guys are tired." But there it was, all written out, and presumably Headquarters knew what they were doing. They wanted Villanueva de la Cañada cleaned up right now, not the next morning. I turned to a runner. "Tell Burns and Sid Levine we're to go forward when a general attack begins. Everybody ready!"

Before the messages got to Headquarters, we heard heavy firing and yelling off to the left, beyond the Washington Battalion. The Dimitrov Battalion had launched the attack, and the English battalion was on the move. At that the other seven battalions surrounding the town joined in. The Lincolns were going forward, yelling, and I ran with them. There were sandbags in front of me, and I jumped over them into a trench and then into a dugout and scrambled up into a street of the village. We had gained a foothold.

Shortly after sunrise the next morning, we were surprised to see men were coming down the street toward us. They had their hands up high. More and more appeared. They were fascist prisoners. The village was ours!

It was not until later that I found out it had not been intended for the Fifteenth to attack La Cañada; that was for another unit. The plan was for the Fifteenth to bypass the village and to occupy the all-important heights of Romanillos in the first shock of the surprise attack, before the fascists could organize their defense. Because of this Headquarters blunder, a day had been wasted, and irreplaceable men had been lost.

Everybody was up at dawn. We went house to house along the streets, yelling for civilians to come out. Details sent back to pick up the dead found about thirty of ours. They were a grotesque sight. Men seem to fall on their faces in an attack; when they are turned over, their bodies are stiff and rigid in a sprawling pose and their faces are distorted. One of the men was George Armitage from Canada. I couldn't hold back the tears when I saw him.

Later in the day, the fascists began shelling La Cañada. The Lincolns moved out of the town into an orchard. There we reorganized ourselves, replacing those killed and wounded. With this accomplished, we moved out again for the heights of Romanillos. We were to attack those heights the next day.

For three weeks the fighting continued. The wave of attack rushed toward the heights, hung for a few days below the crest, and yielded a little. In those days lines were set that remained unchanged to the end of the war. The main assault on the heights came on the third day. Eight little Russian tanks splashed through the shallow stream in the early morning, heading up the hill toward the fascist machine-gun positions, and three thousand men rose cheering from the reeds along the bank to follow. In the face of this attack, the fascists ran.

It was like a fox hunt. The fascists raced up the hill empty-handed but out of range, and the Americans and Spaniards raced after them, stopping now and then to fire. They were exultant; they had cut through the fascist lines like a hot knife through butter. Franco's men had never dreamed that the Loyalists would be capable of sustaining the attack, of crossing the Guadarrama River.

But the tanks topped the ridge before the infantry was halfway up; and behind the tanks, fascist machine gunners set up a deadly fire. There were not enough tanks to cover the wide front; the brigade on the left was stopped by fire from the crest, so the Fifteenth could not go on. We began to dig in, only nine hundred yards from the crest.

The final effort came the next morning. The fascists launched a counterattack and were driven back. Instantly, the brigade saw its opportunity and took it. We drove at the retreating fascists desperately, without much preparation. We figured if we could get to the crest and stick there for a little, the outfits on either side would be able to get up. Machine-gun fire stopped us again. That night we had to fall back to the starting point.

I went over with the left wing, Oliver with the right; the attack stalled in an olive grove, below the lower ridge that we had left. There I learned that Oliver was wounded. They told me he was hit in the stomach. The stretcher bearers took him right away, but he didn't want to go. He kept telling the men not to waste time with him. They said he was hanging on to his belly with both hands.

An hour or two later, the stretcher bearers returned, and one of them reported that Oliver was gone. They had gotten him back about a mile, but he couldn't hold on.

Oliver had been in the U.S. Army for six years. He was talented and had lots of courage, but he was black, so he left the army still a private. In Spain he became commander of the Lincoln Battalion. It was perhaps the first time that a black man had commanded white American troops. He was a building trades worker, very active in the fight for free speech and black rights on Chicago's South Side. His sober attitude had made him close to the men, and a lot of time was spent talking about him after he died.

We withdrew from the low ground to the top of the lower ridge from where the attack had been launched. It was near sundown; I went up and down the line, examining all positions with the company commanders and making arrangements for the night. I was worried about tanks, though I didn't say so. The ground before us had no boulders or trees, only underbrush and grass. This was the logical place for a tank attack. I rang Brigade and asked Major Nathan for an antitank battery.

"We'll have three by tomorrow," he replied. "Meanwhile, I'll have some antitank grenades and rifle bullets sent up. How are things with the Yanks?"

"Okay. You?"

"Oh, I'm a casualty. My boot heel was shot from under me. I'm limping frightfully. Must procure a pair of *alpargatas,* eh? Well, cheerio!"

"Salud."

I wondered what was in this man's voice that was so agreeable to hear.

The phone rang later that night. The brigade commander said, "Steve, we heard that Oliver died this morning. You are in command of the battalion now."

For the first three days, there were few fascist planes overhead. Then they appeared in swarms. Loyalist planes, outnumbered twenty to one, were driven from the sky. The second purpose of the drive, to draw planes away from the north, was proving too successful for comfort. But the Lincolns, veterans of the pick, dug deep, and we were fairly safe from the continual bombing and strafing.

The worst thing during these weeks was the lack of water. There was never enough, and most of the time there wasn't any at all. The river dried up three or four days after the battle began. Sometimes it was so bad that the men couldn't move, couldn't think, didn't know what was going on around them. If a fascist attack had come at one of these times, it would have been too bad. We dug into the river bed, but sand kept caving in on us from the banks. We got down eight or ten feet, and water seeped in to make a shallow little pool. Every man got five or six swallows before the well ran dry. The water tasted of dead mule, but it was water.

We all had stomach trouble and walked around with our pants slit because we had no time to take them off to relieve ourselves. If you've ever had really bad diarrhea, you know what I mean. It was pretty debilitating. I was down to 135 pounds from 155.

True to his promise, Jackie Shirai abandoned the kitchen when the big fight came. He went into action with his good Russian rifle and caught a bullet in the head. Shorty Friedman and a lot of other guys were killed, too. So many were lost that the Washington and Lincoln battalions were consolidated into the Lincoln-Washington Battalion.

The night the two battalions were merged, orders came to go to Villanueva de Pardillo, where the fascists were counterattacking furiously, endangering the gains of the whole offensive. There were no trucks, and the route lay up the bed of a dry river. It was not easy to march in soft sand under full pack. The sand sifted into our shoes and scoured the skin off our feet. Some took off their shoes and tried it barefoot, but their feet became too raw. We couldn't go fast, but we had to go fast; we had to be in position before daylight.

The machine gunners had the worst time. Ruby, Rae Steele, Doug Roach, and Sundstrom "organized" a horse somewhere. When I discovered it, I gave them a good bawling out. "Don't you know this is no way to act in a Republican army—stealing horses?" They were ashamed of themselves. They said, "Okay, Comrade Steve, we won't do it any more." The proprieties having been observed, we continued the march. With the horse.

At sunrise we reached the highway bridge on the road leading to Pardillo and left the river, following the highway for a little over a mile. We were in full view of the fascists, who started shelling. Presently we were given orders to take up a reserve position in a deep winding gully. We spread out along the gully and started digging in, but before we had time for much digging, the shelling began in earnest, and the first planes came over.

All day, in continuous waves, they flew over. They dropped heavy and light bombs and swooped down with machine guns hammering. They fired a field of barley close by with incendiary bombs, and the sharp odor of burning straw mixed with the fumes of powder. The artillery shelled sporadically from nine in the morning to six at night.

The earth trembled and shook in continuous upheaval; whole trees were uprooted, and fragments flew through the air. The blast of the concussions was like a windstorm. It was impossible to believe that anyone but yourself was still alive, and impossible to believe that you could live for long in such an inferno. In the second-long pauses, you listened for voices, for screams, for any human sound, and there was nothing. In all of it, there was one thought of comfort: so long as the shelling and bombing continued, the fascist infantry would not attack. I wanted the bombing to stop, and yet my mind told me that if it did, things might get worse.

Toward dusk the planes vanished, and the shelling ceased abruptly. Lieutenant Miller, Bernie Adis, his political commissar, the runner, and I crept out of the hole we had dug under the roots of a great oak tree. The tree had sustained a direct hit, and torn limbs and branches lay over the opening. We peered up and down the gully. Here and there something stirred.

A Spanish runner slid into the gully. "Comandante—we're attacked—send whatever is left of your men quickly!"

Were there any to send? I ran along the edge of the cut. "Hey, guys, you all right? How many hurt? Make it snappy, we're going up! How many did we lose?"

It was the miracle of the war. Of the seven hundred men in the ravine, only four were killed that day. One man's nerve broke; he leaped up and ran, and bomb splinters got him. Several were wounded; one died later in the hospital. All day the Spanish soldiers had watched the fires flickering over the hollow where we lay. They believed it was impossible that many—or any—could survive. They cheered and wrung the hands of their American comrades as we came into the line.

As for us, we had been in the midst of death, and now found ourselves alive and unhurt. The realization was exhilarating. We crowded into the trenches besides our Spanish comrades. Someone, a Spaniard, started singing the "Internationale." The whole line took it up in Spanish and English.

Later I lay on the floor of the battalion post and listened lazily to the talk of a group near by. Night was the time for talk. The days were a time of tight-nerved watchfulness, but at night the lines came to life. Food came up and picks and shovels went into action. Reports were made and complaints adjusted and the business of living conducted, and then around midnight, when the work was caught up, everybody relaxed, either in sleep or in bull sessions.

I lay listening to John Cookson describe a project for harnessing the Mediterranean Sea by a dam across the Straits of Gibraltar. Such a dam was entirely practical from an engineering standpoint, he said. It would provide electric power for all Europe and Africa. It would make possible the cultivation of countless square miles of desert, now an arid waste. It would increase beyond all calculation the industrial and agricultural wealth of the world. "It's not the engineering problems that are holding it back," Cookson said. "It's the political setup."

The men were thoroughly interested. They asked questions and discussed them warmly. They were soldiers in the midst of battle, yet they were all tied up in talk about science and politics. Cookson enjoyed these "disputations," as he called them, and had a new one every time there was a moment for it.

After three weeks the lines settled down, and the battalion was pulled out and sent back to rest in Ibáñez. That was what the boys wanted, and a motorcyclist went off to tell the villagers that their friends the Americans were on their way back.

The relief battalion was late, and sunrise caught us just leaving the trenches. That was a worrisome thing. We were on our way out; it would certainly be the worst kind of luck to be caught now out in the open in full light. When we were within an hour's march of the place where the trucks were waiting, the planes appeared. Exhausted after three weeks of continuous fighting, we dove for low places, ditches, and hollows. The anti-aircraft guns started firing, but they were too far away to do much good. The planes were low now, following the winding road suddenly bare of men. The first load let go, about a hundred and fifty yards ahead. I counted six explosions, the last two hundred yards behind me. In an instant the road was jammed again. The line moved faster. The attack had stimulated the men's flagging energies.

Ahead, under the trees, we saw smoke rising from a camouflaged kitchen and saw the crews of the anti-aircraft guns moving about. The lovely smell of burro stew floated through the air. Major Nathan, in charge of the withdrawal, strolled across the field with two tin cups. He had been saving some brandy to toast me as the new brigade commissar.

I was astonished, but Nathan assured me there would be official notice shortly. Then we heard the drone of motors again. We ran like deer. The anti-aircraft let loose, but the planes were flying very low. The thud of bombs came from beyond the grove, and instantly the planes were overhead. Nathan yelled, "Drop!" and I burrowed into the dirt. My holster was under me. If I could get the holster out, my behind would come down a few miles. I tugged at the holster, and an enormous crash deafened me. The bomb had burst right beside us. But I was all in one piece.

Nathan was calling, "I'm hit, Steve!" Ralph Bates, an English writer who had just arrived from Madrid, and I ran to him and ripped open his shirt. There was a three-inch gash in his chest but only a speck of blood was oozing out. I thought at first it was just a scratch, but Nathan's face was twisted with pain, and he couldn't speak. I yelled frantically for first aid.

There was an ambulance under the trees a few hundred yards away. I raced toward it, and as I ran, I saw with satisfaction two of the fascist bombers spiraling out of the sky, smoke trailing behind them. The anti-aircraft had nailed them. The other planes scattered and flew away. The Spaniards around the ambulance were on their feet, shouting and cheering. They paid no attention to me as I got the stretcher and started back.

With Nathan on the stretcher, we rushed back to the ambulance. Other men had joined us, among them Lieutenant Garland. We shoved the stretcher into the rack and looked around for the driver. A Spanish major wearing a red cross on his sleeve was running toward us, screaming.

"Take it, Garland," I said. I told the major, "A man has been wounded—a brigade officer," but he was too excited to listen. Garland had the motor going. The major leaped for the running board and stopped short, staring incredulously at my drawn automatic.

Garland drove off, and the other Americans discreetly vanished. The major and I stared at each other. His hands and head and dignified little Vandyke beard were shaking with amazement and fury. He turned away suddenly and began yelling at a lot of Spanish soldiers hurrying toward us.

I began to realize I'd stepped into something. I thought probably the best time to settle it would be later—quite a lot later. I streaked across a field and shot gracefully over a stone wall into a creek knee-deep with water. I splashed up the creek to the shelter of some bushes and started running again. I felt like a small boy chased by cops.

I found a tent, went into it, and sat down, clutching my head. Then

I called the brigade office and reported that Major Nathan was badly wounded. I also reported that I had "stolen" an ambulance to take him to the hospital. Brigade said, "That's nothing—the ambulance will be back soon." They didn't seem concerned about the Spanish major.

So I put a guard outside headquarters with orders to admit no strangers, and I lay low, waiting for Garland to return with the ambulance. Word came from the hospital that they were operating on Nathan.

Garland came back riding on the tailgate of a truck. "Where the hell is the ambulance?" I inquired calmly.

"I left it at the hospital. I don't want to get into no goddamn trouble." Garland was virtuous and indignant.

"Listen," I said, "you get on that motorcycle and climb out of here. Bring back the ambulance! Bring it back!"

Garland departed reluctantly. He drove the ambulance reasonably close to the grove from which he had taken it, blew the horn loudly, and hit the dirt. He came across the field and the stone wall and creek even faster than I had.

A little later a patrol of Spaniards led by the little major appeared in the American camp. Everybody went dumb. A guy with a suede jacket and a pistol and brown pants? Why, no. Never saw anybody who looked like that. The major and his patrol went away again. Toward evening, I called the hospital. They said Nathan had died about ten minutes before.

That hurt. Nathan, wise and capable, strolling along under the heaviest fire, swinging his foolish little cane, his pipe cocked up at an angle—the rawest recruit couldn't be afraid when Nathan was around. For the sake of that example, knowing the effect of his manner on untrained or half-trained men, Nathan had taken the most outrageous chances, exposed himself dozens of times in that grandly arrogant manner. And now death had found him in a bomb splinter.

I felt sick, but I still had to settle things with the Spanish major. I stuck a carton of Luckies under my jacket, just in case, called a couple of men and the battalion interpreter, and set out for the Spanish camp.

"Comrade Major," I said, "I'm very sorry about what happened."

"You will do your explaining elsewhere," the major said icily.

"All right," I said. "The reason I did that was because the wounded man was Major Nathan, our brigade officer."

"Nathan!" The major started. "The tall man with the cane and the pipe? How is he?"

"He's dead. He died soon after the operation."

"Oh, no!" the major cried. "Ah, that is sad! If I had known—why did you not tell me, Comrade?"

We talked for some time about Nathan. To offer the cigarettes just then would have been insulting. I sent them over the next day, by runner.

I returned from making my peace with the Spanish major and went on to brigade headquarters. They had just received orders to march immediately to Quijorna to relieve Spanish divisions that were almost surrounded. We were the nearest troops. Everyone who heard was shocked. It was almost nine miles to Quijorna; they had marched for hours that morning; and they had been fighting for three weeks. This could not happen—even in Spain.

At the meeting of all commanders and commissars that followed, no one wanted to be the first to speak. Finally the commander of the A Battalion broke the silence: "I'll never be able to present that order to the men. Christ, man, you can't get blood from a stone!"

The colonel listened as each officer explained how his forces were depleted and the men exhausted. Then it was my turn. I had had a chance to do some thinking while the others were speaking. I said, "If the order is explained to the men, I think they'll go back in spite of their exhaustion."

The commissar of the British battalion, Wally Tapsell, glared at me. "What are you talking about, Steve? You know bloody well your men won't go back any more than the others will!"

"Okay, what do you propose to do? Our job is to do the impossible when we must. This is the impossible time!"

The colonel rapped on the table. "What shall be done?"

"Let's start with the Americans," I said, "and explain the order to them."

The men gathered around the flat rock where the colonel and the others were standing. The colonel read the order. No one said anything, but you could feel a wave of bewildered resentment sweep through the crowd. When the colonel finished reading, Jock Cunningham of the regimental staff spoke, explaining the military situation.

When he was done, I climbed up on the rock. I couldn't see their faces, and I didn't like that; it would have been easier if I could have seen them. There were murmurs from the back of the crowd, and someone shouted, "For God's sake, Steve, you're not going to tell us to go back!"

"Well, fellows, you heard the order," I said. "I got no more pep left than you. If we judge this order from the point of our physical shape only, we would all agree that it is impossible to carry out. But comrades, there are other factors that we must take into consideration. First, do you want to see the sun rise tomorrow morning and know that three thousand Spanish comrades were surrounded by fascists, and we were nine miles away, and didn't try to help them?"

I paused to let that sink in. "And second—we're on the road in a ravine. There's no chance to hold the lines here. If we don't march nine miles west and hold the heights, the gate to the ravine will remain open, the fascists will break through, and we'll have to run back about nine and one half miles to El Escorial—the only place we can make a stand. That's our choice—either we march nine miles tonight and help our Spanish comrades, or we run nine and one half miles tomorrow without knowing if we can stop them there."

I waited through a thick silence, and a voice came through the darkness, "You're right." I recognized the voice of Paul Block, an artist from New York. No one else spoke, but there were no catcalls. I figured the decision had been made.

The commanders and commissars made the rounds of the other battalions, and the same thing happened. Even the battalions in the worst physical shape formed up in the line of march.

The march began, but before we reached the main road, less than five hundred yards away, another motorcycle came speeding up with new orders. The Spanish comrades had extricated themselves and had the situation in hand. The Fifteenth was to remain in camp. But we had carried out the order to return to the lines. We had been ready to go. That was the main thing. Everyone felt not just good, but proud.

The next day the trucks came to carry the battalion to Ibáñez. I did not accompany them, for I was ordered to the training camp in Tarazona to report on the Brunete offensive and the lessons to be drawn from it.

The training school at Tarazona looked like a movie set of the old West. The buildings were all of pine logs with the bark on, laid corncrib fashion, and the cracks were chinked with clay. The long log barracks and the classrooms were scattered among the pine trees, sheltered from aircraft observation. I made my report on the Brunete offensive. Of the greater lacks, the lack of planes, tanks, artillery, the shortage of all supplies, there was little point in speaking. These questions were decided in Paris and London and Washington, not in Madrid, and still less in Tarazona. The Loyalist army's problem was how to do the most with the materials available.

Vicente Uribe, a Spanish Communist who was minister of agriculture for the Republican government, summed up the situation in a speech at Madrid. The first purpose of the offensive, to cut the Madrid salient, had not been accomplished. But the offensive had succeeded in drawing large forces, including three hundred planes, away from the north. To that extent, it had been successful. Uribe compared Brunete to the battle of Jarama. Jarama, he said, was improvised— fought out of hand, with whatever forces and methods were available. Like many battles in the first stages, it was primarily defensive. Brunete, however, was an offensive. It was planned and organized. It was an operation fought by an army, not by individual units under separate commands. Insofar as it had succeeded, it had proved to the Spanish people that their forces were steadily growing stronger and were already strong enough to beat the fascists in battle. Brunete, then, was a step nearer the goal.

The government was fully aware of the political necessity for a new offensive to follow up the victory at Brunete. Brunete had had a powerful effect on the international setup. If the government could prove its strength by winning a number of victories, there was every reason to believe that the "nonintervention" policy would fall to pieces, and that Spain would be allowed to purchase the supplies and materials it so badly needed. And there was a further military reason for a new offensive. It was known that the fascists were preparing a drive against Madrid. The government hoped, by striking the first blow elsewhere, to disrupt this offensive before it began.

There was yet another reason. In May, soon after I arrived in Spain, an anarchist takeover of the docks and telephone exchange in Barcelona sparked fighting between anarchist military units and those of the Republican government led by Enrique Lister and the Communist Fifth Regiment. Many were killed and wounded. The Barcelona uprising tragically underscored the difficulty of achieving political unity—a problem that had frequently plagued the Republican effort. I didn't know much about what had happened until later. But I did realize that a unified miltary effort could help overcome some of the past divisions.

For all these reasons, the government, moving swiftly, prepared a drive on the Aragon front. After heavy losses at Brunete, there was a major reorganization of the Fifteenth Brigade. It was made into a predominately English-speaking force including the Lincoln, Washington, Mackenzie-Papineau, and British Saklatvala battalions. It also included the Slavic Dimitrov Battalion, the French-Belgian Sixth of February, and a battalion made up of volunteers from Latin America. Vladimir Čopic was in command, and Robert Merriman was chief of staff. There thus appeared for the first time a true peoples' army, a Republican army made up of units representing all political shadings and all parts of Spain. Here anarchist battalions fought beside Socialists and Communists, all alike commanded by brigade officers who might be of any party or no party.

The plan was to drive northwest up the railroad that runs through the valley of the Ebro, toward Saragossa, some twenty miles distant from the starting point. The country there is a high and barren level plain broken by abrupt hills and valleys. The front did not consist of a continuous line of trenches but was a series of strong points—hills or towns strongly fortified, with nothing between.

One such point was Quinto, a town on the railroad. Twelve miles to the west was Belchite, likewise strongly held. The capture of Quinto was the first assignment of the Fifteenth Brigade. We moved up four days before the drive opened, took over the front line, and made preparations for the attack. Quinto fell in two days, and our next objective was Belchite. Napoleon had tried to capture Belchite once but had failed. The city was still stronger a century later, and German engineers had erected a powerful defense system.

Belchite could not be captured, but it had to be, for several reasons. Barcelona believed it had already fallen; to tell them otherwise now would have a very bad effect on morale there, and Barcelona was the industrial center of Spain. Production of guns, trucks, munitions, shoes, and clothes for the army fluctuated with its morale. Military considerations were certainly no less pressing. The bulk of the attacking force had driven deep into fascist territory. Belchite was behind them, a powerful threat so long as it remained in fascist hands. On the positive side, Belchite lay on a road leading straight to Saragossa. Capture of the city would open a new route for attack.

To the men lying in a shallow trench under the walls of Belchite, these matters were by no means clear. They did know that any man who raised up six inches off the ground was going to get a bullet through him. They knew the trench was straight instead of zigzag, so the snipers in the houses at the left were able to enfilade it. They knew the sun was hot, even early in the morning. It looked like a long, rough day ahead for men to lie glued to the ground, not daring to move a muscle.

We had moved up at night into the trench, a shallow ditch running out at an angle from the edge of town. The night before the houses overlooking the ditch had been empty; but in the darkness the fascists had come back, set up machine guns, and posted snipers in windows overlooking the ditch.

The first light brought heavy fire. Our battalion was in a predicament. We had to go forward, yet that seemed like suicide. On the other hand, if we stayed in the trench, we'd be picked off like sitting ducks. And a retreat over bare ground would cost more lives than an attack. Therefore we had to go forward.

I was in the brigade headquarters under a culvert on the road to Mediana, five hundred yards back. The phone rang, and it was Hans Amlie, who had become the Lincolns' commander. He spoke first to Čopic, the brigade commander, and then to Bob Merriman, its chief of staff. Amlie protested that despite his orders, the battalion could not advance. In the regular army that would have amounted to failure to obey orders and led to a court-martial. With us, it meant that the political commissar would have to straighten it out. As I was commissar for the Fifteenth Brigade, I had to see what could be done to get us around this impasse.

I left Headquarters and went down the wash a ways, peeping cautiously at the town. Over on the right, inside the town, was a church; and here, as everywhere, the fascists had made the church the center of resistance. They fortified the churches and put machine guns in the belfries, and then called the Loyalists godless Bolsheviks for attacking churches.

This stone church looked powerful. It was not far inside the northern edge of the town, but the buildings surrounding it protected it from direct artillery fire. The antitanks kept knocking at the machine-gun nests, but there were always more machine guns. The church had to be taken before the town could be taken. Everyone had known that right from the start.

I thought I might as well have a look around by the church. I took two or three men with me, and we worked around to that side of the town. We found a dry ditch leading into the town. The ditch ran close to a mill made of bricks and an olive-oil factory. The mill was right across the street from the church. We didn't know what was inside the factory, but it seemed quiet. We sent back for more men and hand grenades. A dozen men came up, bringing two of the new light machine guns issued before the battle of Aragon started.

We got all set, and at a signal, lobbed hand grenades through the factory windows, waited an instant for the burst, and rushed through a small opening torn open by a shell. There was no one inside. It seems the fascists had pulled out the night before. Quickly we set up the machine guns commanding the approaches to the main doors of the factory on the town side. We had a foothold in the town.

I went out and saw that things were happening in other parts of the town. Captain Bradley and about twenty men charged a street from

the east, under heavy fire. They captured and held a barricade block-
ing the street. From the west another attack was being prepared that
was likewise destined to reach the town. But Belchite was a long way
from being taken. The church was the key. From the plaza behind the
church, the streets ran out like the spokes of a wheel, and so long as
the fascists held the church, they commanded the streets.

A good part of the Lincoln-Washington Battalion moved around to
the ditch and into the mill beside the church. The mill became battalion headquarters and the base of attack. Since we couldn't go through
the streets, we started going through houses. As in all old Spanish
towns, the houses were built close together, wall to wall. The men
started the work of breaking through the earthen walls from one
house into the next. They were expert street fighters now, having
learned street-fighting at Quinto.

Belchite was besieged for several days, and time was running out.
The fascists at Saragossa were striving to push through a relief column to raise the siege. Our guards posted outside the town were
continually on the lookout for fascist reinforcements that could come
and pin us against the city walls. In a matter of hours, the city would
either surrender or be relieved.

I went back to the factory. I hadn't slept for a hell of a while, but I
was feeling better about the way things were going. Inside the mill, I
saw Dave Doran, who was my assistant at the time. Dave shouted
something, and I started toward him. "Steve, look out!" he yelled.
From the corner of my eye, I saw the window high in the factory wall
and the church tower above the window; in the same instant, something hit me hard on the cheek, and a terrible fiery pain struck inside
my thigh and ran up into my stomach. The pain was so fierce that I
doubled up on the floor. In spite of it, I managed to roll toward the
brick walls to keep from being hit again. Part of my mind was taken
up with the pain, but another part considered the matter coolly.
You've been hit, twice.

Had I been hit by two bullets, or twice by the same bullet? I
couldn't decide and never have been able to. Meanwhile, hands were
moving swiftly upon me, cutting away clothing, pressing to stop the
bleeding. I knew the hands must belong to people, but when I opened
my eyes, I could only see some dark bodies swimming vaguely in a
vaguely swimming room. I must have lost a lot of blood in a hurry to
be so groggy all at once. I felt myself lifted onto a stretcher and
opened my eyes again, and a face swam into sight. I grinned at the
face. At least, I intended to grin.

I awoke in a large, poorly lit room. My lips were parched, and my tongue felt as dry as old shoe leather. Everything smelled of ether. A man groaned and called for help. I looked up and saw two long lines of at least fifty low metal beds, full of wounded. I heard a faint sound of artillery fire, and I concluded that I was in a field hospital not far from the front. I knew of only one hospital near the front. It was reserved for head and abdominal cases. Others had to be taken further to the rear. What was I doing here?

As far as I knew I had not been seriously wounded. Perhaps I had been hit on the way to the hospital. I got frightened at the thought, and my hands involuntarily reached under the sheet to feel my body. Then I remembered being brought to this hospital by Dr. Mark Strauss, the Fifteenth Brigade's physician. All the ambulances were gone at the time.

The cries of the wounded became louder and more numerous. I sat up against the cold metal bedstead, looking at the two lines of wounded in the ward. I counted nine beds whose inhabitants lay motionless, their dark blankets removed. I noted that they weren't even taken out of the ward, only covered with a white sheet. A nurse came rushing by, and I inquired, "Are there any Americans here?" She said, "Si, Americanos," pointing to the end of the room. Several men had just been brought in. They were still on stretchers, and their bandages were drenched with blood.

Three beds from me, a man began to moan. He said something unintelligible, but the voice sounded familiar. I reared up. To my astonishment, I saw Paul Block, the artist who had helped carry me when I was hit a short while ago. Paul's eyes opened, but he did not know me. He was sweating and struggling for breath. The nurse and the doctor came, took his pulse and began to work on him. Paul recovered consciousness for a short while and recognized me. He asked for water, grasped my hand, and even while unconscious again, held me tight. He did not recover consciousness and he was covered like the other nine.

What I saw here was worse than anything I ever experienced. The passing of comrades was hard to take. Men were killed at the front, but it never had this effect on me. In action, even at the very moment of death, the fight has to go on, but here it was different. I was frightened. I tried to turn my mind from the dead comrades, but the more I tried, the more vividly I saw them in life.

In the hospital I found out that Belchite had been captured. Dave Doran had gotten hold of a propaganda truck and fitted it with a microphone and loudspeaker. He brought it up to the church where the fascist resistance was centered. Hastily he wrote out a speech which a Spanish boy read into the microphone. "Fascist soldiers, those of you who are Spaniards, listen!" the loudspeaker thundered. "Your leaders are lying to you. Quinto is in Republican hands. You will get no reinforcements. The relief column sent from Saragossa has been stopped at Mediana. There is no relief for you in Belchite; there is only death!

"Why are you fighting for the fascists? The fascists have taken your land. They have oppressed and exploited you and kept you in poverty. But the Republic is distributing land to the peasants. It has brought freedom and democracy.

"The fascists are the enemies of the people. When you are on their side, you are fighting against your own brothers, against the people of Spain. Our side is fighting for the people of Spain. Our side is the people of Spain. Come over to us and live. Drop your arms and come over the barricades one by one."

When the voice ceased, there was a long, unearthly silence. Nothing happened for a long, long time. Finally a lone enemy soldier crept over the barricades. He had a wound in his shoulder and wanted medical aid. They rushed him to Dave Doran. "What's the morale like?" Dave demanded. "Not good. Many are talking about that speech on the loudspeaker. Only fear of the officers holds them, because the officers would shoot them on the least provocation. But many have been killed or wounded, and the church and basement are nearly full of casualties."

"If this is true, could you go back and bring a group of them to our lines?"

The prisoner didn't like the idea at all. Going back was a risky business.

"It's the only choice we're giving you. Come back by way of this building and slip your rifles across the sandbags."

The prisoner crept through an opening in the barricades and vanished into the dark street. Doran had machine guns set up covering this street. Then he waited, sweating. An hour went by, and another hour, and at about midnight, there was a bustle in the street beyond the barricade. A rifle came sliding butt first over the sandbags. Within an hour several hundred fascists had surrendered. The main body of fascist resistance had crumbled—and without the cost in lives of an all-out assault the next morning.

The officers, finding themselves deserted, made a last desperate sortie in an effort to escape, and most were killed, wounded, or captured in the attempt. The next day a few last-ditch defenders were cleaned out of the houses. Belchite was ours.

I needed time to recuperate after I left the hospital. My wounds had become infected, and I was unable to return to the front as long as they were festering. Consequently I took on minor duties for the next six weeks. I escorted Congressman John Bernard, the sole representative to vote against the U.S. neutrality acts, through Republican territory; and when Lillian Hellman and Dorothy Parker, then writing for the *New Masses,* came to Spain, I served as their guide for a few days in Valencia.

At about that time, preparations for the twentieth anniversary of the Russian Revolution were beginning, and it was decided to send representatives from the International Brigades. I was selected to represent the Fifteenth Brigade at the November 7 festivities in Moscow and made arrangements to travel to Paris and pick up a visa for the Soviet Union.

I caught a truck to Barcelona, where I picked up a ride on a single-prop plane flying to Marseilles. The little plane was jammed with fifteen men in addition to the pilot, and we took off in threatening weather. We had barely gotten off the ground when a terrific thunderstorm burst, and the plane simply didn't have the power to climb above the clouds. We had no alternative but to skim along the surface, barely twenty to thirty feet above the Mediterranean. The bobbing up and down had just about everybody on board vomiting, and the pilot had to struggle to keep us on course.

It was a relief to touch down in Marseilles. My first thought after leaving the airport was food. You can't imagine how good the cheese and long loaves of French bread tasted after over half a year in Spain. I caught a train for Paris, checked in with the brigade headquarters, and waited for my visa for the Soviet Union. At Headquarters I received the sad news that Joe Dallet had been killed on the Aragon front. We had been separated after our arrival in Spain, our responsibilities taking us to different theaters of the struggle. The man who gave me this news also told me that Joe's wife Kitty was on her way to Paris from England and due to arrive the next day. She didn't know about Joe.

Kitty and Joe had met in Youngstown when Joe was the Party's organizer there. They had been having some problems before Joe left for Spain and had separated. But when we landed at Le Havre on our way to Spain, she was there at the dock. She and Joe spent some time together, and it appeared that they were working out their difficulties. In fact, Kitty wanted to accompany us to Spain and serve in a medical unit. There was a policy that no wives were allowed in, and although Joe fought it, they couldn't get the rules changed. Kitty went to England where her dad was working and kept in touch with Joe by mail. Joe had written her that I was going to be in Paris on my way to Moscow, and Kitty decided to come and visit with me. I was the one to tell her about Joe. I had watched their romance rekindle just a few months before. It was tough.

I went to the Soviet embassy each day, hoping that my visa would arrive. The Soviet diplomatic service was less than efficient, and there was no sign of my document. After a week I received a cable from Earl Browder, the secretary of the American Party, to forget about Moscow and catch the next ship home. I boarded a steamer the next day and arrived in New York City in time to report on Spain at a National Committee meeting. It was November 1937.

Until then I still thought I would be heading back to Spain. But at this national meeting I was "coopted" (which is how we called selected) onto the National Committee and asked to go on a speaking tour about Spain. I reluctantly agreed. I think the Party felt I had taken my risks already and could be of more use at home. After a brief but wonderful reunion with Margaret, I hit the road.

For two months I spoke at public meetings and met with the press about Spain. I touched down in a lot of familiar places—Philly, Pittsburgh, Detroit, and Chicago—and met with Party groups in Camden, Trenton, St. Louis, and Milwaukee. I talked not only about the urgency of the Spanish situation but of how I visualized the transition to a democratic order if Franco could be beaten. Already railroads, banks, and many factories had been nationalized. Large landholdings had been broken up, and the Church and old military structures dislodged. It seemed almost inevitable that victory on the battlefields would open the gates to the institutionalization of these processes in a democratic socialist Spain. I also tried to say something about the volunteers from each town where I was speaking.

In Ann Arbor I was invited to speak at the university. I concluded my remarks by talking about DeWitt Parker, a friend from the area who had been killed when a shell hit his dugout shortly before I left Belchite. At one point DeWitt had given me his watch because he had an extra, and I needed one. When I was done speaking, a man approached and said he was DeWitt's father. I spent the night talking with the family and gave them back DeWitt's watch.

In Philadelphia I was slated to speak at a large meeting held in the Metropolitan Opera House. I read that day that the fascists had cut through Republican lines, splitting Catalonia off from Madrid. I told myself that this was the end. The cities were thoroughly blockaded, and it seemed only a matter of time before the crushing military

Steve Nelson addressing a Loyalist support rally, Madison Square Garden, New York, spring 1938.

superiority of the fascists wiped out both Catalonia and Madrid. Roy Hudson, a national Party leader also on the agenda, came up to me before my talk and said, "You have to tell them that we're going to win in Spain." I said, "Roy, I can't tell them that because I'm not sure it's true."

I sat on the platform in front of three thousand people and was unsure of what to say. Tung P'ing spoke before me on the struggle of the Communists in China. He was an eloquent speaker and placed their struggle in historical perspective. He assured the audience of their eventual victory, and he was right, if a decade premature. When I got up I talked about the necessity of the democratic countries opening the gate to Spain. If we could convince our government to come to the aid of Spain, the struggle could be won. But if we couldn't we would face fascism in other places at other times.

While in Cleveland I was cabled by Clarence Hathaway, then editor of the *Daily Worker,* to return to New York City immediately. They even sent me plane fare, which was a rarity. When I came back, I was told that liberals within the American League for Peace and Democracy wanted somebody from the Party to work with them. I looked like a good choice because of the prominence I was receiving due to Spain. I asked, "Is my return to Spain a closed question?" Hathaway answered that it was, so I went to work in the American League.

I might have been back from Spain, but the war went on. Men from the Lincoln Brigade fought and died at Teruel in late 1937, in the second battle for Belchite the following spring, and finally in the crossing of the Ebro River and the retreat back across it in the summer of 1938.

It was in New York that we heard of Spain's defeat. Margaret and I were sharing an apartment with another couple in Manhattan. We sat in the living room after dinner one night to listen to the news on the radio, and word came that Franco's forces had entered Madrid. The three of them cried like children, and I sat there dumbstruck. All I could think about were the Loyalist forces encircled by Franco, unable to retreat, trapped with their backs against the Mediterranean. And then we sat there asking each other, "What now?" We had lost the initiative, and we feared Hitler's next steps.

Why did Republican Spain die? It may sound like political rhetoric to say so today, but Spain in 1936–1938 was the front line of the struggle against international fascism. Yet the Republic lacked the backing of the Western democracies. This lack, more than anything else, led to its defeat. Franco was more than adequately supplied and equipped from Germany, Italy, and Portugal, while Spain could count on support only from the Soviet Union and Mexico. If the democratic countries had realized that Hitler was fighting his first round in Spain, perhaps they would have lined up with the Republic. They would have at least permitted the sale of ammunition or medicine and food. As it was Franco's forces received more than a little assistance from the democracies through indirect means. Half of his trucks and oil actually came from the United States.

Also contributing to the weakness of Republican forces, yet on a far smaller scale, were divisions within the Popular Front itself. Republicans, Socialists, Communists, anarchists, and Trotskyists, although all committed antifascists, had differing conceptions of what the struggle in Spain was about. Moreover, there were serious long-standing animosities among them.

There were those who doubted the intentions of the Spanish Communist Party and of Communists from other countries who fought explicitly for the limited program of the Popular Front. Socialists and social democrats, in particular, had been the focus of Communist polemics during and after the First World War. Many of the Socialist parties had supported their countries' respective military efforts then in a war that Communists viewed as a squabble between imperialist powers. Furthermore, many of these parties had given little support for the Soviet Union in the 1920s. These were the litmus tests by which Communists measured respective allies. At the 1928 Congress of the Communist International, these parties were dubbed "social-fascist." This mistaken analysis was coming to an end in 1935 when the Comintern offered a reevaluation, but the damage to Socialist-Communist relations had been severe. We had been wrong to use the label social-fascist, and the consequences were tragic. Even after we attempted to revise our appraisal, there was a lack of trust and respect. This interfered with the broadest possible support for the Republic.

There was something else, which I could not see at that time. Many Socialists were able to see the unsavory side of Stalin's policies in the Soviet Union. We supported them blindly and could not see that any criticism was justified. Perhaps the Socialists figured that if we ever had the upper hand in Spain, we would do with them what had been done to the various oppositions in the Soviet Union. Had the Soviets presented a more democratic image to the world, it would have been easier to establish a broader base of international support.

Coming at the Communists from the other end of the Left's political spectrum were the anarchists, whose range of support in Spain was greater than in any other country; and, to a much lesser extent, the Trotskyists. Both groups distrusted the Communists' willingness to support political and military institutions with which they had serious philosophical disagreements. They also saw the Popular Front's limited aims as creating a situation in which we could "win the war but lose the revolution." Consequently, the anarchists pushed for measures they thought would radicalize the process of social change but which I and many Communists saw as weakening the immediate war effort. I think that some of the anarchist attempts to create agricultural communes and establish worker ownership in all factories—large and small—were premature and hindered the fullest possible mobilization against the fascists. I disagreed with them when they called for settling accounts with the bourgeoisie then and there—even with the owners who were loyal to the Republic. I thought then, and still do, that the first matter was to defeat the fascists.

We were wrong to see in anarchist activities a Trotskyist conspiracy. Unfortunately, that was how the Communists saw anarchism—as a well-intentioned movement with an indigenous base in many parts of Spain that was being manipulated by the Troyskyists. There was, however, a serious disagreement on how to conduct the war, and I still believe that the anarchists' position was self-defeating. With the POUM, the Trotskyist grouping in Spain, there was no dialogue.[4] Historic antagonisms and distrusts were too great to overcome. What is perhaps most significant about these frictions among the parties of the Left is that they limited the unity of forces fighting for the Republic. If we could have agreed on a common agenda and put off some of these questions until they could have received a fuller, democratic debate, we all would have been much better off.

It has been said that tensions on the Left led factions to divert supplies from their political opponents, and even resulted in murder. It's obvious that some irregular things occurred, but by whom I personally cannot say. For example, we will probably never know who took Andres Nin, the Trotskyist leader, out of jail in Alcalá de Henares and killed him. The bitterness that existed sometimes led to serious conflict. There was a mood that said whoever isn't with us is against us. To an extent the Stalinist influence, which led to criminal actions in the Soviet Union, also operated in Spain. There, however, nobody gave orders to "go out and do it." People internalize political attitudes and then operate along the lines they see as correct. I have no evidence one way or the other about these charges. While I was in Spain, nothing of the sort occurred within the Lincoln Battalion or the Fifteenth Brigade. Not one man was taken out and shot, and political differences did not stand in the way of our cooperation with units of a different political orientation.[5]

If I were to make any criticism of the American Communists' role in Spain, it would not be of what we did during the struggle itself. What other American organization mobilized so many men and women to fight for Spanish democracy? But had we taken a broader, more flexible approach over the years prior to Spain, we could have gotten more support for the Republic. There was a point in the United States by the end of 1937 when the bottom of the barrel was scraped. We had no more resources to contribute and could not persuade those outside the immediate belt around the Left to see Spain as their struggle. If we had gained more popular support, perhaps we could have pressured Congress to change its disastrous policy of "neutrality." All Spain really needed was time. We were always sure that Hitler was going to attack somewhere—Poland, Czechoslovakia, France, or the Soviet Union. Another year's resistance might have united the struggle in Spain with the Second World War. That would have averted much tragedy, for the immediate aftermath of Franco's victory was death on a massive scale. Some two to three hundred thousand were killed by execution squads, a million were imprisoned, and hundreds of thousands were driven into exile. Some have only won their freedom from these jails in the last few years, for the pall cast by four decades of Franco's dictatorship is only now breaking up. And as night follows day, World War Two followed the defeat of the Spanish Republic.

The volunteers for Spain remained in the front lines. They fought with the French Resistance and the Yugoslav partisans and in the Russian and American armies. Entire Allied companies were made up of exiled Spaniards. They were in the tanks that led the French army into Paris during the liberation. And they retained the hope that after the defeat of Hitler, the Allied forces would turn toward Spain and depose Franco. How ironic that at the end of the war, the United States emerged as Franco's chief prop.

The International Brigades were withdrawn from Spain several months before the final collapse in the vain hope that such a move might force Franco to remove his German and Italian allies from Spain. In the States many of the returning volunteers received rough treatment. They were termed "premature antifascists" and faced resistance when they tried to join the armed forces during the Second World War. Out of the fifteen hundred who came back, almost half served in the war.

The impact of the Spanish experience on the Communists who were there is difficult to judge. Up to that time, I was a willing soldier in the ranks, accepting every assignment with few questions. But after

Spain I found myself raising questions that I would not have raised in the past. I relied more on my own conclusions drawn from my own experiences, and I think that this held true for many other American veterans. In Spain and in the midst of a battle, you had to take more initiative. You developed the habit of thinking on your own. More-over, when you are leading men into life and death encounters, blind obedience to authority is not enough. Men would follow only if they believed you and felt your interpretation was the best one possible.

Another of the lessons many of us drew from Spain was the neces-sity of working with other popular movements. While it was Dimitrov who raised the notion of the popular front against fascism, it was the Communist Party of Spain that more than any other party put it into effect. The Party's practice had a profound influence on those of us who were in Spain and able to observe its actions from close range. We learned that Communists couldn't go it alone and ignore other democratic forces.

Could the forces unleashed by the Spanish experience have led to a decisive challenge to Stalinism within the Communist movement? Perhaps, but history does not always unfold in a straight path. The coming of the Second World War, and with it Stalin's greatly en-hanced prestige, impeded these new impulses, and the cold war re-channeled them back into the uncritical support of a monolithic Com-munist movement.

Perhaps Stalin recognized this better than anybody. Many of the Russians who fought in Spain, and many of the volunteers from other countries who went there after the defeat of the Republic because they could not return to their own countries, were victims of his purges. Such was the case with Vladimir Čopic, our commander in the Fifteenth Brigade. This was to trouble me greatly in later years.

EIGHT

The West Coast: 1939–1945

We were only in New York City a little more than a year, from 1938 to 1939, but that was enough. It had been a tough winter there. The dailies were filled with news about continuing executions and jailings in Spain, and it was hard for me to buck the sense of despair that this brought on. Nor had I fully recovered from my Spanish diarrhea. And finally, our attempt to bring a new life into the world that spring ended tragically when our daughter died shortly after birth. I would have liked to have returned to the anthracite region after Spain, but the Party leadership had other ideas for me, and the anthracite coalfields were a declining area. The entire region was becoming another casualty of capitalism's uneven development, going the way of the New England textile towns and the steel valleys in more recent years. I did go back briefly. A large hall in Wilkes-Barre had been rented, and a crowd of more than a thousand showed up to welcome me home. Elizabeth Gurley Flynn joined me on the platform to speak about Spain. Someone sent a bouquet of flowers up to me, and I didn't know what to do with them, so I turned and gave them to her. She laughed but took them. She knew how to roll with it.

New York was such a contrast. Margaret and I got an apartment of our own on Third Avenue, and Kitty Dallet moved in with us. Her life was in turmoil then, but she knew she could stay with us as long as need be. After a few months she found herself in a whirlwind romance with an English doctor that ended in a quick marriage and an even quicker divorce. Kitty moved out to California to return to the University of California at Berkeley, and we temporarily lost touch with her. In the meantime I went to work in the national office of the American League for Peace and Democracy, an organization comprised mainly of liberals that had been formed to awaken the American people to the dangers of fascism. We sent out speakers, agitated against doing business with Germany and Italy, and tried to educate people to the meaning of fascism. I considered it useful work, but I felt better with the miners. It was hard to sit in an office after Spain.

My responsibilities with the league did not last for long. The league was caught in the trough between the defeat of Spain and the beginnings of World War II, and its financial support fell. We cut our already small staff in half, and those who stayed on took over an increased workload. I was one of those who left.

Soon afterward Margaret and I were asked if we were ready for a change. The Party, it seemed, could use us on the West Coast. We didn't have to discuss it very long. Our personal situation coincided with the Party's needs, and there was something about California which sounded appealing. We had visions of a better climate, and our friends there had been urging us for a long time to give the coast a try.

The Party subsidized a brand new Plymouth; it was the only time we've ever had a new car. We packed its back seat full of books and some clothes, said good-bye to New York City, and set out cross-country. It was the spring of 1939, and the drive west gave us both a chance to relax and enjoy the country. We drove through Iowa corn-fields and the Nebraska wheat belt and explored the Carlsbad Caverns, the Grand Canyon, and the Painted Desert. We stayed with friends from the Party along the way, occasionally shedding our role as tourists to sit in on a meeting. Before we knew it, we were through the Mojave Desert and settling into a furnished apartment on Bixel Street in midtown Los Angeles.

I had two assignments in southern California; the first was as a troubleshooter. Despite the progress made through the CIO, the labor movement in LA still lagged behind that of San Francisco and the industrial centers of the East. Trade unionism was confined to the AFL building trades, some Hollywood unions, and seamen and longshoremen. Mass industrial unionism among auto and aircraft workers was just picking up steam. Nowhere was the fight for a union tougher than in California's Imperial Valley, a region of fertile agricultural lands worked by itinerant laborers of a dozen nationalities and owned by powerful agricultural interests. The struggle to organize the valley's work force had been going on for over a decade and had resulted in more than a few deaths as well as hundreds of beatings and arrests. The Los Angeles district of the Party considered building the labor movement its top priority. Many Party members had been sent into the Imperial Valley to take jobs as farm workers and stimulate union organizing, but a very high percentage were quickly exposed and fired, brutally beaten, or both. In LA several

Party sections found that many of their members were being fired from their jobs for no apparent reason. It was more than coincidental. The Party and the young trade union organizations were obviously being infiltrated.

I was to help figure out what was going on and put an end to it. I was assigned to work with two other Party members on a special control commission whose existence was known only to a few Party leaders. One of my co-workers possessed a certain technical expertise that enabled him to detect wiretaps and electronic surveillance. The other was an old Armenian dentist, Dr. V. T. K. Tashjian. An extreme disciplinarian with a shaved skull, he appeared as stern and gruff as they come, but was really an extremely sensitive man. We spent a good deal of time discussing what was going on and talking with people who had come back from the valley and could report on the terror there. Our question was, who was behind it?

The LA Police Department had a vicious Red Squad, led by William "Red" Hynes, which had often served as the arm of the open shoppers. But the thoroughness of the firings made Tashjian feel that this infiltration wasn't their handiwork alone. We decided that the Associated Farmers, the organization representing the interests of the large agribusinesses in the valley, had to be behind it. They already maintained their own security force, which included a squad of thugs, and it was not at all beyond their scope of activities to try to infiltrate the Party or trade unions.

We managed to get a young Party member employed as a clerical worker in the Associated Farmers' offices in LA. We thought he might be able to get his hands on some files or find out who was in charge of the stool pigeon operation. After working there a month, he couldn't find out anything. But one morning in the men's room, he overheard that the Associated Farmers had just had their records subpoenaed by the government. We put two and two together. The LaFollette Committee had recently appeared in town at the request of the AFL and the American Civil Liberties Union (ACLU). The committee, set up under the leadership of Robert LaFollette, Jr., the progressive senator from Wisconsin, investigated abuses of civil liberties by business in its attempts to defeat unionism.[1]

We thought it would be difficult to crack the Senate committee, but one morning I met Tashjian for coffee, and he was grinning from ear to ear. A young person employed by the Associated Farmers had somehow managed to get in touch with him and had offered us access to the files subpoenaed by the LaFollette Committee. Tashjian wouldn't identify the source, and I didn't want to ask. He would only say that this young person had had a change of heart after becoming aware of the impact of the Associated's policies. I thought it was probably someone working around the office as a courier or clerk.

Each night for several weeks, Tashjian met with his contact and returned to an apartment with a batch of files. We set up a camera and quickly photographed the reports so that the contact could replace them before morning. If we had to, we developed prints; otherwise we worked from negatives. This went on as long as the LaFollette Committee was holding hearings. When they finished, our contact informed Tashjian that it was now too risky to continue.

By then, however, we had managed to photograph about seven or eight hundred of these reports. A typical one might state that the informant, identified only by a number, had been at a meeting Tuesday night with Jack Moore, Lou Barron, and Matt Pelman to discuss a certain phase of organizing. We would go to Jack, Lou, and Matt, who were obviously not agents, and ask who else had been at the meeting. By a process of elimination, we concluded that there were about thirty informants inside the Party in the LA area. We boiled it down over a few months to those we were absolutely positive were working for the growers.

Once we knew who the stoolies were, we figured out how best to expose them. We thought we should try to make an impression not only on them, but on all informants. Two of the Associated Farmers' agents were prominent in a Party section of about three hundred members. They were married; he was the membership secretary, and she was the section's literature agent. They were the kind of members who were always willing to take on some routine task like putting out a mailing or typing a report, but they rarely had much to say. The husband had a good cover. He claimed to be consumptive and unable to socialize much. His livelihood was dealing in rare birds, and he disappeared every now and then for two or three weeks to go to Mexico to purchase birds for dealers. We decided to start with them.

Not long afterward there was a picnic for the *People's World (PW)*, a radical paper on the West Coast with close ties to the Party. Seven or eight hundred people were there, including this couple, enjoying a lazy California day. Around sunset a bit of entertainment ended on the platform we had set up, and a member of the District Committee who was chairing the meeting got on stage. "We've got something to announce," he began in a friendly tone. "I want to call two people up here who deserve special recognition. I want you all to remember who these people are." Most of the people in the crowd of course thought he was going to praise the couple as he asked them to come up on the platform. When they were standing on either side of him, he took hold of their hands and smiled. Raising their arms in the air, he announced that they were stool pigeons for the Associated Farmers. "We have the goods on these two." There was a gasp from the crowd, then silence, and all of a sudden the couple bolted from the stage and ran for their car while most of the crowd burst into laughter. We never saw them again, and I think stool pigeons learned to stay away from our picnics after that.

We handled the other informers more quietly. We would call a meeting and warn everyone else not to show up. When the informer arrived, we'd tell him or her to come in for a talk. Essentially we told them to get the hell out or else. Fortunately, we never had to determine what "else" might be.

Everybody was curious as to how the Associated Farmers' stool pigeon operation had been exposed, but only a handful knew how it had been done or who was involved. Till this day I don't think many people realize that I was on the special commission. Thirty-five years later, I was fishing on Gull Pond on Cape Cod with a man who was more or less an acquaintance. We had fished for trout together from his small boat a few times before. We got to talking about old times, and he mentioned he had been in California in the late thirties. We were sitting there lazily casting into the early morning mist when he started to chuckle. "You know, as a matter of fact, I was working with the Associated Farmers." I almost dropped my rod into the water. "You might as well meet me: I'm the one who fed you that information. I know all about you, Steve." I couldn't believe that after all these years, I was meeting the elusive contact. I bought him a drink.

My other task in Los Angeles was to act as an intermediary between the National Board and the Japanese Bureau of the Party. The Japanese Bureau, located in LA, had responsibility for the 125 or so Japanese members of the Party nationally, most of whom were on the West Coast. It was the smallest nationality group in the Party. The bureau coordinated the work of these members within the larger Japanese organizations in this country. There was a certain element of anti-Japanese hysteria on the coast at this time, and several newspaper articles had accused Japanese fisherman of spying for the imperial government. Moreover, Japanese Party members were fairly isolated within the Japanese-American community and were regarded by nationalists as traitors to imperial Japan.

I met with them for a few months to help coordinate certain activities. The history of the Russian Party had just been published, and the Japanese Bureau was asked to translate it into Japanese and put out several thousand copies. The Party had raised about $2,000 for the printing, and I brought the money with me. The translators and typesetters were working gratis, night and day, on this project. In addition to publishing this history, we worked on several pamphlets and leaflets agitating against the Japanese government's war in China and appealing to the Japanese people not to become tools of reactionary forces.

We wanted to get this material into Japan, for under pressure from the secret police, the Communist Party there had splintered into regional bodies. Unable to reconstitute itself on a national basis due to constant pressure and infiltration, the Japanese Party was powerless to oppose Japan's membership in the anti-Comintern pact with Hitler and Mussolini.

We went up and down the coast, from Seattle to San Pedro, wherever we had contacts with seamen or longshoremen. Most readily agreed to sneak these pamphlets onto cargo ships bound for Japan. Some were stuck into crates, and other were left lying about the holds in the hope that Japanese longshoremen would find them. Each month at least one thousand copies of the *Doho* (The Comrade), an eight-page tabloid put out by the Japanese Bureau, were shipped out. We sunk a lot of labor, money, and feeling into these activities even though we knew we were shooting in the dark. We didn't get any feedback on our efforts until after the war, when an American seaman told me he had talked with a Japanese longshoreman who said he had read about the American labor movement in *Doho* and once found leaflets in a packing crate. Another Japanese said he had seen our leaflets blowing in the wind when a crate he was unloading slipped out of its sling and smashed open on the docks.

Although partially oriented toward getting materials into Japan, the Japanese Party members believed their primary task was to participate in the American labor movement. Many young Japanese worked as clerks and deliverymen for fruit stands in southern California. They were the base of the Party in the Japanese-American community and helped organize a union of clerks and deliverymen.

I was no longer connected with the Japanese Bureau when the United States entered the war and large numbers of Japanese on the coast were interned. Conditions within the camps were terrible, and their thousands of inhabitants suffered a great deal. It bothers me to this day that I went along with the Party in backing the government's detention of Japanese. I believed government and media claims that there were many spies hiding within the Japanese-American community and accepted the notion that what is good for the war effort is good for the country, the Party, and the struggle for a better world. The Party encouraged its Japanese members in the camps to work with the administration to facilitate the delivery of health care and ameliorate conditions. These internees told their fellows that the Allies, despite having placed the Japanese in camps, were right, and the imperial government of Japan wrong. That was hard to say. They were accused of being stooges for the Americans, and many were beaten up. In retrospect it is easy to see that we were terribly wrong in justifying this treatment of the Japanese in the name of national interest.

Although we departed LA for San Francisco in the fall of 1939, we first had the pleasure of meeting Woody Guthrie. A friend writing for the *PW,* Ed Robbin, had the kind of sensitivity that attracted him to all sorts of people. He could mix it up with anybody. He heard a guy singing folksy songs on the local radio station where he did a weekly news broadcast and was impressed enough to track him down. What he found was a young Oklahoman singing without a note or lyric in front of him, talking about the Dust Bowl and bankers and, in his own natural way, saying things that had social meaning.

Ed invited Woody to his house for dinner one night and asked me over to meet him. I was amazed at Woody's facility to talk with his guitar. Words just poured out of him. It was almost as if he couldn't talk without it. 'So you're the guy who was over in Spain?" was the first thing he asked me. "What was it like over there? What was that guy Franco like?" I was amazed he knew who Franco was. Then he asked me, "Did Mr. Hitler help him much?" Nothing inhibited him, and the questions rolled out, one after the other. He sat there absorbing my answers like a sponge.

I couldn't describe him when I went home to Margaret that night, and we invited him to our house a few days later. Woody walked in, handsome and gangly with a disheveled head of bushy hair, and two young women, our other dinner guests, decided immediately that they'd make him presentable. Before we started eating, they sat Woody down and tried to get a comb through his hair. They were no more successful with that than they were trying to convince him to put on a sporty shirt. Woody liked the attention but couldn't understand why he ought to get spruced up. "Don't you want to get somewhere?" one of the women demanded. "Not particularly," he smiled back.

When we got to the table, Woody had a big dish of spaghetti set in front of him, and a bowl of meat sauce sat to his right. He looked at it for a while and asked, "Say, what's this?" He had never eaten spaghetti with meat sauce before. He turned to Maggie, saying "Mrs. Nelson, do you have a can of red beans around here? I want to make a chili out of this." So he took the beans and mixed them with the sauce and exclaimed, "Boy, I never had anything like this before." But he didn't trust the spaghetti, it just wasn't in his background. The chili, that he knew. We had a marvelous time with him, listening to him sing and play and answering his questions. We loved him right away.

In no time he became a correspondent for the *PW*. He wrote a column, "Woody Sez," that was only an inch long but usually a gem. And he sketched a little picture to go with it. He used to read the *PW* and the *Daily Worker* constantly and had questions for me whenever I saw him. He read about Russia, and we'd discuss socialism.

"Oh, that's like a big union where the boss is no longer around?"

"That's right," I'd answer.

"What'd they do with the bosses?"

"They sent some to jail," I responded, "some fled, and others had to be shot."

Woody paused a bit and answered, "They had it coming. They lived off the fat of the land for a long time. What are you going to do about that here in this country?"

That startled me. I explained that we were trying to organize unions now and said where we hoped that would lead.

"I can see that, but boy, you tackle those bankers that took over my daddy's farm, and you're not going to be on a picnic."

Some people ask a question to disparage you, drive you into a corner, or pick an argument. Not Woody. He would question only to seek knowledge. It made me feel rejuvenated just to talk with him.

On August 22, 1939, the Soviet Union signed a pact of nonaggression with Nazi Germany. I felt like I had been hit by a bolt of lightning. The very heart of our policies and struggles over the last decade had been the fight against the spread of fascism, and in that fight the Soviet Union had played a central role. But there was a logic to the pact I could understand.

Even before Franco's rebellion in Spain, the Soviet Union had repeatedly offered to form collective security agreements with the Western democracies and the nations of Eastern Europe. Despite fascist victories in Spain, Ethiopia, and Albania, both England and France sat back, spurning Russian advances. It seemed to me that the Western countries were willing to let Hitler advance, hoping that he would move first to the east against the Soviet Union. The historical record indicates that at the very least, they were willing to appease Germany's expansionist gambits until the invasion of the Low Countries. The Soviet Union feared an attack from Hitler—possibly with the acquiescence of the Western countries. In any case it did not appear that the Soviets would be able to count on Western support if Hitler invaded. Consequently I could understand the Soviet Union's desire to secure itself from hostilities and buy time to develop its defenses. But I was devastated by the morning paper with its shocking photo of Foreign Minister Molotov and Stalin toasting Hitler at the signing of the pact.

I went to a meeting of a longshoremen's local with Bill Schneiderman, the chairman of the California Party, soon after the signing of the pact. The question "How do you justify it?" came up from the floor. Bill stood up and replied, "The Soviet Union had a problem, just like you could have when you're negotiating your next contract. What if there's one shipping company that's ready to sign with you and another that's holding out? Would you treat both of them the same way? I doubt it. You'd probably sign with the one that was ready to go along with what you wanted, right? And you'd break up any chance of an employers' alliance against you. The Soviet Union is doing just that. They tried to get a security pact with France, Britain and the other democratic countries, and they wouldn't line up. So the Soviet Union said, 'All right, Hitler is ready to sign a pact that says he's not going to attack us. The other guys wouldn't sign one to form a joint defense, so the hell with 'em!' If you split the employers up, it weakens them, and it strengthens your union's position." And I think that most of the longshoremen thought that was a pretty reasonable answer.

Perhaps because I had been to Spain, I was more bitter than most people about British and French indifference to Hitler. When the Nazis attacked Poland in September 1939, and Britain and France were forced into war, my feelings were that "the sons-of-bitches had it coming."

What the Soviet Union did was one thing; what the American Party did, however, should have been another. Sadly, it was not. The American Party rapidly shifted its attitude toward events in Europe, arguing now that the United States should not get involved. By October the Party adopted a position labeling the war one of imperialist rivalry in which "both sides were equally guilty." The key principle motivating our activities of the last five years was no longer operative. Antifascism would be relegated to the back burners.

We called off our campaign to boycott Nazi goods, disbanded the Anti-Nazi League in Hollywood, and watered down our educational efforts to alert people to the dangers of fascism. Not only did the Party abdicate leadership in the fight against fascism; it also found itself aligned with isolationists. When Britain entered the war, we opposed U. S. assistance and objected to the Lend-Lease program, which sent Britain some mothballed destroyers. We raised the slogan "The Yanks are not coming!" And despite the invasion of Poland on September 1, 1939, and the Nazi's savage campaigns through Eastern and Western Europe in the following year, we maintained that position. We paid for it, though.

The Party's standing, which was quite good on the West Coast, started to slide. It wasn't that we hated fascism any less, but people saw us as mechanical pawns of Soviet foreign policy. How could we vociferously oppose fascism for all these years and suddenly mute our criticisms? Some people left the Party over this change of policy, and others withdrew quietly from activities or simply stopped coming around to meetings. There was some minimal disagreement within the Party over these policies, but most people either quickly fell into the groove or left. Either way, we didn't have to continually argue over the question. There was scarcely any debate within the Party either on a local or national level.

We were hurt particularly among intellectuals and the Jewish community. Left-wing Jews were as sectarian as the other members of the Party and suffered the consequences. They tried to justify their position with the mass organizations, but people wouldn't buy it. Their support within fraternal organizations declined, and Jewish left-wing papers lost readers. Jewish Communists had long been engaged in factional fighting with the Socialists, who were stronger in the Jewish community. Now they found themselves isolated. In addition, certain intellectuals became disillusioned with a movement that could make such a blunder. More fundamentally, our position on the pact weakened our ability to work with New Deal Democrats on issues of mutual concern.

In retrospect I can see these dissidents were right. Instead of recognizing the situation of the Soviet Union and saying, "You do what you think is right, but we don't agree with you and will continue to fight fascism here and elsewhere," we fell into line behind Soviet policy. We treated the Soviet Union as the single pivot in the world around which everything else was centered. Nothing else mattered.

We could have taken a position like that of Harry Pollitt, secretary of the British Communist Party. When France and Britain were attacked, he differed with the contention of both the Soviet and the American parties that the war was imperialist. He said we should see the greater danger of a Nazi victory and therefore find ways to critically support the British. For that he was booted out of the leadership of the British Party.

It would be wrong, however, to blame the Soviet Union for the decisions of the American Party. The blame is ours because we did not make our own analysis. We had the mentality that the Soviet Union was always right and that its interests were paramount. It wasn't that someone in Moscow pushed a button and we pulled a new position out of the drawer. We ourselves justified our actions. Unless revolutionaries take an independent view and hold positions consistent with the problems of their own countries, they will find themselves out of step with their people and the times.

In late 1939 hostilities broke out between the Soviet Union and Finland. Since the brutal Finnish civil war in 1918 between Left and Right, in which the Right had emerged victorious, Finland's leaders had sided with Germany against the Soviet Union. The latter, eager to protect the approaches to Leningrad in case of war with Germany, negotiated pacts of mutual security with Estonia, Latvia, and Lithuania. The Soviet Union then began negotiating with Finland to neutralize the threat that the strategically located Karelian Isthmus posed to Leningrad. The city lay exposed as long as this area along the Russian border was in hostile hands. The Soviets offered to compensate the Finns if they'd move their lines back. Mannerheim, the Finnish leader who had won his spurs in the court of the czar, had fortified the isthmus with pillboxes, tank traps, and barbed wire and had greatly enlarged the nearby air bases. This Mannerheim Line had awesome offensive capabilities for an attack on the Soviet Union. British and French influence had penetrated the Finnish government, and the result was an intransigence toward settlement with the Soviets. When Finland declined a Soviet ultimatum, the Soviets attacked.

The war lasted only till mid-March when, despite the wild claims of the American press that the Red Army was pillaging Finland, a fairly moderate settlement was imposed. The treaty indicated that the Soviets had aimed all along simply to get concessions necessary for their own defense. Failure to secure this border would have had disastrous consequences during the Second World War.

Sometimes you look back, and actions that seem awfully serious at the time look silly in retrospect. When the Soviet Union attacked Finland, we didn't know which way the Nazis were going to go. There was a sense that the heavens were about to cave in—that there was going to be war between Germany and the Soviet Union. I didn't dare adopt an optimistic perspective. We figured if the United States continued its "neutrality," the Soviet Union could find itself under attack from Japan on one side and Germany on the other. Given a domestic situation where our alliance with New Deal Democrats had been temporarily broken due to our position on the Hitler-Stalin Pact, the Party began deliberations over what we should do in case of war.

The leadership concluded that someday, maybe soon, the American Party might have to function from the underground. An elaborate shadow organization based on groups of three members was set up. The three would know only each other, with one member in contact with a member of another group. It was hierarchically structured and theoretically, at least, highly resistant to infiltration and exposure. The shadow organization extended from the national leadership through state and district organizations down to the branch committees.

In January 1940 Margaret and I went "on the shelf," as we called going underground. We were part of a group of about twenty Party members in the California organization who dropped out of public activities and left town. We departed San Francisco and went down the coast about twenty miles, stopping in Redwood City on the San Francisco Peninsula. We found a cottage and told the man from whom we rented that I was a writer. Stuck back away from the road in a cluster of trees, our cottage was a cozy little place. The rent was cheap because it was the off-season, and we were able to get by on the $35 a week that we were getting from the district.

We changed our names. I took that of a friend with whom I had fought in Spain. Generally our job was to lie low, follow the news, and be ready in case of war and repression of the Party to step into the leadership. These eventualities never materialized, and life on the shelf was closer to a vacation than a harried underground existence. I'd listen to the radio and read the newspaper, and occasionally someone from the state organization would take some roundabout way down from San Francisco and stay overnight to brief us.

When I told the cottage owner I was a writer, I wasn't just creating a cover. I had been wanting to tell what Spain had been like. I thought I could write a novel about my experiences and weave into it what other people had told me about what had happened to them. As it turned out, a man and woman came to stay with us for about a month. Each day I would sit down with this fellow and talk, and he'd take it down in longhand. When I looked at his notes, I didn't think I had anything in front of me. After I got off the shelf, I went to see a writer friend, David Lamson, who had written about the Canadian frontier for the *Saturday Evening Post* and other popular magazines. A man about forty, Lamson was tall and tough-looking, more like a lumberjack than the superb writer he was. Years before this he had been unjustly accused and convicted of murdering his wife and was sentenced to death. He maintained his innocence and wrote a book, *And We Who Are About to Die,* about his life on death row in San Quentin. After seven years he was finally absolved of the crime.

Lamson read over my notes and felt there was something there. He and his wife Ruth had often listened to me talk about Spain in their kitchen until late at night. I stayed with them for a week, and between the two of us, we knocked out a draft. I called it "The Volunteers."

I sent copies to a number of Party leaders—including Henry Winston and Bob Thompson—but they couldn't bring themselves to read it. Nobody wanted to hear anything about Spain at that time; people didn't want to be reminded of defeat. "The Volunteers" lay around unread for a number of years and came out only in 1953, when I was in jail.

The end of the Finnish-Soviet war in March 1940 brought our temporary stay in the underground to a close. It no longer looked as if the Party was about to be knocked off balance by arrests and repression. The funny thing about this three-month period is that we had been stashing away equipment up and down the coast. Ink, mimeograph machines, and reams of paper and stencils were hidden away in the woods, and later on we had a rough time tracking them down. There's a lumberjack somewhere in northern California with a mimeo machine rusting in his shed, and he probably doesn't remember how the damn thing got there.

A little over a year later, while we were back in San Francisco, Germany broke the nonagression pact and invaded the Soviet Union. It was June 22, 1941. I was home alone, reading in the living room, when news came over the radio that the Soviet Union was under attack. I can still remember jumping up and racing outside to the car to head over to Bill Schneiderman's house. I never even thought of calling. I knew he was hosting a birthday party and figured a lot of the state leadership would be there. I had to drive through Golden Gate Park to get there, and I listened to the radio the entire way over. I walked into the house and, to my amazement, they were partying. I cried out, "Do you know what's happened?" When I told them the news, the party broke up. People went home to listen to their radios, agreeing first to meet early in the morning.

The invasion of the Soviet Union changed the character of the war.

I think that it was Hitler's biggest blunder. If he had attacked the Soviet Union first, he might have been able to defeat it while the Western democracies sat things out. But Churchill's realization that his house could burn too caused him to extend his hand to the Soviet Union when it was attacked.

The first couple of months of the war were disastrous. The Red Army was unprepared, and hundreds of thousands of Russian troops were captured as the Nazis rolled right through to the Ukraine. Some drew the conclusion that the Soviet Union would never be able to reverse the tide after such devastating defeats. Nightly radio commentators like H. V. Kaltenborn predicted doom for the Soviet Union. Those of us who had some military experience and had analyzed the nonaggression pact as a device to allow the Soviets a chance to prepare for war were shocked and angry. Why hadn't they been using that time to build up their defenses! We later learned that the defeats were due in large part to Stalin's decimation of the Red Army officer corps down to the lowest echelons.

But as the war continued, the Soviet Union joined with the Allies and began an unbelievable mobilization. Entire factories were moved to the East. Virgin forests were leveled and steel mills and foundries to produce metal armaments were thrown up almost overnight. Stalin had hesitated during the preceding months, but when he moved, he did so with incredible energy and single-mindedness.

Stateside, our policies shifted once again, and the Party came back into the antifascist movement, where we were to stay throughout the war. The ambiguities of the Hitler-Stalin Pact months were cleared away. The interests of the Soviet Union and the political principles for which we struggled throughout the thirties were no longer at odds. The world was at the crossroads, and we saw what role we should play. In many ways I was relieved.

There was a freshness and vitality to the Left in California that made it an extraspecial place to be a radical. With our difficulties with the government at an all-time low due to our cooperation in the war effort, we rode the crest of a wave in the early forties. But the upswing was more than a temporary phenomenon. The Left and the Communist Party in California had an authentic niche in the state's cultural and political heritage and reflected the vibrancy of its working-class movements.

California was known even then as a sort of maverick state. All kinds of people had drifted there during the Depression, and they provided the basis of support for a variety of populist and radical ventures.

There were still remnants of the old Wobbly tradition of roaming hoboes and footloose men and women riding the rails and following the
harvest. And there was a clearly identifiable financial and industrial
class to target for responsibility for the state's problems.

The labor movement had tackled these interests time and time
again, with spectacular cases like those of Tom Mooney and Warren
Billings and the McNamara brothers to attest to the intensity of its
struggles.[2] During the Depression a quasi-populist doctor, Francis E.
Townsend, had a mass base among the unemployed and elderly for
his "ham 'n eggs" movement. "Why should we be hungry when there
is plenty of ham and eggs?" he'd ask. "We've got more eggs than we
know what to do with!" His ideas of redistributing the nation's wealth
touched a responsive chord. Upton Sinclair, the socialist author and
muckraker, had campaigned for the governorship in 1934 on a radical
program called EPIC—End Poverty in California. Sweeping through
the Democratic primary, Sinclair was defeated only by a massive and
concerted counterattack by the state's ruling interests. But the radical perspective gained sway over a portion of the Democratic Party,
and in 1939 a liberal Democrat, Culbert Olson, became governor,
ending forty-odd years of Republican hegemony, and we envisioned a
move leftward. For one thing, Tom Mooney and Warren Billings were
at last freed.

The Left had participated in these struggles, and it prospered in
California's fertile political soil. Radicals were not outside the working class looking in but were a part of it. The overwhelming majority
of Communists were workers. Whether technicians, stagehands, or
carpenters in the Hollywood branch, longshoremen in San Pedro and
the Bay Area, or aircraft, auto, and office workers in LA, they were
conscious members of an American working class. And in California
there were many of them.

Perhaps six or seven thousand people were in the Party during the
war. This working-class orientation in both membership and strategy
led the Party to emphasize work within the labor movement. We were
an organic part of that movement and had participated in the desperate struggles to organize the CIO, and people recognized that we'd
paid our dues. Scores of locals elected Communists as their union
leaders, and hundreds of others were willing to cooperate with the
Party, for we were seen as a strong ally of the labor movement.

In such a favorable atmosphere, the California Party flourished
during the war years. We participated in the labor movement and in
electoral politics with a flexibility and energy that won us friends,
recruits, and a relative degree of success for our common struggles.

The Party did not have unlimited power, but it had enough to make it a respectable political force.

The California Party also enjoyed more autonomy than most districts because the national leadership was over three thousand miles away, in New York City. Moreover, the state Party members were overwhelmingly American-born and included many native Californians. We were less encumbered by the dogmatism that foreign-born Communists were especially prone to. We were also more familiar with American culture and politics and less likely to dismiss them out of hand. In many ways we set our own course. There was a lively internal life to the organization, due in part to an iconoclastic Western mood. It was the healthiest Party district I'd been in. People talked back to you—they argued their points and did it in plain language, freer of leftist jargon than in most places. Moreover, the leaders of the California Party were not removed from local practice, sitting back in an office righteously issuing policy statements. We had a saying there, "The guys who eat have to wash the dishes too."

And they were pretty good dishwashers. California had a group of rank and file elected leaders that surpassed those of any other district where I had worked. Bill Schneiderman, the state chairman, who, like me, was in his late thirties, was an articulate guy with a keen sense of state politics. Nothing in the legislature or Congress passed him by. He was a cool, collected sort of man, almost shy in some ways. I valued his friendship. In LA Paul Cline was the party chairman. He was a driving force for a broad, flexible policy. Cline wasn't afraid of being "contaminated" by bourgeois associates, and he cultivated relationships with church leaders and Democratic politicos. He'd say, "Look, I'm a Communist, but I want to know what you as a Democrat think about this." He was open-minded and listened attentively to what was said in the political arena.

Around these men were a score of other men and women. Rudy and Walter Lambert, Louise Todd, and Archie Brown, a Spanish Civil War vet and a longshoreman, were all active in San Francisco. Slim Connelly headed both the LA and California CIO Federations. Close to 250 pounds and well over six feet, with the mannerisms to fit his size, Slim was a powerful organizer. Dave Jenkins was director of the California Labor School, which attracted hundreds of Bay Area activists. Ben Dobbs, Jack Moore, and Nemi Sparks worked in LA, and Pettis Perry, Matt Crawford, Herschel Alexander, and Ray Thompson worked in the black community. Pettis Perry had been a sharecropper in the South and had taught himself to read and write. He started studying Marxist literature and applied it to the problems of the black community. He could work with a black minister as easily as with a guy from the poolroom. Ray Thompson was the first black man I met who described the problems of black youth to me. He knew about stickups, gangs, and trouble with the cops from first-hand experience. When the Party considered running Ray for city council in Oakland, he said, "Hold on. Are you ready to face this?" and explained that he had a juvenile record for petty crime. We talked things over, and Ray helped me to realize what that meant in terms of the black community. Until then we had taken an almost puritanical attitude toward petty crime, especially as it pertained to people joining the Party. If a person had even a minor criminal record, he or she could not join. But Ray forced me to confront experiences that were different from my own. I realized that I still had a lot to learn about black people. Here I was, a man in my thirties dealing with some of these things for the first time.

California could also boast of an exceptional group of women in leadership roles. Anita Whitney, then close to eighty, was a member of both the State and National committees. She had been a suffragette and early Socialist Party activist and had been prosecuted for her opposition to the First World War. Louise Todd had been accused of illegally collecting signatures on a campaign petition in the thirties and she spent sixteen months in the Tahatchapi prison. She later became the state organizational secretary and a nationally known leader. Oleta O'Connor Yates, later to become chairman of the San Francisco district, was a local Irish-American woman well connected with Irish fraternal groups. She blossomed into one of the most eloquent radical spokeswomen in the state. Bernadette Doyle, another Irish-American woman who was my co-worker in Oakland, at one time ran for state superintendent of public education and received something like four hundred thousand votes. She was a strong determined woman and was one of the reasons I was so happy working in Oakland. And last there was a young woman who impressed me the first time I met her. Dorothy Healey was a lively and quick-witted organizer blessed with a beautiful smile and a lot of guts. She got her start working among farm workers in the thirties and has been an outstanding leader in radical movements both within and outside the Party on the coast till this day.

There were a slew of longshoremen and seamen who were marvelous rank and file leaders, among them Bill Bailey, B. B. Jones, and Walter Stack. Walt still amazes me. The first thing he does in the morning is run down to the bay and dive in, no matter whether it's winter or summer. Some time in his fifties, I think, he started running, and my neighbors down the road saw him breeze by in the 1978 Boston Marathon, still going strong. I never met anybody on the waterfront as acid-tongued and militant as Stack. He could be devastating, and many a foreman blanched when locked in argument with Walt over a grievance. Bill Bailey was with me in Spain. He was one of those who pulled the Nazi flag off the *Bremen* when it docked in New York Harbor in the 1930s. B. B. Jones always had a wad in his mouth and a watch cap on his head. He'd never put on Sunday clothes and professed little respect for bourgeois niceties. There was also a Yugoslav, Padavan, who had been a seaman, fisherman, and longshoreman. During a waterfront strike he had been beaten up so terribly that he became totally blind. Yet he was the life and leader of the Party section in San Pedro. He was able to keep up with things simply by sound and by having somebody read to him. He knew the waterfront and could identify hundreds of people just by their voices.

Al Richmond and Harrison George, an old Wobbly, were two of those who made the *Peoples' World* such a respected and influential newspaper. Although not formally a Party organ, the *PW* was for all intents and purposes the Party's voice on the West Coast. It was more popularly oriented than the *Daily Worker* and had a mass following outside the ranks of the Party. It was especially popular with the labor movement. The *PW* was a daily while I was on the coast, and it was the kind of paper that anyone could pick up and read. There was a constant stream of fund raisers for the *PW,* some hosted by labor unions who saw the paper as an ally worth supporting.

Al Richmond was the managing editor and the picture of a newspaper man. He never appeared hassled, and the words just rolled off his typewriter. And there were reporters like Ed Robbin, who introduced me to Woody Guthrie, and Mike Quin. Mike was really an unusual human being. Slim, with big horn-rimmed glasses and a serious appearance that concealed a rapier wit, his prose was like poetry. Mike came out of the Bay Area and had hardly more than a high school education. We worked together on little pamphlets like *Why Socialism for Maritime Workers?* He bowled me over with his capacity to make things convincing and clear. I recall his coverage of the trials of Harry Bridges, the Australian-born longshoremen's leader who was constantly harassed because of his trade union activity and radical political beliefs. The International Longshoremen's and Warehousemen's Union (ILWU) had a nightly radio show, and Mike got on the air every night for months to report on each day's trial proceedings.[3] Without using a lot of legal jargon, he put complex courtroom maneuverings into everyday language. That radio hour was like religion all over the waterfront. People would gather around a radio and listen to Mike's crisp, machine-gun diction. There was no waste of words, no crazy embellishments or phony put-ons—but a working-class approach with a good measure of sarcasm.

There were also a couple of old-timers around the San Francisco Party. One was Pop Falkoff, a man past seventy-five. He had been a garment presser and was paralyzed in one hand. Pop was a self-educated philosopher who had read all the Marxist works and could talk about what they said and how they fit into the development of Marxist thought. Even the academics in the Party respected his grasp of philosophy and dialectics. He was also responsible for raising a good deal of money. People admired him, and if they wanted to make a donation to the *PW,* they would come to Pop and pass the money through him. There was another Pop, but he was Falkoff's polar opposite. A Georgian Russian with a huge impressive head, Pop Hanoff was as hard as nails. He wanted to come across as an old Bolshevik. When trying to recruit someone into the Party, he'd say, "You had better join the Party now, because we'll remember you when the revolution comes!" Hanoff claimed to have been in the Russian Party before the Revolution. He would appear periodically in my office and demand to know the status of our membership registration. He sent one of my co-workers into a panic every time he showed up.

I was in San Francisco when the United States entered the war, and I remained in the Bay Area throughout the conflict. The state committee had asked me to help with work on the waterfront there after I finished my tasks in LA. The last seven or eight years in San Francisco had been tumultuous ones with a jumble of organizing drives and walkouts, a general strike in 1934, and the emergence of a strong, progressive, and militant labor movement based on the CIO.[4] A lot of loose ends needed to be pulled together, and the Party figured that I could help. I worked with Jim Torme, a young hod carrier. We made a good team, encouraging rank and file Communist longshoremen to function as progressive groups in their locals, issuing Party labor bulletins, and planning pamphlets about socialism and waterfront workers.

San Francisco's tremendous harbor facilities made it the center of West Coast shipping, and teamsters, longshoremen, warehousemen, and, during the war, shipyard workers joined the Party in large numbers. Waterfront workers were at the very heart of the Party, much as the waterfront was the base of life for a good chunk of the city's population. There were about forty to fifty Party members in one longshoremen's local alone. Working different shifts and often living in different parts of the city, it was difficult for them to meet. Many of the wives of longshoremen were active in the Ladies' Auxiliary. They really added a punch to the labor movement, turning out in large numbers for demonstrations or picket lines. They had an effect on everybody because up till that time women hadn't played that visible a role in the local labor movement. But when they came marching down Market Street to the Embarcadero and the docks twenty-four abreast and dressed alike in white caps and blouses with red kerchiefs, they made an unforgettable impression.

Seamen were perhaps the best supporters of the Party in San Francisco. They'd come off a ship after a few months at sea, drop over to the Party offices, and announce, "Before I go out on the town, I'm here to pay my dues to the Party." And they'd plunk down a couple of hundred bucks. They had real spirit—an "I'll take no crap" attitude—and a camaraderie with other men who went to sea. Sometimes guys would suggest a particular project, a leaflet of some kind they wanted to see written and distributed to other seamen. Not only would they sit down and write it, but they'd pay for it out of their own pockets. Most were well-read guys who took trunkfuls of books with them whenever they sailed. Many brought Party literature along to sell on ship. "I'm working day and night, brother. Half a day for the boss—half a day for the Party," was the way some put it. A handful of seamen could always be found at the Seamen's Bookstore down on the Embarcadero. Run by left-wing seamen like Bill Bailey and Walt Stack, the bookstore was a dropping-off point for messages and mail. A log was kept that indicated on what ship a man was working. Fellows would drop by to check on their mail, drink some coffee, and argue politics or union affairs.

Not long after I began working in the Bay Area, I was elected chairman of the San Francisco Party at the county convention. We found a little apartment in the Mission District that we fixed up and got ready for the birth of our daughter Josie. After losing our first child, we both experienced a lot of anxiety during Margaret's pregnancy, and we were ecstatic about the birth of our baby girl. In the meantime I had begun working out of the Party offices on Haight Street in Haight-Ashbury. We stayed there for about a year and then moved to the Twin Hills section of town. We lived on the second floor of a two-story wooden structure, and below us lived a young couple, Jack and Tillie Olsen. Jack was a warehouseman and Tillie was active in the Ladies' Auxiliary of the ILWU.

Tillie, a writer of working-class background, had been brought to

Hollywood fresh out of a Midwest high school. Hollywood quickly disillusioned her, and after a child and a divorce from her first husband, she met Jack. She was a wonderful neighbor and comrade, often helping out with Josie. One of Tillie's daughters would come upstairs in the morning every so often and wander over to the fridge, and Margaret was often downstairs having coffee with Tillie. Tillie was always happy unless the subject of her writing came up. She wouldn't show anybody anything she wrote. Only years later did *Yonnondio* and *Tell Me a Riddle* find their way into print and attract attention.

As chairman of the district, I felt a little further away from the grassroots. I would be called on to make statements, give interviews, and deliver speeches for the Party. At conventions I would have to prepare reports and help set agendas. I worked out of the office but spent a lot of time meeting people on their own territory. I couldn't sit back in an office all day and operate from there. I'd go to people's homes, and I spent night after night away from my own home and family. It was more demanding than other jobs I'd done, but I knew my limitations and was able to allocate work to a fine staff. If it came to doing some research that would take me hours in the library, I'd ask someone else who might be able to cut right through it. When I had to write something up, I would scratch out a draft and give it to somebody else to polish up. I had no hesitation asking for help, especially from professionals in and around the Party.

There wasn't enough time for personal things then. Evenings were booked up so often we hardly had time to go to the movies. Maggie was tied down with Josie, and Party responsibilities made it difficult for me to share the housework and child care. I did what I could, but there was no question that Maggie did the bulk of it. When Bobby, our son, was born in June 1943, that made life around the house even more hectic.

The Bay Area was tightly organized, and San Francisco was perhaps the strongest labor town in the country. The Party reflected this in its own composition and in the everyday life of its branches. Many revolved around the waterfront. Probably two thirds of a meeting would center on waterfront problems—contract negotiations, safety on the docks, the internal life of the local—with the remainder of the time devoted to educationals and discussions of national and international events. Neighborhood branches tended to focus more on local elections and community issues.

I met regularly with the district Trade Union Committee. Composed of representatives from the area's various locals, it tried to coordinate the activities of Party members in the labor movement. We discussed everything from contract demands and strike support to who we wanted elected to the San Francisco central labor council. A lot of energy went into separating substantive problems from those stemming from the inability of some comrades to work together. But in addition to this day-to-day trade union work, we also stressed the need for recruitment. It often boiled down to who would talk to prospective members, what Party literature we might give them, and whether there was some class or other function to which they could be invited.

National policy was set at the Party convention, and the district would try to translate it into a general approach for the area. The Trade Union Committee would help carry out these policies and deal with problems that were not within the vision of the policy makers at the time programs were drawn up. There was give and take with rank and filers. Leaders learned that they had to justify their positions or be ready to accept the wisdom of members in the shops or on the docks when it contradicted basic policies. Realities often changed preconceived notions. Essentially our main goals were to get every possible benefit for workers in their fights with management and to cement the left-liberal coalition of labor and the New Deal. These objectives were to change, however, with the entrance of the United States into the war.

I was in New York City for a National Committee meeting the day of the attack on Pearl Harbor. We immediately issued a statement indicating our support for the war effort. I left the meeting and caught the next flight back to the coast. We usually took trains, but with visions of a possible Japanese attack on California, it was decided I had better fly. Even that took sixteen hours. The next day I went straight to the draft board to volunteer. I was told that at thirty-seven I was too old for the army. I found out, though, that I probably could get in the navy. When I got back to the Party office there were objections to my enlisting. I wasn't entirely convinced by their arguments, but I submitted. The Party was ready to shift into high gear to do everything it could for the war, and it couldn't afford to lose many of its leaders overnight.

Many Party activists enlisted or were drafted. The section organizer in Oakland, Bob Cole, was one of the latter. Paul Crouch (who later turned out to be a stool pigeon) replaced him but proved incompetent. When we discussed how to deal with the Oakland situation in the State Committee, I suggested that I go there to fill in. It seemed to me that Oleta O'Connor Yates, a native of the city and well known because of her campaign for county supervisor, would be a natural to chair the San Francisco district. When I suggested she replace me, some people asked how a woman was going to handle longshoremen. It never turned out to be a problem. As for me, I was already well known to the membership in Oakland, and they readily accepted me as their county organizer.

We moved there early in 1942 and found ourselves sinking roots easily. Politically, Oakland seemed an ideal place to organize. The trade union movement was young and virile, and there was plenty of room to try things out. In San Francisco the workers were spread throughout the city. Seamen were often away, and it was damned difficult to organize meetings. Oakland was more compact. In Richmond and Oakland were two of the biggest shipyards on the coast, and they dominated the life of the city.

Virtually all the CIO unions in Oakland—the auto workers, the electrical workers, and several warehouse locals—were led by Communists or progressives during the war. Most of the members were younger than I was. The Party had perhaps five or six hundred members in Alameda County, and over a hundred were working in the shipyards alone. Scores of members were activists in their locals and in the CIO Council, so many, in fact, that the Party was at the core of the Oakland labor movement.

I enjoyed Oakland more than I did San Francisco. Perhaps it was a bit closer to the earth somehow. With the war in progress and the shipyards working night and day, Oakland had an upbeat atmosphere. The shipyards were attracting all sorts of people. We had a sign painter in the Oakland branch who quit painting to work in the Richmond shipyard. He ended up painting name plates on ships and lettered *John Reed* on one of them. Unskilled workers from the South, both black and white, were also lured to California by defense jobs, and many ended up in the yards. Racism became a big problem there, for many white workers resented having blacks alongside them in the yards or getting promotions to skilled positions. For many it was their first on-the-job contact with blacks, and for many blacks, it was their first crack at heavy industry.

Party members gave a lot of attention to these problems. Even where there was only one man or woman on a gang, they were often able to turn a nasty situation around, or at least cool things down. I remember the poster put out by the War Production Board. It had a double-barreled shotgun on it and the slogan, "Give It to Them with Both Barrels! Black and White!" Our people bought them in stores, paying for the posters themselves, and plastered them up all over the place.

Two kinds of problems came up repeatedly in the shipyards. One concerned racist remarks. It was tough to overcome prejudices built up over years but often possible to convince a worker that at the least, harmony between the races was vital for the war effort. We cautioned our men and women in the yards not to use a sledgehammer approach. They were not to let racial slurs slip by, but they also had to be careful not to permanently alienate the speakers. The other problem was to win a fair share of upgrading and promotions for black workers. We worked with black community groups, churches, and the NAACP to this end. Delegations would go to management and demand that the companies follow government orders about promotion, and often we were successful. If it was the workers or the union that balked, we'd go to them. When white workers in the Kaiser shipyards were preventing a black from being promoted to shipfitter, a number of us went to the shipfitters' union and argued it out on the floor of the local. We had a determined bunch who were able to mobilize a lot of workers, both black and white, behind us, and the man became a shipfitter.

With the entry of the United States into the Second World War, our priority became simply to do everything possible for the war effort. We swept aside anything that interfered with the mobilization. One of the first concrete products of this attitude was the adoption of a position categorically opposed to strikes in war industries. The National Committee proposed a no-strike stance the day after Pearl Harbor. We did not discuss this policy but implemented it from the top down in the heat of the moment. It was a sudden reversal from our earlier position, for Communists had led several militant West Coast strikes in the aircraft industry in the winter of 1940 and spring of 1941, prior to Hitler's invasion of the Soviet Union. When I announced these policies to the district leadership, the committee accepted the no-strike decision almost without question. The suddenness of the war on the West Coast, with air raid alarms and blackouts and the overpowering urge to get on with the fight against the fascists, built up a momentum of its own. Anything that had to be done to ensure victory was acceptable.

In other industries the no-strike pledge met with significant rank and file opposition. I don't believe that was the case in the Oakland shipyards, as the yards were working on a cost-plus basis. What did Moore and Kaiser, two of the biggest companies, care if they had to pay shipwrights a bit more than they used to pay? Cost-plus meant they were guaranteed a profit on top of whatever costs they had. With the companies' share a sure thing, conditions became fairly good in the yards, although problems over safety and the pace of work remained. Wages were relatively high, and work was steady. In fact the yards were going three shifts all the time, and workers were making much higher wages than most had ever earned before. I recall no wildcats over grievances or contractual issues during the war in the Bay Area shipyards. As long as work was guaranteed and the companies could be certain of their profits through their agreements with the government, labor relations were quite smooth.

The war was not an abstract thing to most workers in the yards. Many had a brother, father, husband, or son overseas. With rationing of gas, meat, and sugar, with returning casualties and reports of those killed, everybody felt a part of the effort. People felt a great deal of responsibility. You'd tell yourself, "Damn! I'm not out in the field bleeding and dying. I'm working here in a nice little shipyard. I go home and sleep with my wife and see my kids." You'd think twice before challenging things.

So far as the unions were concerned, productivity became a top goal. People who had been leading strikes just a few years before were now urging their fellow workers to get out maximum output for the war. Party members served on joint production boards with management, seeking to eliminate obstacles to full production. We justified this as long as the ammunition was produced and the ships built.

However, there were times when we went beyond the call of duty. We overstated the harm that a strike or work stoppage would have caused war production. We didn't realize that a momentary halt to production might be worth it if it ensured that the workers got their fair share too. It would have been possible to improve war production and make the employer come up with more at the same time. The companies were making exorbitant profits, and what means did workers have for their defense other than the refusal to produce? Besides, in many instances the sacrifice of working conditions did little to help production. It only helped to increase profits. And when grievances festered, it certainly hurt workers' morale, thus slowing production.

When I went to Pittsburgh after the war, I found that the Party's no-strike stance had hurt it deeply in the coalfields. Under John L. Lewis's leadership, coal miners went on strike despite the wartime no-strike orders from the government. The mine operators tried to use this decree to break the union, and Lewis took up the challenge. The only miners out of kilter with Lewis on this were those influenced by the Party. One fellow, a miner all his life and the Party organizer in the coalfields, took his lunch pail and tried to go to work.

That was the end of his career as a miner. His fellows saw him as a scab and refused to work alongside him ever again.

Outside the workplace, Party members joined civil defense organizations. They went door to door with non-Communists and saw to it that people covered their windows and doused their lights at night. Margaret went off a few hours a day to learn machine shop work in case she was needed in a defense factory, and at one time I considered enlisting in the Coast Guard. And like everyone else, Party members served and died in the war.

The Party played down its advocacy of socialism during the war. Anticapitalist work didn't have the same priority as before. Discussions of socialism were limited more to smaller internal meetings, and our public espousal of it was limited. We allowed the immediate crisis to overshadow our long-range perspective. The Party's image, of course, was quite good. We were seen less as a foreign import, and because of the courageous role the Soviets played, anti-Soviet attitudes were negligible. During the war the Comintern was dissolved in the interests of unity on a world scale. By that time I personally didn't see that the Comintern had been playing much of a role. It had lost its validity somehow as the parties throughout the world matured and stood, I thought, on their own feet.

I worked in the Oakland Party office along with Bernadette Doyle. We were surrounded by a small but energetic Local Committee. It was the happiest bunch I ever worked with. When we had meetings, we couldn't break them up. We had to stay and chat for a while afterward. There was a mutual sensitivity and involvement of people in each other's lives. We had a railroad engineer on the committee who would lay over for a week every time he came back from a run. He and his wife would come by and work night and day around the Party office. Others on the Local Committee worked on the docks, in the shipyards and warehouses, and in the nearby auto plant or were housewives or clerical workers.

After Bobby was born, we lived in downtown Oakland on Grove Street near McArthur Boulevard and the Bay Bridge. It was a comfortable old house, and we had an apartment on the second floor. When Margaret's mother passed away in Pittsburgh and left her $1,500, we thought about it a bit and plunked the money down on a little bungalow in the hills. With a government loan and a thirty-year mortgage, we paid $17 a month. When I went to the bank to ask about a mortgage, the young woman handling my application asked, "Mr. Nelson, by whom are you employed?" When I replied, "the Communist Party," her mouth fell open, and she turned a little red, but the mortgage was approved. The house wasn't much more than a shack, but with the help of friends we fixed it up in no time. It was built on a hillside and shook every time the refrigerator went on.

Almost by chance, a number of our neighbors were Party or union activists. One man was a warehouse organizer, another a seaman, and a third a cleaner and dyer whose wife worked in the shipyards. As a welder and feminist, she carried two torches in the yards. When a black dentist and his family tried to move into our neighborhood and met with resistance, our street undertook to see that they could move right in. There was a sense of neighborhood and camaraderie that we all recognized was something special. I could have remained there for the rest of my life.

The California countryside exerted a strong pull on us while we were on the coast. When we first arrived in LA, we found ourselves getting out of the city to drive through the deserts and the mountains and picnic in the valleys. Tashjian, the old Armenian dentist I worked with on the Control Commission, had a big touring car and delighted in taking us for outings. We'd leave early Sunday morning and meet with friends in the mountains, often up in the redwood country. He'd prepare the fixings for shish kebob the night before and have them marinating in containers on the ride out. I remember coasting back from somewhere around the Mount Palomar Observatory, descending into the desert through clouds and being unable to see a thing, even LA. Some people we knew from the Hollywood section of the Party had us to their cabin in the mountains, and others put us up at their beach house a few times. Even in Oakland we'd slip away for the day into Muir Woods and to Mount Tamalpais.

Harrison George, a fine popular writer and the executive editor for the *PW,* insisted I learn to fish when I was in San Francisco. He was a crazy fisherman, almost compulsive about getting out at least once a week. I think he had an ulterior motive about teaching me, because he needed someone to drive him up the coast to his favorite spots. We made it into a weekly ritual. We would get up at two or three in the morning on Saturday, and sleepily drive till we found our destination, and then climb out on the rocks and cast into the morning surf. These trips made us close friends. Harrison was a marvelous old guy. He had been jailed as a Wobbly during World War I for opposing the war. I think he enjoyed these mornings as the homespun fisherman best of all.

Even though Maggie and I had only limited contact with the Hollywood section of the Party, there was something exciting about reading novels and seeing movies created by comrades you knew. Movies were our main entertainment, and Hollywood was coming out with good political films at the time. Chaplin's *Great Dictator* and *Modern Times* were two of my favorites and I got a kick out of seeing movies that had something to do with the struggles we had been in. In *Casablanca,* for instance, Bogart's character, Rick Blaine, alludes to having fought in Spain on the Republican side. These movies were romanticized versions, but we were glad somebody was telling the story.

There was a fairly large group of party members in Hollywood, perhaps 150 people. The professionals—writers, actors and actresses, and directors—were in one branch, and the technical people—stagehands, carpenters, technicians—were in another. The fight against fascism, first in Spain and then during the war, had touched a responsive chord in Hollywood. Many people used their creative talents in this struggle, and it carried over into support for the labor movement as well. As I had been in Spain and was thus a personality of sorts, I was invited to a few parties there to give little talks and answer questions. I never did completely shake my awe at meeting some of these people, though. There was still that inescapable Hollywood glamour.

Josie and Bobby made a big difference in our lives. After Spain we agreed that we wanted to try to raise a family. We didn't try to figure out how we were going to pay for things. If necessary, I would have gone back to carpentry. People in the Oakland Party knew that we had kids and usually showed a lot of understanding and sensitivity. I was able to sit at home and read and make reports and line things up by phone and thus avoid a lot of legwork. Margaret did get bogged down with housework even though I managed to come home every day to help with dinner and clean up before I rushed out to a meeting. In some ways I think she was pleased to stay home after twenty-five years of constant radical activity. On the other hand, her enforced separation from politics sometimes upset her.

Child care was unheard of at meetings in the forties. Nor did people bring their children to lectures—picnics and socials, yes; but not more serious get-togethers. Margaret frequently swapped baby-sitting with another woman down the block but that couldn't always be arranged. Once, when Elizabeth Gurley Flynn was scheduled to speak at a meeting, Maggie was determined to hear her, even though she couldn't find a sitter. She finally decided to take Josie, who was about two at the time. When there were meetings at our house, which was often, Margaret or I would tell Josie it was "talking time" and let her know we would appreciate her silence. This time, Maggie told her it was a "big talking time." Josie, sitting in the audience before the program started, realized she knew everyone on stage. She had met Elizabeth Flynn before and knew Bernadette Doyle and Kenneth May quite well. Ken, who worked with me in the District Office, had stayed with us at the house for a few months and was the source of a lot of head pats and treats for Josie.

Turning to Margaret, Josie announced, "Talking time for Daddy, talking time for Kenny, talking time for me, too!" She stood up as I began introducing Flynn to the crowd of five hundred and started to walk toward the stage. By the time she made it up there, I was back in my chair and Elizabeth was at the podium. To some applause and a few chuckles, Josie climbed into my lap, chattering away. She proceeded to make the rounds and visited with Bernadette and Ken before marching back to her seat and promptly falling asleep. But Elizabeth, who stood there patiently smiling, wasn't about to let the incident drop. She worked it into her speech and emphasized how difficult it was for women to participate in anything outside the home and their work. It is to the credit of the women's movement of more recent years that it brought these issues into the center of political discussion and is developing alternative ways of handling these responsibilities.

Soon after arriving on the coast, I made the acquaintance of a very amazing man, J. Robert Oppenheimer. I had gone up to Berkeley to speak about Spain and help raise funds for Spanish refugees. Oppenheimer, whom I had never heard of before, was the main speaker and gave a good talk about the significance of the Spanish fight. After the session he came up to me and with a smile, exclaimed, "I'm going to marry a friend of yours, Steve." I couldn't for the world think who that could be, so he went on, "I'm going to marry Kitty." Kitty Dallet! I remembered that she had come to the coast after staying with us in New York City, but we had lost touch.

Not long after that, Oppenheimer invited me to his home to get together with some of his friends from the academic community who wanted to meet someone who had been in Spain. After we moved to Frisco and Oakland, the four of us, Maggie, Kitty, Robert, and I, saw each other socially a few times. On Josie's second birthday, Margaret answered a knock on the door, and there was Robert, his blue eyes twinkling under the porkpie hat he always wore, with a birthday present. I also saw Robert at Berkeley now and then because I was responsible for working with people from the university, getting them to conduct classes and discussions. A number of Oppenheimer's graduate students in the field of physics were quite active. Our contacts were more on their terms than ours. They lived in a more rarefied intellectual and cultural atmosphere, although they were friendly and not at all pretentious.

Oppenheimer was a tall, thin, loose-jointed man who chain smoked and often seemed a bit agitated or impatient. He always expressed himself in perfect English, as if the words were written out ahead of time. He told me what first attracted him to the Left was the menace of the Nazis. While studying physics at Heidelberg he had encountered them first hand. Later on, he casually remarked, he took along Marx's three volumes of *Das Kapital* for a three-day train ride to New York City. When he got off the train, he was through all three volumes and had found them quite logical. I gulped when I heard that and thought about how many times I had tried to get through the first volume and understand just a bit of it. His memory was incredible. He learned Sanskrit, for example, in a few months and spoke half a dozen languages fluently.

Oppenheimer had such intellectual presence that almost everyone deferred to him. I was very impressed with our discussions and began to admire him. He and Kitty and his brother Frank and Frank's wife Jacquenette were all sympathetic to the Left and made contributions to the Party.

Now and then we met to exchange opinions on political issues, but we never became close friends. Our relations ended rather abruptly when he left town during the war. He called me up and said that he was going away and would like to meet for lunch. We met at a restaurant on the main strip in Berkeley, and he appeared excited to the point of nervousness. He couldn't discuss where he was going, but would only say that it had to do with the war effort. We chatted, mostly about Spain and the war, and exchanged good-byes. His last comment was that it was too bad that the Spanish Loyalists had not been able to hold out a little longer so that we could have buried Franco and Hitler in the same grave. That was the last time I ever saw him, except on television, for Robert's connection with the Party had been tenuous at best, anyway.

His name, of course, started coming up in the news after the use of the atomic bomb in Japan. He made statements expounding the potential of atomic energy—he said that a quantity of uranium as big as a baseball could power an automobile twice around the globe. After Hiroshima, he denied that the bomb would have long-range effects. He was wrong. I wasn't surprised to find that Oppenheimer was involved in such a stupendous undertaking. I recognized his genius early on. Later the cold war and McCarthyism brought my friendship with him back into the public arena and cast it into a bizarre and fantastic conspiracy.

In the latter part of the thirties and during the years of the Second World War, Communists found it increasingly possible to work with people of different political views. Working on a day-to-day basis with the CIO, the left wing of the New Deal, and the Allied war effort stimulated reevaluations of theory. Some within the Party began to grapple with the significance of our united front efforts and considered where they were taking us. What, especially, did the postwar period hold in store? Were our theoretical and organizational principles sufficiently thought out?

No one played a more prominent role in these deliberations than Earl Browder, the Party's general secretary. During the factional turmoil of the late 1920s, Browder had been working for the Comintern in the Far East. Consequently he appeared to be a neutral choice for Party secretary after the expulsion of Lovestone and the temporary stewardship of Max Bedacht. Although not publicly identified with any faction, Browder had the confidence of the Comintern, which had interceded in the struggles within the American Party.

I first met Earl at our New York City apartment during the late twenties, when Margaret and I held a party to raise funds for the *Daily Worker*. Then and in subsequent years, I saw him as a personable guy, if a bit shy and aloof. He was tolerant of people and rarely sharp or nasty. Occasionally, when I was talking to him, I felt he was somewhere else. You couldn't quite confront him squarely, but you realized that he was observing everything that was going on. He was an effective speaker with a wry sense of humor. His speeches, full of American idioms, were different than the old type of radical harangues. He still had some of the characteristics of his boyhood in small-town Kansas—or "Kaansas," as he used to say.

Browder sketched a new blueprint for postwar international relations and advocated certain domestic policy changes for the American Party. His view of international affairs was heavily influenced by the ability of the Allies to cooperate during the war. The Teheran Conference in December 1943, when Stalin, FDR, and Churchill met for the first time, was in the Party's eyes the capstone of unity between the Soviet Union, the United States, and England. Teheran not only guaranteed Hitler's eventual defeat but also strongly suggested a postwar continuation of international cooperation between the Soviet Union and the West. Browder took Teheran as a demarcation point, arguing that capitalism and socialism would be able to coexist peacefully after the defeat of fascism. He believed that a return to an earlier period of hostilities between the West and the Soviet Union was no longer necessary. In a sense he saw Teheran as the institutionalization of the wartime relationship into the postwar period. Given the actions and remarks of both Stalin and the Western leaders, such an international perspective seemed quite plausible.

The implications that Browder drew for the American Communist movement were significant. Between January and May 1944, he called for the Party to reject a simple view of class vs. class as the determining factor in our participation in politics. Fearing a return to the right in domestic postwar politics, Browder was willing to lead the Communists into tacit support for the sector of the American ruling class willing to "coexist" with the Soviet Union and not retreat on the gains of the New Deal. Browder's ideas did not suggest, however, a fundamental break in terms of the American Party's relations with the Soviets. He saw his views of peaceful coexistence as being well within the foreign policy considerations of the Soviet Party.

Browder saw an opportunity for the Party to gain a greater legitimacy in American politics. The experiences of the last decade suggested that flexibility in our electoral and trade union work often brought greater results. Our real impact had not come through the "go it alone" attitude of the TUUL, when Communists chartered independent, left-led unions, or through electoral campaigns in the Party's name. On the contrary, the Party had been most effective within the context of the more politically diverse CIO and in the coalition electoral work in Wisconsin, Minnesota, New York, and California. In these places grassroots movements in which the Communists participated alongside nonleftists had brought electoral and legislative results. Campaigning as "Communists" had often in fact, seemed an obstacle.

Under Browder's leadership the American Communist Party reconstituted itself as the Communist Political Association (CPA) at its May 1944 national convention. Browder argued we could better carry on political activities, especially in the electoral arena, through other means than the Party itself. We could work with forces in COPE (the political arm of the CIO), the left wing of the Democratic Party, or in independent electoral coalitions with other groups. To me that made sense. In California the Democratic Party seemed more of a people's movement than the arm of the other branch of the capitalist class. Moreover, it was clear that large numbers of people were not about to abandon their uncritical allegiance to the two-party system. As long as they wouldn't, our electoral efforts relegated us to "sect" status. I saw Browder's push to transform ourselves into the CPA as an attempt to overcome this.

Although the sudden decision to transform the Party into the CPA came as a bit of a surprise, I accepted it willingly. I understood it to mean that we could continue as a revolutionary political organization but alter the form of our electoral work. By then I already saw our election campaigns as formalities and thought it was a hopeful thing that we were leaving them behind. Even then, I was searching for something and felt this might be on the right track.

Furthermore, Browder had long advocated the need to study American realities. At the beginning of the war, he was convicted of violating a minor passport regulation. When he went off to jail, his final speech emphasized understanding American traditions and values. One's political activity, he said, should flow from study of one's own country. I took this to mean what Lenin advised when he urged Communists from other countries to "shed their Russian clothes." These ideas were beginning to penetrate the Party and many of us began to see the need to draw our basic sustenance from American reality and history. I myself saw a value in the system of checks and balances, for example. Certainly it favors those who have the power, but it was a novel concept. Even the bourgeois democratic electoral system, with all its limitations, had positive aspects. The will of the people does break through at times. We should not scorn the fact that people have a certain degree of freedom when it comes to where they live and work. Instead, these rights should be valued as the basis for pushing for even greater freedoms.

Many of us who were active in mass work in various parts of the country believed the Party would become more accessible to large numbers of Americans if we could overcome some of our narrowness. This is not to say that the American Communist movement was abandoning the concept of a Marxist-Leninist vanguard party, or that we denied the need to fight for socialism. But frankly we did not think the postwar period would end in a direct clash for power. We did, however, want to gear up for what we saw ahead.

There was little open disagreement within the Party about its transformation to the CPA or about the theoretical arguments behind the change. Only a few in California conveyed serious reservations. My best barometer was our trade union group in Oakland. Of the fifteen or so business agents and local presidents, only one fellow questioned the action. These were people who liked theoretical discussions, and they welcomed the changes with open arms. However, it would be an exaggeration to say that this period was one of great dynamism and creativity in applying Marxism to American conditions. The experimentation was terminated within a year, during which time we continued much the same as before. Nor were there any elections in which we could test the new policies.

It is difficult to tell what might have happened had the process of experimentation been allowed more time. In May 1945 I was building a chimney for my neighbor Jack when the storm broke. Jack's house was built into the hillside just like ours, and we had to go twenty feet up before we reached the first floor. We were about to put the angle irons in to build the hearth of the fireplace. I was standing on scaffolding when I heard over the radio, that Jacques Duclos, a leading French Communist, had just published an article challenging the American Party's transformation into the CPA. He called it a dangerously revisionist rejection of the class struggle. I dropped everything and, with the mortar still wet in the box, ran home to make a few phone calls. As I was getting confirmation that the American Party's decisions were the subject of searing international criticism, Katrina, Jack's wife, came flying over and begged me to get back to the house. The mortar was beginning to set, and Jack was trying to put the mantle in. Unfortunately, he didn't have the know-how. I ran back and helped him straighten things out and cautioned him to let it stay there until I had time. I went back to my house to make calls, and Jack sadly went back to work on the chimney. Once past the roof, he threw all discretion to the winds, and his crooked chimney stands as a mute testimony to the crisis that came with the Duclos article.

Our District Office was wired a copy of the article the next day. Although published in the French Party journal *Cahiers du Communisme,* Duclos's article was immediately interpreted as a direct blast from Moscow. The piece objected to the picture of international relations Browder had been outlining and called the CPA the liquidation of an independent party for the American working class and the dissolution of the Communist movement in the United States. Although unambiguous, the article was nonetheless puzzling. Given both the actions of the French CP and the course of world diplomacy, I could not see why our picture of postwar development was so out of line. Even more mysterious was the question of who had actually pushed for such a public denunciation of the American Party. For, no mistake about it, that was what the article was. It was as if the "Communist heavens" had thrown a thunderbolt or two at us.

I was deeply shocked and confused. At first I thought that maybe we did go overboard. We had a good deal of respect for the French Party and saw behind it the collective weight of international Communist wisdom. We were not that certain of our own position and, as it turned out, were all too ready to reject our experiment and return to the fold. The reaction of Party members on the coast was similar— there was a great deal of confusion and indecision, with many quickly falling behind the Duclos position.

A National Committee meeting was scheduled for June a month after the Duclos article was read in the United States. The highest leadership body of the Party, the National Board, had been meeting off and on in the interim, although its deliberations were not yet publicized within the Party. I rode the train to the New York meeting with Bill Schneiderman and Louise Todd. We couldn't figure out what was going to happen and were especially concerned about the now open conflict between William Foster and Browder. We thought that it might come down to losing one or the other. When we hit New York City I went to see my old buddy from Spain, Bill Lawrence. Bill was in bad shape. He had been working in the Organizational Department of the Party, a mill that could grind people to death. His wife had just died, and he was faced with raising two little girls alone. He filled me in on the latest developments at the National Office, and we wondered what the next few days would bring.

It soon became clear that the National Board had lined up behind the Foster and Duclos position, with Browder alone refusing to accept its critique. Whatever support Browder had at this level had eroded during the course of the past month's board meetings. After his initial address Browder hardly made an appearance at the three-day National Committee meeting. While the fifty or so delegates and the dozen observers met on the fifth floor of the Party office building, Earl remained alone on the ninth floor, refusing to come down and argue for his position. I chaired one of the sessions and became particularly upset at Browder's absence. He should have listened and taken part in the discussions. Perhaps his presence would have brought more sense to the arguments. At one point I criticized his absence and remarked that never again would we give anybody that much elbow room to do whatever they wanted. Turning to Foster, I added, "And that includes you too, Bill." This prompted his quick reply, "You don't have to worry about me, Steve. I'm not like him." I wasn't so sure and said as much.

When the vote came on a set of draft resolutions calling for the reestablishment of the Party along the lines pressed by Foster and Duclos, Browder alone refused to go along with it. I hadn't wanted it to come to that, but I now realized that Browder was history.

The summer months were agonizing. When we got back from New

York in June, we reported that the reconstitution of the Party would be the subject of an emergency national convention in July. Acrimonious discussion and criticism began within the California party and continued up to a particularly rough state convention. The state leadership was under attack for having accepted the Browder position in the first place. In Oakland the criticism that came my way was not that bitter. It took the form of "Steve, how could you do it?" But in San Francisco Schneiderman and others had rougher going.

I had difficulty explaining what was going on and spent sleepless nights. I remembered two young women, active in the YCL, who were on a committee to discuss these policies with me. They put me through a grilling, and I couldn't answer all their questions adequately. In the back of my mind, I realized that many of those who were attacking the state leadership so vitriolically had swallowed the same pill I had. But as a leader I bore more responsibility.

Preoccupied with its internal convulsions and with confidence in its leaders shaken, the Party lost members and retreated to the more traditional and hence secure methods of past practice. The feeling that we had stepped out of line with the major Communist movements of the world and that we were offending the main theses of that movement destroyed whatever confidence we had in the past year's initiatives.

The concept that we couldn't promote a Soviet model of communism in the United States had begun to register, but nobody had the guts to stand up and say it in so many words. Thus when the crunch came, we went back to the old mold. The Party, however, was never the same again. We were being prepared by our own experiences for a new way of thinking but were not ready to break out of the shell. Browder deserves credit for attempting to get the Party to consider American conditions more closely and look for new ways to organize for socialism. In a sense his efforts foreshadowed the arguments heard in 1956 and 1957, when the Party was once again wracked by crisis.

As an elected delegate to the emergency national convention, I voted along with everyone else to reconstitute the Party. I was reelected to the National Committee, and when the group met I was pressed to run on a slate for the National Board. The national leadership, smarting under criticism that they were perpetuating themselves in power, sought to include someone who had not been at the center of things. John Williamson and Benjamin Davis, then board members, maintained that I could represent a fresh, more proletarian viewpoint. That, I suppose, was the kind of image I had.

Frankly, I didn't have a fresh new political strategy to offer. I disagreed strongly with those who sought my candidacy. I didn't want to leave California. People vehemently argued, "You've got to do it. The Party's in a crisis, and you're one of the outstanding rank and file leaders." Eventually I relented, and it was to be a very tragic decision for Margaret and me.

The Browder-Duclos crisis coincided with serious changes in my own life. I had never wanted to be a full-time Party functionary, and even in Spain I had not sought leadership. It just happened. I never learned how to say no and thus wound up in positions of increasing responsibility. While on the coast I felt that I had been in harness long enough, and I had considered getting another person to take over my position in Oakland. I wanted somebody else to make the reports, and I wanted to hear them from the floor. This had been my ambition for a few years but circumstances had been such during the war that I always had to fill in. First I had wanted to go to work in the ship-yards but that had been impossible. Now, with the war over, I felt that I could be more effective working in a shop and within a union. I was not a top-notch theoretician or writer and didn't feel that I was indispensable. And I never had been afraid of work. I was the kind of guy who couldn't sit still—still am, I guess—and I could have kept active as a rank and file Party member. Most of all, at the age of forty-three, I needed a change of pace.

I thought that when we bought the house in Oakland we had finally settled down. It was a congenial place to live. The climate was nice, free of the pollution of later years, and we had friends there. Complicating matters was the fact that we now had two youngsters. What would moving to New York mean for them? But for two decades I had seen myself as a PR—a Professional Revolutionary—and this self-image was too much to overcome. I knew I wasn't going to be happy in New York, yet I accepted the call.

After I was elected to the National Board, I went back to California to wind up my affairs. I was getting telegrams from Williamson every other week. "When are you coming? We have to reorganize work, and you're needed." It was not easy to settle matters in Oakland and find a replacement. But the time came, and I said, "Margaret, we have to go." "I know," she smiled, "Let's go."

We sold the house and got on the train with Bobby and Josie and some baggage and crossed the country in three days and three nights. We arrived at a little hotel, the Albert, a lousy old fleabag across the street from Party headquarters. We had a hell of a time.

NINE

On the National Board,
New York City: 1945–1948

The years following the Second World War saw a dramatic turn-around in the fortunes of American radicalism. The Communist Party came out of the war with a solid membership of over fifty thousand and with its credibility strengthened as a result of its role in the war effort. We were also encouraged by a massive strike wave which engulfed the economy in 1946 as millions of workers from steel, auto and electrical plants, packinghouses, and elsewhere took to the streets to cash in on their collective strength. Although most of these workers had been organized in unions since the late 1930s, the downswing of 1937–1938 and then the war itself had prevented them from using their bargaining strength to force concessions from man-agement. But in 1946 it looked like the CIO had gotten its second wind. The Party also moved freely within the left wing of the Demo-cratic Party and in a host of grassroots organizations like the Ameri-can Slav Congress, the National Negro Congress, and the National Citizens' Political Action Committee.[1]

But the flush of victory from the 1946 strikes soon faded, as did the seemingly strong position of the Party in a viable progressive move-ment. At the same time, relations between the Soviet Union and its wartime allies deteriorated, and storm clouds gathered over the Med-iterranean and Europe. They soon crossed the Atlantic and let loose a thunderous torrent on the Party and the movements within which it fought for social change.

FDR's death in April 1945 and the ascendency of Truman to the presidency had more than a symbolic impact, for over the next sev-eral years, the wartime antifascist coalition crumbled, and the cold war became the focal point of American domestic and international policies. Browder's projections of postwar cooperation between East and West were soon proven wrong. Hiroshima, United States efforts to bolster the French in Indochina, the Truman Doctrine in Greece and Turkey, and the Marshall Plan all pointed to an aggressive American drive to assert hegemony on a worldwide scale.[2] As ever, international developments had severe domestic repercussions.

The labor movement was soon checked by the Taft-Hartley Act, and the CIO unions closest to the Party found their very existence threatened.[3] The progressive wing of the Democratic Party realized that the New Deal was quite dead and that Truman offered little hope in either his domestic or foreign policies. As radical politics in labor, the Democratic Party, and the mass progressive organizations came under attack, the government unleashed an offensive aimed at the Party itself. Hundreds of Party leaders were soon under indictment, imprisoned, or in hiding. By the time the postmortems had been delivered on Henry Wallace's abortive third-party presidential bid in the fall of 1948, the tide of domestic reaction was running high. What had begun as a promising period for the Communist Party turned within a half decade into the nightmares of McCarthyism and the cold war.

Although I was at the center of the Party during these years, I did not fully understand why the changes were occurring. The Party was unable to shake off a post-Browder stagnancy in its political analysis. Creativity suffered as a fairly dogmatic, uncritical brand of Marxism dominated National Board discussion. At a time when we needed above all else a frank evaluation of our practice and a flexible approach to changing political conditions, we lapsed into a hard-line sectarianism from which the American Party has yet to emerge.

Margaret and I found New York City no more congenial in the fall of 1945 than it had been in either the late twenties or the thirties. With the severe postwar shortage in housing thwarting our efforts to find a place of our own, we remained trapped in the Albert Hotel. The beds were impossible, and neither Josie nor Bobby could sleep. During the day Margaret waged a secret campaign to get us thrown out of the place by allowing the kids to run screaming through the halls as they played. Finally a friend suggested I try looking around Nyack, a community up the Hudson.

In Nyack someone told me about an old house in considerable disrepair. A commercial artist and his wife, a nurse, lived on the first floor, but the second floor was deserted. I tracked down the landlord and asked if I could build an addition consisting of a bathroom and kitchen onto the second floor. He was skeptical about how it could be done, but I told him that if he bought the material, I would put it up.

I took three days off and built the addition, putting in the pipes and wiring myself. In about a week we moved into this old shack and made it home in no time.

When you're in the Party, you don't move into town the way a normal family would. In a sense you already have friends there. There's an ongoing community that you automatically become a part of. In Nyack there was a small Party branch made up mostly of professionals and middle-class people. If Bobby and Josie were sick, there was usually someone to help out and a sympathetic doctor would treat them. At Christmas time, just a few months after we moved in, one of our neighbors gave Bobby a train set. At three and a half he was organizing an imaginary Brotherhood of Lionel Railway Workers under the kitchen table. The couple downstairs, Julian and Nicky, were both Party members. An immigrant from Scotland, Nicky was a nurse at a mental institution. At night we'd often sit downstairs with them and she'd tell about the obsessions and fixations of the patients. I frequently thought of her stories a few years later when the cold war and domestic reaction made me feel that the entire country had become an institution for the insane.

Julian was a commercial artist from Texas who had become a Red somewhere along the line. Both Julian and Nicky were a bit older than we were and had no kids. But they loved children, and Julian would make up comic strips for Bobby and Josie. Bobby especially would run downstairs to watch Julian work. He had a peculiar way of conversing with him that only the two of them could understand.

At this time you could still swim in the Hudson, and it was quite the thing to take the kids there on Sunday morning to watch the fishermen pull in their nets of shad. With boat rides and hiking trails, Nyack was a congenial place to live. The only problem was that it was so blasted far from the city. I was driving an old Model A Ford then. After the war you still couldn't buy decent tires, and the retreads split almost as soon as you got them on the car. I drove the Ford down to the George Washington Bridge, took the bus across, and then rode the subway to Twelfth Street, where my office was located. It took me about an hour and a half each way, and with meetings often not breaking up till ten-thirty or later, it was common for me to get home after midnight. Finally I got so fed up with commuting and being away from Margaret and the kids that we decided to move into the city.

We found a place on Seventh Street in the East Village, right around the corner from Cooper Union, and took in some friends to make the rent bearable. With all sorts of community activities for

Bobby, Josie, and Margaret to plug into, the Village was nicer than I had expected it to be. We remained there for as long as we were in the city.

Living on the thirty or forty dollars a week that we got from the Party, we managed to scrape by. We picked up second-hand clothing and were usually able to get a doctor or dentist without paying. Although we sometimes wondered whether we were providing enough for the children, we knew they weren't starving and that their health needs would always be cared for. I quit smoking at the time. As Margaret put it, it was a choice between buying tobacco or a quart of milk for Bobby and Josie—and Bobby was already developing a taste for milk that knew no bounds.

Movies were our big extravagance, with an occasional night at the theater if someone gave us tickets. Most of our entertainment and recreation, however, was self-created. We'd visit with friends, play chess or listen to classical music on the radio. In the anthracite fields Harold Spencer and some librarians who used to hide us from the cops had briefly exposed me to classical music. In New York I actually began to enjoy it. We had a good radio, and Margaret and I would sit on the floor with the kids and listen to concerts on Sunday afternoons.

But these Sundays were brief interludes in an otherwise intense and often hectic work pace. Life in general wasn't the same in New York. Office work was boring, and the overall political climate was worsening. I still thought about going back to carpentry or to some other work, but it seemed too far-fetched at the time to be realistic. Besides, there was the feeling that the Party always came first.

When I got to New York, I started serving on the National Board, the highest elected decision-making body in the Party. There was a feeling of confidence—we believed we had gotten ourselves back on the road we should have been on all along. The period of internal division and confusion was officially over, and the prevailing mood was a desire to pitch in and get to work.

Soon after I arrived, there was a full meeting or plenum of the National Committee. Gene Dennis, the general secretary of the Party, spoke at length, outlining what was to become the Party's perspective on the postwar scene.[4] Dennis predicted a major economic crisis for the United States as it shifted away from a wartime economy. The capitalist system, he argued, could plan for itself during periods of war, but it reverted to its essentially anarchic nature during peace. Thus we could expect drastic cutbacks in production resulting in layoffs for millions of workers. The return of demo-

bilized soldiers demanding their old jobs would compound the hard-
ships. Dennis foresaw a crisis rivaling that of the 1930s unless
comprehensive plans were made to convert from war to peace. The
government's role as a planner and director of the economy, assumed during World War II, must be carried into the postwar era.
Instead of turning out planes, tanks, and war materials, production
could be oriented toward housing, schools, hospitals, domestic goods,
and public power projects. The Party's role was to help place these
demands on the political agenda.

The plenum singled out two groups as needing special attention;
returning veterans and black workers. Blacks had entered heavy industry in unprecedented numbers during the war. Because they were
often the last hired and lacked seniority, they would be especially
vulnerable to layoffs and firings. We kicked around various ideas as
to how to prevent black workers from being forced out of the plants.
Some suggested proportional layoffs based on race, and others that all
black workers should automatically be given five or ten years extra
seniority to compensate for past discrimination. These measures, of
course, conflicted with many of the seniority arrangements that the
unions had only recently won. Seniority was the key determinant of a
worker's job security and his rank in the plant. It replaced the arbi-
trary decisions of management with a system that seemed fair to
most workers. As a result it was something of a sacred cow, and to
suggest changes that would penalize some workers to help others
could create a volatile issue. Many trade union officials and activists
were particularly uncomfortable with these suggestions.

The other group of men and women who came up for discussion
were the returning veterans. How could we help to see that there was
useful work available for them and that they had access to housing,
education and loans? Our answers returned us to the problem of planning for a conversion from a wartime to peacetime economy.

Given these potential problems for large numbers of black and
white workers, we saw the possibility for large-scale struggles. We
felt that we had a vital contribution to make that could help stave off
widespread depression, and this influenced our policies in the trade
unions and mass organizations and in the electoral arena. Frankly we
did not foresee the Keynesian fiscal policies that would at least temporarily avert a depression or serious recession.[5] We operated with an
almost classical sense of economic determinism and believed a catastrophe was imminent.

At my first National Board meeting I was asked to undertake
nationality-group work. The other board members already had their

tasks, and I was happy to take on the job. Until I left New York in 1948, nationality work was my primary responsibility.

The Party had a language bureau for each nationality group with which it worked. These bureaus coordinated activities within the larger fraternal organizations and often put out their own newspapers and literature. Communists were active in over a dozen nationality groups and were particularly prominent in Finnish, Jewish, and Slavic organizations. I was both troubleshooter and adviser as well as an observer with the responsibility for working out policies for Communists within the various ethnic communities.

There was a continual stream of political controversies and problems that needed resolution. Some might be as simple as finding a replacement for the retiring editor of a language paper. Others were of a more serious nature, as was frequently the case in the late forties, when many fraternal organizations came under government attack. I might get a report that the International Workers' Order (IWO) had been subpoenaed. I'd meet with the local and national leadership of the organization and discuss how they could respond. I might be able to arrange legal assistance or suggest how they report the situation to their membership. Or when the government used deportation as a weapon against foreign-born political and labor activists, I met and worked with the Committee for the Protection of the Foreign-Born.

I was responsible for helping the different language bureaus carry out the policies of the Party within their respective communities. How could Finnish Communists, for example, best mobilize for the 1948 presidential campaign of Henry Wallace? Many activists within the fraternal groups were very enthusiastic about Wallace. They saw him and the movement around him as a means of preventing further deterioration of the nation's political atmosphere, in which attacks on nationality groups were mounting. Finnish Communists might set up a campaign committee within the Finnish community and urge lodges to endorse Wallace. They might ask for contributions from members or try to persuade a singing society to do a benefit concert for the campaign. The idea was to work in these mass organizations and reach out to people through them. In such a way fraternal groups had played a tremendous role in the organization of the CIO. They were seen as a vital component of the movement for social and political change.

I was well suited for the work. I was familiar with fraternal lodges, both as a rank and file member and as an officer, and I was sensitive to many of the traditions and historical developments within the various ethnic groups. Moreover, I could attend virtually any Slavic meeting without a translator. Besides Serbo-Croatian, I could follow the drift of conversations in Slovak, Czech, Russian, Bulgarian, Polish, and Ukrainian.

One of the fringe benefits of working with the nationality groups was that you often got a good meal. I was always getting a phone call from a nationality-group leader with a problem or complaint and the offer, "How about getting together over lunch? It's on me." The Jewish comrades had a deli where they liked to go, the Greeks a restaurant on the waterfront where all the radical seamen hung out, and each of the other groups a favorite ethnic haunt.

Periodically I reported on my work to the entire National Board. The reports occasionally provoked discussion on the changing nature of the ethnic community. Among Croatian immigrants to the United States, for instance, a strong grassroots radicalism had flourished since the turn of the century. Yet in the context of postwar America, the viability of that radical tendency was called into question.

Agents of industrial corporations had recruited large numbers of Slavic men to work for American coal, steel, and manufacturing companies during the late nineteenth and early twentieth centuries. They literally picked the biggest sons in the family to come to America. The recruitment primed the pump, and a seemingly endless number of Slavs migrated here until World War I temporarily shut off the flow. Crammed together in coal and mill towns, often boarding in groups of seven or eight to a house, these workers were mostly single men without much family responsibility, and they dared to join radical outfits that guys with big families hesitated to approach. It was especially among these young single Croatians that radicalism caught on. The presence of prolabor Croatian leaders, including newspaper editors and even an occasional priest, also fostered a left-wing consciousness among the Croatians almost from the time that they arrived in the country. This attitude carried over into the fraternal organizations like the CFU and the SNPJ, the Slovene society, where radicals were active early on. Radicalism was less developed among the Serbs, who seemed to be more dominated by priests and other traditional leaders.

The importance of political work within these organizations, which had received less attention since the late 1920s, became clear during the effort to build the CIO in the 1930s. Then the support of fraternal organizations brought immigrant workers and their sons and daughters into the CIO en masse. Lodges became organizing centers for the SWOC (Steel Workers Organizing Committee), the CIO union in steel, up and down the Monongahela Valley near Pittsburgh. During the Second World War, these groups organized the American Slav Congress, a united front of all Slavic groups to back the war effort.

In the course of these activities, the organizations had grown larger and more centralized. Some had learned how to build youth lodges, sports programs, and cultural activities. They had sound insurance operations and were effective in delivering the goods. Yet by the late forties, the nationality groups seemed to be losing their central position in the ethnic community. The children of immigrants, as they grew up, were staying away from the lodge.

We asked ourselves what was happening to the foreign-born in this country. Were they becoming integrated into American society? Even within the ranks of the ethnic leaders, there were those who argued that the foreign-born were fading fast as a distinct constituency. They maintained that when a Bulgarian peasant migrated to America, got a job in a mill and became an industrial worker, his ethnic identity waned. Others saw the ethnic community as a permanent fixture. I could not agree fully with either position. I saw important aspects of an ethnic cultural tradition that would be tragic to lose, but I also felt that the ethnic organizations must, in a certain sense of the term, Americanize. If they rejected American realities and social dynamics out of hand, they would only further alienate their youth.

It was a fact of life—the older generation was not pulling the younger into the movement. Increasingly, first and second generations not only spoke different languages but also opted for different lifestyles. While the young men wanted to play football, the old men would shake their heads and say, "They're crazy! What's football? Now, soccer, there is a game!" While the elders complained about the quality of American food and longed for the culture of the Old World, their children were rapidly entering the mainstream of American society. World War II was a watershed. Sons who went to high school and then served in the armed forces thought in far different terms than their fathers. Daughters who worked in the shipyards and electrical plants were a world away from their mothers' experiences with domestic service and boarders. Industrial workers after the war were no longer just pick and shovel men. Machine tenders who enjoyed the security provided by unions with established channels for collective bargaining could not appreciate the chronic insecurity of the pre-CIO era. Life was changing, and we had to urge the old ones to understand and accept it.

But despite our recognition of these changing cultural patterns, we were limited in what we could offer, for we were still trying to present a socialist vision based on the model of the Soviet Union. The sons and daughters of immigrants, often far better-educated than their parents, couldn't accept our claim that the Soviet model represented a better life. Thus some immigrants' sectarian attitudes toward American life combined with the Party's sectarian radicalism to create a rift across generational lines.

I went to a meeting in Duluth where we discussed this problem in the Finnish-American community. Although the Finns were the most radical of all ethnic groups, they too had problems capturing the interest of their second generation. When they decided to include an English page and a sports column in their paper, some old-timers reacted as if it meant the extinction of the Finnish community. Others, less worried, thought national-group traditions would remain even when the people ceased to speak the native tongue. But while emphasizing the need to study American life and become involved in the larger society, I was trying to distinguish this tack from simple assimilation into the dominant bourgeois value system.

Although I experienced the changes in working-class values and culture primarily in terms of the foreign-born community and their children, I can see now that the entire American working class was undergoing a transformation during and after the war. I was to learn this with a vengeance during the fifties. The Party, which had historically been rooted in a heavily immigrant working-class culture characterized by economic insecurity and political alienation, was unable to adjust to these changes. We could not evaluate the significance of the changing composition of the work force and its new patterns of community life and consumption. In a sense the activities of the Left were undercutting the role of the fraternal groups in the ethnic community. Gains such as unemployment compensation and social security as well as the greatly enhanced sense of security brought by the CIO unions made the fraternal organization less necessary in meeting the needs of working people. At the same time, participation in the labor movement and especially the war effort through the American Slav Congress and similar broad-based organizations among Jews and Armenians, for example, eased the process of acceptance of the foreign-born and their children.

If the long-range question confronting nationality groups was how to redefine their purpose and methods to meet the changing dynamics of postwar America, the immediate problem we faced was how to defend ourselves against the onslaught of the cold war. As the postwar pattern of stability and cooperation between the Soviet Union and the West envisioned by Browder collapsed, its domestic counterpart was an across-the-board reaction against radical and progressive politics. Within a decade after Teheran, the Communist Party was reduced to a mere shadow of its former self, the progressive CIO unions had been smashed, and many foreign-born radicals had been deported or intimidated. This attack on the Left and its progressive allies began in a piecemeal fashion, and I first experienced it through the difficulties that our fraternal organizations began to encounter.

While I was coordinating nationality-group work, the International Workers' Order came under attack from the New York State Insurance Commission. Nationality groups had traditionally provided their working-class members with cheap health and life insurance, and the IWO had evolved from this practice. Over the course of several decades, certain nationality groups became dissatisfied with their own organizations' insurance programs and affiliated instead with the IWO. By the late forties, the IWO had over one hundred thousand members distributed in various nationality sections. Margaret and I both had policies with it. Run to provide a service and not a profit, the IWO provided good insurance at rates working people could afford. It was especially popular in the coalfields and mill towns. The IWO took a militant stand against large commercial insurance companies and demonstrated in practice that coverage should not cost what these companies were charging.

The IWO also projected a political image. It had participated in conferences to mobilize the ethnic community for the CIO and had endorsed radical initiatives and electoral campaigns. In some cases these political stands went beyond the bounds of what the rank and file membership would have supported. Although the IWO endorsed Browder's presidential candidacy in 1936, for example, it could not deliver the votes of its members, who overwhelmingly backed Roosevelt.

These two practices, undercutting the commercial insurance companies and asserting itself politically, led to a concerted attack on the IWO by the insurance companies and the government. The attack was spearheaded by the investigations and harassment of the New York State Insurance Commission, and it sought nothing less than the total dismantling of the IWO. The organization's endorsement of Browder in 1936 gave the commission a blank check on which to write "Moscow-dominated." Examinations of the IWO's books revealed contributions to the American Labor Party and some local Communist candidates. While the commercial insurance companies certainly filled Democratic and Republican campaign coffers, the commission used the practice as a pretext to take over the funds of the IWO. Its policies and assets were turned over to companies like the Continental Insurance Company.

We tried to fight this both publicly and in the courts for two years, but the mood of the country was clearly against us. We were forced to salvage what we could, and we advised some of the nationality sections to transform themselves into another association before the IWO was completely destroyed. Our case was still being fought when I left New York in 1948, but it was a harbinger of the future.

Soon after I came on the National Board, political differences began to develop. While it is very easy to project back onto these arguments and theoretical debates positions that only became clear in later years, after I left New York, I think the situation was as follows. The experience of the American Party with the Popular Front activities of the thirties and during the Second World War catalyzed a healthy internal discussion. Due in part to Browder's prodding, the Party was poised momentarily on the brink of a major reevaluation. At this critical juncture, in May 1945, the Soviet Party intervened in the form of the Duclos letter, which had first appeared as an article in the French Communist Party's theoretical journal. The result was a crisis of conviction in which the more traditional style of politics reasserted itself in the form of William Z. Foster and those closest to him on the National Board. The opportunity for change was lost, internal discussion stifled, and initiative paralyzed as the Party chose Foster's politics over those of Browder. In retrospect the choice we might have made, but that was lost in the shuffle, was for neither position. Neither Browder nor Foster advocated any fundamental shift in our relationship with the Soviet Party. More than at any other point in its twenty-odd-year history, the American Party could have engaged in a process leading toward greater internal democracy, a reorientation toward American realities, and independence vis-à-vis the Soviet Union.

In rejecting Browder's World War II theses projecting harmony among the wartime allies, we also rejected his efforts to stimulate a deeper study of American history and political realities. We could have tried to embark on a new course, but our lack of self-confidence and forceful leadership prevented us from trying to find a more viable direction for American communism.

Fresh from his victory over Browder and buttressed by the Duclos letter, Foster and his allies on the board, especially Robert Thompson and Benjamin Davis, drove the Party back to the old position in which our dependence on the policies of the Soviet leadership was central. They emphasized the ultimate importance of the Soviet

Union's place in the postwar period. In their eyes it was essential to follow Soviet priorities in determining the American Party's domestic stance. They spoke in terms of purity of principle and resolution of will. Decisions jeopardizing the Party's place in what had once been a popular front of labor, New Deal Democrats, and the Left were urged, despite the repercussions.

Opposition to this view was fluid and rarely as coherently organized as the Foster bloc. It stemmed from a fear of losing our influence in the CIO and with progressives within the Democratic Party and finding ourselves isolated from the main currents within which we had worked for years. Those in opposition were more likely to hesitate before placing the needs of the Soviet Union ahead of American realities, but frankly it was more hesitation than assertion of an alternative. And when the cold war intensified, we drew the wagons into a circle around the Party, and internal disagreements on the board died down.

There was a personal or stylistic dimension to these internal struggles. Those aligned with Foster seemed less likely to consider, much less accept, human frailties and problems and more apt to push for an organizational, bureaucratic solution to problems of both a personal and political nature. Their style was decidedly more heavy-handed and manipulative.

The Foster bloc did not, however, run roughshod over the board in the late 1940s. It was often decisively defeated on issues. Opposition was frequently offered by Elizabeth Gurley Flynn, the only woman on the board, Eugene Dennis, who replaced Browder as general secretary, Jack Stachel, Irving Potash of the Furriers, John Gates, myself, and others. But while Foster, Thompson, and Davis constantly conferred over policies and board politics, we were more a reactive and shifting coalition that came together on certain key issues.

A brief discussion of three issues confronting the board might illuminate the Party's political dilemmas in the postwar era. The first concerned our political activities within the black community. I found myself, along with others, arguing with Ben Davis over the ways in which the Party should relate to the struggle for civil rights and equality. Davis, a charismatic black community leader who was several times elected to the New York City Council, argued for the creation of a Left organization to work among black people. He also resurrected the theoretical position that blacks constituted an oppressed nation with the right to self-determination.[6]

On the other hand, a number of us urged working within the NAACP and other already existing though hardly radical black organizations. While Davis's militant class strategy was not as sectarian as the Party's earlier position, which pushed for an independent black republic in the black belt, I saw it as an unnecessary turn away from our work in alliance with other elements in the black community and toward the old class-against-class politics. Did we go it alone with untainted principles or stay part of a politically heterogeneous but larger movement?

A second issue, revolving around the stand Party activists would take within the labor movement on the Marshall Plan and the third-party candidacy of Henry Wallace, had a far greater impact on the Party. Many radicals within the CIO were particularly aware of how precarious our position was. Although elected to leadership in several unions and various city and state CIO councils, the Left could not count on mass rank and file support outside of a few unions. Within the CIO the Left had traditionally depended on an alliance with the Center forces represented by CIO and Steelworkers' President Phil Murray and Sidney Hillman of the Amalgamated Clothing Workers. The Marshall Plan, which called for the infusion of massive amounts of U.S. aid to war-ravaged Western Europe, had obvious political implications. The United States sought to cut off any possibility that the European Left might come to power by integrating European economies with its own. Consequently the various European Communist parties fought the Marshall Plan. Our own Party transmitted a blunt message to its labor activists—oppose the plan. The Soviet Union's vehement opposition to the plan added force to the Party's stance. Similarly, the Party urged its labor activists to back the Progressive Party candidacy of Henry Wallace. But Phil Murray met with the CIO left wingers and made it clear that the CIO would not endorse Wallace and would support the Marshall Plan. For the radicals to take any other position would risk rupturing their link with the CIO Center.

After these decisions alienated the Left-led unions from the CIO, the question of whether we might be pressing too hard arose in the National Board. When Jack Stachel, who had been an authority on trade union matters for years, suggested that we might be able to maneuver around the difficulties and avoid a head-on collision, it was as if the heavens had fallen upon him. While Flynn, Irving Potash, and I came to his defense, Thompson, Davis, and Foster jumped on him, charging him with revisionism and calling him a "Browderite." By the end of the discussion, Stachel was in tears.

The third issue was the split that developed between Tito and the Soviet Union. It reveals just how much we were still in the habit of tailing the Soviet Party. In June 1948 Tito stood accused of collaboration with the West and was summarily excommunicated from the Communist fold. Although we had received only the Soviet version of the events, the American Party reacted quite automatically in support of the Soviet position. We accepted the evaluation that the Yugoslav Party was jeopardizing both socialism in its own country and the international solidarity of the Eastern European nations. As has so often been the case, international events had their inevitable impact on the Party and its domestic relations. The American Party felt obliged to ruthlessly attack the Titoist position, and I carried the ball among the Yugoslav members of the Party in New York City. At a decisive meeting I strongly condemned Tito, and of the hundred-odd Party members present, only two dared to vote against the position I presented. We didn't have all the details then, but I can see now that many would not have listened to Tito's side even if we had. I lapsed into the classical description of the Soviets as the leading party, a stance that still had currency. It now seems evident that Tito was resisting Stalin's encroachments, which would have drastically altered the development of socialism in Yugoslavia. I later learned that Stalin was attempting to place Soviet generals in the high command of the Yugoslav armed forces. Stalin's plans also called for the integration of the Yugoslav economy into that of the Soviet Union. The result would have been an "international division of labor" with the Yugoslavs in a precariously dependent position. But we didn't know all that at the time and readily agreed that anyone who parted with the Soviet Union was a renegade.

It was questionable if the American Party could have withstood the ferocious assault unleashed upon it in the late forties even if it had opted for internal democracy, independence from Soviet priorities, and a reorientation to American conditions. But it is certain that we contributed to our own isolation and thus intensified these attacks. Our position on foreign relations, for example, did not allow us to even consider that it took two sides to heat up the cold war. While the United States bears the major responsibility, the Soviet Union's hard line in Eastern Europe and its unwillingness to allow the development of democratic politics there played into the hands of the West. There was, of course, not a whisper of criticism on the National Board. Similarly, the Marshall Plan and the Wallace campaign helped provide the Right in the CIO and the Democratic Party with issues to use in their move against the Left. The Party lacked both the flexibility and the initiative that movements for radical social change need to rise to the challenge of crises like the cold war.

The bitterness of political divisions on the National Board spilled over into everyday working relations. I never really came to socialize with many of the other Board members. When I wanted to *schmooze* or go out for a cup of coffee I went downstairs to the fifth floor and found one of my buddies from the New York State organization—usually a Spanish vet or someone active in fraternal or trade union work. I don't recall ever visiting at other board members' homes or having them over to our place all the time we were there. Elizabeth Gurley Flynn was the only exception.

It didn't have to be this way. In some parties the internal life was different. I once represented the American Party at a session of the Canadian Party. After the meeting we went out for a beer. The secretary of the Canadian Party, Tim Buck, suggested that we relax a bit by going over to a bowling alley. That never happened in the American Party in New York City. We were too rigid and compulsive about our work. A Communist was judged by the number of hours he or she put in, and when a meeting was over, people couldn't wait to get home.

I had my own office and plenty to keep me busy. Between reading, meetings, and administrative work, I rarely had time to develop deeper personal relationships with other Party leaders. There was a certain level of civility on the board but it broke down occasionally in heated political exchanges or office backbiting. I quickly found myself on the outs with the Foster bloc, to which I represented revisionism in the Party. I could always talk with Davis though—although we argued repeatedly, we maintained a mutual respect and would often go out for coffee. He'd insist that we couldn't influence these petty bourgeois organizations and I'd heatedly respond, "But Ben, I can't see how you can wipe off the existing black organizations just like that." With Thompson and Foster, my relations were more distant.

Foster was not the kind of guy you could go out to lunch with. He brought his own lunch and ate in his office while he worked. When Bill was through with his work for the day, he grabbed his briefcase and went home. He was a prolific writer. Waking at five in the morning, he read the papers and came in with an article for the *Daily Worker* by eight. Once, after a particularly bitter exchange, he caught up with me on the street outside the building. He referred to an article I had written for one of his birthdays in which I spoke glowingly of the 1919 steel strike and his many other contributions to the labor movement. Foster looked a bit confused and asked, "How come, Steve, you said that about me then and now . . . ? I replied, "I still believe that you deserve the credit for that, but that doesn't make you perfect forever." He was genuinely shocked and turned away from me quickly.

These frequently chilled personal relations on the board coupled with the presence of many members working as paid staff people profoundly affected the nature of the Party in New York City. The American Party had a fairly strong financial base for its size. A substantial number of small business people and professionals contributed generously, as did a number of Party-owned small enterprises. The latter included several drugstores and cleaning establishments—nothing big-time. The nature of the Party's financial connections was known only to a few, and I was only peripherally aware of it. But one thing I can attest to is that there was no "Moscow gold" pouring into the Party coffers in those years.

This financial base made it easy for the Party to staff itself with full-time people. In other places a few staffers might be paid, but in New York there was a whole additional echelon of people working full-time. A New York section might pay section organizers, an organizational secretary, a literature agent, and even an educational director. There were more full-time people than the size of the membership warranted. When you have a lot of people spending the whole day figuring out what other people who are coming to the meeting that night are going to do, there is a tendency to overplan. Although it's all well-meant, the tendencies toward bureaucratization and the pressures on rank and filers to engage in a wide range of activities lead to a tremendous strain on rank and file and organizers alike. Tasks are piled on that the membership is incapable of fulfilling. Goals are set that appear to be impossible to everyone but the section leadership. Bureaucratic pressure is a sure way to discourage workers, already tired from their jobs, from participation in a radical movement.

Such organizational problems, however, paled in comparison to the mounting government attacks. In 1948 the cold war started to get personal. Before I left New York City, I was subpoenaed by the House Un-American Activities Committee (HUAC).[7] The committee informed me that it wanted to ask questions pertaining to my activities in California. Although the subpoena was vaguely worded, there was enough of a hint to show what HUAC was after. There was already a campaign underway to prove that the Soviet Union's development of the atomic bomb was the product of espionage. It dovetailed closely with the escalating cold war.

HUAC thought it could tie me up with J. Robert Oppenheimer and other scientists on the West Coast who had progressive or Communist views. It was certainly no secret that Oppenheimer and I knew one another or that I had been in the leadership of the Party in the Bay Area at that time. Oppenheimer himself had already been grilled in security clearance hearings. As it came out later, he first tried to deny that he had any left-wing associations. When the government contradicted his story and demanded to know his links and those of his brother to the Party, he acknowledged having made donations and having acquaintances among the Left. He named names and in so doing destroyed the careers of a number of his former graduate students and several other promising young scientists. Brilliant young men ended up working on oil rigs and construction crews, their futures in research ended. Oppenheimer apparently wanted to make himself acceptable to the authorities and didn't take into consideration the impact his answers would have on others. I wasn't particularly surprised that my name came up in the Oppenheimer hearings, but I actually thought very little about it until my first clash with HUAC.

There were a slew of people in the corridors as I was ushered into the hearings, including a number of the young scientists and students who had worked with Oppenheimer. Cameras were rolling as I walked right by them without acknowledging their presence. I was afraid that any further publicity linking these guys to the Party would be just another strike against them. The hearing room was packed. Several trainloads of people had come to protest the Mundt-Nixon Bill, which was designed to outlaw the Communist Party, and some of them decided to carry their demonstration into the hearing room. While they were an orderly crowd, their presence was felt. Richard M. Nixon, a young congressman from California already engaging in the kind of heavy-handedness that was to ensure him a place in history, seemed particularly upset with the audience.

By the time I was called as a witness, HUAC had held extensive hearings into purported espionage activities concerning the atomic bomb. What emerged from them was the kind of television plot that wouldn't have had the slightest credibility but for the domestic atmosphere of reaction. The FBI/HUAC scenario went as follows: I was sent to the Bay Area in 1940 with the underground assignment to gather information regarding the development of the atomic bomb. Under my guidance the Radiation Laboratory at the University of California at Berkeley was infiltrated, a cell of five or six young physicists established, and contact made with Kitty and Robert Oppenheimer. Late one night in March 1943, an individual identified by HUAC as "Scientist X" came to my home. I arrived there about one-thirty in the morning, and Scientist X proceeded to pass a formula to me. Several days later I met Peter Ivanov, the Soviet vice-consul in San Francisco, on the grounds of the St. Francis Hospital. At our rendezvous I transferred something to him. A few days later the third secretary of the Russian Embassy in Washington came to San Francisco and visited me at home. There he paid me ten bills of unknown denomination. I was, In HUAC's words, the "Communist espionage agent . . . who had secured information regarding the development of the atomic bomb."[8]

All in all, it was pretty hokey stuff, backed up only with the false testimony of FBI agents and informers. In the first place, I never had any links with Soviet espionage in the United States. I had known a number of YCL members at the university and had met with them in my capacity as organizer in Oakland. I had also spoken with Vice-Consul Ivanov about Russian war relief and American-Soviet Friendship Council matters.[9] But I had no knowledge of what kind of technical work these young physicists were engaged in and probably couldn't have understood the nature of their work if I had tried. I never heard the term "atomic energy" nor knew anything about the bomb until Hiroshima.

There may have been a Soviet espionage network operating in this country, but common sense would dictate against recruiting prominent Party officials. As it came out in these and later hearings, I was under constant surveillance throughout the forties. I found recently from files obtained under the Freedom of Information Act that I was on an FBI detention list during these years. Any espionage agent worth his salt would have known this and avoided me like the plague. Moreover, it would have been political suicide for the district leader to risk implication in any illegal activities.

Most of the allegations concerning my role in the "theft of the atomic bomb" were already public by the time I sat down in the old House Office Building in June 1949. With me as counsel was Emmanuel "Manny" Bloch, who was later a lawyer for Ethel and Julius Rosenberg.[10] I had already decided how I would respond to what was essentially a HUAC fishing expedition. I would be a very "uncooperative witness." I knew that to identify people would be the same as to label them Communists and, given the growing political hysteria, would jeopardize their jobs—or worse.

The hearing was largely consumed by questions concerning my immigration to the United States and various hassles I'd had regarding passports for the USSR and Spain. I thought I understood the use of the Fifth Amendment to refuse to answer a question on the grounds that to do so might be self-incriminating. Apparently I didn't. Despite Manny's warnings and advice, I talked back to the committee and refused to answer any questions that I didn't think they had the right to ask. Somehow I wound up with thirty-three counts of contempt, each with a possible sentence of one year in jail. I couldn't distinguish between the legal and political aspects of the Fifth. I saw no harm in replying that I was proud to know Bill Foster, Elizabeth Gurley Flynn, or Mother Bloor, while Manny squirmed next to me and tried to advise against this approach. It turned out that, according to law, I couldn't then turn around and use the Fifth when they asked me about other people.

I should have listened to Manny. I thought I could deal with this without a lawyer. Nixon was threatening me with contempt before the hearings were five minutes old, and he succeeded in getting several votes through unanimously directing me to answer the questions. That I wouldn't do. Besides, I didn't like Nixon trying to bully me into talking. I lucked out on the contempt charges when they came up for trial six months later. Milton Freedman was my lawyer. He said, "Steve, this is how it stands. While we usually urge jury trials, there's not a jury in D.C. that would let you off. They'd send you up for sure. We've got a chance on constitutional grounds, and I think we'd better settle for a judge with no jury." We managed to get a judge who, though conservative as hell, was a strict constitutionalist. He listened to the lawyer's analysis of the Bill of Rights and recessed to draw up his opinion. When he called court into session that afternoon, he began by saying something to the effect that I might be the worst son-of-a-bitch in the world, but . . . . As soon as he said that Milton grabbed me by the arm and whispered, "You're off!"

Just what the FBI was going to do with these atomic bomb charges remained unclear. They hung over me for the next several years. It was convenient publicity for a period in which the cold war and repression of the Left were in vogue. Cedric Belfrage has argued in his *American Inquisition* that the government wanted to build up an atomic spy conspiracy linking me to Oppenheimer.[11] He and I were bigger and probably more plausible targets than the Rosenbergs. As a foreign-born Party leader with schooling in Moscow and service in Spain, I probably fit the government's propaganda needs better. Certainly Oppenheimer was in the most sensitive possible position connected with the development of the atomic bomb. There was not the slightest evidence against either of us, however, and the investigation was eventually dropped.

In 1948 nationality-group activities were winding down. Thrown on the defensive, organizations like the IWO curtailed their political activities and concentrated on beating off government prosecution. Some energies went into the newly formed Progressive Party and Wallace's campaign, but the optimistic vigor of the CIO and Slav Congress days was dissipating. At this time reports came into the office from nationality groups in Pittsburgh complaining of problems with the district organizer there. On the ninth floor of the Party building, Henry Winston could be heard grumbling that the Pittsburgh office wasn't coming through on recruitment, registration, or its quota of *Daily Worker* subscriptions.

Roy Hudson had been the district organizer in Pittsburgh since the end of the war. He had been a seaman and trade union activist for years and was the National Board's specialist on labor policy during the Browder period. He had come under attack with Browder and, while remaining in the Party, he was dropped from the board and sent to Pittsburgh. But Pittsburgh didn't have a radical labor movement to match its role as the nation's industrial heartland. In fact, it had become known as a dumping ground for organizers and had gone through at least a dozen in the years since the Party was founded. Frustrated in his work with the labor movement, Hudson also met difficulties in his relations with the nationality groups. They saw him as a taskmaster and were unaccustomed to his essentially trade union approach, with its emphasis on discipline and accountability. Relations soon degenerated into mutual recriminations.

The Party's organizational apparatus frequently had the notion that if things weren't going well in an area, it was probably because the person in charge there wasn't any good. Consequently many of us were shipped around the country in hopes that we would be the cork to float the bottle. Actually the whole situation was beginning to crumble in Pittsburgh, and Hudson couldn't have done much to stop it. Nevertheless, before I knew it, discussion was under way. "Steve! He's a nationality guy. He's got ways of working with people. Steve, you've got to go to Pittsburgh and see what you can do."

I had to be persuaded. I didn't want to uproot the family again. While I didn't care that much for New York City, I didn't like the idea of being shifted around like a chess piece. But it turned out that Margaret was somewhat more happy than I about the prospect of returning to Pittsburgh. She felt even less at home in New York City than I, and she had grown up in Pittsburgh. She asked how long we were going to blunder around from place to place now that we had kids; why not settle in Pittsburgh? The Pittsburgh district leadership started sending people to New York to convince me that we'd make a good team. They had exaggerated opinions of what I could do, but I finally agreed to go.

I can't say I was terribly optimistic when I left the National Board and headed across the Alleghenies for the Steel City. Events, both on a worldwide scale and within the United States, had moved too fast for the radical movements that had come out of the war with such promise. The Party, along with these movements, had been thrown on the defensive and lacked a sense of how to regain its momentum. After three years on the National Board, I was troubled. I had doubts about what we were doing, yet I couldn't articulate them. Perhaps, after twenty-five years in the movement and hitting my forty-fifth birthday, I was getting a bit stale.

TEN

Pittsburgh: Under Attack

In *The Great Fear,* David Caute called Pittsburgh the "violent epicenter" of postwar domestic reaction.[1] I cannot say whether or not Pittsburgh experienced rougher times than other places during the cold war. I do know that the devastating effects of McCarthyism were felt throughout this country, and that for myself and Margaret, and possibly Bobby and Josie as well, these were the toughest years of our lives.

In later years it was never very easy for me to return to Pittsburgh. It's tough even now, some thirty years later, to convey a sense of the times and their meanings. I will try, however, to do just that, because I think these years in the late forties and early fifties must be confronted if we are to comprehend our recent past. The cold war or McCarthy period represented a fundamental change in American politics and culture whose legacy has only been denied in the last few years.

Margaret, Josie, Bobby, and I arrived in Pittsburgh in the summer of 1948, in the midst of Henry Wallace's third-party campaign for the presidency and on the eve of a prolonged attack against Left and progressive social movements. Before we left in 1957, we saw hundreds of men and women fired from their jobs, driven out of town, deported, or jailed. Moreover, the movements these people participated in were, by and large, crushed. Radicals in labor unions were curbed, progressive fraternal organizations intimidated, and the Communist Party hounded into impotency.

Soon after we arrived in town, the Party held a district wide convention at the Carnegie Library on the North Side. As soon as I walked in the room, I could sense that people were feeling under pressure. Many were hesitant to announce their names although the meeting was open only to delegates. The convention allowed me to size up the state of the organization and see how dramatically it had changed since the twenties.

The Party organization in the city itself had always been small, the guts of it were out in the coalfields. Back in the twenties there were over two hundred coal miners in the Party, spread all over the western end of the state in towns like Rural Ridge, Canonsburg, Uniontown, and Bentleyville. When they were young, strong, and vital, so was the Party. But by 1948 they were aging men. Many had married late or not at all, so there was no second generation to replace them. And where there were children, the father could not bring his son or daughter to think as he did because his mentality of socialism and politics was expressed in terms they could not accept. I doubt if we had more than thirty miners left in the Party when I arrived in 1948. I suppose the 1927–1928 strike had been the high-water mark for the Party in the coalfields.

There were perhaps three hundred Party members in and around Pittsburgh in 1948, with the largest groups among steel and electrical workers and their wives and husbands. Many lived in the little industrial towns scattered along the Monongahela, Allegheny, and Ohio rivers, and others formed small groups in Sharon and Erie. Party activists, working through their fraternal lodges and the young CIO unions, had played a vital role in cracking the hegemony of the steel and electrical trusts in the mill towns near Pittsburgh in the thirties. And if the Party had little strength in the city proper, it could nevertheless speak with some authority to many within the working-class ethnic communities of Homestead, Duquesne, Etna, Braddock, and New Kensington. Many steelworker and electrical worker locals, as well as a number of the fraternal groups, elected Communists to key leadership posts. The real capabilities of the Party lay within the activities of these organizations. It wasn't so much a matter of Party members following Party directives within these groups but of whether Communists, who were working-class ethnics themselves, could work with a larger group of people who shared many of their ideas about work, community and politics. Given the wrenching nature of the changes wrought by the CIO and the New Deal in these towns, it should be no surprise that there were many who shared a radical social vision for American society.

If the Party could not boast a membership in the thousands here, it could reach tens of thousands through its work and that of allied progressive forces. Between weekly radio shows on WLOA in Braddock and the newspapers printed in their East Street workshop, the fraternal groups sustained a large and fairly responsive membership. Progressive ideas still retained currency in the United Electrical Workers, the hotel and restaurant local, some steelworkers locals, and a few mine locals. And many of the small-fry politicians in the mill boroughs owed their election to radical support. Yet this political power was expressed through and built in relation to the CIO and the New Deal branch of the Democratic Party. That was both its source of strength and ultimate weakness, for progressive policies within the labor move- ment and the Democratic Party were rapidly waning by 1948.

The postwar years dispelled any hopes that the United States, Western Europe, and the Soviet Union would continue their alliance. With fascism defeated the victors soon commenced squabbling among themselves over the future political coloration of the globe. Moreover, indigenous revolutionary movements that had resisted the German and Japanese invasions were shifting their sights toward the capture of political power. Right-wing, anti-Soviet voices within the Demo- cratic Party had been relatively mute during World War II, when the Soviet Union was an indispensable ally. But with the death of FDR, American foreign policy veered sharply to the right. Apparently, Stalin read in this the reversion of Western policy to the earlier goal of crushing the Soviet Union. He responded with undemocratic and provocative measures in Eastern Europe. His actions, along with the obvious strength of the Left in war-wracked Western Europe, China, and Indochina, crystallized cold war sentiment in the United States.

By 1948 we could see little difference between Harry Truman Democrats and the Republican Party. Conservative forces in both parties were mounting an intensifying campaign around foreign pol- icy and domestic security. The labor movement had been slugged with Taft-Hartley, and there was less and less room to maneuver within the CIO and the Democratic Party. And then along came Henry Wallace, vice-president during FDR's third term, who talked a different ball game. He challenged Truman's policy toward the Soviet Union and offered peaceful coexistence as an alternative to cold war. His ideas about domestic issues were grounded in the best of New Deal progressivism. That appealed to us. We had to decide what to do. It was becoming painfully clear that there was not much of a chance to change things in the Democratic Party. When Wallace was denied a spot on the Democratic slate, an independent campaign for the presidency began.

No one expected victory, but many felt that Wallace could poll between five and ten million votes on the Progressive Party ticket. In the early months of 1948, the Progressive Party and Wallace had considerable strength. There was still some momentum carrying over from the New Deal, and many saw Wallace as the true heir of the FDR tradition. Even the bourgeois pollsters talked of five million votes. "We're not responsible for that blasted Truman. Wallace is carrying the banner." It appeared that he was getting substantial grassroots support. Progressives in fraternal groups under attack by state agencies and unionists who found the CIO moving rightward all saw Wallace as both a means of protest and a way out of a political dilemma. There was a brief moment of euphoria. The trouble was that we were reading the votes of the Party "fractions" or progressive caucuses in local unions and assuming these results indicated how the majority of the members would vote. Endorsements did in fact come from many mill locals and fraternal lodges, but few national labor leaders or politicians followed suit.

As the campaign progressed, the Truman forces in the Democratic Party undermined the Wallace movement through red-baiting and by stealing the Progressive Party's domestic program. Truman eroded Wallace's support by differentiating himself from Dewey on issues affecting blacks, Jews, and labor. More and more, Wallace was left only with the foreign policy issue of peaceful coexistence—and on that the American people would not go along, especially as they were presented with a picture of a surging Communist tide in central Europe and Asia. There were also serious shortcomings in the approach of the Progressive Party and the Communist Party both on an organizational and theoretical level. There was too much emphasis on big meetings and publicity and not enough on precinct work, and we had trouble handling the red-baiting issue. Some in the Progressive Party tried to steer clear of any Communist connection, while others insisted on defending the Soviet Union above all else. Finally, there was that bane of all third-party efforts in America, the "don't waste your vote" argument.

The Wallace ticket, red-baited from the beginning in the almost hysterical atmosphere of 1948, polled only about one and a quarter million votes. The Progressive Party was a fiasco. The rank and file we were counting on continued to vote Democratic, despite the exhortations of their often radical local leadership. They were too closely wedded to the old Democratic Party apparatus of ward heelers and local politicians. The CIO–New Deal alliance, which the Party had helped along, retained its hold on workers in spite of Truman's turn to the right. Perhaps more significantly, these working men and women were not about to break with the Democrats over the kinds of international issues we were raising. Many believed that they must support the government against the foreign enemies they read about daily in the press. The bottom line was that the issues over which the break was to be made were not sufficiently domestic.

We eventually realized that an independent party couldn't be built on wits and wishes. There had to be a broad base of support, and the progressive base was actually shrinking in 1948. There was not enough momentum to demonstrate logically to millions of people why they should leave the Democratic Party. We had read our hopes into their minds. Had we had our ear to the ground more, we might have found ways of trying a third-party effort on a smaller scale, perhaps in a few selected congressional districts where the chances were better. As it was we further isolated ourselves from the mainstream of political life. It is difficult to know whether different political decisions could have reversed the impact of the cold war, but it is clear that this disastrous defeat simply quickened the crumbling of our foundations of support. The Communist Party and its progressive allies stood vulnerable in defeat, and their enemies were quick to attack.

Red-baiting was nothing new in American political life. But the Party, after emerging from the underground in the 1920s, had built a fairly strong base of support for its work in the thirties and during World War II. While a substantial membership and range of support were not absolute protections against attack, they certainly deterred a frontal assault by the government or rightwing forces. Party members were sometimes jailed, beaten, and even killed in the course of the struggles of the thirties, but no all-out attack was launched on the Party's very existence. During World War II, of course, the Party was held in some esteem as a valued ally in the war effort. All this was to change in the postwar epoch.

An American in the late forties whose sole source of news and information was the newspaper or radio would see a threatening global situation. The "Reds," once again Public Enemy Number 1, were on the offensive worldwide. War had broken out in Korea in late June 1950, and soon the major world powers were involved. The Party's stance against United States intervention made most Americans see us as traitors. At home HUAC was uncovering Communists everywhere, and major spy trials and investigations were in the headlines almost daily. It is difficult to capture in a few words how shrill and intense the red-baiting was. And it was having an impact on the working people we wanted to reach. The poor vote for the Progressive Party in November 1948 was to an extent an indication of that.

Efforts to drive the radicals out of various unions and fraternal lodges, had been going on for some time. But in the midst of the cold war, these attacks gathered momentum and fused with a nationwide attack on the Left. In 1947 leaders of the Joint Anti-Fascist Refugee Committee were convicted of contempt of Congress for refusing to give HUAC the names of contributors. A few months later, the Hollywood Ten were indicted.[2] On July 20, 1948, on the very eve of the Progressive Party convention at which Wallace was to receive the nomination, the government arrested twelve members of the National Board of the Party for violation of the Smith Act. They were charged with conspiring to teach and advocate the overthrow of the government by force and violence. Their trial began at the Foley Square Courthouse in New York City on January 17, 1949, and went on for ten months. All were found guilty, and ten received the maximum five-years sentence and a $10,000 fine.[3] They were not convicted for committing overt acts but simply on ideological grounds—or at least the ideology the government "proved" existed in court.

All this was beginning to have a chilling effect. But it took a meeting held on the North Side of Pittsburgh in April 1949 to show me how desperate the situation was becoming. As recently as May 1947, the Party had sponsored a meeting at the Carnegie Library Lyceum where some seven hundred people heard District Organizer Roy Hudson and Robert Minor, than a special correspondent for the *Daily Worker,* speak without incident. The headlines in the *Pittsburgh Press* told the story after we tried to hold a similar rally on April 2, 1949. "Mob Violence Flares As Thousands Protest Red Rally on North Side."

The Carnegie Library had a lyceum built in the nineteenth century that was available for lectures to whoever paid the hall's rent. It seated five or six hundred comfortably, and we reserved it for an early spring evening so that people could listen to Henry Winston, the Party's organizational secretary and a Smith Act defendant, speak on the trial then in progress in New York. We expected some disturbance because local veterans' groups had been calling for a picket line to protest the meeting, and Father Charles Owen Rice's Association of Catholic Trade Unionists would not let an occasion like this pass without incident.[4] There were several hundred placard-carrying protesters on the street as people filtered into the hall. Members of the American Legion, the Disabled War Veterans, Catholic War Veterans, and Local 601 of the United Electrical Workers (then under right-wing leadership) jeered and jostled those on their way in. One sign I'll never forget read, "Uncle Sam's Vets Vs. Stalin's Stooges." Unknown to us at the time, Matt Cvetic, who several months later was revealed as an FBI informant and was on the organizing committee for the meeting, was keeping the protest's planners fully informed of the measures we were taking to assure the meeting would be orderly.

I was inside trying to chair the meeting. Disrupters had gotten into the hall and were challenging speakers and generally raising hell. We managed to quiet these guys down and make them leave, but scuffles were breaking out on the street. When we tried to end the meeting, we had to run the gauntlet of demonstrators, now in the thousands. A *Pittsburgh Press* reporter wrote that the crowd of twenty-five hundred to three thousand protesters "mussed up men and women alike, pummelling some with fists. Boxes and stones were hurled. . . . A trolley window smashed and a taxicab almost upset." The campus editor of the *Pitt News* was mistaken for a "Red" and kicked and beaten by a group of five or six vets. All this time a Local 601 soundtruck was screaming anti-Communist slogans and exhorting the crowd. The initial police force of fifty men was augmented by fifty reserves from the North Side station house and then by motorcycle cops and the entire mounted force. Bedlam had broken out on the corner of Federal and East Ohio Streets, and it continued unchecked for over an hour. R. H. Jones, a cabbie, indignantly reported to the press that "a whole bunch of people piled into the cab and someone in the crowd pointed at them and hollered, 'They're Commies!' I told them 'I'm not hauling Commies,' and they split. But then the crowd tried to turn over my cab!"[5]

We were lucky no one was seriously hurt and that we got Winston safely away. That night and for the next few days, we were pretty shook up. We had no way of knowing there was going to be such a concentrated attack. In various small towns you might expect this kind of thing, but in Pittsburgh it was a shocker and did not bode well for the future. While we could take limited defensive measures, our weaknesses were graphically revealed, not only to ourselves but to the whole city.

The movement's vulnerability was confirmed at another meeting soon afterward. This time the International Workers' Order, which had some thirty-nine thousand policy holders in western Pennsylvania, was holding a regional conference in downtown Pittsburgh. About three hundred delegates were attending a morning session at which they heard John Middleton, president of the English-speaking section. All of a sudden a delegate gazing out of a second-floor window started to gesture wildly for the floor. TV camera crews had set up outside, focusing on the doors leading out of the hall, and a crowd was gathering. Soon loudspeakers were calling attention to the meeting and denouncing the IWO as a red front. This terrified a lot of people, especially those from the coalfields who didn't want their pictures taken and broadcast. It broke the meeting up. We agreed that when people went out for lunch, they shouldn't return.

The attack on the Left in the fraternal community took various forms. Legal actions were brought against the IWO and other nationality groups. The Serbian Progressive Club in Wilmerding, for example, was placed in receivership by the courts for having a radical leadership. Three progressive foreign language papers—the Serbian *Slobodna rec,* the Croatian *Narodni glasnik,* and the Slovak *Ludovy dennik*—had their headquarters in a building on East Street on the North Side. These papers had a combined circulation in the tens of thousands. In 1947 the *Pittsburgh Press* ran a series on Communist activities in the ethnic community and singled these papers out for a special measure of abuse. Not long afterward unidentified people started smashing the windows of the East Street offices at night and harassing the printers. Finally the risks became too great, and the papers were moved to Chicago. At about the same time, radio programs by the American Slav Congress and Croatian and Slovak organizations were forced from the air.

More importantly, the effects of these attacks in the daily press were beginning to make the members of the fraternal lodges leery of associating with radicals. Some groups asked us not to circulate our papers there because they feared losing their liquor licenses. It was difficult to get people to renew subscriptions, and financial support fell off. The FBI was contacting people who received radical papers through the mail and threatening to turn them in to their bosses or the Immigration Department. The fear of losing one's job or deportation was not to be taken lightly. Hundreds were confronted with both in Pittsburgh alone. And for every individual singled out for harassment, dozens of others got the message.

The press and the newly formed Americans Battling Communism (ABC) found that they could hang the "Un-American" tag most easily on the foreign-born.[6] The Right's tactics were less a direct assault on progressives within the fraternal lodges, in which they offered opposing slates, than a smear campaign. They sought to single out progressives and Party members for public scorn, and the local press obliged them by printing names and addresses along with a few spicy descriptive clauses. Those men and women who failed to crumble under the pressure were frequently hit with deportation proceedings or fired. Not strong enough to challenge for leadership directly, the Right felt it could achieve the same results by making an example out of the progressives and thus intimidating the mass of members.

Perhaps only twenty or thirty of these deportation cases ever went the full route in the courts. Many others ended in voluntary deportation or political neutralization. The Committee for the Protection of the Foreign-Born defended many of these men and women, and Pittsburgh was blessed with two hard-nosed lawyers who went every inch of the way with their clients. Hy Schlesinger and Yee Steinberg were conscientious progressive men who refused to be cowed by a repressive judiciary. But ultimately the decision whether to fight or submit was made by the individual. In Pittsburgh, there were a lot of men and women who fought.

George Wuchenich was head of the American Slav Congress in Pittsburgh and one of the more visible progressive leaders in the ethnic community. He spoke frequently in public and did a weekly radio show on WLOA in Braddock. Wuchenich wasn't a Party member, but he held many similar political views and was a fellow I always liked. He'd been a captain in the OSS who fought with partisans in Yugoslavia during the war and had gone to China on a U.S. mission to assess the potential for military collaboration with the Communists.[7] He rode two thousand miles on horseback to get to the Communists' base in Yenan. Naturally the red hunters wanted him badly, and it was only a matter of time before he was subpoenaed to testify before some congressional committee. George was a straight shooter and told me he wasn't going to Washington simply to plead the Fifth Amendment. "I'm gonna expose the bastards!"

The counsel for the committee was a big hulking man with a crewcut. When he called George "Mr. Wuchenich" George said, "Make that Captain Wuchenich." The lawyer said, "Well you're no longer a captain." George knew he still had the right to use the title, and he responded, "I earned my stripes. I was dropped in Yugoslavia behind the lines. Where were you when I was over there? Behind some desk in London, right? And you have the nerve to question me? Why do you wear that crewcut? What gives you that right? You're so goddamn big they couldn't throw you out of the plane if they tried." The guy was so flustered that he could only mumble a few words. George continued, "I'll tell you what I did during the war, . . ." and he proceeded to do just that. The hearing ended in a shambles. The committee was unable to bring George under its control and finally decided to get rid of him. George was a marvelous guy who wouldn't give an inch to the ABC and other right-wing outfits, but even he was eventually forced to leave town when he simply couldn't get work in Pittsburgh anymore.

Besides Wuchenich, the Immigration Department went after Allen

McNeal, a veteran of the Spanish Civil War and a UE organizer, and Nick Lazari, the business agent for the Hotel and Restaurant Workers local in town. And there was Vincent Kemenovich, a Croatian immigrant who had come to western Pennsylvania in the 1920s and was a leader in the National Miners Union struggles of those years and later in the UMWA. He was living in Trafford City and working in a foundry. He was never able to get his citizenship papers because he had been marked as a radical early on. The *Pittsburgh Press* ran a story on Vince in September 1949. It began: "Another pinko manipulator of the bloody 1931 mine strikes is up for deportation."[8] There was an old Greek restaurant worker who must have been sixty-five then, a skinny, sickly-looking man with a wife who was in even worse shape than he was. They wanted to send him back to reactionary Greece, which would have meant a death sentence. Most of their children were scattered about the country, but one young daughter stuck to her father and worked like hell with the Committee for the Protection of the Foreign-Born to save him.

Big Charlie's story illustrates the extremes to which the Immigration Department was willing to go. Charlie was a Croatian immigrant to the coalfields who had worked in the mines for some forty years. He was a huge man, over six and a half feet tall, but the black lung had gotten to him, and although he was only sixty-five, he looked like eighty. He could barely breathe, and his lungs heaved constantly as he spoke. Charlie was illiterate, but he associated with the Party and kept getting the Party paper written in Croatian, which his kids read to him. Immigration decided to deport him because he received the paper. What sort of threat to domestic tranquility could Charlie possibly have been?

Charlie's case was not doing so well and he had one last crack with the Appeals Committee of the Immigration Department. I don't know who had the idea, but I suspect it was Hy Schlesinger who said to Charlie, "You've got to make the case yourself." So Charlie, Hy, and Evelyn Abelson, who was extremely active on the defense committee, decided to go to Washington. For some reason they couldn't get a car or go by bus. That stumped Hy and Evelyn but not Charlie. He just told them to meet him on the corner the morning they were to appear in D.C. They were there, and Charlie drove up in the back seat of a Yellow Cab. Now whoever heard of a miner taking a cab to Washington, D.C.?

They appeared before the Appeals Committee and Schlesinger, after the preliminary motions said, "I'm the attorney, but gentlemen, I'd like to have you hear the defendant himself present the argument." The committee hesitated but agreed, and Charlie stood up. Breathing heavily but still a powerful-looking man, he put up an innocent sort of defense. "What harm did I do to the United States? I dug a pile of coal that's as big as the biggest mountain and what did I get for it? I've got seven children and they all went to American schools and believe in America. Now when I'm old I'm being told I'm not wanted here anymore. Is that fair?" And he sat back down. Somehow he got to the men on the committee, and they dismissed the case. I guess they decided he wasn't an enemy of the state after all. That must have made quite a story for the driver.

Despite the changing composition of its work force in the 1970s, Pittsburgh has yet to shed its image as a shot and a beer town. Its place in popular consciousness has always been closely linked with its role as a steel and manufacturing city, and rightly so. The steel and electrical industries have been Pittsburgh's historic lifelines and have shaped its development in myriad ways. Work in the steel mills and electrical manufacturing plants that dot the three rivers leading to and from Pittsburgh attracted tens of thousands of migrants and their families, first from the British Isles and later from Eastern and Southern Europe and the American South. Their labor built the fortunes of the city's elites but brought the migrants little more than a position at the bottom of the heap.

The unwillingness of these men and women to accept their conditions generated struggle after struggle against the steel and electrical trusts. For brief periods, such as in the decade following the Civil War, Pittsburgh's working classes asserted their political and industrial rights and established strong trade unions and control over city government. But in the expansion of the late nineteenth century, the strength of the labor movement was splintered. In the boroughs along the three rivers, the industrialists established their own fiefdoms and following the defeat of the Amalgamated Association of Iron, Steel, and Tin Workers in the historic Homestead lockout of 1892, the bosses reigned unchecked.[9] Civil liberties had as little place in Homestead, Braddock, or McKeesport as trade unionism, and that was mighty little. It was to this environment that most of the Southern and Eastern European and black migrants came.

In the iron and steel industry, unionism withered after Homestead. United States Steel won its "open-shop kingpin" spurs in the following decades and made sure no one forgot it. But in the massive workers' mobilizations of the World War I period, the immigrant steelworkers were not to be denied their shot at the boss. In 1919 hundreds of thousands of iron and steel workers filed out of the mills and vowed to stay out until they won union recognition and a decent contract. The peak of workers' militancy had already passed, however, and these workers were not able to withstand the terror and violence of the coal and iron police and the almost unlimited powers of the companies.[10] Consequently steel unionism was a dead letter throughout the 1920s and only became a possibility after the Great Depression brought political changes in Washington and a new consciousness to the mill towns.

The electrical industry, although somewhat smaller and later in coming to the Pittsburgh area, was also a significant employer. It literally dominated the Turtle Creek area with its imposing factories and political power. Westinghouse was no more to be trifled with than was U.S. Steel. But for a variety of reasons, strong veins of radicalism had always existed in the electrical industry's work force. Since the beginning of the twentieth century, skilled electrical workers and machinists had filled the ranks of the early Socialist Party, the IWW, and finally the Communist Party. Workers managed to build fragile unions and take on the companies in epic, often life and death battles. But like the steelworkers, they lacked firmly established trade unionism and political rights in the decades before the organization of the CIO.

The CIO and the New Deal represented a monumental breakthrough for these working men and women. They were part of a social and political process that brought much more than the creation of unions and a change in local government. The thirties saw political and social rights extended to the ethnic, black, and native-born working-class communities of the Mon Valley and the Allegheny and Ohio rivers. These victories depended on the close ties of workplace and community activists and the supportive context of working-class mutualism and culture. The latter was often provided by the nationality groups, which played a key role in the CIO struggles and in municipal elections. Radical working-class men and women, in and out of the Communist Party, were at the center of most of these fights. That is not to say they were the most important element of these struggles, but to underscore that they were a vital aspect of the fight for industrial unionism.

During the late thirties and the war, many steel and electrical worker locals selected radicals to guide them. Perhaps these radicals were most skilled at articulating the members' needs and sentiments and at the same time were trusted not to seek office simply to exploit their positions. The United Electrical Workers (UE) was as progressive a union as existed, and Communists were free to work within it as members, staff, and officers. The United Steelworkers of America (USWA), however, was quick to rid its staff of the radicals it had brought on during the early days of organizing. Only a few Communists and progressives were able to retain jobs within the national organization, although many still were elected to local leadership.

By the time I reached Pittsburgh in 1948, these radical steelworkers had been ousted from their positions in several locals but were still holding on in Etna, Lawrenceville, and Duquesne. The USWA had passed an amendment to its constitution in 1947 barring Communists from holding office in local unions. The organization's leadership, grouped around Phil Murray, who was also the president of the CIO, was moving decisively against whatever radical opposition existed. The USWA was organized in a top-down manner in many of the mill towns around Pittsburgh, and the national organization consequently exerted enormous influence. In the atmosphere of cold war, the radicals were increasingly isolated from their union brothers and sisters.

In the late thirties some steelworkers had come out openly as Party members. The climate had seemed right for it. But by 1948 these steelworkers were out on a limb, and the limb was being sawed off. They were faced with the choice of maybe holding on to their jobs—if they remained silent—or leaving town if they didn't. Elmer Kish, one of those who had publicly announced membership, was a trustee for Local 1397 of the Homestead mill but was removed by a vote of the membership soon after the international union ruled against Communists holding office. In only a few locals were Communists, by dint of their ties with the rank and file, able to withstand the tide.

In other Pittsburgh area locals it didn't matter whether men had announced Party membership or not. Allegations of Party-related activity or involvement in the Progressive Party campaign were sufficient grounds for the local newspapers and the USWA to mount an attack. Steelworkers like Tony Salopek, the secretary-treasurer at Duquesne, Alex Staber at Jones and Laughlin Steel, Joe Robinson, and a score of others were driven from union office, fired, blacklisted or forced into political silence. And with the ouster of these progressive voices from the union, alternatives to the Phil Murray brand of steel unionism largely disappeared.

The battle to oust the "Reds" from the UE was not so one-sided. For one thing, the national leadership was quite progressive, and many leaders were close to the Party. For another, Communists and progressives had been the founders of the local union at many plants. Left vs. Right fights had gone on as early as the Hitler-Stalin Pact in

1939 but were quieted by the general political unity of the New Deal and World War II. With the cold war, however, the UE became a major battleground in the Right's efforts to purge left-wingers from the labor movement. Nowhere was the conflict more intense or more important than at the huge East Pittsburgh Westinghouse plant.

In November 1949, when eleven international unions were expelled from the CIO because of their radical politics, the UE was clearly the main target. With over six hundred thousand members and a militant, often class-conscious rank and file, the UE stood well to the left of Phil Murray and the mainstream CIO leadership. The International Union of Electrical Workers (IUE) was chartered by the CIO with the explicit mission of raiding UE locals. The CIO wanted to destroy the UE, and Local 601 at the Westinghouse plant was a major objective in its campaign.

The Westinghouse workers in East Pittsburgh, with their long tradition of militancy, had maintained some semblance of organization and opposition to management from the 1920s on. Communists there were a part of the group that founded UE Local 601 in the mid-thirties, and they were frequently prominent in the local's leadership and active in its internal affairs. In addition, the workers could rely on an ethnically diverse but close-knit community located next to the plant in the Turtle Creek Valley. Social ties and the support of fraternal societies had long been critical for electrical worker unionism. Radicals were a legitimate part of this social network and not to be easily dislodged.

Although what became known as the Progressive Caucus had been elected to leadership an overwhelming number of times since the founding of the UE, the local had a history of factionalism. The Party's influence during the early part of World War II, when its slogan was "The Yanks Are Not Coming," had cost the Progressive Caucus the 1941 local elections. The caucus had a fine bunch of rank and file activists and leaders and exerted a political influence that was felt not only in the plant but in Turtle Creek and the labor movement regionally. Many of its members, men and women like Margaret Darin, Logan Burkhart, and Tom Fitzpatrick, were among the founders of the local and were generally older skilled workers. They were opposed by the self-styled right-wing Rank and File Caucus, which used anticommunism in its campaign to gain office and its later efforts to replace the UE with the IUE.

The Rank and File group would never have beaten the Progressive Caucus if the matter had been left solely to the members of the local. The Progressive Caucus had a good record on shop floor and contract issues. That's how they got where they were. But the Rank and File Caucus, and later the IUE, could count on the tacit support of the Westinghouse Corporation, the intervention of HUAC, the sensationalism and smearing of the local press, and the blessings of a young labor priest, Father Charles Owen Rice. Rice had been a pro-CIO priest and was an ardent anti-Communist throughout the forties and early fifties. In later years he regretted that he had contributed both to the cold war and anticommunism, and he acquired quite a reputation for radicalism himself, especially through his opposition to the Vietnam War. But in the forties Rice was the chief tactician for the Rank and File Caucus. His contact with the various parishes in the Turtle Creek Valley and his regular radio show gave him considerable influence. His message came through clearly in the sermons and newsletters of several churches.

Westinghouse indirectly aided the right wing within the union with timely firings and by taking an increasingly tough position in negotiations with the UE after the war. Employment had fallen from over twenty thousand in wartime to about thirteen thousand when I arrived in town and this weakened the standing of the Progressive Caucus. Some workers probably felt the company would be easier to deal with if the local got a more conservative leadership. The press, for its part, took every possible opportunity to red-bait guys like Tom Fitz (as everyone called Fitzpatrick) and Tommy Quinn. National magazines like *Life* were just as bad. The peak of the hysteria came when HUAC subpoenaed Progressive Caucus leaders to appear in Washington, D.C., on the eve of a local election in April 1949. Soon afterward, Pittsburgh's Number 1 informer, Matt Cvetic, went public and included Tom Fitz, Quinn, and other Progressive Caucus members in his long list of subversives.

In April 1950 it came down to an election between the UE and the IUE for the right to represent the workers of Local 601. The IUE made the issues out to be anticommunism, patriotism, and adherence to the Church, while the UE stood on its record. Both sides threw every possible weapon into the fight. The priests of the Turtle Creek Valley called for a pro-IUE vote from their pulpits the Sunday before the election, and Judge Michael Musmanno electioneered at the plant gate with a company of National Guard in full regalia at his side. The UE, on the other hand, brought in outside speakers and sent the local whatever funds it could. Almost 12,000 of the 13,000 workers voted in the April election. The IUE won—5,763 to 5,663. Since it did not pull a majority due to votes for "No Union," a runoff was held in June. The IUE won that too, by the slim margin of 5,964 to 5,706. The decisive Westinghouse local had been raided successfully, and the achievement was an important boost to the IUE's campaign nationally. In retrospect, given the political climate, the UE had done quite well. But several years of concentrated red-baiting had taken their toll. Workers said, "Chuck it, I'm tired of this stuff. Tom Fitz is a great guy, but he's way the hell out of line on these foreign issues. We can't have this Russian thing jamming us up forever. Maybe this IUE outfit will be all right."

I can't judge how effective the IUE has been in regard to shop conditions since 1950, but I do know that the labor movement was the real loser when it kicked the UE out. Men like Tom Fitz and Tommy Quinn were eventually canned by the company, and 601, after its anticommunism had run out of steam, lapsed into political apathy. The ouster of progressives from the ranks of labor, however, has done little to quell shop floor dissent. The day-to-day battle with management over control of working conditions continues. But labor has lacked articulated alternatives to its role as an appendage of Democratic Party politics. It no longer can even be considered as a left-leaning force within the Democratic Party. For Pittsburgh and the Mon Valley, this lack of alternatives is most fateful. The mills still belch iron dust and sulfur smoke into the air, but the future is uncertain. Westinghouse was down to less than five thousand employees in 1979, and there was talk of a total shutdown. The Mon Valley mill towns have seen their sons and daughters move away, and few newcomers have taken their places. There are simply fewer and fewer jobs. Many of these towns will likely wind up as industrial ghost towns, a grim historical reminder of the uneven and unplanned growth of capitalism. It is the legacy of the cold war and domestic reaction that the voices which might have been able to offer an alternative were prematurely silenced.

A somewhat sad epilogue to the UE story occurred a few years later. The Party decided at the national level that given the retreat of progressive forces, an effort should be made to save something wherever possible. The Party attempted to get back into the "mainstream" of labor, and Party members tried to take whole locals of the UE into some other union. That created a lot of bad feelings between the Party and UE leaders, who felt abandoned. Around Pittsburgh we viewed every situation separately. In Erie, Sharon, and Farrell and at the Westinghouse Airbrake plant in Turtle Creek, it looked like the UE could hold out, and we urged it to do so. Elsewhere, where there was little chance, people tried to get into any union where they could continue to fight another day.

McCarthyism was not confined to the nationality organizations and the labor movement. It seemed to be almost everywhere in those years. Anybody even remotely connected with the Left, whether through the Party, the Wallace Campaign, the labor movement, the Civil Rights Congress or a host of other activities, was fair game for HUAC, the press, local anti-Communist groups like the ABC, and the courts.[11] Workers fired for refusing to cooperate with HUAC found their unemployment benefits withheld. A few single women supporting children on welfare had their benefits cut off after being "named" by Cvetic. People cited in the local press were unable to get credit at stores.

Perhaps the Right's biggest weapon was its capacity to get people fired. It has been estimated that over one hundred people actually lost their jobs in Pittsburgh, many of them in the steel industry. Many, many more were threatened and either dropped political activity, withstood the pressure, or left town. Steve Devunich, a skilled machinist at the Armstrong Tile Factory, was within six months of qualifying for a pension. A founder and officer of the local union, he was accused of Party membership, which was illegal for union officers under the Taft-Hartley Act. He was forced to risk his pension if he continued to be active in the union. Dorothy Albert, an English teacher with almost twenty years experience at Taylor Allderdice High School, was fired because of her political beliefs. Even though Dorothy had the support of her students, she was shunned by the leaders of the Jewish community and forced to leave town. Max Mandel, a violinist with the Pittsburgh Symphony Orchestra, lost his union membership after being named as a radical by Cvetic and the *Pittsburgh Press* and was automatically fired by the orchestra. He too left town. Two social workers, Evelyn Abelson and Sunny Sartiskey, lost their jobs. Secretaries, an engineer, and even a deputy sheriff in nearby Washington, Pa., were all summarily fired after the press published their names, addresses, and places of work. Cvetic alone named almost three hundred people in the city and environs when he surfaced before HUAC in February 1950. The *Pittsburgh Press* had already published a list of some one thousand people who had signed nominating petitions for Henry Wallace in 1948.

I was directly affected by this atmosphere of repression when the city council of McKeesport introduced an ordinance that would bar Communists from speaking in the town. It was decided that I should go there to speak and point out how unconstitutional the measure was. I was spotted in the corridors of the town hall and arrested before I entered the meeting room. As I was dragged to a cell, I only had the chance to shout into the meeting that what was happening was the destruction of democracy for Communists first and then other people. With my one phone call, I reached Margaret. There was a meeting going on at the house, and they interrupted it to discuss how to raise the $35 bail. Bobby, who was about eight, piped in, "Let's go down to the bank and get it." He thought banks were places where you got money when you needed it. Margaret got me bailed out without Mellon Bank's assistance, we gave Bobby brush-up lessons in economics, and I never set foot in McKeesport again.

Over the years it became impossible for many people to stay in town. All they could expect was notoriety and unemployment without benefits. The hysteria made it difficult to work in any sort of organization. Ruth Kish, for example, was president of the Glen-Hazel Mothers' Guild for the Hazelwood housing project. She was forced to resign from the presidency even though many of the other women considered her a close friend. Eventually she could no longer even belong to the guild as a member. Similar experiences persuaded many people to pack it in and get out of town. Margaret and I estimated that some seventy or eighty families, over two hundred people, took this route. And as they left and others simply stopped coming to meetings, we were left with a smaller and smaller organization. We continued to try to keep things together, but it became more and more difficult. Finally, they came and arrested some of us.

The area least affected by the cold war and domestic reaction was the black community, which never accepted the "Red Menace" at face value. The local black paper, the *Pittsburgh Courier,* was the only paper in town that covered the Wallace campaign objectively and seriously discussed the issues it raised. Most black people seemed to have a greater suspicion of McCarthyism than did whites. While whites would often shun me, I can't recall a single black person who refused to talk to me during these years. I think this was mainly due to a historical skepticism of white authority, although the Party did have a good track record in the black community.

Black Communists, to be sure, took a lot of heat. But the government and the press were not so successful at isolating them from the rest of the black community. Fellows like Ben Careathers, Bobby Jones, and Ashton Allen had worked too hard around issues of concern to black people to be suddenly cast aside. Some of them were active in a campaign to desegregate the Highland Park swimming pool in the summer of 1948, when we arrived in town.

It had been a hot, sticky, typical Pittsburgh summer, but most swimming facilities were off limits to blacks. The swimming pool in Highland Park was a natural place for black people from East Liberty and Homewood to go, but it was still de facto segregated. There had been discussion about this in the Party's District Committee, and it was decided that some of our people could raise the question in their unions. The first local to react was the UE local at Westinghouse. They decided to bring a racially mixed group to swim there on a Sunday in early August.

About twenty union members, mostly white, as well as several blacks, including Bobby Jones, a cab driver in the Party, went down to the pool. When they tried to swim, rocks and bottles were thrown, and eventually the police stepped in. Instead of arresting those throwing things they grabbed Nate Albert, a UE steward, and accused him of inciting a riot. For shouting "Let's swim!" he was sentenced to eighteen months in jail. We organized around Nate's defense and continued to keep pressure up on the pool. Black organizations and churches began to speak out, and the *Courier* supported the campaign.

Interracial groups kept returning to Highland Park, and the rock-throwing and jeering continued. It took that whole summer and some of the next, but gradually resistance was worn down. I went a few times with Bobby and some of his black friends, and by the end of that second summer, blacks could swim there peacefully. It was an important victory for the black community and represented one of the points of continuity between the tremendous changes in the black community during World War II and the civil rights movement of the fifties.

Wars generally have a radicalizing effect on those involved, and World War II had been no exception. Like World War I, it caused sweeping changes in patterns of employment and residence. The migration of the World War I years toward urban-industrial centers was repeated during the early 1940s as heavy industry and manufacturing employed record numbers of blacks and women, too. The impact of these demographic changes, the role of blacks in the armed services, and the generally progressive racial policies of the New Deal (mind you, often as the result of pressure from black people) contributed to a more assertive consciousness in the black community and led to many struggles similar to the one to desegregate the Highland Park pool.

My evidence of these changes was frequently more impressionistic and personal. When we first came to town, we lived in Harmarville, a coal-mining town about fifteen miles outside of Pittsburgh in the Allegheny River Valley. The Hudsons had bought a house there when Roy was assigned as the district organizer, and they figured it would be nice living in the country. They both had cars and didn't have kids, so it worked out pretty well for them. But it was tough on us. Margaret was stuck out there with the kids when I had meetings at night, and it was terribly expensive to go back and forth every day. We stayed out there a year, but when the political pressures starting mounting, we decided we had to get into the city. We rented a place on Mellon Street in East Liberty for a while, a three-room apartment over a bakery, and finally put some money down on a house in the Hill. The Hill had been a traditional gathering point for immigrants to the city but was largely black when we moved in. We bought the center house of a triplex on Iowa Street in what was referred to as the aristocratic part of the black community because so many ministers lived nearby. It was a lucky break for us. We could shop nearby and the kids went to Herron Hill School. Most of all, we were accepted in the community at a time when I was being crucified in the local press.

The house was under almost constant surveillance by the FBI and assorted police agencies while we lived there. At certain times, particularly Halloween, the coverage was suddenly increased. I don't know what they expected to happen, but the FBI could be counted on to double its coverage every Halloween. Whenever this happened, kids from the neighborhood, who treated it like a game, would come by and tell Margaret, "Mrs. Nelson, the men in the black car with the notebooks are down the block again." Our neighbors for the most part laughed about it. One young professional couple, however, took the whole espionage business more seriously. They were approached by two white men who identified themselves as government agents on assignment and in need of a place to stay to observe some prominent subversives in the neighborhood. The couple took them into their house, and the "agents" stayed with them for a few days. They drank their liquor and joined the couple at the dinner table. After about a week the couple began to tire of their house guests and asked them to leave. Rather than do that, the two men tied up their hosts and ransacked the house. It took the couple a few hours to untangle themselves and call the police who of course knew nothing of the two "agents." The *Courier* had a field day with it, wryly noting that this incident ought to teach a lesson to those who want to work with police agencies.

Even before I left the National Board, discussions had begun concerning how the Party should react to the cold war. Paramount importance was placed on safeguarding the existence of the organization so that it could continue to function no matter what happened. When

I was in Pittsburgh, it was decided to set up a shadow underground organization that could survive the terror of fascism. In other countries Party organizations had been able to function primarily because they had undertaken such preventative measures. Clearly under a reactionary threat, the Party believed fascism was imminent. We took between a hundred and a hundred and fifty lower-echelon leaders and set them up underground with an apparatus to step in and take over leadership when those above ground were arrested.

There was an underground District Committee in Pittsburgh and other cities, made up for the most part of people we figured would likely escape detention when conditions worsened. There were also people sent in from out of town whose identities were unknown to us. A parallel organizational structure was built from the National Board down to the district level, based on the historic principle of units of three to five members who are linked in a pyramid but who know only one member in another cell. As the National Office disintegrated as an effective body due to the lengthy prison sentences imposed on its officials, there was a period in which the shadow organization vied with it for leadership. More to the point is the fact that little effective leadership was exerted nationally at all. The districts were left pretty much to fend for themselves.

In retrospect it is easy to see that going underground was a mistake. We were under a reactionary threat, something that has occurred periodically in American history, but there was still a lot of elbow room to operate openly. Our vulnerability was accentuated by our lack of roots in the American soil. We did not attach enough importance to American democracy. We didn't consider that there might be people who disagreed with us but would still defend our right to exist. When I was out on bail between trials I was asked if I would go underground. Although I was under a possible lengthy sentence, I felt it would be a mistake for me and the Party, and the idea was dropped. It would be easy to say that I suspected going underground was wrong, but that would be overstating it. Like almost everything else, I believed that we had to defend the organization and that the European model of an underground was the best bet.

We were under surveillance, and the organization was infiltrated by the FBI. Even going to small unannounced meetings was a chore for many of us. I would often drive somewhere and ditch my car, get picked up by somebody, and then be taken on a long roundabout way to throw off my "tail." One of the reasons we did this was that we didn't want to lead the FBI to the house of some worker who would subsequently be canned from his or her job.

The Party was of course losing members rapidly. From a peak of some seventy-five or eighty thousand members during the war, we were down to a little over forty thousand in 1950 and thirty thousand the following year. Sadly, the Party itself contributed to the decline in membership by choosing this moment to conduct an internal campaign around the problem of white chauvinism. This activity quickly deteriorated into a witch-hunt.

Although a serious problem, white chauvinism was not the source of our predicament. When you're knocked off your base, as we were, you often develop an abstract issue and make it into a major concern. The campaign against white chauvinism only further demoralized an already beleaguered group of people. Under the supervigilance of those then in control of the National Office, an internal control commission began to investigate alleged instances of white chauvinistic behavior or attitudes. Some accusations had merit, but many did not. People who had done tremendous work in the past, especially in the New York City area, were humiliated or expelled. The campaign did little to improve the Party's ability to fight racism but did inject more chaos and bitterness into the ranks. I don't believe we expelled anyone in Pittsburgh, however. To be truthful, we didn't have anybody that we wanted to get rid of. There was criticism where problems existed, and perhaps sometimes where they only appeared to exist, but hardly an organized campaign. What we heard about the issue elsewhere troubled us, but then we were on our own, for the Party was almost unable to function as a cohesive national organization in the early fifties.

In the midst of this I began a six-year-long roller coaster ride in the courts and prisons of Pennsylvania that took me through two state sedition trials, one federal Smith Act trial, and appeals all the way to the Supreme Court. Looking back on it, I suppose I should not have been too surprised when I was finally arrested. When we arrived in 1948, the *Pittsburgh Press* greeted me with an editorial in which I was labeled an "inspector-general for the Soviet underground." The article concluded, "Whatever else Steve Nelson's assignment to Pittsburgh might involve, one thing is certain, it won't be in the interests of democracy, American style." Moreover, the local anti-Communist group, the Americans Battling Communism, announced in March 1950 that there was enough evidence to indict me and other local figures. But when Margaret and I returned from a movie around midnight on August 31, 1950, and found two detectives flashing badges and telling me I was under arrest, I could only wonder, for what?

Margaret, as usual, was quick to react. Storming up to the detectives, she demanded to see their warrants and hear the charges. One of them pulled out a flashlight and mumbled something about sedition versus the state of Pennsylvania. That was a twist. As far as we knew there had not been any state sedition charges brought against Party members anywhere since the cold war had started. We weren't given much of a chance to mull it over, however, as I was hustled into the back seat of the squad car and was soon riding down Centre Avenue to the downtown police station.

On the way downtown I overheard enough from the squad car radio to realize that I was not the only one arrested. Soon after I was placed in the lockup I was joined by Jim Dolsen and Andy Onda. Jim, then in his sixties, was the correspondent for the *Daily Worker* in Pittsburgh and had decades of experience in the movement behind him. Andy, who was a few years younger than I, directed Party activities among steelworkers. He had grown up on Pittsburgh's South Side and worked in the Jones and Laughlin mill there. In the thirties he threw himself into the CIO drive to organize steelworkers and once was almost elected to office in Cleveland on the Communist Party ticket. They were to be my codefendants.

We were charged with attempting to overthrow by force and violence the government of Pennsylvania and the United States under the 1919 Pennsylvania Sedition Act. Initially designed to deter labor organizing, the act had been a dead letter since the 1926 prosecution of a handful of workers from Jones and Laughlin's Aliquippa works. Why then were we suddenly arrested and charged with violation of it?

In the first place, the federal government was not the force that came after us. There had not been any prosecutions under the federal Smith Act since the July 1948 arrests of the National Board members of the Party, and there were not to be any more until June 1951. The federal government was waiting for the U. S. Supreme Court to dispose of the appeals from the 1948 National Board cases before proceeding with any more Smith Act prosecutions. Ours was a state charge all the way and it was the result of local conditions and personalities.

As far back as 1948 the ABC had been campaigning for the arrest of local Communists. In early 1950, at the same time that Matt Cvetic testified in Washington, surfacing as an undercover agent for the FBI, the ABC conducted local "investigations." Cvetic's testimony received headlines in the Pittsburgh papers, which clamored for the prosecution of radicals as loudly as the ABC.

At this point another local character entered the drama. And I do mean character. Michael Musmanno, then judge of the Court of

Common Pleas of Allegheny County, was not an easy man to figure out. On the one hand, he had publicly supported Sacco and Vanzetti in the late twenties and the CIO in the thirties. He had written a book called *Black Fury* that was turned into a sympathetic movie about coal miners starring Paul Muni. On the other hand, Musmanno had publicly praised Mussolini for his "purification of the Italian soil" in a letter to the *Pittsburgh Press,* and he appeared to many as simply an opportunistic politician. I questioned the man's mental and emotional stability. In later years he acquired a reputation for eccentricity due to his frequent disputes with other judges and his often quasi-hysterical defenses of Columbus, rather than the Vikings, as the "discoverer" of America.

In 1950 Musmanno was running for lieutenant governor, and it seemed that he thought red-baiting was his best bet to get elected. With the federal government hesitating to go after further indictments under the Smith Act, Musmanno personally forced the issue. In July 1950 he went to the Party's offices on the fourth floor of the Bakewell Building on Grant Street and purchased some books and pamphlets. In his *Across the Street from the Courthouse,* he describes the offices as the equivalent of an "advance post of the Red Army" that "Russian agents had planted" in the critical industrial bastion of Pittsburgh.[12] On the basis of his purchases, Musmanno personally filed criminal informations charging the three of us with sedition, and as a result we were arrested a few days later. The Party offices were subsequently raided by Musmanno and Cvetic, during which they seized the books, papers, and documents with which they were to accuse us in court. Ironically, most of the material was already available at the Carnegie Library.

Meanwhile, Jim, Andy, and I were in the county jail. Bail was set at $10,000 for each of us, and friends finally raised enough money to get us out. It was accepted for Dolsen and Onda but refused for me. Musmanno had personally intervened again, this time petitioning the courts that my bail be raised to $100,000. It gained him daily publicity and kept me behind bars another month until the state supreme court finally put it back to $10,000.

In October, after Musmanno, Cvetic, and Harry Alan Sherman, president of the ABC, testified before it, the grand jury returned identical indictments for sedition against the three of us. On January 8, 1951, our trial began. In essence, we were charged with encouraging others to hold the government up to hatred and contempt and with possessing and distributing literature of a seditious nature that might encourage others to commit violence or other unlawful acts.

The trial took place under conditions that can best be described as hysterical. We had been convicted in the press and in the election campaign speeches of a number of politicians long before the case went to jury. I, however, was severed from the case in late May.

After the end of a Friday in court on May 28, 1951, I left for Philadelphia to speak at a meeting to raise funds for the trial. As it was a weekend, Bobby and Josie came with me. The trial had prevented us from spending much time together the last five months, and having them with me was a pleasant change of pace. As I approached the city I stopped to make a phone call, and then we started on the last leg of the trip. It was around midnight when we suddenly crashed. I was pinned behind the steering wheel and had pains in my chest and legs. When I tried to move my right leg, I couldn't control it. I reached over to where Bobby lay slumped against the door. He was still breathing but knocked cold. Josie was lying on the floor in the back but seemed all right. I must have passed out, because the next thing I remember is waking up in the hospital with interns preparing me for surgery. I had broken my right leg just above the ankle where I had broken it only a year before on a hunting trip. In the operating room my troubles were compounded when X-rays revealed that my kneecap was also broken. When they wheeled me out I was encased in a cast all the way up to my crotch.

After a short sleep, I awoke to see my lawyers, Basil Pollitt and John McTernan, Margaret, and several other people at my side. Besides the leg and knee, four ribs were broken, my left arm was dislocated, and my head was pounding. They told me that the children were safe. Soon the nurse made them leave, but not before they told me that an assistant prosecutor, Gilbert Helwig, was downstairs looking over my records to see if they could be transferred to Pittsburgh so that the trial could continue. Loran Lewis, the prosecutor, and Musmanno were eager to get me back in court, but the doctors in Philadelphia said there was no way I could be returned to Pittsburgh. I think the two prosecutors were motivated by political ambitions. Musmanno, defeated in his race for lieutenant governor, was soon running for the state supreme court. Lewis meanwhile successfully sought a seat on the county court. The trials, as you might expect, figured prominently in their campaigns.

After spending June and July in the hospital, I was able to go to the Philadelphia apartment of Harold Spencer, my friend from the anthracite region, to rest and recover. I had to stay in Philadelphia because of a new operation performed by another doctor, who used a stader splint. This consisted of steel pins drilled into the bones to hold the lower part of the leg in place. The knee was operated on right away so that stiffness would not result. The splint, however, required weekly checking, and I was thus unable to return to Pittsburgh, despite repeated demands by Lewis and Musmanno.

August in a Philadelphia apartment is hot. Harold went to work, and Margaret was shopping. While she was gone someone knocked on the door. I was stretched out on the bed with the right leg in the steel splint raised high, so I just said, "Come in." The door opened and who should it be but Musmanno, accompanied by two strangers. Grinning, he looked around the apartment and came toward me. "How are you, Steve?"

"What are you doing here? What right do you have to come in here?" I shouted at him.

"I came to see how soon you were coming back for your trial."

"Get out of here, you rat," I said and reached for my crutch. At that he turned and scampered out without looking back. One of the men with him stayed behind and said, "I'm sorry about this."

"What are you sorry about, and who are you?"

"I was ordered to come with him. I'm a city detective, and I'm assigned to go with him when he campaigns." At this moment a storm broke loose. The wind was howling, and rain blew into the room. Seeing how helpless I was, the detective asked, "Can I close the windows for you? I really am sorry about this."

It was a shocker. This big Philadelphia flatfoot was embarrassed by the judge. The dick was a decent sort.

The apartment where I convalesced was located on a busy one-way street where cars were not allowed to park. My friends noticed that three autos loaded with several men, all looking alike, parked cattycorner from Harold's apartment. They were always there. There were cars at the back entrance to the building too. As I made my weekly trip to the hospital, two cars followed the taxi right to the hospital door. At the hospital they parked at the front and rear doors. About eight men were scattered at strategic points, and two followed me to the clinic as I hobbled along on my crutches.

This went on for nearly two weeks as the trial of Onda and Dolsen in Pittsburgh, from which I was severed, was drawing to a close. While Onda was making his argument to the jury, surveillance was increased at my Philadelphia residence. The FBI came to the door under various pretenses. I was still on my back, hardly able to move, with four-inch steel pins sticking out from my leg.

One morning, two rather nervous young men came into the apartment while I was on a high chair, my broken leg propped on a dresser, shaving in the bathroom. Without introducing himself, one of them pulled out a picture and brought it close to me. "Nelson, you know this man? His name is Jackson, and he's a fugitive. You know where he is?"

"Get out of here, you bums! Who do you think I am—one of your kind?" I must have yelled pretty loud, because they left quickly, although not before they looked to see if there was someone behind the closet door.

Later that day there was a knock at the door. Margaret and Harold were preparing supper, and I was sitting in bed, applying medication around the pins to keep my leg from getting infected. Six men crowded into the small apartment, holding their hands on their hip pockets like gangsters in a movie. When Margaret demanded to know by what right they had entered, one of them pulled a paper out of his pocket and announced, "Nelson, you're under arrest for violation of the Smith Act." Actually, that wasn't such a big surprise. Three months previously, in June 1951, federal prosecutions under the Smith Act had resumed. Arrests were made in New York City, then in California and Maryland, and now it seemed it was Pittsburgh's turn.

"You can see he's sick," Margaret cried. "Did you get a clearance from the hospital?"

They had. I sized up the situation and prepared to leave while Margaret continued to demand, "Where are you taking him? What's the bail? Wait until I get his medicine!"

The six men were in a hurry to get out. Margaret was raising hell with them, and if there was one among them with a conscience, he knew it right then and there. They took me out the back door and whisked me off to the Federal Building on Chestnut Street where a judge was waiting to set bail. Without batting an eye, he set bail at $50,000, although I was already out on $10,000.

The radio was on in the marshal's car, and the regular program was interrupted to announce the news of my arrest and those of Dolsen and Onda at their sedition trial, just as Onda was making his summary to the jury. The new victims added to the list were Ben Careathers, Bill Albertson, and Irving Weissman. I could see them shackling Onda in front of the jury. They'd never get the benefit of a reasonable doubt after that.

Onda and Dolsen were found guilty and their bail increased. They were put in the Allegheny County Jail, where Onda suffered his first severe heart attack. Their sentencing was postponed pending my retrial. Margaret tracked me down and eventually got me released.

Although I was still sick and compelled to use crutches, I was ordered to appear in court in Pittsburgh to begin the state sedition trial on September 28, 1951, exactly four months after the accident. I told the presiding judge I couldn't go ahead because of illness, and that if it weren't obvious to him he could get a doctor to examine me. He appointed two physicians who recommended a two-month postponement of the trial. I wasn't very sure that would be enough time to get better and find a lawyer.

All our efforts to get a lawyer failed. Margaret and various friends saw over eighty in Pittsburgh who said they were too busy or that they didn't practice criminal law. Some frankly admitted that they didn't want to become another Schlesinger, the local progressive attorney who had been, at one time or another in 1950 and 1951, arrested, brought up for disbarment, and held in contempt of court, all because of his politics and whom he defended. Upon my return to Pittsburgh, I visited more than twenty-five lawyers myself and wrote to fifty others out of town. Some were willing but unable to go to court without a delay of several months. Most simply refused.

December 3 arrived, and the trial was scheduled to start. I was still without counsel and was in pain as I hobbled into the courtroom. I told all this to Judge Harry Montgomery and asked for a postponement. He replied that there had already been too many delays, and that the trial would start. I pointed out to him that every racketeer could and did get postponements. But there would be no more "dilly-dallying," as the judge told me. I demanded that doctors be appointed to examine me, and he complied, appointing them himself.

Montgomery had good reasons for rushing the trial. I believe he wanted to get the conviction in before filing candidacy for the state supreme court. In this he would only have followed the examples of other officials who had figured in the previous trial. Judge Gunther had become a superior court justice, D.A. Rahauser a county judge, and prosecutor Loran Lewis also a county judge. Musmanno, who had raided the Communist Party headquarters personally and who appointed Montgomery as trial judge in this case, had got himself elected to the state supreme court for a twenty-year term. Montgomery wasn't going to miss his chance. He got himself a few headlines in the local press complaining about my "stalling and delaying tactics" and then appointed the head doctor for U.S. Steel to examine me in West Penn Hospital in Bloomfield.

I had to take various tests, including one in which the fluid was drained from my spine and a dye pumped in. This allowed the doctors to take x-rays to determine if there was damage to my neck or spine.

The test is intricate, and the patient must lie flat on his back for at least twenty-four hours afterward to avoid complications. Five hours after my tests, while I was lying in bed, a man entered the hospital and demanded to see me. He came up to the end of the ward where I was and asked the man next to me, "Are you Steve Nelson?"

I couldn't see him very well at first, but when I did I knew I had never seen him before. He came toward me with his hand in his pocket and said, "So you're Steve Nelson."

"Yes, but who are you?"

"I came to tell you that I just got a telegram today that my brother was killed in Korea." He shoved his hand further into his jacket and pulled out a gun as he came over to my bed. I jumped up and despite the flash of pain in my head, pushed his gun away. My neighbor, an old miner, jumped out of bed and grabbed him from behind, and I was able to disarm him.

At that, doctors, nurses, and orderlies rushed over, scolding me for getting up as I collapsed back into bed. I demanded to have my assailant arrested, but nothing happened. Meanwhile, this fellow was glaring at Margaret and threatening her. He then walked out, with no one trying to stop him. At least I had the gun, which I turned over to a hospital guard. We never found out who my attacker was. He might have been the person who sent a bullet through the window of our home a little while afterward.

I was pronounced fit to stand trial, and the proceedings began on an appropriately cold and dreary day. The courtroom was almost empty when we arrived. Chills broke over me, and I felt dizzy. Margaret kept looking at me anxiously. I had decided that I would have to ask the judge to help me secure counsel. We had contacted dozens of lawyers around Pittsburgh and Philadelphia. The overwhelming majority had not even answered. Of those who did, most rejected the case outright. Some wanted a fortune to represent me, and others wanted several months of preparation time. It all added up to my facing trial without a lawyer. When I explained this to Judge Montgomery, he said simply, "There will be no further delay."[13]

I tried my last card. "Your Honor, since you apparently don't believe that I cannot get an attorney in this city, I request that you appoint a panel of attorneys with whom I can discuss the case and see if I can get one to defend me."

He hesitated but gave me the names of four lawyers who I could try to see, but I should "be prepared to go to trial tomorrow morning." I protested that no attorney could be ready to go to trial in one day. He must have other clients, whom he could not drop, and he must have time to become familiar with the case. The judge, however, refused to reconsider.

Still, I thought any lawyer was better than none. That night was a busy one. I interviewed three of the attorneys on the list, but they were unacceptable. The fourth, whom I located fifteen minutes before court opened, was only interested in his fee of fifty dollars a day.

Court then began, and Judge Montgomery asked me if I was ready to proceed. I explained that I had no attorney, but that there were three willing to represent me if they could get thirty to sixty days' time. The judge pointed out that he had done his duty by suggesting a panel, and that I was actually refusing everybody he had recommended. He denied me any more time. The trial would proceed the next day, and I was to be my own lawyer.

That night I sat up looking over old cases, trying to become a lawyer. I knew that I could begin by filing certain motions, and I asked the judge for time to do so. He gave me fifteen minutes to write them up and present them. Margaret and I scribbled furiously and handed them over, but he hardly glanced at them. My final motion stunned the judge. I demanded that he disqualify himself because of his deep participation with those who had been behind my arrest and trial. I pointed out that among other actions showing his prejudice was the sentence he gave Nate Albert for attempting to break down Jim Crow at the Highland Park pool. I asked him if it wasn't a fact that he was one of the founders of Americans Battling Communism, which had demanded my arrest and circulated propaganda against me. He admitted that he was one of the officers, but "at the present time, inactive," and he refused to disqualify himself.

The next day a panel of ninety prospective jurors was brought in. The judge asked the tipstaff to go out into the corridor to find a lawyer. The man he found, Pierce O'Connor, was as surprised as I was that he had become my attorney. He did not know what kinds of questions to ask the prospective jurors, outside of the routine ones about residence and occupation, although as we went along he became a little more familiar with the questions I wrote for him. In about an hour he examined fourteen prospective jurors and used up four of my eight challenges when the judge refused to excuse people who had shown obvious bias.

After a while O'Connor had to leave because a case of his was coming up shortly. I looked at Margaret, and we couldn't help laughing when she whispered, "He may give you Harry Alan Sherman as an attorney."

The tipstaff went back into the hall, and presently Harry Glick was ushered into the courtroom. I could see he disliked being roped in, but he didn't protest openly. Despite his total unfamiliarity with the case, his questioning was sharp, and in the course of several hours he managed to get almost the whole remaining panel dismissed on grounds of prejudice or fear. When a prospective juror indicated he or she might try to be fair, the prosecution used its challenges. A man was challenged because he was a UE member and worked at Westinghouse. A coal miner's wife from up the Allegheny River was challenged because her husband was a UMWA member. And so on. By the close of the day, only five jurors had been selected. The judge called Glick and me up for a side-bar conference and said that from now on we could no longer ask so many questions but would be limited to ten, which were to be written out and submitted after a ten-minute recess.

I wrote down ten questions that we thought might work. We asked, for example, whether my membership in the Communist Party or opposition to the Korean War would create a bias that would make it difficult for the juror to render an impartial verdict. But if we were not allowed to examine witnesses personally, it would be almost impossible to get someone dismissed for cause. Indeed, the jury box was filled in no time.

That night the children came home from school showing signs of strain. There had been an air-raid drill, and they had to huddle under the seats. The teacher had asked questions. Bobby said that when she asked who the "enemy" was, some answered Korea, others China and Russia, and a few said "communism." Some kids had told him that his old man was a spy.

Art Shields, who was covering the trial for the *Daily Worker,* Jim Dolsen, and Ben Careathers came over to the house. After dinner they ushered me out of the kitchen. The dishes were usually my job, but not tonight. Everyone wanted me to rest. I decided I would take another crack at some law books someone had sent me. I reached for one and read some of it, but nothing I read seemed to help.

In the morning I rolled out of bed, helped the children with breakfast, and got them off to school. They wished me luck as they left. We piled into a cab and headed to the courthouse. In the hallway were two coal miner friends who became regulars during the trial. They were self-appointed guardians, and whenever I had to go to the bathroom during a recess, these friends "had to go," too. They took the opportunity to hand me money collected for the defense and bring me regards from friends. We exchanged a few words and went into the courtroom. There, Margaret and I sat at the defense table alone. She had a few sharpened pencils and a yellow legal notebook at her side.

As the trial started, the courtroom was packed. Looking at the jury, prosecutor Cercone, who was Musmanno's nephew, began, "You have been sworn to try . . . the case of Steve Nelson . . . , who is charged with . . . the felonious crime of sedition. . . . Sedition under our laws is committed when a person, either individually, or in combination with others, brings, publishes, writes, or by cartoon, utterance, or conduct intends to make or cause to be made any outbreak or demonstration of violence against the state of Pennsylvania or of the United States of America. . . . Sedition itself includes any writing, publication, printing, or other literature which advocates or teaches the necessity of crime [or] violence . . . or the sale of or gift or distribution of any literature, publication, printing, or writing which advocates sedition."

At one point Cercone said they would put on witnesses to prove I was a member of the Communist Party. I told them to save the bother, that I admitted my membership proudly, but I reminded the judge that he had stated that the Communist Party was not on trial here. He snapped back that any objections were to be made later.

Eventually Cercone started to wind up his opening remarks. He told the jury what his various witnesses would testify to. One would relate how "Steve Nelson infiltrated the City of Pittsburgh with the Communist Party-planned program of propaganda and sabotage." I moved for a mistrial, charging the prosecutor with making speeches for his election campaign. The judge, to my surprise, ordered the remarks stricken.

Cercone ended his speech in less than forty minutes, with half that time taken up by my objections. When the judge said he would order remarks stricken later if they were unfair, I told him that people's minds, unlike spigots, could not be turned off and on. It was of little use to threaten me with contempt. Since the charges carried a maximum of twenty-year sentence, a few more years for "contempt" would not make much of a difference.

Prosecutor Lewis, who was handling the case until Cercone's uncle Musmanno was through testifying, then called the first witness. It was city detective Becker, who had arrested me and been present when Musmanno raided the Party offices and bookstore. He had little to say, but I objected to most of it anyway, and that rounded off the day's session.

The second witness, on the following day, was Musmanno himself.

When I had last seen Musmanno, I was with Pat Cush, a retired steelworker. We had watched him strut up Liberty Avenue at the head of the St. Patrick's Day Parade. Old Pat was furious. "You'll observe," he said, "that this lowdown individual found a way to get at the head of this Irish parade. He'll always find his way to the front, no matter what. He knows it's good politics." Here in the courtroom, Musmanno was strutting again. Margaret leaned over and whispered, "What a clown."

The prosecutor motioned to one of his assistants, and the door in the back of the courtroom opened. Three men pushed in a factory-type dolly loaded with books and pamphlets. Lewis proceeded to introduce into the record the titles of over a hundred books. He included nearly all the works of Marx, Engels, Lenin, Stalin, and other communist leaders, including American ones. He introduced maps of the USSR and Pennsylvania, magazines, leaflets, and posters. I protested that the introduction of all this material simply proved that this was a trial of ideas; that the jury and courts were incompetent to pass on this quantity of books and pamphlets; and that the procedure was contrary to all the claims made about freedom of thought.

But the judge paid no attention to my protests. He seemed in a hurry, and the books and papers were admitted by the carton or bundle. I suggested that perhaps the material should be weighed and presented by the pound and insisted that if these books were to be introduced, over my objections, then at least a charlatan like Musmanno shouldn't be the one to interpret ideas to the jury. The judge instead proposed that he himself interpret the literature, and I continued to object to either of them explaining any of the books or my ideas. As they introduced *Daily Worker* issues, leaflets, pamphlets, and books by the bundle, I continued to protest that "no jury should be required to pass on what another man should read."

In the first trial, the prosecution had built its case on our opposition to the Korean War. They didn't have any trouble proving that, for we made a point of it. At this trial the prosecution still seemed to hope to profit by the war atmosphere, but they pulled their horns in considerably. To their claim that the Communists opposed the war, I answered that we certainly did, and that many people in our country's history, including Abraham Lincoln, had opposed wars declared by the government. Montgomery interrupted me, but I still tried to continue. He instructed the deputies to restrain me, and the court was then recessed.

After a break Musmanno was back on the witness stand, and the prosecution rushed ahead. They didn't bother to qualify him as an "expert" on Marxism as they had at the first trial, but Lewis kept asking him to interpret Marxist analysis and strategy. Finally it was my turn to cross-examine.

How could I make use of my one night's study of *The Art of Cross-Examination?* I didn't yet have the record of the previous day in court, and there was no time to write out any questions. Margaret saw my predicament and said, "Look, you know Musmanno. He's a lot of hot air. Just prick him, and he'll go up like a gas balloon." Fortunately, there wasn't very much about him that I didn't know. I knew he was terribly egocentric, that he had written a book in which he proposed himself as a candidate for president, and that he was exceedingly vain. In another book of his, this one about Germany, he had appeared in every one of the sixty-odd photographs, including those with the photographer, the chauffeur, the secretary, and Hitler's dog.

He would do almost anything for a chance to get his name in the paper. Once, while sitting as a judge, he had sentenced himself to the county jail for three days for a traffic violation. I knew that he had praised Mussolini and was sorry that Roosevelt hadn't supported Hitler and Mussolini against the Soviet Union, as Hearst and Dulles had advised.

But for all that, I knew he was dangerous. First, he was still an unexposed McCarthyite in the Democratic Party with a "prolabor" past. People who would in time see through him hadn't done so yet. Second, he had the support of the presiding judge, who would let him shoot his mouth off. It wouldn't be enough to show he was a fool and a clown. Finally, how does a layman go about cross-examining anyone—and a judge of the state supreme court at that?

I asked him why he went to the Communist Party offices in July 1950. " . . . To obtain literature," he answered. Did he have any trouble buying it? "No," he finally said, after a long wrangle. Did he or did he not know that the Party offices had been across the street from the courthouse for eight years? It took nearly half an hour to get a simple "Yes." He had called the office a secret hideout, but after another twenty minutes he admitted that it wasn't secret. To my question, "Did you find any weapons in the Communist Party office?" he answered, "Yes, the place was filled with weapons, because I regard these books as weapons."

We went round and round. My cross-examination of Musmanno took days. I have never encountered such a long-winded and argumentative man, even on trivial issues. Despite a fairly constant chorus of "I object" from the prosecution and "Sustained" from the judge, I grilled him on his sympathies for Mussolini, about the right of a citizen to read books in a democracy, and on his own political activities.

At four different times I took up the question of who had appointed the trial judge for this case. I couldn't get the two of them to admit the simple truth—that Musmanno appointed Montgomery. So I came back to it whenever I had to gain some time. I almost enjoyed seeing these two do fancy legal footwork to cover up. All I had to do was say, "I still don't know who appointed the trial judge," and they were off to the races as people in the courtroom rolled their eyes.

I finally began to wrap up my questioning. Did he not keep a person named Alice Roth from being a grand juror because she was supposed to be a Communist? He admitted he did. Did he know his action was illegal? That the Supreme Court had reversed him on this? He admitted weakly that he had been overruled. Didn't he resort to the illegal use of a padlock on Communist Party headquarters? Wasn't he reversed when he had my bail raised to $100,000? Didn't he illegally arrest attorney Hyman Schlesinger and have him thrown into jail, and didn't the Supreme Court overrule him on all these matters? When I was through, Montgomery called a long recess.

As the crowd settled down the next day, a man walked in, and without waiting to be told, marched straight to the witness stand. He gave his name as Paul Crouch. For a full day he identified various Marxist books he had seen in my office in Oakland, California, and tied me in with each one. To speed up the process, the prosecutor introduced the books in lots of two hundred and by bundles and boxes. Finally Montgomery let us off for the day with Cercone and Crouch still at it. The last newspaper edition came out with columns devoted to Crouch and his seditious books. Bill Burns, a radio and TV commentator for KDKA who pushed what was to me the most objectionable sort of journalism, devoted his whole program to Crouch.

That night, as I prepared questions for his cross-examination, Margaret and I talked about how people in Oakland had caught on to Crouch. They had demanded that he be removed from his post in the Party years ago after he had proposed policies that members felt would lead to violence at street meetings. A number of other questions had been raised. He spent a lot of his time drinking alone in bars. It was known that his son was sick, and people tried to be sympathetic, but after a while they felt Crouch was not responsible enough to hold a leadership position.

The next day I questioned Crouch on his activities as a strikebreaker on a Miami newspaper. When he admitted to that, I moved on to his record as a government witness. Referring to him as "Mr.

Stool Pigeon," I asked if he had not testifed against Harry Bridges although he never saw the man and had nothing to do with him, according to his own testimony at another hearing where he was under oath. The judge refused to allow him to answer.

When I asked him where he lived, Crouch, visibly upset, said that if he divulged his address, his life would be in danger from me. This time I jumped up, protesting that the judge should not permit such prejudicial remarks to be made and requesting a mistrial. Montgomery laughed off my complaint. When Crouch made a similar statement in the afternoon, I again moved for a mistrial. As I did so, I walked to the witness stand and asked if he knew of a single case of assassination in the entire time he was in the Communist Party. He had to admit he knew of no such thing. I continued questioning him about his role as a paid witness. It was not hard to show that he had testified to different things at different trials.

I knew who the next witness would be. My friends had noticed Matthew Cvetic enter the D.A.'s office. When Cvetic testified before HUAC in February and March 1950, he named hundreds of people as Communists and caused many of them a good deal of grief. It wasn't just that he informed on people; he lied and slandered them as well. In a three-part series in the *Saturday Evening Post* entitled "I was a Communist for the FBI," he and his ghost writer Pete Martin claimed I was "one of the biggest shots in the United States Communist Party . . . spent fourteen months in a Moscow school for training saboteurs . . . was a member of the Red Army Reserves and was on call for military activity anywhere in the world."[14] Frankly, I despised him.

Cvetic, a short overweight man dressed in a gray suit, sat in the witness chair. As I made myself comfortable in the large oak armchair, Margaret said, "At least we know what to expect from him. He spilled his guts at the previous trial, and he can't say very much that's different from what he said then." She was right. Cvetic, the key witness against me as he was the only one who testified to things that supposedly took place within the period covered by the indictment, was through for the government in less than an hour and a half, and I proceeded to cross-examine.

I wondered where to begin my questioning since he actually had testified to very little, even by this court's standards. His chief testimony against me concerned a Communist Party convention that took place in Carnegie Library—a public place—which he referred to as a secret meeting where Communists had discussed "infiltration of the steel industry." It was in fact a regular convention such as any union might have held. He also stated that I had said, "Now that we have the A-bomb, they won't be in such a goddamn hurry to start a war." I was also supposed to have said that "I didn't tell those bastards anything" after returning from an appearance before HUAC. It wasn't much.

However, I saw no reason to start with these matters. I believed it would be more effective to show that this character was using his past connection with the Party and his presumed knowledge of it for his private gain. He had been made into a hero in the press, on the radio, and even in a motion picture, *I Was A Communist for the FBI*. I decided to itemize his anti-Communist activities, in each case adding up the amount of money he had earned by "piecework," as I referred to it at that time. I asked him how much he had gotten for the picture and the articles in the *Post*. After several heated exchanges, it was brought out that he had received a total of $18,000 for the articles and motion picture rights. I finally managed to get the admission that he had retained 40 percent of the proceeds, with 30 percent going to Harry Alan Sherman, local leader of the ABC, and 30 percent to Pete Martin.

I asked whether the story he sold the *Post* and the motion picture he marketed with Warner Brothers bearing his name were based on lies. The movie, a fantasy that was greeted by one New York Film critic as a "hissing and horrendous spy film," portrayed Cvetic as a valiant undercover agent and a character based on me as a ruthless murderer. It premiered in Pittsburgh during our first trial with most of the local politicians present. I never saw the picture, although I have heard parts of the radio serial that aired under the same name with Dana Andrews playing Cvetic. I wanted to show that Cvetic had been paid for lying, and that that was all he was doing in court.

Montgomery at first wanted to make me refrain from asking questions about the picture, but he finally said that it should be stipulated "that the movie is fictional to some extent." He said that Cvetic was not responsible for what Warner Brothers had done as it was assumed they took a "dramatic license." Cvetic fell back on that license for the next hour or so.

I asked him whether he had fingered a number of steelworkers at the Isabella furnace in Etna. The judge objected to my term *fingering*. How, I inquired, could Cvetic's work be dignified by any other name? I went on to ask about similar groups of workers at U.S. Steel in Etna and a Crucible Steel plant. Cercone objected to these questions, and Montgomery sustained him. Had he testified, I asked, against a certain glass worker? Against a coal miner, a schoolteacher, a musician, a mother on assistance, Hy Schlesinger? He admitted to each instance. Had he been paid by the head? Again the prosecutor's objection was sustained.

Cvetic's composure was disintegrating on the stand. His answers became inaudible, and he kept pleading with the judge that he couldn't answer questions while this man was shouting at him. After two days of testimony, Cvetic left the courtroom in a distinctly dizzy condition. He was subsequently thoroughly discredited. It turned out he was an alcoholic, and he was later rejected even by his employer, the FBI, for unreliability. But not before he caused a lot of damage.

The prosecution ended its testimony with two other witnesses who testified to things that supposedly happened in the early thirties. I spent very little time on them, and thus ended the government's case against me.

No matter how many trials one has been through, or how similar they seem, each engenders its own suspense and anxiety. My second trial closely resembled the first—the same parade of government witnesses and their stools—yet when the prosecutor said, "The state rests," I asked myself if that was all they were going to do. With such people and such lies they wanted to take away my rights and put me in prison?

But there was not time to think about that. A trial is like a treadmill. When the tipstaff yells "Court!" in the morning, you have to be there, and the show, which in this case was more of a circus, must go on. Frequently I felt sick, and my leg gave me trouble, but I had to drag myself to the courtroom or face contempt charges. So I kept my shirt on and went through the act. I was on time and as ready as I could be each day.

We did get one night out in the midst of the trial. We saw Arthur Miller's play *The Crucible,* which deals with the Salem witch trials. In the front row were seated my prosecutor, Cercone, and his uncle Judge Musmanno. I wonder if these two understood Miller's play was as much about cold war America as seventeenth-century Salem.

On January 16, my witness took the stand. This time the prosecution had to guess what was up, and I think the FBI surveillance was increased. I suspected, and it was later confirmed, that our house was bugged. By now even Bobby knew what the score was, and when we got a little careless, he'd say, "Daddy, did you forget that the walls have ears?"

My first witness, Herbert Aptheker, had sat in the courtroom several hours a day to get a feel of the atmosphere but had not drawn any attention to himself. We did not even greet each other. He left after lunch to work on his testimony alone. Finally, we talked the night before he was to take the stand. I was becoming confident we could handle our case even though we didn't have time to rehearse the whole thing.

When we began, my initial questioning disclosed that he was a Ph.D. graduate of Columbia University, that he had written many articles and books, particularly on the Negro question, and that he was an associate editor of *Masses and Mainstream,* a radical cultural magazine published in New York City. Aptheker said that his studies had been interrupted by World War II, when he joined the army as a private. By the end of the war he had risen to the rank of major. He stated he had joined the Communist Party in 1939 and was proud of his membership.

Since I was on trial because I was a Communist, my witness and I were prepared to go into all the necessary details about the Party—what it is and what it stood for. But when I asked my very first question about this subject, "Why did you join the Communist Party?" the prosecutor objected, and the court sustained him.

Our aim was to challenge the prosecution's distorted presentation of Marxism-Leninism and to describe our own ideas and activities. We undertook to answer the indictment, which had been drawn up by Musmanno and consisted of thirty-three quotations from various leftist works. Our plan was to read the quotations cited in the indictment, discuss what book each was extracted from, and then explain its real meaning when considered in that context.

If most of the jurors had been well-versed in these matters, we might have gone into greater detail, but it became evident right off that they couldn't follow a complicated discussion of Marxism. So Aptheker tried to tackle things in the most elementary way, using American examples. Herb was not a guy who could explain things in workingman's language for he had too many years in academia behind him. But we had to try to offset Musmanno's testimony about Marxism. Since Musmanno had selected and arranged quotations so as to put special emphasis on "class struggle," "revolution," and "force and violence," Aptheker explained each one of these as clearly as he could.

We had had a bit of an argument ourselves over how to deal with the "force and violence" explanation. When you start with the premise that the ruling class never gives up without a struggle, it leads you into a discussion of the forcible overthrow of that class. I wanted to make the point that we did not favor force but preferred to reach our goal by democratic means. Herb was afraid he would be distorting the classical formulations. I said, "Look, I'm on trial, We're not writing the program of the Communist Party with the jury. We're trying to win the case without compromising principle." Herb called the National Office and eventually agreed to tone down the rhetoric a little.

He was wonderful when it came to discussing the history of the United States and really conducted a mini-course in the courtroom. His explanations of American history captivated jurors and audience alike in a way his theoretical presentations simply did not. The prosecutor became very impatient at times and once complained that it would take a week to explain some of these things. I answered, "Listen, Mr. Prosecutor, I've got plenty of time; you are trying to put me away for twenty years." That annoyed the judge, who retorted "We have had enough of that. We are not going into all the reasons why Abraham Lincoln was elected president."

While Aptheker was still testifying, I was busy discussing with my friends what to do next. Should we put on more witnesses or should we rest with one? I favored putting on a few more. Even though the theoretical discussion of Marx had been handled, I felt we should tackle the lies of the other stool pigeons, especially those of Cvetic. We wanted to expose his yarn about "infiltration" of basic industries and to explain what happened at the "secret" convention at Carnegie Library. And we wanted to contradict his claim that force and violence were taught in the local Party schools. But to put a person up there to testify opened him up to potential trouble. "Are you a member of the Communist Party? If so, who else is a member?" and so on. I was fortunate to get Aptheker to testify for me. He was the one guy both competent enough and willing to do it despite the risks.

We settled on one or two more witnesses. The first of these was the local black Communist leader of many years, Benjamin Careathers. I had met Ben and his brother Ernie in the 1920s when I first came to Pittsburgh. Ben used to travel around western Pennsylvania on a motorcycle, with white motorists trying to run him off the road because he was black. I had wanted the evening to go over questions with Ben, but he had to take the stand a few minutes after Aptheker left since the judge wasn't going to lose any time. Ben didn't seem to mind. "Look," he said to me, "perhaps the less we prepare the better. If we can't handle these little fascists by now, another night won't change things." Ben was like that—the kind of guy you always wanted next to you when trouble was about to happen.

He testified that he had first met me in the early thirties on the steps of the state capitol in Harrisburg during one of the hunger marches. He had led a delegation of several hundred from Pittsburgh, and I was with a similar group from the anthracite. Careathers introduced scores of leaflets to show what he and the Party in Pittsburgh were doing. The prosecutor didn't want the leaflets read, but the judge couldn't very well keep them out after the prosecution had brought in tons of literature. In less than an hour, Ben and I covered a lot of ground. His answers were short and to the point. He described his part in the Steel Workers Organizing Committee and his role in the organization of the Jones and Laughlin Aliquippa Works. Ben discussed various labor struggles and the role of the Party in them and then turned his attention to the conditions of blacks in Pittsburgh.

An hour and a half later, Ben's testimony was finished, and Cercone jumped up to cross-examine him. Striding up to the witness chair, and without the ordinary courtesy of addressing Ben as "Mister," he began to shout questions at him. Ben sighed and calmly told Cercone to step back and not shout at him, that Cercone should know better than to try to intimidate him. He'd answer the questions in time. Cercone tried to rattle Ben and diminish the credibility of his testimony. He was successful at neither. It was one of the high points of the defense.

The prosecutor wound up his case with a bit of Fourth of July oratory, and the judge proceeded to rule against all my motions. Things he had promised to act on were forgotten, and scores of dubious charges were permitted to remain in the record.

The morning the judge was to deliver his charge to the jury, the courtroom was packed. At nine-thirty Montgomery was ready, but one of the jurors, a man who had been present and on time every single day during the weeks of trial, was missing. Montgomery motioned Cercone and me to approach the bench and suggested replacing the missing juror with one of the two alternates. I asked the judge if he had tried to locate him. On the tried and tested principle that what was good for the prosecution could not be good for me, I insisted that he instruct the county detectives to go out and find the man. I maintained I had a right to know why the juror was not present. Perhaps something had happened. Besides, if the man had been able and willing all these weeks to fulfill his duties, he had the right to be an hour or two late before being replaced.

Finally the judge permitted the detectives to see if they could find the man. Two hours later they came back with him, and the entire room was thrown into a turmoil by his appearance. A good part of his face was painted with iodine, and a patch covered the bridge of his nose. His eyes were blackened. The judge, after conferring with the detectives, announced that the man had had a slight accident but was now all right.

Montgomery then read his charge to the jury, and his presentation gave me little hope. There was nothing to do now but wait and look at the clock and the light above the jury room that comes on when a verdict has been reached. When the court day ended at four o'clock with no decision, the judge suggested that I go home. He was to call me when the verdict was reached.

At nine o'clock the jurors retired for the night. Scores of friends came over to the house, and even while playing, Josie and Bobby listened to our talk. As they went to bed, they wished us luck. Bobby started to choke up but made it upstairs before the tears came. He and Josie realized that twenty years in jail was a long time.

The next day at nine-thirty we called the clerk and found out the jury was still deliberating. At noon there was still no sign of a verdict. We went down to the courtroom to watch for the light, but nothing happened. As the time went by, my spirits started to rise. Perhaps one of the jurors was holding out for us. The judge once again suggested that we might as well go home and wait. Finally, after twenty-three more hours, the jury reached a verdict. We rushed downtown and to my surprise, the courtroom was filled. All other cases were adjourned for the occasion. The jurors filed in, and I suddenly knew there was no hope. Not one of them would look at me.

Montgomery called for a report, and the foreman replied, "Guilty on all counts." I asked the jurors be polled individually. They answered, one by one, some rather weakly, others almost inaudibly. I stood before them while they answered. When the last one had responded, I came close to the jury box and said, "YOU KNOW I AM NOT GUILTY. NOW LET IT BE ON YOUR CONSCIENCE, NOT MINE."

The judge was at a loss. It was highly irregular for a defendant to say anything to the jurors after a verdict. Friends could not believe what had happened. The jurors left, and the press went off to call in the news. We walked down the street talking about the verdict and were stopped by a woman who was on her way to the courtroom to hear it. When we told her what it was, she said, "What a shame," and wished us luck. We didn't know her, but somehow her words made it easier to tell the children that we must not lose heart.

The trial ended in late January 1952. For a few months we all remained free on bail and motions for appeals to both trials were filed. On June 26, 1952, our motion for a new trial was denied, and we were placed in the Allegheny county jail. On July 10 we appeared before Judge Montgomery, and he pronounced sentence of twenty years imprisonment, court costs and $10,000 in fines—the maximum.

I was pretty upset when I heard him say twenty years, even though

I knew it was coming. I think I was ready to cry. I recall looking back over my shoulder as I was led away and seeing Margaret and a few others crying. I felt very helpless. When I was put in a cell, the other men asked what I got. When I said "twenty years," one of them remarked "Holy shit!" and the others just shook their heads. Then one guy said, "You're not going to serve it, Nelson." I don't know why he said it, but it did me a lot of good.

ELEVEN

In the Hole

After we had been in the county jail for six weeks, I was suddenly ordered to get my belongings and be ready to go. I wondered what was up. The judge had ruled that I was to be held in the county jail while appeals were pending and the fight for bail went on. As I came to the checkout point, I was thoroughly searched. Every little item was scrutinized; each book was leafed through; and even the seams of my clothes were turned inside out. I extended my hands for the handcuffs, but instead the chief deputy took out a large leather-and-iron-reinforced belt about four inches wide and a half inch thick. He put it around my midriff and snapped the handcuffs hanging from the belt onto my wrists. The doors opened, and I stepped outside, surrounded by several deputies. We descended the granite steps toward the street facing the back entrance of the courthouse.

Cameras clicked and TV crews turned their klieg lights on. People were lining the courthouse steps, and there was no mistaking the character of this crowd. I recognized many from the courtroom. At least there they had maintained some small semblance of restraint. Here, they shouted and swore at me. It was almost a relief to get into the sheriff's car and leave the stone jail on Ross Street behind as we headed for the workhouse in Blawnox.

Forty minutes later, the old gray walls of the workhouse came into view. Rising high where the ground dips toward the Allegheny River, the walls are capped by castlelike pieces of architecture that serve as guardhouses. We drove through the one break in the wall, and I was led inside. My "chastity belt" was removed, and the transfer of papers accomplished. The inner door then opened and a man motioned me in and told me to stand against the wall and wait. I was in a corridor about as large as a good-sized hall with a skylight window some twenty-five feet overhead. I stood leaning against the white tile wall.

For a moment I thought I was alone, so soundless were the men passing back and forth. I looked to see if I could recognize any of them. They moved along silently, glancing curiously at me, the new-comer in street clothes. They were all dressed in dirty gray patched and shapeless pants and shirts.

A prisoner passed nearby, and I spoke to him to find out if he knew a certain man I had met in the county jail. He looked at me with frightened eyes and didn't answer. I was about to ask the same question of another man when a voice from behind the iron gate spoke out.

"Don't talk—do you want me to put you in the hole?"

"No, what did I do?"

"You're trying to be smart, Nelson. I know your kind. You're in jail now, mister, and don't forget it."

Fat chance, I thought. I got tired and impatient leaning against the wall, although I knew there was nothing particularly good to look forward to inside. I shifted from one foot to the other. Finally I was taken to the shower room. When I had stripped and showered, a guard said, "That's your stuff there," pointing to an old navy duffle with a stick about two inches wide and eighteen inches long tied to it. My name, prison number, and "20 years" were painted on the stick. "Your clothes won't keep that long," he chuckled. "Maybe you ought to send them to your wife."

"I'll just put them in the bag," I answered. My eyes were riveted on the stick as I slouched on a bench.

Other men were brought in and put through the same routine. Two officials came in. One in a black uniform with two gold bars on his elevator cap was the boss of the place. He had various names, as I soon learned, among them "the General." He took over. The young guard placed a big ledger in front of him and beckoned to a prisoner to come forward. He told him to stand within a yellow chalk circle on the floor.

"What are you in for?" demanded the General.

"Nonsupport."

"Huh, woman trouble. Well, we'll fix that. What's your trade?"

"Coal miner."

The General looked him over and told the young guard to stick him in the boiler room. "You'll stoke your coal there for a while."

"What's your name?" the General asked.

"Steve Nelson."

"What are you in for?"

"Political prisoner."

"That isn't what it says here," he replied, pointing to the commitment papers. "It says 'sedition' here."

"It's the same thing, sir, only in different words."

"Oh, is it? How long a sentence did you get?" He went through the usual set of questions and concluded with, "Put him in the chair shop. And stick him on the West Range, Cell P-47."

On the way to the chair shop the guard, whose name was Buck, stopped at his desk. There was nothing on it, not even a paperclip, but he said with a serious air, "You guys step back against the wall. I got to check some papers." Then he walked over to one of the cells and picked up the morning paper. He sat down behind the desk, turned to the sports page, and started reading. The men standing against the wall exchanged words in low tones. The man next to me introduced himself as "Nick—though they usually call me 'the Boxer.' " Nick, I was to find out, had led a hectic life. Brought up in a coal-mining area, he had begun work in the mines when he was only fourteen. While still young, he had injured himself when he brushed against a live trolley wire. It impaired his speech and hearing. He left the mines and took up boxing, keeping it up till he went into the army at the age of thirty. Now he was thirty-eight, paunchy and slow, but still powerful. Still a boxer at heart.

Buck came over and tapped Nick on the shoulder. "I see you're talking again. If you know what's good for you, you'll keep that big mouth of yours shut. If I catch you talking once more, I'll put you in the hole."

"Sir?" Nick asked, cupping his ear, "were you saying something to me?" He moved forward slightly, and Buck retreated a step before Nick's imposing torso.

"Did you say you can't hear? Okay, okay then." Turning, Buck went back to his desk and finished the paper. Nick's actions bolstered my confidence. He had backed the guard down.

Soon he put away the newspaper and led us out of the building, across the yard, and into the furniture shop. As the shop doors opened, a bell rang, and about fifty men automatically turned toward us. I got to learn why. The bell broke the monotony. Its ping could mean that something new was happening: a letter from home or maybe a money order that one would have to go to the library to sign for. That would take all of fifteen minutes but be a break nonetheless in the damnably long day.

The shop was an old structure a block long and half that wide. Its work spaces were arranged so that the men worked fifteen feet from each other. It was like a cow barn. The noise of the machinery—

power saws, drills, turners—made it impossible to hear anybody speaking. There was the smell of steamed wood, glue, tobacco spit, and sweat. Almost all the men chewed because it was forbidden to smoke in the shop. The sweat stank more than usual because there was no ventilation, and the prisoners could bathe only once a week. The gray shirts were more or less clean for they were changed weekly, but the pants had to be worn for a month and they showed it, especially in the seats.

Near the door stood a raised platform with a dirty glass-topped desk and two high armchairs flanked on each side by three-foot-high spittoons. In one chair sat a skeletonlike figure of an old man with small black eyes. Eighty-six years old, he was the foreman of the shop and had spent fifty-three of his years in this place. His name was Bill Mauser, but here he was "Skeleton." Everybody sooner or later had to listen to him tell how he had made chairs in the old country and had been employed in different prisons since coming to the United States. He had started at the workhouse in 1900.

"The furniture I designed thirty to forty years ago is still the standard product of this shop. That'll tell you something, won't it, boy? And now I'll teach you how to make a chair. I'm in charge of production, and the guard here is the boss. He sees to it that order is kept."

The guard pointed to a spot fifteen feet away from his chair and indicated to me that it was my work spot. Nick was put one space behind me.

Inmates all around us worked busily away. A man was assigned to teach us what to do, but he also initiated us newcomers into prison life. The work required a certain experience and skill, and it was evident that our instructor had been here for a few years. The instructors were known as "pushers." They got their jobs by a "drag," a special favor from the guard, known as "Big Shot," who ran the furniture shop. While they had to eat the same food and undergo the same restrictions as the rest of the inmates, the pushers could get little favors from the guards. There were half a dozen of them in the place, and although nearly half the inmates were black, all the pushers were white.

The Skeleton rose from his cushioned chair where he had been sitting motionless except for the constant roving of his little black eyes and the periodic spitting of tobacco juice. He stepped off the platform and walked around the full length of the shop. Drawing near me, he eyed me up and down and said, "Nelson, you got a long time to spend here, so you might just as well learn how to make a good chair. Think you can make one? I suppose you can. Now I don't care what a man is in here for—never ask him, either—but a man's got to produce in here or I'd just as soon put him in the hole as not."

He stood so close to me that the stench of chewing tobacco on his breath and of the juice running down his throat made me feel as if my face was pressed against a spittoon that hadn't been emptied in weeks. I stepped back to avoid the shower of tobacco that sprayed from his mouth as he spoke.

"I see you were a carpenter. That should make you feel at home here." Shoving aside the pusher who had been showing me the ropes, the old man started to weave. His skinny fingers moved fast as he weaved without even looking at what he was doing. "It's nothing, nothing at all," he said. But the furious pace he kept up was exhausting him, and the pusher gave me a knowing wink. It seemed that everyone humored the old man.

He walked over to the nearest spittoon, spat, went to the fountain for a drink of water, and walked back, continually chewing the same cut. "You know," he said to me, "I actually believe the reason I've lived so long is that I've chewed since I was fifteen years old and I've swallowed a mouthful of the stuff at least twice a day all my life."

The pusher, Mike, had spent six years in the workhouse and thought he could make better chairs than the Skeleton. He was in charge of production when the old man was sick or on vacation. I soon found out he detested both Skeleton and Big Shot, the guard.

There is nothing more confusing than to be told to do something and to do it in a hurry when you haven't the slightest idea what it is all about. A wicker chair in the making is just a bunch of sticks, wires, and fiber, all loose with hundreds of ends sticking in all directions. Nick seemed baffled and discouraged. He walked over to the old man to ask if he could be given a simpler job, like sweeping the floor or carrying the heavy fiber, but the old man turned him down flat. Nick turned back to his bench. His expression kept me from asking to be changed to woodworking, which I could handle without problems. I didn't want to give Skeleton the satisfaction of refusing me. Mike came over and quietly said, "You just look at the way I'm doing this job, and don't act like we're talking. You have to be careful here; they're laying for you. Big Shot did his best to get you assigned here, and he's got you now. He's been bragging he'll have you in the hole before the day is over." Big Shot, meanwhile, had gotten off the platform and was heading our way. Mike continued to demonstrate the correct way of making a chair. "When you want to form it into this shape, take your hammer and tap it in lightly. Be sure that you don't bruise the fiber, or you'll get the wrong shape. That rat told me to start you off wrong so that you'd mess up and he could bawl you out."

Big Shot motioned Mike over to him and apparently scolded him for talking with me. I, in the meantime, was left with a maze of mixed-up fibers. Where to start? Which one goes over the other first? The other men looked on and grinned at my predicament. Some signaled directions to me, but none dared to come over. I looked at Nick who was talking to himself and shaking his head while he held a pair of wire-cutting pliers in his hand. By going back and forth to the spittoon, a walk of three steps, he seemed to be finding some relief from the tension.

In time I began to get the hang of it, and my complicated maze of fibers began to look like a chair. But Nick, who was being pushed as much as I was, was having a rougher time. We agreed the first day that we would try to keep the same pace. No loafing, but no racing, either.

Mike made his rounds regularly, with a short stop at each work place. When the guard was out of the room, he stayed longer and went through the motions of instructing me as he told me the secrets of the prison.

"This place is racket-ridden, everywhere you look. You'll get an earful when you get out in the yard. But look out for stools. You can't trust anybody. They'll come over to you, but for Christ's sake, don't trust them. The officials have their stools everywhere. You know who the stoolie is in this place? Maybe it would be better to ask who isn't a stoolie in here. I guess there are a few guys who wouldn't sell you out, but the majority I wouldn't trust further than I could throw them."

I asked him if that wasn't true in all places where people were unorganized, and he said, "Yeah, but this is different. There was a strike here last April. We went on strike demanding the state's minimum wage for prisoners, a measly ten cents a day, and the strike was broken. The guys blamed for it are still in isolation. That was over four months ago, and they're still deprived of the yard and their other privileges."

"You mean the state's minimum is ten cents a day for prison labor?"

"Yeah, ten cents. But this damn place is county-run and says the law don't apply to them."

"How many men went out on strike?"

"Hell, everybody."

"What did the administration do?"

"They shut down the shop and kept us all in our cells, twenty-four hours a day. They kept the canteens locked, and no one had any tobacco or candy, no newspapers, no mail, nothing. We couldn't write letters or work on parole papers. They stuck a few of the guys who they called the ringleaders in the hole and kept working on the rest of us. They filled the hole to capacity. Finally the strike collapsed. I'm telling you, the coal and steel companies could learn a lesson in strikebreaking from this gang."

"Where did the strike start?"

"In the rag shop."

"How did you know?"

"It don't take much time to know what's going on in any part of this place at any time."

"Was there a committee leading it?"

"Well, there was sort of an informal committee so the guards wouldn't know who was in charge. But with everyone locked in, it was pretty tough, and anyone that spoke out got thrown in the hole."

"What were the other demands?"

"I don't remember them all, but you name it around here, and it's needed. Bad food. Some real medical attention. A chance for some recreation. Since then, by the way, the administration did build a tennis court, a volleyball court, and some horseshoe rings out in the yard. They bought some sports equipment too. The yard out there is called the "Sahara Desert." The place is dusty and full of rocks in the summer and muddy and full of rocks in the winter. There's nowhere to sit down and not enough room for more than a few guys to do anything. Everyone else just sits around."

The bell at the door rang, interrupting our conversation. Skeleton was shouting "Chow!" and everybody dropped their work and ran to the dirty-looking, cracked cement troughs at the far end of the shop. A tiny piece of soap was passed from hand to hand, and rags were used as towels. When the bell rang again, everyone made for the door. Big Shot opened it, and the men lined up in single file. The ancient factory whistle gave a short blast, and we started walking toward the main building. Lines of prisoners from other shops were converging on the mess hall, each row following a painted line on the cement walk or a line made of bricks set in the ground where there was no concrete. Nothing was heard but the shuffle of feet, for no one was allowed to speak. It was like the march of the dead. We descended a long stairway. Its two-inch pipe railing shone, polished three times a day by eight hundred men rubbing against it. The mess hall had closely lined concrete tables less than a foot wide, with small hinged drop seats. Musty-looking tin cups and spoons were set for ten men at each table. Our lines passed the kitchen crew, who were dressed in uniforms that probably had been white at one time, and soon eight hundred of us were jammed into the small hall.

The noon meal, called dinner, consisted almost entirely of inedible tasteless beans cooked with no fat or flavor. They were supplemented by a kind of flour pudding and a black brew called tea. Most men ate the bread with salt. That was the standard dinner, with potatoes or flat-tasting macaroni alternating as the main dish. Suppers were the same except for a watery soup; breakfast was flapjacks with sugar water four times a week and a glass of milk and bread the other three days. Sometimes we got coffee made of cereals. "Meat" was served twice a week in the form of meatballs that the men called "bread-burgers." For Sunday dinner we got a slice of pork shoulder so thin that it curled up like a piece of bacon when fried. The men lived mainly on bread and potatoes, for not even Blawnox could succeed in making these two staples totally inedible. When the last man entered, the doors to the mess hall were shut, and the guards stationed themselves around the walls. The only sounds were of spoons, metal plates, and cups, for talking was punished by a stretch in the hole. Conversation was limited to "Pass the salt."

It soon became routine. In the chow line I always walked between Nick and a young fellow from Erie, an ex-GI called "Cabbage Head." One hot day the fan was on the blink, and the men in the mess hall near me were sniffing and looking from side to side and under their seats. You couldn't look back—that was enough to get you sent to the hole. I stuck my head rather low and was about to ask Cabbage Head what smelled so bad when I noticed that all the men near me had started to snicker and laugh. It was plain that the joke was on us newcomers, but I couldn't figure out what it was.

Someone from the back bench said in a stage whisper, "It's Cabbage Head's feet." The laughing swelled till a guard known as "Hollywood" stepped over. Looking at me, he bellowed, "I seen you—you been talking and agitating ever since you came in. I been watching you. Step out here. And you too," he added, pointing at a black prisoner named Pete who sat behind me.

The place got very quiet as Pete and I were ordered against the tile wall. Pete started to say something, but Hollywood cut him off. "Don't you tell me anything! Ain't I got eyes to see? I don't need you telling me anything. You talked, and that's against the rules. Go up to the front office, and you too, Nelson."

We were soon in a small room with a half dozen guards, "on trial." Hollywood read the complaint, which consisted of three words: "These

guys talked." The head guard said, "OK—you both heard the charges.
What have you got to say for yourselves?"

Pete stepped forward and was ready to speak when one of the
guards told him to stand back from the desk and watch his manners
in front of the head guard. Flustered, he apologized, then told the
story of Cabbage Head's feet. Although I explained we had not been
talking, the guard said we had broken the rules. The sentence was
quickly delivered: no privileges for seven days.

After supper Pete and I were locked in our cells. Our doors
slammed shut at four-fifteen by the remote control lever while the
other prisoners were allowed in the yard for an hour. I looked at the
faded ivory paint on the rough concrete walls and the battleship gray
of the bars on the door. The cell was short and narrow, and there
wasn't much to look at. A twenty-five watt bulb screwed high in the
wall gave the only light. There was a wash bowl, toilet, and a straw
bed. I lay on the bed staring at the ceiling and thought about being
locked up here from four in the afternoon until six-thirty in the morning with no one to see and nothing to read for a week. There wasn't a
sound in the place. The silence was twice as oppressive for someone
like me, a newcomer, who wanted to ask questions.

I heard some footsteps and sat up to see who was passing by. As the
steps sounded on the concrete floor, which was laid on a steel frame
like a tightly stretched drumskin, I realized the man was one or two
flights below. In a few minutes, I heard them again, closer this time
but still below me. I figured he was bound to pass my cell, and soon
the footsteps were coming my way.

They came to an abrupt stop. It was a guard. "How you doing,
Steve?" He spoke in a rather pleasant voice, which surprised me, for
he was the first official there who seemed human. "I see they got you
in double-lock already. Didn't surprise me. Hollywood was laying for
you." Then he looked around and said, almost in a whisper, "And he
ain't the only one. But I guess you know that already." As he was
about to leave, he asked, "Was that you talking a while ago? You
know you can't talk to anyone while you're in the cell." He then
winked and walked away.

The hour was almost up, the yard period over. Several hundred
men were coming up the iron steps all at once. The prison seemed to
come alive as the sixty-five range doors opened for five seconds and
the men stepped in. But before long the place was quiet again. It was
five-fifteen, and there was not a thing to expect until six-thirty the
next morning. I wished I could sleep it away, but I knew I wouldn't be
that lucky.

Just to be doing something, I started to clean my cell. I washed down the walls, the floor, and small wash bowl. I wiped and dusted the bars. I washed my handkerchiefs, socks, and underwear. My thoughts kept turning to my friends outside. I made a mental roll call of many of them. They'd be on the job and thinking about me, I told myself.

It was late that night before I fell asleep. I first chewed over every little bit of knowledge I had gained during the few weeks I had been in the workhouse. From what I had seen, I sensed a certain friendliness toward me on the part of the inmates. One guard had even seemed less hostile than the others. I recognized that I must not give in, even though I couldn't come to any decision about just what that meant. Finally, I told myself that I would listen and learn and check things out first. Above all, I would not let myself be isolated from the other prisoners.

At six-fifteen the next morning, the lights went on, and the place came back to life. I was too fast with my washing and dressing and was ready and waiting for the doors to open. I noticed that the factory whistles along the Allegheny River blew at various intervals, echoing against the hills. Later I learned to tell time by the sounds of the different whistles, but the first few weeks it was all confusion.

Finally the doors opened, and I stepped out of the cell into the range with the other men. We walked toward the stairs that led to the mess hall in the basement and the breakfast of cold flapjacks and sugar water. Usually the men went straight to the shops as soon as they finished breakfast, but this morning no one moved out of the mess hall. I very carefully asked the fellow next to me why, but he only shrugged his shoulders. Another man muttered that it was due to fog. He was right. A fog had settled over the area, and the officials apparently didn't want to risk letting the men go through the yard. This precaution, I was told, hadn't been used in a long time. Why now? Someone said it was because of me. I could hardly believe that, but I began to wonder. Perhaps the administration wanted to turn the other men against me, for no one liked sitting in the mess hall all morning. We were kept in for three mornings in a row until the fog had lifted.

After a week without privileges, I was able to go out to the yard every day for about an hour. The yard hadn't a tree, flower, or blade of grass nor a bench, box or rock to sit on. If a man wanted to take the load off his feet, he had to use the dirt and gravel. Usually there was a ball game going, but this involved only a few of the eight hundred inmates. Only about a hundred men could participate in sports because there just weren't the facilities. There was no room for the others to do anything but mill around and talk.

For all that, the one hour in the fresh air was the best period of the day. Almost everyone looked forward to it eagerly and made preparations to get the most out of it. In the yard friends from other parts of the prison could be seen. Here men exchanged small articles, borrowed items, and relieved the isolation of being cooped in a cell. I was reminded of an old-time market place, where one could not only buy and sell but also pick up the day's news, as in Pakrac, the county seat back in the old country. At Blawnox the "news" was pretty specialized, so one soon found out where to get what. Sports had its enthusiasts, and those following it knew just where to get or pass on information. A large group of men would sit around and hash over the Pirate games daily, second-guessing managerial decisions. The ones interested in applying for parole had their center where a number of "jailhouse lawyers" loafed, prisoners who liked to talk about jazz had their spot, and so on.

But nearly every prisoner was interested in all the news about the "place" as the jail was called—what went on, which guards were quitting, who was in the hole, and why. These discussions went on day and night in undertones, and even the most timid prisoners expressed their sentiments.

As soon as I got to Blawnox, I found myself in the midst of these discussions. It seemed that all prisoners who had opinions saw to it that I soon learned them. In this way I quickly picked up the history of the place without making any special effort to search it out. In fact I had decided I was just going to listen and learn who was who before saying anything except to explain, when asked, why I was in jail and how I was framed. While I made no attempt to recruit anyone to my politics, I didn't hesitate to tell what they were and what they were not.

The administration kept a close eye on me and on the men who spoke to me in the yard. Some men started passing me notes instead of talking. One prisoner told me he had been called in and questioned about talking with me and told to keep his nose clean. I had expected this but was amazed that the prisoners were willing to tell me about the pressures the administration was applying. One inmate, who they tried to buy with the promise of three years' time off, came to me and told me he had agreed to work with them but begged me not to hold it against him and, above all, not to tell anyone else about it.

As it turned out, men took risks to associate with me and wouldn't give in to threats from the guards. It infuriated the administration but made me feel a lot more secure. I was stopped in line frequently and searched. Any piece of paper, even a newspaper or magazine, could serve as an excuse to throw a man in the hole. Even carrying an extra piece of clothing, such as some socks that one might want to wash in the shop, could lead to punishment.

There got to be a regular group of men who would come over and chat with me in the yard. Sometimes it was just to kill time, but sometimes I was privy to what was on their minds. I heard many of their beefs and quite a few secrets. Some of their proposals and plans were simply fantastic, especially those concerning escape. I was a good listener but for the most part deferred passing judgment on their plans. At first I asked them why they came to me. Some frankly expected me to be able to do something about the problems they hadn't been able to solve themselves. They had read in the newspapers about what a powerful threat the Party was, and they thought it might be able to do something about conditions in the workhouse. Others just shrugged and said that if I couldn't do anything, at least it was safe talking to me because it was so apparent that I was the pet hate of the administration.

The list of grievances was almost endless, and the question of what to do was raised in almost every conversation about them. I didn't want to act hastily, but I couldn't listen to these complaints forever, knowing how true they were, without considering some action to change things.

Various proposals were advanced. One idea that received a lot of support, but which I sharply opposed, was that of a prison riot. A great majority of the men held this idea, among them a number who seemed to be the natural leaders in the various shops and wings. They advanced this plan for a couple of reasons. First, other means had failed. The strike four months earlier for ten cents a day minimum pay had been broken, and the leaders stuck in solitary confinement for months. Second, there was a rash of prison riots throughout the country, and this news strongly influenced them. Those who pushed for a riot argued that it was impossible to strike inside a prison. I couldn't agree with them, but I was hard-pressed to suggest something that I thought would work.

A riot broke out in the state pen at Bellefonte, Pennsylvania, and there were rumblings at Western Penitentiary at Woods Run nearby. The air inside the workhouse was charged, and I felt that something might happen at any moment. Men were getting bolder about their complaints and openly griping about the food and medical care.

About this time I was temporarily transferred to the county jail because of the pending federal Smith Act trial with Dolsen, Albertson, Careathers, and Weissman. Andy Onda had been severed from our case because of his heart condition. The administration was happy to see me go. They issued a statement to the press saying they didn't want me at Blawnox because they didn't have the facilities to keep a "big criminal" like me. While they couldn't catch me doing anything "against the rules," they were sure I was "the cause of all the trouble." They wound up by saying that they had to get rid of me because the inmates didn't want me there. They also started circulating a petition among the prisoners demanding my transfer. It was signed by just five men out of eight hundred and hastily withdrawn.

There was a delay in starting the Smith Act trial, however, and I was returned to Blawnox. I found the administration there cracking down. Every complaint or even expression of mild dissatisfaction was punished with a "cure," usually three to nine days on bread and water in the hole or being put on the "shelf." The shelf was the milder form of punishment, since the inmates got their regular food. But still a man there was totally isolated, locked up twenty-four hours a day and not allowed mail, writing privileges, or visitors. While the time spent on the shelf was longer, sometimes from three to six months, the hole was more dreadful, as I was soon to find out.

One of the prisoners thrown in the hole was Nick. In fact, I heard about it before I was brought back to Blawnox because it was tied up directly with me. The day I left the workhouse for the federal trial, Nick had come over to my workplace in the furniture shop and asked me to buy him some chewing tobacco in the commissary. Because he was hard of hearing and was forbidden to use his hearing aid, you had to shout at him if he was to hear you. He was standing there talking to me when Big Shot came down off his platform and began walking toward us. I warned Nick that he was coming, and Nick walked over to the spittoon to get rid of a mouthful of tobacco. As he was turning, he saw that Big Shot was saying something to him. Cupping his hand over his ear, he stepped up to the guard and said, "Pardon me, were you saying something to me?"

"You know damn well I was talking to you!"

Nick looked surprised and stepped closer. He seemed calm, but I was sure he was mad. Big Shot demanded to know what he was talking to me about. Nick replied that he wanted some chewing tobacco.

"Don't tell me that," Big Shot said. "You got plenty of tobacco."

"All right, search my pockets and my cell. If you find any tobacco, I'll buy you a cigar as soon as I get some dough. OK?"

"You trying to be smart with me? You always talk to him."

By now Nick was red in the face and not about to grovel in front of the guard. Big Shot had stepped back, and I could hear him tell Nick to come down to the office. That meant the hole, for certain.

Everyone in the shop was watching Nick. He had said that if they tried to put him in the hole, it would take more than one guard to do it. Nick put his tools away while Big Shot stepped over to the telephone. I was afraid Nick was going to be beaten by the guards. I had tried to persuade him that he would gain nothing from a fight with them, but I couldn't convince him. He was going to use his fists to defend himself. I could see him getting set, shadow-boxing while he waited for the guards to appear. No one said anything to him, and he was silent himself.

Just as the clock struck the ten-minute morning smoke period, the General and two guards appeared. They went over to Big Shot and then over to Nick. I was resigned to what seemed to be shaping up as my first trip to the hole. Nick was taking up the fight for the right of an inmate to speak, and I had let the whole thing pass without saying a word. At this moment I wished I had spoken out, instead of merely standing there. Now I'd be going to the hole for nothing.

The General came over to me and gave me my chance. "You're the cause of this trouble, Nelson. If you don't stop making trouble you'll be going to the hole with him."

"What trouble did I cause?"

"You know what trouble. This whole place has been in an uproar since you came."

"Sir, all this man did was to ask me to get him a plug of tobacco, and now you're taking him to the hole." Having said that, I felt a little better.

Nick was told to go to the office. He asked if they would hear his story there, and they said yes. Believing them, Nick went without protest. Evidently he thought he would get the chance to talk his way out of it. He didn't. On the way to the hole, he put up a fight. It took five guards with blackjacks to subdue him, and they cut him up pretty badly in the process. He spent nine days there, without medical attention, stripped of his clothing and given only bread and water. His cuts healed slowly, but he came out of the hole with his pride intact. Every inmate in the place knew that it had taken five guards to put him away and that some of them had suffered bloody noses and black eyes.

I was not punished at the same time as Nick, as I was sent to the county jail, but I knew I would not get off. While I was in the county jail, I warned my friends that I would probably be placed in the hole when I was returned. In fact, I wasn't back at the workhouse more than an hour before I was called out of the furniture shop. I was brought to the head guard's office for my "trial" and then to the basement and the hole.

I followed Big Shot through an iron door into a large room, and the other guards followed me. We went across the room toward still another iron door, the gate to the hole. Big Shot's body nearly blocked the entrance as he stood fidgeting around with the brass key, which must have weighed a half pound. Finally the crude mechanism ground, and the door opened. Flicking the electric switch, he stepped into a long dreary room with blank wall on three sides and a line of fourteen cells on the fourth. From where I stood, I could see several naked men peering at me with sunken eyes from dirty unshaven faces. At first I felt like I was looking at skeletons in a wax museum. I didn't have much time to think about it, because Big Shot was ordering me to strip. I was then told to take a shirt and pair of pants from an old barrel containing what passed as clothes. They were terrible-smelling rags worn by the inmates in the hole and hardly ever washed. Grimy and hardened by sweat and dirt, they felt like weatherproofed canvas. The air in my cell, near the end of the row, was suffocating, and the cell was empty except for a seatless commode that was automatically flushed once every twenty-four hours. There was no stool, not even an iron bed. No water either.

The guards left, and the place became almost completely dark although it was only ten in the morning. I didn't put on the shirt and pants, for they were so crusted from human dirt that they stood up like frozen clothes on the line. My feet were especially uncomfortable. The unfinished concrete floor cut my soles so that they really hurt. The smell was awful. Gradually my eyes became accustomed to the bit of light that came from the small bulb at the other end of the corridor. While I couldn't see much, I doubted that I was missing anything as I had nothing to read or do or look at but the walls. Nevertheless I missed the light. I felt the walls with my hand. They were damp and grimy. I walked over to the door, held on to the bars, and stared into the empty darkness.

By my reckoning it should have been close to ten-thirty, the dinner hour in the mess hall above. That meant it was close to our bread and water "dinner" in the hole. I heard no movements of any kind to indicate food, but what noise could there possibly be in here? There wasn't a cup or spoon to make noise with. When several inmates began shrieking at each other, I figured this was the "predinner" noise of the hole.

As I strained my ears, I finally began to distinguish various sounds. At first all I could hear was a loud echo such as I had never heard before. It seemed as though each word was repeated three times. I realized this was because the hole was bare of anything that might have absorbed sound. An echo was something I had always associated with a canyon or a narrow and deep valley, only there it would have been thrilling and delightful. Here it was weird and depressing. On top of that, five or six men were all shouting at once. Maybe the confusion and unpleasantness were worse for me because of my separation from the others by six empty cells.

I heard a man calling my name but couldn't make out what he said. Others were trying to repeat it, but it was still unintelligible. I called out, "I can't understand you!" For a few moments there was silence, then one fellow started to say something, and soon the bedlam had resumed. As time went on my ears got used to the sounds, and I could make out some of what was being said. It was mostly insults.

"You're crazy as a bedbug."

"It's you that's crazy, you son of a bitch."

"Who's an s.o.b., you goddamn bastard? You should be in the loony bin down at Woodville."

"You say that again, and I'll knock your black head off when I get you in the yard."

"You and who else, you dumb hick, you moonshine-drinking hillbilly. If I get hold of you, I'll cut your goddamn throat from ear to ear."

The language was some of the foulest I had ever heard. The shouting got more violent, and I was relieved that people were locked up so that they wouldn't be at each other's throats. Nine days of this, I thought to myself! How to stop it? I felt sure that this environment had brought the men to the brink of madness, and I didn't want to go that route myself.

I tried to break into the shouting, but no one seemed to hear me. Suddenly a heavy tread was heard approaching the door. All speaking stopped. The key turned, and the lock ground. By the sound of the feet over the iron threshold and two iron steps down to the cellblock, you could figure how many men came in. It sounded like five or six. I craned my neck to steal a glance at the newcomers. Perhaps this was dinner time.

My head was pressed against the bars at the end of my cell, but I couldn't see a thing. I realized the men weren't bringing food because if they were, they'd be making noise. I must have missed mealtime in the hole by a few minutes. That was bad. I wouldn't be fed anything until four o'clock. The very thought of it made me ravenous.

Finally two men came into view, each naked and carrying an old army shirt and a pair of pants. They were put in cells eight and nine, partially closing the gap between me and the other inmates. For the moment I was too pleased at that to reflect on the fact that two more men were being subjected to the hole. Everything was pretty quiet while they were locked in. After the guards left, a man started singing. He was "the Shoemaker," the man in the first cell with the loud voice whose monologues usually brought on the first cries of "Shut up!" Somebody was yelling at him to pipe down, and he was yelling back that he wouldn't.

My head was pounding. I decided to sit this round out and wait until things calmed down. One of the new inmates had asked a question, but no one could understand him. Suddenly there was a snatch of silence. I broke it by saying, "Listen, fellows. What's the sense of us yelling at each other? We didn't put each other in this hole! Why should we take it out on ourselves? This only pleases the rats that put us here."

No one interrupted me. I was amazed that I was hearing things much more clearly. I went on, "If we talk one at a time, we'll be able to hear each other, but if we talk at once, we'll get on each other's nerves for no reason."

Someone down the line said, "That's right, buddy, but how in hell are you gonna shut this crazy nut up?"

I didn't understand him, but someone closer to my cell repeated it for me. The fellows in cells one and two, Shoemaker and Hillbilly, were calling each other names and hollering again, and it looked like my remarks were in vain. It lasted a good hour till they got tired and the screaming slackened.

During the lull someone said, "Hey, Steve, tell us about your outfit. We heard all kinds of stuff about you on the radio and in the papers. Tell us why you got that twenty-year trip."

"Okay, but later, not now. Let's get to know each other, and then we can discuss it. How about if we introduce ourselves first? A 'Who's Who' in the hole?"

That suggestion got a better response than I expected, and everybody but the occupants of cells one and two agreed. Shoemaker said, "I don't care to listen to anyone else's troubles. I got enough of my own, and it's nobody's business anyway."

"Okay, you don't have to, but for Christ's sake, pipe down so we can hear each other," another voice answered.

"Bullshit! All you want to do is talk all the time!"

"That's right," I cut in. "One or two of us can't talk all the time. Why don't we sing or tell jokes?"

Someone asked if anyone could sing, and eventually someone cautiously ventured that he could. It was, of all people, the Shoemaker.

"Well, let's hear you."

"Hell, he can't sing."

"I can too."

I was afraid things were sliding back downhill, so I coaxed him to sing. There was no response, so I shouted, "Hey, buddy, you in cell one, what's your name? Shoemaker?"

"No, damn it, that's not my name. It's Jamison. Just because I was put to work in the shoe shop, everyone calls me that. It's Jamison."

"Okay, Jamison," someone else said. "We might as well get our names straight. Let's call off the cells and hear who you are and why you're here."

So roll was called, and each inmate gave his name and explained why he was in the hole. In most cases the explanations took some time. As the roll call ended, Jamison began to sing. He chose the theme song of the workhouse band, "Oh, why don't you believe me?" It was the only song the band knew, and they played it for all occasions. But Jamison sang it well.

Someone else led off with a song everyone knew, and most of the fellows joined in. The singing went on for almost an hour, and while it often wasn't much, it was a lot more tolerable than the wild shouting and quarreling. During the lulls the conversation became more orderly. We devised a rotation system so that one man spoke at a time. Then we sang again. Jamison was soon accorded the respect of a celebrity as he had the best voice in the hole and knew an endless number of songs.

I was happy over the turn of events. But when was it going to be time for the bread and water? Would four o'clock ever arrive? It had to be close, and conversation soon turned to it. There were several false alarms, but finally the door opened and footsteps were heard on the iron steps. The lights went on, and talking ceased.

Later the guards came in to do their last chore of the day. A board was shoved into each cell, and an old blanket dropped in front of each door. I pulled mine in, folded it, and laid it on the board. The bottoms of my feet were very sore, and I sat down on the blanket in such a hurry that I nearly collapsed. The blanket stank of sweat, unwashed feet, and mildew from the old barrel in which it was kept. Now that I could stretch out on the board, I swept my hand along the floor fishing for crumbs of bread that I might have missed. I found something but wasn't sure what it was. I laid it on the crossbar where I would be able to see it when the guard put on the light to punch the clock at night.

Stripping off my shirt and pants, I rolled them into a pillow. Still I couldn't lie down to rest. I walked up and down on my board and blanket enjoying the softness on the bottoms of my soles. The perspiration rolled down like water after a shower. I had never before realized how objectionable one's own body odor could be. The place stank. I lay down again, but the thought of putting my face on that heap of vermin-infested rag made me recoil, and I sat upright. But I had no choice, and like everyone else, I lay on my back and soon fell asleep.

The other prisoners were talking as I woke up. I asked how long I had been asleep and was disappointed it hadn't been longer than an hour or so. A conversation was underway in which a black vet named "Sailor" was being asked about various things. Sailor had been a guard at the Nuremberg trials and was telling how he had escorted Hermann Goering to his cell during breaks in the proceedings. The Sailor was well-known at Blawnox because he was one of the men who had been singled out as a ringleader of the April strike. He had spent six week on the shelf and time in the hole because of it. Having been in the hole before, he was asked the questions. He knew the meaning of every sound and movement about us.

"That's the last count—now they're gonna flush the toilets," he said, and soon the toilets were flushed by remote control. The stench was awful.

Suddenly an inmate was yelling, "Holy smoke, my toilet is overflowing! Sailor, what can I do to stop it!"

"Not a thing, buddy. Just hold your nose and try to keep your clothes and blanket dry. You'll get moved to another cell when the guard comes down to punch the clock."

It was a hot stuffy night, and the smell from the overflowed toilet didn't help any. I rolled and tossed on my board and blanket bed. Every time my face touched the stinking blanket, I turned to lie on my back. The last time I woke up was when they handed me my three slices of bread and cup of water. Other prisoners were pushing out their boards and blankets. I pushed mine out and stepped onto the rough concrete floor.

Before the guards left, which wasn't more than a matter of minutes, I was through with my bread. The water tasted like the nasty tin cup from which I drank. I made sure I got it under the lower lip of my mouth.

"Let's have a quiz," I called out.

"Nah, I don't like them," a voice came back. "Too much like school."

Nobody else said anything, and feeling like a camp counselor, I said, "Well, we're going to do this one differently. We can make our own rules. We don't need to try to act smart. We don't have to try to stump each other, and besides, it'll help pass the time."

"Hey man," the Sailor spoke up. "Let's hear what it's like. What have you got to lose? You start it and we'll see."

"Nah, I'm not interested. You go ahead."

"Okay, Steve," the Sailor called. "Let's get it started. I want to win a DeSoto, and I'll tell 'em Groucho sent me!" He broke out laughing at his own joke.

"I don't get it. What's the joke?" another man asked. It was clear he had been inside the joint for years and had never heard the Groucho Marx show. One of the other guys filled him in and did a few of Groucho's routines. You would have had to have been there to appreciate it. Pretty soon the ball was back in my hands. I figured that the most common area of facts among the men would be some branch of sports. "Which one of you men knows the score on baseball, boxing, or some other sport?"

"I know boxing, baseball, and football," the Sailor said, and another man said he knew basketball pretty well.

"Okay, let's get the facts on heavyweight champs up to date."

We spent a good hour on heavyweights and then branched off into other sports. Almost every man had something to contribute. I asked what socialist had played shortstop for the Pittsburgh Pirates and stumped them. Someone guessed Honus Wagner, and when I said that was right there was general disbelief. I gave my one political rap of the day, and we were back to sports. We kept up the conversation, and when the guards came into the cellblock, the Sailor was asking where Johnson had fought Jess Willard.

The young guard went about his routine without paying any mind, but Sergeant Stazie, a small guard with gray hair, came over to see what the talking was about. He approached Sailor's cell to bawl him out, but Sailor took him by surprise.

"Hey Stazie, you know a lot about boxing. We can't agree on where Jess Willard and Johnson fought for the championship. The fellow down here says it was in Salt Lake City, and I say it was in Havana. What do you think?"

For the first time in the collective memory of the hole, Stazie spoke civilly to a prisoner. He thought about it a moment and said, "You're right, Sailor. Havana, Cuba."

Sailor came back with, "Hey, I told you guys Stazie would know. He used to be a boxer when he was young, right Stazie?" I could imagine Sailor laughing to himself as he soft-soaped the guard. He kept on firing questions at Stazie and marveling at his fund of knowledge.

When the guards left everyone broke out in a fit of hysterical laughing. It was as if a major victory had been won. We talked about who would bell the cat next time the guards came down to the hole and clinch our triumph. Most of all, it was a boost to our own self-respect.

In the next few days, we went from sports to literature and history. At the end of the fourth day, my attorneys came to visit me. They informed me that my trial for the federal Smith Act charges was about to start and that I would be transferred back to the county jail the next day. I hadn't exactly been looking forward to the trial, but since it would be getting me out of the hole, it took on a new light. When I told the other men in the hole about it, they thought it was a new trial. I had to explain that it wasn't a retrial but a whole new set of charges, this time under a federal law, the Smith Act. When I went into the differences between the state and federal sedition laws, a couple of the guys thought it was double jeopardy and that I shouldn't be tried twice for the same offense.

Before I left someone proposed that we should meet in the yard some day and organize an "alumni of the hole" society. They thought I would be good at getting that together. When I did leave later that day, I felt a twinge of sorrow at leaving these men, most of whom I knew only by name and voice, behind me.

I spent the next three months in the county jail in downtown Pittsburgh preparing for the Smith Act case. We had been able to get two sympathetic lawyers from out of town to work along with Schlesinger on these charges. The judge, however, got sick and later died, delaying proceedings. While in the county jail, I had been writing as many as seven or eight letters a day, some of them to people overseas, asking for support. In return I began to receive up to twenty letters a day, many pledging support and some sending money for legal defense or copies of protest letters written to the D.A. and governor. Friends from the Veterans of the Abraham Lincoln Brigade (VALB) and the Civil Rights Congress and certain nationality groups responded with a great deal of support.[1]

At this stage our fight was directed toward getting the governor and attorney general to grant bail. Judge Montgomery was in the midst of his campaign for the state supreme court, running on the slogan, "I sent Nelson to the workhouse for twenty years." Vice-President Nixon came to town on behalf of the Republican ticket and praised the local judges for their conduct in my case.

Montgomery was getting a lot of letters about the sentence. He stated he had "enough of them for Nelson to paper his cell" and that he was turning all of them over to the FBI. He lost the election, however, and soon had me transferred back to Blawnox till a new judge was appointed for the Smith Act case.

I was lined up on sick call in the county jail because of a nasty infection in my right ear when I heard a guard yell, "Nelson, to go." I knew immediately what that meant—back to the hole. I still had five days to put in there. I could just see myself in that dungeon with an infected ear and a cold. Fortunately, they picked a Wednesday to transfer me. That was the day Margaret came. I figured that when she came and didn't find me, she would know the score. She already knew I had been having ear trouble and was getting penicillin shots.

I was forced to leave the sick line before I got my shot, and I soon packed my stuff and sent back the books I borrowed from Carnegie Library. The deputies were in a hurry and drove fast. My ear was pumping and pained me a good deal. There were snow flurries blowing across the road as we drove through the Highland Park Zoo. I noticed the large open-mouthed whale in the Children's Zoo was boarded up for the winter. The cliffs on the far side of the river were bare but starkly beautiful. A few barges loaded with coal were floating down the Allegheny River.

But at Blawnox, nothing had changed. The large iron door opened, and I passed through. I was ushered into the large corridor that reminded me of the cattle run of a slaughterhouse. Soon I was back in the hole.

Big Shot himself had escorted me there. "Look," I told him, "I want you to tell the office that I'm sick. I've got an infected ear. I should see a doctor. And tell them I want my clothes and shoes. I can't lie on a cold concrete floor with an infection without clothes."

That was a bit much for him. "Listen here, smart guy, no one else has got his clothes and shoes here. This is the HOLE, mister, not a sanitarium. He wants his clothes! He wants his shoes! And a doctor, no less. . . . It's no wonder you're here, Nelson. But you'll get used to it, don't think no different." He turned the lights off and went out.

"They got you back, Nelson. How much time do you owe them?" someone asked.

"Five days," I replied, and that was the end of the conversation.

It was cold in the hole. I was lying on the damp floor, and the pain in my ear was severe. I didn't pay any attention to who came in and why. When guards brought the supper of bread, I was feverish and didn't feel like eating. I put the cup of water on the floor and the three slices of bread on top of it.

After the guards came in for the final count for the night, a fellow called down, "How's about joining us for a quiz, Nelson? Or are you too sick?"

"I'm afraid I am, but you fellows go ahead."

The others went on with the quiz, and I was amazed that the men now in the hole were still following the same idea we had developed months earlier. After the key question was decided upon, they elaborated on the subject for hours.

Later on the guards returned to give us our blankets and boards for the night. I was shivering and unable to bear the thought of spending a sleepless night with a cold and the pain in my ear. The ear was throbbing and discharging. There was nothing to wipe the discharge with, so I used my finger for wiping the pus and the palm of my hand to pump out my ear, as children do when they are swimming and diving. This relieved the pressure a bit.

When the guard came over, I asked for some aspirin and a roll of toilet paper to wipe the discharge with. I was surprised when he answered that he already had been told to give me two aspirins. He got me some toilet paper and before leaving dropped a second blanket in front of my cell.

I began to feel a good deal better but kept up my demands to see the chief before he went home. "I want him to know," I told the guard when he came in an hour later, "that he will be held responsible for whatever may happen to me. A lot of people know about this and they won't let anything happen without doing something."

"They're doing their damnedest to give us trouble now, but that ain't gonna help you any. You're only causing more trouble for yourself, that's all. You're not going to change this place—you ought to know that. But I'll tell him, as soon as I find him."

The effort to talk had knocked me out. I fixed my "bed" and hoped I would fall asleep. But the door soon opened, and the lights came back on. I turned onto my belly and propped my head on the palms of my hands. I could tell by the footsteps that there were several men. Soon the General was standing in front of my cell.

"Nelson, what's wrong with you? I mean, how'd you get all this fuss stirred up, people calling and sending wires like we were trying to kill you or something." Margaret must have really got things going.

"What do you call this, anyway?" I asked. "You knew I had a fever when I was brought in, but you stick me in here anyway."

"Well, you got a blanket and some aspirin, didn't you?"

"What good is that for an infection? Whatever happens, you'll be held responsible," I shouted.

"You'll never be satisfied. Other prisoners don't make all the complaints you do."

"Well, they ought to. Besides, I'm a political prisoner, and I know your guards have instructions to really give it to me."

"How did you come to that conclusion, Nelson?"

"Big Shot told me that I wouldn't last two years in this place—that I'd be hanging off the bars before then."

"Oh, is that what he told you? I'm surprised at that. Well, we can't get you a doctor tonight. You'll have to wait until morning. They'll take you over to the infirmary as soon as the doctor comes in."

He walked away saying to himself, "Why they sent this guy here is beyond me." A few minutes later he was back, and to my astonishment, he was holding my old shoes and socks. The guard behind him had my regular prison clothes. "Here's hoping you'll be satisfied now," he said.

"No, I'm not satisfied," I called after him. "And I won't be till I'm out of this place. And how about shoes and socks for the other men in here?"

Stalking back to my cell, he yelled, "No! Damn it! No!" Whirling, he walked away.

As the door closed behind him, a loud joyful pandemonium broke out. The discussion went on far into the night as to whether or not the others would get their clothes. Later on I found that people on the outside had been protesting my mistreatment. A constant barrage of phone calls and telegrams had forced the General to act.

At daybreak two guards came into the cellblock and told me to come with them. I put the old shirt and pants on top of my regular prison garb because I figured it was cold outside and the morgue, as the prison hospital was known, was some distance away. Then I wrapped the blanket around me. I was right about it being cold out. The wind had a sharp sting. The guard walking in front of me set a slow pace, his collar turned up and his hat pulled down over his ears. He seemed to be taking his good old time. As I kicked up against his heels, he looked back at me, but I couldn't convince him to pick up the pace.

When we entered the morgue, it was as deserted as a real morgue. I edged over to the radiator, but it was as cold as ice. Fortunately I didn't have to wait very long and was soon being examined by a strange man whom I assumed to be the doctor. He prescribed regular shots of penicillin and administered the first himself. Returning to the cell, I almost ran ahead of the guards to get out of the cold. I wasn't in more than a few minutes, however, when the guards returned. My lawyers were there to see me.

Upstairs in a conference room, I found them seated at a long oak table. They seemed worried when they saw me, and I suppose I looked a mess. I hadn't showered for several days, my ear was stuffed with gauze, and the whole side of my face was painted with merthiolate. My double set of prison clothes didn't improve my appearance. However, they saw no legal way to get me out of the hole. I listened to their report on preparations for the trial, and I sent a message through them to Margaret. When we saw the crew going by with the hot water and canned pea soup, the lawyers locked up their briefcases and said good-bye. I was feeling worn out from lack of sleep and hunger, and I couldn't wait till I was back in my cell so I could eat. I gulped down the bread and the strange soup concoction we were given with it that night and was soon asleep.

The next five days and five nights I spent in the hole were much the same. Each morning I was given a shot of penicillin, and the pain and infection subsided. I was participating in the quiz games again and carrying on discussions. Many of the latter developed on the subject of prisons. Everybody had an opinion on this subject and was willing to express it in the hole. Ironically, the hole was one of the few places you could talk without interference from a guard or fear of a stoolie.

Listening to the talk and asking questions, I learned a lot fast. I also had a lot to say, and for the first time in a long time, the chance to say it. I tested many of my ideas out on the other men and was forced to rethink several things. I found out too that some men were circulating a petition in the wings and shops that raised most of their demands and grievances. It was being signed with an "X," and only a few men had refused to sign it.

A new fellow was brought down on my last day. He was told to strip in the usual fashion, but after his clothes were searched, he was given them back and allowed to take them with him into the cell. That was new, and it became the topic of conversation. Later a crew of guards came in and took all the grimy clothes that were in the barrel and burned them in the yard ovens. They washed the floor in the corridor and spread carbolic acid in the corners just as we had in the Perpignan prison in France when we were caught trying to get into Spain. Some rags were brought in, and each man got one to use as a towel after a cold water wash-up following the morning meal.

While these changes were sensational, most of the men insisted that they were only temporary and made simply to appease me because I had a lot of friends on the outside. I pointed out that if we continued to fight, we could win even more improvements.

The time came for me to leave. Toward the end of my stay, we agreed that the day one was to leave the hole, he wouldn't eat his three slices of bread; he would leave them to be divided by the rest as an act of solidarity. My share was divided, but no one ate till I was through the door.

I was led to the shower room where the crew from the boiler room was washing up. A tall fellow with corn-yellow hair edged over to me and muttered, "She's ready to blow—any minute. You'll hear about it."

"What's going on?" I asked.

"You'll see—she's ready I'm telling you. All the guys have signed the petition, and we're gonna do something."

"What?"

"Saturday night we aren't eating the beans," he replied, and sidled away.

It was near supper time on a Monday when I came out of the hole. The menu hardly ever changed, so I knew what to expect—noodles topped by tomato juice thinned with water to make a "sauce." Even before I sat down, I was eating the bread, which I had grabbed off the tray as it went by. Hurriedly pouring salt over the noodles, I swallowed them almost without chewing and without thinking of the effect they might have on me later.

The fellows near me asked if I wanted any of theirs. I took some food from Nick and thanked the rest. Nick usually kept totally silent in the mess hall, but he did manage to ask in a whisper whether I knew about the plan not to eat the beans. I was a little worried about that leading to a riot. When I brought this up, my tablemates assured me that it was nothing like that. But everyone had agreed to refuse to eat the slop.

Good news traveled swiftly at Blawnox, and people were full of questions about the changes in the hole. Afterward it was back to the cells. I tried to walk fast to get there before the doors closed. You almost had to run to make it, but I couldn't as my leg still bothered me. Just as I reached the cell next to mine, the doors slammed shut. Two other inmates and I got locked out. I swore at the guard who had thrown the switch and sat down in front of my cell. You weren't permitted to go anywhere and simply had to wait for a guard to come by and let you in. Eventually I was inside, and I marveled at how I was able to welcome that cell as home. It had only a box of letters and some legal documents for the trial, but somehow that made the place a little more bearable. Especially the letters.

There was one from Margaret that must have come just that day.

Dearest Steve,

This is a letter from the three of us to you. This morning Bobby saw me writing and thought it was for you, and said, "Mommy put something in for me." Josie came along afterward and said to say something for her, too. So this is a three-in-one combination.

First, the kids are all right. Bobby has got himself a thirty-five-cent pop-pop boat which he runs all day by a candle which makes steam and makes the boat run around in the bathtub going put-put. He finds that very exciting. Of course, he could set the house on fire with the matches he has to use lighting the candle to supply the power. Josie brought a lamp home from school that she made. It is partly woven and pretty nice, made out of a couple of boards, and I would say it is quite an accomplishment. Maybe we can open up a lamp shop and sell Josie's originals. With the furniture we should be able to pick up from you and Josie's handiwork, we'll have a substantial operation. I am sure some of the aspiring politicians around here wouldn't mind having your handiwork around.

The day is one of those in which the air is polluted. I noticed it when I got up and have felt it all day. The air is very bad, and we need a change, either colder weather or a good rain. All the smells and poisons from the mills are hanging in the air today.

I have taken it upon myself to write some friends on the West Coast about your fiftieth birthday, with the idea of getting some messages to you and a little action stirred up, also maybe some money for the defense. If you have any suggestions on this, I will try to follow through on them. I have a selfish motive. I would like you to get a bunch of mail, and I would like to remind people that you are still in jail, and there is no bail.

Well, now that you are back at Blawnox, I suppose you will miss the basket of food I used to bring to the county jail. There was something about bringing that basket in that always made me feel that it was just another way of making me feel degraded. At best I never looked forward to it; I guess I still remember the days of women taking lunch pails to the mills at noon for their men working there.

Last night the kids made a ghost house and made me go through it. They hung strings all over the room and tried to scare me. They had a good laugh and said I hollered too much, and they had to push me around. They made me bump my leg, but I enjoyed it as much as they did.

I sent you a small chess set, but I suppose you never got it. The kids wanted you to have it. I don't suppose you can do much with it, but they want you to have something and thought this would at least make you laugh. They constantly ask for you. They are going to get some color pictures to send to you.

Love and kisses from the three of us.

Margaret

Without Margaret and the efforts of scores of people, many of whom were only names to me, I doubt if I could have endured those months in prison. Not only did the letters and messages of support keep my spirits up; they also deterred further punishment by the prison and the courts. They came from all over the world. Some were from internationally known Communist leaders like Harry Pollitt and Luigi Longo, while others were signed simply "an anthracite miner" or with a first name only. Bob Minor was one of those who wrote to me regularly. His radical roots went back even before the 1920s, and he had been associated with the anarchist movement before joining the Party. First a brilliant cartoonist for the *St. Louis Post-Dispatch* and later for the *New York Evening World,* he eventually became a full-time Party worker. We got to know each other when he was in Spain as a *Daily Worker* correspondent. He kept urging me to have confidence in American democracy despite its then nightmarish appearance. He wrote me more than once that if "those bastards" carried their dirty pitcher to the well often enough, it would crack as sure as night follows day.

In the chair shop things looked about the same as they had three months ago. Even the men were the same, except for two new ones. One of these occupied my old work space. The runner gave the guard a slip of paper with my name and number on it. Big Shot looked at me and then pointed to a spot a few feet away. The spot he indicated was wet from a leak in the old concrete roof, and the seepage formed a pool of water. I objected that it was wet there, but he yelled back that that was where he wanted me.

I didn't know what to do. My ear wasn't well yet, and I had eaten little since coming out of the hole. Yet if I refused to work there, he'd put me back in the hole. I walked about the place pretending to gather my tools and materials to give myself a chance to think. If I took this from him, it was going to be bad. If I went to the hole, it would be worse. I decided if I had to go back, it ought to be for a better reason than this. Getting some sawdust, I threw it in the puddle of water, swept it up, and then threw some more down.

I could sense Big Shot staring at me, but I didn't look back at him.

Just at this moment, the General happened to come in with a few men I thought were probably state prison inspectors. I walked over to him and said, "Look where he put me to work. I demand that I be treated no worse than the other prisoners." The General seemed surprised and replied that there were other spots where I could work. When I responded that Big Shot had put me there over my protest, he sighed and went to the guard to talk it over. When he returned he moved me to a drier spot.

The following days were tense. Men were being searched at every turn, and several were thrown into the hole. One young black prisoner who was due to leave on parole was put in the hole on the charge of being "Nelson's stooge." I guess they hoped he would blame it on me. The administration had accused me of "using" black prisoners just to cause them trouble.

Several men from other shops were framed the same way. They were accused of circulating "Nelson's petition." It looked as if I would join them shortly. My cell was searched daily, and I was often skin-searched on my way to and from the shop or mess hall. I worked on my chairs absent-mindedly, almost forgetting where I was. But I didn't walk away from my spot, and I was careful about what I said.

The only break in the tension came when Margaret was allowed to visit me and bring the children. I had last seen Bobby and Josie during a day in federal court for the Smith Act case months ago. Bobby had run toward me as I stepped out of the courthouse elevator, but I couldn't pick him up or hug him because my hands were cuffed to the iron and leather belt I wore.

At the workhouse prisoners and visitors were separated by a thick screen. Bobby had brought some gourds that grew in the yard that summer, and Josie was trying to show me some Indian corn that we had planted in the spring, but it was impossible to see anything. The General himself stood in the cage watching us. I said to him, "Look at the way men have to see their families—through this," and pointed to the screen, two layers of mesh four feet apart.

The General answered, "It's always been this way, and it's always going to be this way."

I calmed down and enjoyed the visit, but the thirty minutes were quickly up. We said good bye, and they walked out, Josie holding herself together but Bobby and Margaret with tears in their eyes. I had trouble keeping from crying.

By Friday evening the uneasiness had reached its height. News of riots at Bellefonte and Woods Run made the men get more edgy, and there was talk of a riot at Blawnox. As I was going to supper that night, the General had me step out of the chow line. "Hey, Nelson, I just want you to know that we're having beans for supper tomorrow night." Men were passing the spot where I stood and looking at us with some surprise.

"What? You say we're having beans for supper Saturday? That's nothing new. It would be news if we had something edible for a change."

A few chuckles could be heard down the line, and the General reddened and repeated, "We're going to have beans for supper tomorrow night."

The whole prison heard about the exchange, and it seemed to harden the men's resolve. Word went around that no one was going to eat the beans, and that "plates would fly through the skylight."

As we went to breakfast the next day, the General pulled me out of line again and asked me if I knew anything about flying plates. I had been thinking of passing up the meal but realized I would lose a lot of respect if I did. When the lines formed for supper, I was where I always was.

But as I passed the crew dishing out the beans, it was obvious they knew something I didn't. The fellow who handed me my plate scooped around the bottom of the vat and came up with some solid objects in the beans—meat. I brought the plate up close to my eyes and looked again. For the first time, there was actually meat in the beans.

I sat down at the mess table and wondered what would happen. What would the men do? What should I do? That came first. I reached for the bread and then daintily picked out a piece of meat about a half-inch square with my fingers, shook off the beans, and put it in my mouth. I sat back and drank some of the dark brew they called "bug juice." I then proceeded to pick out the other slivers of meat. Shoving the plate to the side, I ate some bread and drank some more juice. I looked around and saw most of the men were doing the same. Some ate a little of the beans, but from the looks of their plates, most of the men left them untouched.

The garbage detail came in with its barrels and hauled out the beans minus the sixty or so pounds of pork thrown into the pots that day. The men had managed to eat the bait without falling into the trap. Best of all, everyone stayed cool, and no disturbances broke out.

The guards were furious, and two days later I was thrown into the hole again. This time it was full to the brim. After five days six of us were moved to the shelf and were charged with being responsible for the trouble. We were locked in individual cells twenty-four hours a day. The day we landed on the shelf there was a strange demonstration whose meaning I at first could not understand. Just as the men were locked in for the night, every cell door in the place began to rattle. The noise was terrific. Soon someone yelled from below, and I understood. "How is that, boys? You guys on the shelf, we haven't forgotten you." We could hear guards threatening to turn the fire hoses on the men, but it did little to quiet them down.

The next day fire bells were heard, and the fire whistle blew in the yard. As I strained to hear what the noise was about, an inmate several floors below yelled that the broom shop was on fire. That was met with shouts of approval, but I didn't like it. I figured it would only lead to more reprisals. Later someone called from below, "Hey, Nelson! The evening paper has a story that the warden said you started the fire." The other guys on the shelf laughed.

That night we were fed later than usual. The man who brought the food up to the shelf had a newspaper clipping sandwiched between my slices of bread. While handing me the plate, he winked at me. The clipping was a story that I was behind all the trouble at the workhouse and that today's fire would likely be connected with me.

When night came the inmates shook the bars again and again. Guards were patrolling the tiers, taking men out of their cells at random and sticking them in the hole. It went on like this for days. Some men began cooperating, but most kept up at least a passive defiance of the administration. In the midst of this, however, I was again transferred to the county jail.

Although I didn't know it at the time, that was the last I was to see of the workhouse. I was soon released on bail and able to return home to await the start of the federal trial for violation of the Smith Act. I was happy to leave most of the preparation to our lawyers. Besides, I had a little detective work I wanted to do.

It had begun before I left the workhouse. I was in the barber shop one day, mainly to kill time. A line of men awaited their turn in one of the four chairs. One barber seemed to be fooling around with his work, making it take a little longer, so I would wind up in his chair. It wasn't very overt, but you become sensitized to that sort of thing in prison. Eventually I wound up in his chair, an awkward contraption raised well off the ground on two by fours. As he snipped away, the barber (also a prisoner) whispered to me, "I know one of the jurors who was on your case."

"Who's that?"

"I can't tell you now. I'll tell you in the yard." That was reasonable enough as there were guards in the barber shop. We agreed to play chess during the exercise period.

I was impatient to find out what this guy had to say, although it wasn't clear to me that it was going to mean anything. We met in the yard and found a relatively isolated spot and sat down to play. Once again he opened with, "I know one of the jurors." After a pause he added, "He was on your side."

I couldn't imagine who that could have been and asked who it was.

"South—he's my neighbor in Millvale.[2] He drinks at the Eagles' bar there, and he let on he didn't think there was much of a case against you. The night before it went to the jury, a couple of guys beat him up on his way home because he wasn't going to vote against you."

I pumped him for any extra tidbits, but he had told me everything he knew. I asked Hy Schlesinger to come and see me, but when he came I couldn't tell him anything because there were guards in the conference room with us. I wasn't sure what to do, but then I was transferred to the county jail and granted bail pending appeal. I was back on the streets.

I contacted an investigative reporter I knew in New York City, and he came to Pittsburgh. He brought me a tiny Swiss tape recorder and showed me how to set it up inside a briefcase. A few days later I knocked on the door of Frank South's house on Maryland Avenue in Millvale, a small industrial town across the Allegheny River from the Lawrenceville section of Pittsburgh.

South wasn't home, so I introduced myself to his wife. She said he'd be back in fifteen minutes and asked me to come on in. "This is it!" I told myself. "She's welcoming me into her home." She ushered me into her living room where the TV set was blaring away to three kids. I didn't think the tape recorder would pick up anything as long as the set was on, so I asked the kids if they liked ice cream. I gave them half a buck and they ran down to Yetter's to buy some homemade ice cream, leaving us in peace. Pretty soon South came in and while surprised, he didn't seem put off that I was there.

I said, "I understand that you had some difficulty at the time when you were serving on the jury. I understand that some men attacked you—and I wondered if you'd be willing to make an affidavit to that effect for me."

"Well, Steve, I don't know. I don't want to get myself in any difficulties of any kind—you know what I mean. You got to understand my point of view too—although I wish you all the luck in the world with your appeal and all."

South was willing to tell me what he remembered about being beaten up and why he was late in getting to court that day. He also told me that during the deliberations he had gotten sick and that a doctor was brought in to give him a shot of something. After that he remembered very little.

From what I pieced together from other sources, there had been four jurors for "not guilty" on the first ballot. Gradually they had been worn down by the other jurors. I couldn't help but think that South, who was obviously one of the holdouts, had been given some sort of sedative and had caved in under its effect. I had my hunches about who the other sympathetic jurors were but was unable to confirm them.

I thought about calling a press conference at which I could present the evidence about South's beating. I figured it would get me a new trial. I was thinking about inviting some people with a national reputation, like Ernest Hemingway and Herbert Matthews, both of whom I knew from Spain, and seeing what sort of coverage I could get. But I didn't want to get South in trouble, and so I hesitated. As I was trying to decide what to do we got our first major break—the Pennsylvania Supreme Court threw out the state sedition convictions.

Victor Rabinowitz made the argument to the state supreme court, and in all those months of sitting in courtrooms, rarely had I been more impressed. He attacked the sedition laws on a number of points, and for once I could sense the judges were listening. Essentially, the court ruled that the federal Smith Act superseded the state sedition act. Because we were being tried under both of them, they held it to be double jeopardy and threw out the state convictions. Years later Bobby moved to Pittsburgh to begin graduate work at Pitt. He moved into an apartment on the North Side and was chatting one day with the young woman who lived upstairs from him. It was Victor's daughter Joni, whom he had never met during the trials. They became close friends and worked together for years in the democratic-socialist New American Movement (NAM).

When the sedition convictions were overturned, the state quickly appealed to the U.S. Supreme Court. Pennsylvania was joined by the Justice Department and thirty other states that feared the ruling would nullify all state sedition laws. With these matters on appeal, and with the twenty-year sentence at least temporarily reversed, we began the Smith Act trial.

Andy Onda had been severed from the case due to a heart condition, but Jim Dolsen was once again my co-defendant. The third defendant, Bill Albertson, was a native Pittsburgher who had been expelled from Pitt in the twenties for student radicalism during the administration of Chancellor Bowman.[3] About seven or eight years younger than I, he was organizational secretary for the Pittsburgh district. He had been active in the trade union movement in New York City before returning home. About the same age as Albertson was Irv Weissman, Party organizer for West Virginia. Both he and Bill were married with two children. Irv had been to City College in New York and had fought in Spain. Both he and Bill got socked with sixty-day contempt citations during the trial. Our last co-defendant was Ben Careathers, who had testified for me in my sedition trial.

The trial took place during the spring and summer of 1953. As in the sedition trials and the other Smith Act trials taking place elsewhere in the United States, it was our ideas and politics that were at issue. We were accused of "conspiring to teach and advocate the duty or necessity" of the overthrow of the government by violent means. The government paraded the usual number of informants to the witness stand, including Cvetic and Joseph Mazzei, the manager of the Art Cinema Theater, where innumerable meetings had been held and, unknown to us, tape recorded. The government made a mistake in using Mazzei, for his perjured testimony was of use during our appeals. While there was a degree of civility to these federal proceedings that distinguished them from the circuslike atmosphere of the state sedition trials, it didn't affect the verdict. We were all found guilty in mid-August 1953 and soon sentenced to the maximum five years and $10,000 fine. I was playing chess with Irv Weissman in the corridor while awaiting the verdict and recall the caption to a picture of the game in the next day's paper. It said, "Red Leader Checkmated." I'll have you know I was ahead by a knight at that point in the game.

It was back to jail, but only for a few weeks. We were granted bail pending appeals and entered a sustained period of legal limbo as the higher courts took up both the sedition and Smith Act cases. Frankly, we didn't know what to expect. At first I thought we didn't have a chance, but since the Pennsylvania Supreme Court had ruled in our favor, and because we were granted bail, I began to feel that things were changing and that there were some grounds for hope.

It was now fall of 1953, over three years since the arrests. It was to be another three years before most of the legal problems were resolved. During those years I wondered a great deal if I would spend the next twenty years in prison. I had spent over a year of the last three behind bars and almost another in court, and I had no desire to see either place again. But at times I felt that the waiting was just as bad as imprisonment. These were not the best of years.

I began to realize just what it took to stand up to it. I saw courage in others and learned from them. Most of all, I learned from Margaret, Josie, and Bobby. As pressures intensified during the early fifties, however, and more and more people were exposed to trouble on one

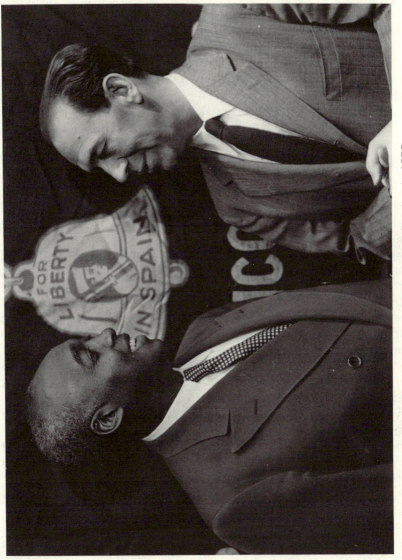

Ben Careathers and Steve Nelson during the Smith Act trial in Pittsburgh, 1953.

level or another, our base of support gradually shrunk. For me and the others on trial, this was keenly felt. We saw our defense as something that could not be confined to the courtroom if we were to remain free. We needed a public, visible defense as well. Margaret did much of that for me. She worked with Alex Steinberg and Miriam Schultz from the local Civil Rights Congress along with Alex and Anabelle Staber, Teresa Onda, Bess Steinberg, Jack Sartiskey, Evelyn Abelson, and Ted and Eileen Rolland.

Margaret organized much of the protest activity that took place on my behalf, speaking at meetings and writing letters at a nonstop pace. When I was in a particularly vulnerable position in jail, as in Philadelphia after the Smith Act arrest and in the hole at Blawnox when I was sick, somehow she found out and was able to get me out of the jam by applying enough pressure on prison officials. During my second sedition trial, she was in effect my co-counsel. Sitting at the defense table with me day after day, she was a constant source of advice. I still can't find words to express the emotional support she provided me throughout the years.

Perhaps her toughest job was helping Bobby and Josie understand what was happening. Bobby was seven and Josie eleven when I was arrested. We had never attempted to keep things hidden from them. On the contrary, we tried to explain things whenever they came up. Even when they were small, they knew that there were those who worked for a living and those who didn't. They learned about discrimination early on and grew up with black and foreign-born friends. When, for instance, some sort of racist remark was made on TV or the radio, Margaret was very conscious of the need to explain it to them and to do it with sensitivity.

A few adults in the community tried to help Margaret out, but it was difficult because the house was under almost constant FBI surveillance. Becky Horwitz frequently came by with soup or a cake, and Nina Stamler, who later married Ben Davis, came from New York to live with us during the Smith Act trial and to work on the defense committee. She gave the family a lot of personal support and was especially helpful with Josie, who found Nina someone she could talk things over with. Sometimes gifts arrived around the children's birthdays or at Christmas from friends out of town. Spanish Civil War vets frequently came to the trial, and they once brought a bike for Bobby.

One Saturday when I was out on bail, Josie asked me to drive her and a girl from the neighborhood to the movies. We went over to her friend's house, and Josie went up to the door. She came back alone with tears streaming down her cheeks. When I finally got it out of her, it turned out that the girl's parents didn't want her associating with Josie because of me. On another occasion Josie planned a cookout in the backyard for some friends of hers from school. The four or five girls she invited all said they would come, and Josie went merrily ahead with preparations. The night of the barbecue, not one of them came. Their parents had stopped them.

Because we lived in a black community and they went to a virtually all-black school, most of the children's friends were black. I think in some ways that helped because the anti-Communist hysteria was simply less intense in the black community. But it was felt there too from time to time. Once Bobby came home from school looking pretty miserable. Margaret talked with him, and it turned out that the kids at school were saying that the Reds were going to poison the water in the reservoir. Margaret told Bobby to tell them that we drank that water, too, and to ask them if they thought we would poison ourselves. That made a lot of sense to him, and he cheered up. He often got in fights, but that seemed to bother him less than occasional tauntings. As far as shooting marbles at recess or playing ball down the block, he had no more problems than the next boy.

When he was eleven, we asked Mr. Hoowe, the mailman who lived across the street, if Bobby could join the scout troop he led. The troop met at the church at the end of the block, and at the meeting of adults to consider his application, it was rejected. But someone (Mr. Hoowe, I suspect) took the matter up with the black city councilman from the fifth ward, who intervened. He argued that it was as senseless to oppress a kid because of his parents' politics as it was because of race, and he convinced the committee to reconsider. Bobby became the only white boy in the troop. Because I had a car I often drove a carload of boys to their outings and hung around to get to know the other fathers.

If there was anybody that Bobby did have a problem with it was the FBI agent who periodically tailed him. This agent started calling him by the name of Butch. "Hi, Butch, how ya doing this morning?" That was the one thing that would make Bobby speak to him. "Listen, mister, my name's not Butch."

The summer camps helped a lot because Bobby and Josie met other kids who were faced with similar problems. Camp helped overcome their isolation and their fear that they were different from everybody else. Bobby was a buddy of Frankie Grayson at summer camp. Frankie's father was one of the Martinsville Seven, black men falsely convicted of rape and electrocuted in 1951. The people running the camp were progressives who put on little skits about some of the trials. One of them came up to Bobby and Frankie and told them that

I would be all right. After the man left, Frankie looked at Bobby and said, "Don't believe him. They're not going to save him. They killed my dad, and I'm sad to say they'll kill yours too." Of all the dangers Margaret and I faced in the fifties, losing touch with our children was one of the greatest. While things were often difficult, we somehow managed to survive with our relations intact.

After the federal trial, the political climate gradually began to change. In April 1954 Senator McCarthy was publicly shamed by Edward R. Murrow, and much of the wind seemed to be taken out of the cold warriors' sails. By that time the whole business of political trials was beginning to wear. It was fairly obvious that the trials had brought no criminal acts out into the open. There was no proof that the Communist Party was doing anything to prepare and organize for the violent overthrow of the government. Also, more people and more organizations like the Quakers and the Women's International League for Peace and Freedom were taking a public stand. In this context the courts started ruling in our favor.

In November 1955 arguments were heard before the U.S. Supreme Court on the Pennsylvania Supreme Court's decision to throw out the sedition convictions. In April 1956 the U.S. Supreme Court handed down its ruling. By a six-to-three majority the justices decreed that the states had no power to try individuals for sedition. Led by Chief Justice Earl Warren, the Court nullified the Pennsylvania Sedition Act and indirectly those of thirty other states. They held the federal Smith Act to take precedence. We were off that hook for once and for all. That left us only with the five-year sentences for the Smith Act convictions.

These went to the Supreme Court in the fall of 1956. In October the convictions were wiped away by another six-to-three ruling. The court declined to rule on the constitutionality of the Smith Act but was willing to throw out the verdict because the government was forced to admit that one of its key witnesses in the trial, Joseph Mazzei, was a perjurer with a record of adultery and bastardy. This decision came at a time when a number of professional informants were being exposed as petty criminals and liars. Mazzei had given contradictory testimony at different trials. The court, probably wishing to avoid a general ruling on the Smith Act, took this out to overturn the convictions.

But we weren't out of the woods yet—the government could still retry the case, and we were once again having trouble finding lawyers. We got a real break, however, when we managed to convince an extremely prominent local attorney to intercede with the Bar Association to provide us with legal assistance. I think that's a pretty good indication of how much things had changed. When this happened the government apparently thought it had better let matters die, and it was decided not to put us back on trial. After six years the prosecution was just about over. I had a few more hassles with the Immigration Department over denaturalization proceedings and with the Subversive Activities Control Board during their continuing witch-hunts, but these didn't amount to much.[4] What mattered was that we weren't going back to prison.

With our troubles at last winding down, I, along with many others, felt a need to understand just what had been happening in the country and why the Party had been so vulnerable. During the attacks the tendency was to pull in and get our mitts up so we didn't get knocked out. I figured that we were under attack because we opposed the Korean War and because we were for real trade unions and real social change. It wasn't hard to see why the government and corporate elites would join in such an attack. It was harder, though, to understand why we were so isolated. I do believe that the attacks were largely orchestrated from the top down: that certain politicians, labor leaders, and businessmen were able to use the press, television, and the radio to create and foster an atmosphere of hysteria. What we now refer to as the "mass media" were catching on big in the early fifties, and I think their influence was staggering. I don't believe the common people turned against the Communists as much as other people seem to think. I do believe that a climate of fear was built in which most working people suspected radical political activity, but there was no mass movement of working people vs. radicalism per se.

On the other hand, we were never really able to come to grips with the issues that were separating us from the average American worker. Some of us were increasingly aware of how our stand on international issues was hurting us, but we were still unable to express these feelings within the Party. And for the most part, we rationalized our lack of support as due to fear or cowardice. Later on I began to put things together, and I realized that much of what we stood for just didn't go down well with many Americans. That forced me to search a little harder for answers to questions such as, why, after having fought so hard for all these years, we had so little support, and how could we recoup? There had to be something more than trying the same old things the same way as before.

I was in the middle of my fifties. I had begun to wear glasses and felt the beginnings of an ulcer. I was far from a physical breakdown or personal crisis, but I was troubled.

TWELVE

The Crisis: 1956—1957

It's difficult to recapture the greatest crisis of your life at a distance of more than twenty years. After almost a decade of vicious government attacks throughout the late forties and early fifties, factors inherent to the movement itself forced me to recognize that the organization to which I'd dedicated my life was no longer a viable means to achieve the kind of social change I envisioned. The depth of this tragedy, which I shared with many other American Communists, must be understood, for it might hold lessons for future generations of radicals. For this reason the story of what happened to American communism in 1956 and 1957 is not wholly negative. Out of this crisis and the ideas which it spawned, I hope that a more effective and democratic socialist movement will grow.

Some accounts of this crisis give the impression that it was somehow produced by specific events in 1956, namely Khrushchev's disclosure of Stalin's crimes and the Soviet intervention in Hungary in the fall of that year. These were certainly turning points in the life of the Party, but for me and many of the people I knew, the crisis of confidence and the conviction that a complete reassessment of the Party's policies and theory was essential had been growing for some time before this. Ironically, many of those most active in the movement to reform the Party, as well as those most opposed to it, had spent some part of the early fifties in prison.

In my own case, the trials were a tremendous personal strain, but they also caused me to reevaluate and even to question what we were doing and why. At the same moment that I was defending Marxist theory in the courtroom, I had to question our methods of applying it. The utter isolation in which I saw myself and other comrades forced me in this direction. My orientation to the Party had always stressed mass work, and until the late forties I could feel that we were moving in this direction. By the end of World War II and for some years after, the Party had a fairly strong public image and considerable influence in some of the most important mass organizations in the country— several CIO unions and various fraternal, ethnic, and black groups. Not only was the Party itself vital and growing, but it was an important part of a broad, progressive, working-class movement. By the time I went on trial, this position had almost completely eroded. The Party had lost or was in the process of losing its most important bases of support in mass organizations, and its own memberhip had fallen dramatically. Why had this happened?

The attack by the government and the various right-wing organizations provided part of the explanation. I was in a particularly good position to see the destructive effects on a local Party organization, and I personally experienced the full range of pressures brought to bear on individual Communists. This tide of reaction certainly helps to explain the Party's decline, as I have tried to show. But it was not the whole story. Those who sought to destroy the Party did so by isolating it from the broader labor movement and the American people in general. The fact that they were successful, that the Party was not able to withstand the attack, seemed to call for a fuller explanation than Foster's argument that our decline was due solely to the government and right-wing offensives.

As I thought the problem over, I began to realize that in some cases we had isolated ourselves, or at least made the reactionaries' job easier by following policies that didn't fit American realities. Notable failures loomed in the recent past. One obvious example was our rigid stand in the CIO Council against the Marshall Plan. Our opposition split the Center-Left coalition and opened the way for a purge of the left-wing unions. Another was our hasty commitment to the Wallace presidential campaign. We simply overestimated its appeal. The more distant past provided other examples: the Nazi-Soviet Pact, our early World War II slogan, 'The Yanks are not coming," and then blind support for the no-strike agreement during the war. It seemed that these were more than tactical errors; they were direct results of our mechanical application of Comintern policies to American problems. Our enemies had always tried to smear the Party as a foreign conspiracy that was more concerned with the needs of the Soviet Union than with those of American workers. Such policies lent credence to these charges, especially during the hysteria of the early fifties.

The fact that those in prison were separated from the daily Party routine also encouraged this sort of reflection. For most of us the time in prison stood in stark contrast to our normal lives; we could sit back and consider what was happening. Those on the outside had less time for such introspection.

Because of the attacks and an understandable preoccupation with defending ourselves, there was little formal discussion before 1956 of the questions that were troubling many of us. In fact, the National Committee never met between 1951 and 1956. During those years most of the national leadership and a good number of the district level leaders were in prison, on trial, or in hiding. Local organizations were swamped with the daily work of trying to stay alive, and a cumbersome underground apparatus made contact between the National Office and the districts difficult. This was another mistake. At the critical period in the Party's history, some of its most capable leaders were put out of commission, and leadership was handed over to less experienced people. The worst part was that all of this was based on the false premise that fascism was on the way. Ironically, the government's campaign may have forestalled the Party's crisis by forcing everyone to close ranks for mutual defense. Unfortunately, it also put off an overdue reexamination of our policies.

This situation meant that the Party was not able to confront developments in the international situation that were beginning to raise doubts in many minds. In 1948, when Tito was branded a renegade for his attempt to remain autonomous from Soviet control, I carried the word to Yugoslav comrades in our Party. Accepting the Soviet interpretation, I argued that Tito was placing himself outside of the socialist camp and siding with the reactionaries. It must have been a difficult thing for some of these immigrant workers to accept. The Yugoslavia they remembered was a bitterly poor, semifeudal collection of hostile ethnic groups. Tito had not only fought valiantly against the Nazis and the native fascists, but he now seemed to be successfully building a modern socialist nation. They were proud of the achievement. But they were Communists before they were Yugoslavs. They respected me, and most of them accepted Stalin's analysis as interpreted by the Party. Now Khrushchev admitted that this too had all been a mistake. He took the initiative in reconciling the two countries by traveling to Yugoslavia, all but explicitly renouncing the wrong-headed policy I had urged upon my comrades and countrymen in the United States. Asked how such mistakes occurred, Khrushchev could only say that Beria, head of Stalin's secret police and long since executed, had misinformed the Soviet leaders. This raised more questions that it answered.

During the late 1940s the various Peoples' Democracies of Eastern Europe held purge trials. It seemed that in each party some prominent leaders were jailed or executed; Anna Pauker in Romania, Slansky in Czechoslovakia, Gomulka in Poland, Stochiev and others in Bulgaria, Kadar and Rajk in Hungary. The trials themselves had been a shock, but about 1955, as part of the de-Stalinization process, each government released some of the revolutionaries from jail, rehabilitated the reputations of those it had executed, and recanted its "mistakes." The revelations were bound to set people thinking. Who ordered the trials? Why were executions thought necessary? Why so many "mistakes"?

Also around 1955 came revelations of Stalin's attempt to wipe out a separate Jewish culture in the Soviet Union. He had liquidated many of the most important figures in the Jewish cultural movement, such as the famous writer and poet Itzak Feffer and the Yiddish actor Solomon Mikhoels. All Communists had admired the Soviet struggle against anti-Semitism, and many American Communists, Jews and non-Jews alike, including myself, were outraged at the news of these killings. Even more disturbing were reports that anti-Semitism had not died with Stalin, that it still existed at the highest levels of the government and Party leadership.

I was not the only one with questions. In spite of the chaos produced by the attacks and the underground misadventures, a vigorous informal discussion of the Party's problems had already begun among the former prisoners and in certain districts by January 1956, when the Smith Act defendants from the Party's Central Committee reentered active political life. I was in contact with one of the centers of the developing movement for Party reform, the New York state organization, through my friendships with George Charney, Bill Lawrence, and others there. The discussion got a boost from speeches by Eugene Dennis and John Gates at a public celebration of the *Daily Worker*'s thirtieth anniversary in January. The paper carried the text of the speeches, and for the first time many of the issues that would be at the heart of the debate over the next two years were brought before the membership. It would be wrong to see Dennis as launching the movement to change the Party. He was not the sort of person to single-handedly mount a frontal attack on the Party's old policies, and he was certainly aware of the rising sentiment for a thorough reassessment. Still his report to the National Committee in the spring of 1956, later published as *The Communists Take a New Look*, encouraged and provided a rallying point for those of us seeking change.

Around the same time I wrote a letter to our Pittsburgh District Committee. It was not a sophisticated or polished theoretical work; I was looking for answers rather than seeking to provide them. But the letter raised many concerns I had in common with what, for want of a better term, I will call the "reform group."[1] The primary theme was the need for a thorough reassessment. I argued that our general goal should be an independent American party of socialism based on American realities. We had, for example, grossly underestimated the vitality of the American economy, and we had failed to base our approach to the American people on their very real commitment to democratic values. Related to this was an appeal to reconsider the idea of dictatorship of the proletariat through a one-party system. The concept was alien to American politics and supported the reactionaries' claim that all Communists were basically authoritarians. I emphasized that while comradely criticism by other parties was a good thing, it must flow both ways. We should reserve the right of criticizing other Communists, including the Soviets. They could take our criticism or leave it, but we should assume the same attitude toward theirs. We had already heard reports on some of the speeches at the CPSU's Twentieth Congress and were aware of some of the revelations, at least about what had occurred since World War II. Such errors hurt the cause of socialism throughout the world, I argued, precisely because the various parties had always been so closely identified with the Soviet leadership. The revelations underscored the need for a reevaluation of this relationship. Finally, I urged that we emphasize the prospects for a peaceful transition to socialism through existing democratic procedures. The experience of my own trial had convinced me that we had made it far too easy for the right wing to focus attention exclusively on the rhetoric of revolutionary violence in Marxist writings, diverting attention from the essentially constructive and democratic character of socialism.

Although I was encouraged by similar ideas being raised in other districts throughout the country, I was disappointed to find that most of my Pittsburgh comrades were not willing to take up these questions. Some apparently saw such ideas as a fundamental break with the concept that the Soviet Party was the only proper interpreter of Marxist theory. I could only hope that if a majority of the national membership shared my views, the Pittsburgh people would go along.

By 1956, and certainly before the disclosure of Stalin's crimes, the national leadership of the Party was already crystallizing into two factions. One group, which I came to call the "tankmen," was led by Foster, who explained the Party's weakness solely in terms of the right-wing attack. He argued that for this reason no serious reevaluation was in order. At the national level, Foster got his strongest support from Ben Davis and Bob Thompson. I called them tankmen because they were tough and brave but like soldiers inside a tank, they had only a limited field of vision. They were trapped inside the "historical tank" of the old Bolshevik-style Party. They sometimes failed to recognize that the United States was not czarist Russia.

The other group, which tends to be identified with John Gates, then editor of the *Daily Worker*, insisted on probing the reasons for our failure. What caused us to lose our base of support in the trade unions? Had we made an accurate political and economic assessment of the country in the decade since the war? Why were we so isolated? Above all, this group demanded a broad-based discussion of what had happened to us and what changes were called for.

Not everyone fit neatly into one or the other of these groups. Eugene Dennis, for example, and to some extent Jack Stachel and Elizabeth Gurley Flynn, occupied a middle ground. Dennis, sensing that a majority of members wanted change, usually sided with the reform group, but he seemed to have an unlimited capacity for vacillation. In the end he remained locked into the old groove.

I now can see that there were patterns in the way people lined up. The tankmen tended to be from an older generation whose ideas and style were forged in the days when the Party was an outlaw organization here and the Russian workers had just established the first socialist state in history. This group had been reinforced by immigrants from Russia and its border states who had entered the Party in fairly large numbers during its early years. The leading revolutionaries from this generation had spent many years working as functionaries at various levels of the Party organization.

The bulk of the reform group came from the secondary leadership, the people who actually had to carry out Party policy at the local level. They tended to be younger, and many had entered the Party by way of the mass organizing of the thirties. Naturally there were variations to these patterns. With my background and ties, I should have been with the tankmen. I had become active in the mid-twenties, experienced both the Lovestone and Trotsky purges, and studied in the Soviet Union. But my experiences in Detroit, Chicago, the anthracite fields, the West Coast, and Spain pushed me toward a more flexible understanding of Marxism than many from my generation were willing to accept.

In spite of the Soviet leadership's acknowledgment of countless "mistakes" during Stalin's rule and the growing feeling that the worst was yet to be revealed, most of us retained our faith. In rereading my letter to the Pittsburgh District Committee, I am not struck by the fact that I was raising such questions, for I felt that many others were moving in the same direction. What stands out to me, in retrospect is the continuing strength of my commitment to the Party. And this was a feeling I shared with most of those in the reform group. We were asking questions. We were dissatisfied and wanted a change, but we had no serious doubts as to whether or not we should remain in the Party. Up to the spring of 1956, the crisis was in the nature of a cloudburst, but at the beginning of May a real storm broke, unleashing a deluge of doubt that shook the commitment of thousands of lifelong Party members.

At the end of April I traveled to New York for a National Committee meeting. Until then we had heard only rumors concerning the last speech at the Soviet Party's Twentieth Congress, which Khrushchev had delivered in a closed session. Now someone from the National Board announced that a comrade had just returned from England with the text of the speech and that because of the document's length, it would occupy the entire afternoon agenda. As we adjourned people filed out, chattering nervously. We ate lunch with queasy stomachs, and most people returned early from the break, a rarity at such conferences.

The National Committee itself consisted of about 65 people, but this meeting was a plenum, which meant that many of the key people at the district level—trade union and Party organizers, for example—were invited. I was elected to chair the session, and I took my seat at a table facing about 120 people, the collective backbone of the Party. I'd never enjoyed chairing meetings. It meant always keeping one eye on the clock and sometimes cutting people off when they exceeded their allotted time, but it was especially uncomfortable to chair this session. The air buzzed with 120 variations of the same question: What's going on? Someone from the administrative committee that made the arrangements for the meeting asked that we remove all notebooks, pens, and pencils. There were to be no notes taken. This had never happened before at a National Committee meeting. Everyone sat up, waiting for something extraordinary to happen.

The comrade who brought the speech rose and proceeded to read it in its entirety, which took an hour and a half. For twenty years we'd labeled the stories of Stalin's atrocities as lies and distortions. We'd suppressed every doubt, feeling that a Communist Party could never have perpetrated such crimes. Now the secretary general of the Communist Party of the Soviet Union confirmed all these accusations and added documentation of many more. Of 1,966 delegates to the 1934 Seventeenth Congress of the Soviet Party, 1,108, including many members of the Central Committee, were arrested, and many of them executed by 1936. Seventy percent of the 139 members and candidates for the Party Central Committee elected at the Seventeenth Congress, a group comparable in stature and experience to the comrades sitting before me, were arrested and shot, not by the guns of the class enemy but by those of other Communists! An entire generation of leadership—the cream of the Bolsheviks, the men and women who made the Revolution—was wiped out. You might prove that one guy was a rascal, that he had dealings with the White Guards, that he had been stealing from the people. Perhaps you could prove this about two or even a dozen, but 70 percent of the Central Committee? This was a massacre. As the speech was read, the list of atrocities seemed endless. Even the idea of Stalin allocating millions of pounds of copper for a giant statue of himself seemed monstrous to anyone who realized that thousands of Russian workers were homeless at the time.

The words of the speech were like bullets, and each found its place in the hearts of the veteran Communists. Tears streamed down the faces of men and women who had spent forty or more years, their whole adult lives, in the movement. I looked into the faces of people who had been beaten up or jailed with me and thought of the hundreds that I had encouraged to join the Party. My head was swimming. I thought, "All the questions that were raised along the way now require new answers, and there's no longer one seat of wisdom where we can find them. We're on our own."

As chairman, I broke the deafening silence that followed the last sentence of the speech. I had made my sacrifices voluntarily and never thought of myself as a martyr, but now I felt betrayed. I said simply, "This was not why I joined the Party." The meeting ended in shock. I found myself in a car heading across town with friends and comrades I had known for years, but not one of us could bring him or herself to speak. I spent the next couple of days discussing the implications of the speech with those to whom I felt closest, Spanish veterans like Bill Lawrence and George Watt and other comrades like Sid Stein, Dorothy Healey, George Charney, Mike Russo, Fred Fine, and Martha Stone. I wanted to call Margaret, but how could I break this sort of news over the phone?

Above all, I was angry, not with the Russians or Foster or even Stalin, but with myself and others who had been so blind in our adherence to Soviet policy and so mechanical in our application of Marxism. All of our lives we had pointed to the Soviet Union as the model for what we were trying to achieve. This was the sort of system we were asking people to fight for in place of capitalism. I, and I'm sure many others who were at the meeting, vowed that our Party would change in order that nothing like this could ever happen again.

The most astounding thing was that some people were so rigid that not even this shock could move them. Foster and others acknowledged that it was a terrible thing but insisted that we were still on the right track and that the Soviet leaders would overcome the problem. A few even defended Stalin, arguing that he should still be respected for his great accomplishments. The emotion produced by the shock seemed to harden the division that had been growing for some time in the national leadership, and for the first time I feared there might be a split.

The worst part was going home. The fact that we'd been asked not to take notes clearly suggested that this information was not to be conveyed to the membership, but I never had a moment's hesitation. Everyone with whom I worked was just as committed as I and deserved to know the truth. This was especially true of Margaret, with whom I had shared everything over the years, but it was terribly hard to break the news. The past few years had taken away any tears we might have shed, but it would have been better had we cried. We were both sick with grief and spent days brooding around the house. At night we laid awake, discussing the next step and worrying about how to tell the kids and our friends.

I reported on the speech to an enlarged District Committee meeting a few days after I returned from New York. Naturally there was a terrible shock, but somehow the information didn't have quite the effect it had had in New York, despite the fact that I was indignant and argued once again for a thorough reassessment. The majority of my people still opposed the shift I was suggesting, and one even questioned the propriety of my reporting to them on the secret speech. There were probably other people who would have preferred to just bury the thing, but most were thankful for the report, and a few came around to my view as a result of it. When the story appeared in the *New York Times* a couple of weeks later, they could at least feel that they had been forewarned.[2]

I was trying to help the members in my district grapple with the issues raised in the speech, but I had to admit to them that I was still confused myself. I said things like, "The crisis has never been so deep" and "The revelations call our whole approach into question." For some who had lived and worked with the security that Marxism-Leninism was a science, interpreted and applied by the Party, such answers were not enough. The most difficult questions came from the few who were still active in mass work. "How can I go into my local union and hope to explain this to people who know and have accepted me as a Communist?" People were often more patient with us than we were with ourselves. The most sensitive ones still respected and often felt sorry for individual members, even if they saw the Party as discredited. But some members concluded that their lives had been wasted, and these people just drifted away. The decline precipitated by McCarthyism now accelerated.

I saw the full significance of the revelations in the reaction of Josie, now fourteen years old. During the trials she may have been under more pressure than any of us. I was insulated to some extent from the sort of experiences she had because I spent so much of my time in courtrooms and jails. She and Bobby faced nasty attacks on a daily basis and nearly became outcasts as a result of my trials and convictions. Still, she sustained her faith in Margaret and me and in what we believed throughout the ordeal.

Margaret and I had barely recovered from the shock ourselves when the June 5, 1956, edition of the *New York Times* hit the streets. It carried a front-page story that quoted large sections from Khrushchev's speech. At first Josie thought it must all be some fantastic lie. "It isn't true, is it?" she asked. When we told her that it was true, I could almost see her reliving the past several years in her mind. Just as we couldn't shield her from the attacks during those years, so we couldn't shield her from the feeling of betrayal which she shared with us.

The fall of 1956 brought another crisis that seemed to prove that the Soviet Party was still determined to dominate the policies of other parties throughout the world. In June Polish workers had struck and rioted in Posnan. What was the Polish government doing that workers should feel it necessary to rebel? Before we could figure out what was going on, Soviet troops had entered Poland to quell the disturbance. In October the Central Committee of the Polish Party elected Wladislaw Gomulka, who had just been released from jail, as Party leader. His election suggested that the Poles were moving toward a much more independent relationship with the Soviet Union. The Soviet leaders tried to block Gomulka's election and even threatened to send in troops once again, but the Poles stood firm. Later on Gomulka was to become a rigid bureaucrat in his own right and had to face worker unrest, but at the time he had the support of the Polish workers and his election seemed to be a major breakthrough.

The lesson was not lost on the Hungarians. Their Party was one of the most rigid in the world, more Russian than the Russians'. Their army wore Red Army uniforms, towns were renamed for prominent

Russians, including Stalin, and the Hungarians had carried out one of the most notorious purge trials. Rajk, a world-renowned revolutionary, was executed in 1949 for fictionalized "crimes against the Party." He was posthumously rehabilitated in 1956 under a rather halting de-Stalinization process when it was revealed that he was guilty of no more than devoting his life to the cause of socialism. This and other revelations may have fueled a movement for greater independence from Soviet influence. When security police fired into a crowd of demonstrators at the end of October, 1956, Erno Gero, the Stalinist party leader, called for Soviet troops. Street fighting dragged on, but Gero was forced to step down and allow Imre Nagy, who espoused a more independent brand of Hungarian socialism, to assume control of the government. Fearing that reactionary elements that had clearly been active throughout the revolt would gain the upper hand, the Soviets intervened in Hungary on November 4 with massive force. They crushed the rebellion and executed Nagy.

John Gates and many others who were identified with the reform group unconditionally condemned the invasion as a crime and sided with the insurgents. I disagreed with what I saw at the time as a simplistic view. Many well-intentioned people, including Communist Party members, were certainly swept up in the revolt, but the Hungarian crowds differed from those that had been active in the Polish uprising. In the Polish case, Communists and other militant workers rose in order to achieve or to protect a more democratic form of socialism. Many in the Hungarian crowds were former collaborators or Hungarian fascists, supporters of the right-wing Horthy dictatorship that lasted from the early twenties until 1944. They saw the street fighting as a chance to introduce a reactionary government. During the war Hungary had been a launching site for German invasions of the Soviet Union, and the Hungarian army had even served alongside the Nazis on the Russian front. Soviet intervention was based on a fear of fascism in Hungary, and I felt that the fear was justified.

I did not completely support the Soviets' actions, however. The best way to fight the right wing would probably have been to bolster Nagy's government, which had the support of the people, instead of shooting him. Still, I couldn't bring myself to unconditionally condemn the Soviet action, especially since I feared that it might lead to a split within our own ranks. I therefore supported a compromise resolution that refused to either condemn or condone the invasion.

About two years after the invasion, my misgivings about some of the elements involved were strengthened when I had a chance to meet a Hungarian "freedom fighter." Bobby was being harassed because he refused to join the Eighteenth Street Assassins, a collection of racist hoodlums who spent their time painting swastikas on buildings. They jumped Bobby one day in the hall of our building, and I was stabbed when I came to help. At the hospital they put me next to a recent Hungarian emigré who had lost a leg when he was pushed or fell in front of a subway train. In his pain he screamed the worst sort of anti-Semitic epithets at the "Jew doctors and nurses." It was hard to envision him as a champion of freedom and democracy.

The Hungarian issue strengthened my conviction that we must follow an independent course; a democratic and independent Hungarian Party could have handled the situation. But this was not an issue over which to leave the Party. I still felt there was a chance for change and wanted to try. ·

Our chance to make this change came in February 1957, when the Party held its Sixteenth National Convention, the first since 1950. In September 1956 the National Committee had produced a draft resolution, a suggested policy statement that would be put before the convention for consideration and discussion. From that point up until the day of the convention, the issues were debated in District Committees and local branch meetings, in the columns of the *Daily Worker,* and around dinner tables in Party homes across the country. I can't remember another period in which interest and discussion had been so intense. Despite the precipitous decline of the Party, there was a sense of optimism as the convention began, a feeling that finally we were going on the right track.

Although it was much clearer and more systematic, the draft resolution raised many of the same points I had made in my letter to the Pittsburgh District Committee. It discussed specific policies that had helped to isolate and weaken the Party and identified most of these as "left sectarian" errors, meaning that a rigid adherence to abstract theory had clouded our view of what was really needed. While not completely breaking with the concept of Leninism, the resolution held that the theory must be interpreted by each Party according to the situation it faced in its own country. No one Party had the Marxist-Leninist "franchise." On the question of proletarian internationalism, the resolution urged a supportive but more independent position for our own Party in relation to others. In general, the committee that drafted the resolution, assuming that a majority of the Party membership shared its perspective, went further in its call for change than Dennis had in his April 1956 report. Certainly the National Committee as a whole supported the document; Foster was the only one to vote against it. This was not surprising in light of the fact that it was obviously a repudiation of his analysis. Seeing the resolution as an attack, he became more obstinate. Since the Khrushchev revelations, he had been inclined to try to get along with the reform group, but now he went on the offensive, maintaining that the line he followed had been the proper one and that the reformers were leading the Party in the direction of revisionism.

At the time revisionism was a serious charge to make against another Communist. Essentially, it meant that in putting forward certain ideas one had deviated from the established body of Marxist-Leninist thought and violated a tenet of the revolutionary science. Such a deviation, if followed by the Party as a whole, could throw it off the tracks and set the whole revolutionary process back. Normally the charge would have caused a stampede, but in this case it seemed to have little impact. Foster, Davis, and Thompson repeatedly accused us of revisionism, but people generally held their ground. If Foster insisted that any attempt to interpret the ideology in light of the problems we actually faced was revisionism, then we were prepared to live with the label. At the moment it seemed to be the least of our worries.

Between the adoption of the draft resolution and the convention, divisions in the reform group, which had always been present, began to show. On one end of the spectrum, Dennis, whom we had expected to support us, started a strategic retreat. He expressed support for a minimal change in moderate language and attempted to placate Foster. Foster's supporters, especially Davis, had been vicious in their attacks on Dennis, and he seemed to be buckling under the pressure. On the other end, I sensed that Gates had really given up, perhaps feeling that he had already compromised too much. He seemed to want to scrap everything, but his idea to replace the American Party with a "political action association," was vague. Foster accused the reform group as a whole of being liquidationist, that is, prepared to dismantle the Party organization. Gates came closest to deserving the label. For the time being, Foster's attacks brought all the reform elements together. Many felt it would be difficult to rebuild things if there was too much disagreement among us.

The convention itself seemed to herald great changes. A panel of outside observers, headed by A. J. Muste, the aged pacifist and labor radical, was invited, and all observers reported favorably on the vigorous debate and the apparent commitment to change. Foster and his supporters fought every step of the way, but the main political resolution, which clearly reflected the reform analysis, was passed essentially intact. There were heated arguments, but there also was an atmosphere or at least rhetoric of rededication. Significantly, the convention closed with the delegates singing "The Star-Spangled Banner." The Communist Party USA, it seemed, had turned its face in a new direction.

Yet in the two decades since the convention, the CPUSA has remained one of the most backward parties in the Western world and one of the most rigid in its adherence to the Soviet line. What happened? Given the apparent victory at the convention, why weren't we able to change the Party?

The place to begin is with the knowledge, which we all recognized even as we struggled against Foster, that had we won we would have faced an enormous task of rebuilding in a period when the dominant political climate was still decidedly conservative. One of the bleakest reports at the convention was a description of the virtual bankruptcy of the *Daily Worker*. Between its highpoint in 1949 and the time of the convention in early 1957, the paper's circulation had fallen by 80 percent; it was on its last legs. Some members refused to support it because they objected to its "revisionist" editorial policy under Gates, but the prime reason for its decline was that there was hardly anyone around to read it, let alone sell subscriptions. According to the Party's own registration figures, membership, which had already fallen from at least seventy-five thousand in 1945, stood at slightly more than twenty thousand in the beginning of 1956. Within the next two years, it dropped by 75 percent to less than five thousand. Whoever won the struggle would have inherited a tiny sect with a bankrupt newspaper.

But the failure to achieve change must also be blamed upon the reformers themselves. We had never been a homogeneous group, and we lacked the will to take power away from the tankmen and run the organization. The clearest theme of the convention was unity, not change, and this was because we lacked self-confidence. The most depressing moments were when we caucused, searching for someone of the stature to replace Foster. At one point some wanted me to run, but I rejected the idea outright. It seemed to me that the chairman of the American Party should be a native-born citizen and perhaps representative of some particular mass organization. I was neither an outstanding writer nor a strong speaker. I felt we could find someone better suited for the job. We approached Bill Schneiderman, but he just shook his head. The logical choice would have been Dennis, but he had vacillated so much over the past few months that most people felt he was no longer reliable. Feeling weak and facing the prospect of leading a Party that had already been decimated, we feared that a further split would finish the organization off. As a result we held back. The convention elected a "unity" Secretariat or National Board that included Foster and several of his supporters. This opened the way not for unity but for more factionalism in the months that followed.

Our ignorance of what was happening internationally was one of the things that undermined our confidence. In some parties there wasn't much turmoil. But in the case of the British Party, for example, there was a reform group that projected a policy of peaceful transition to socialism, by implication rejecting the concept of the dictatorship of the proletariat. The leadership tried to muzzle this group and eventually forced its members to resign. Apparently they were influenced by the fight we were putting up and actually published American material in their little journal, *The Reasoner,* including a letter I had written in support of the *Daily Worker*'s editorial on the Rajk affair. In Italy, as early as 1945, Togliatti had raised some of the same issues that were troubling us. But we didn't know all this at the time, at least I didn't. In fact, Foster often argued that ours was the only Party having trouble readjusting after the Khrushchev revelations and Hungary. It made us feel that we were way out on a limb.

It's been gratifying to see many of the European parties embrace some of the ideas we were trying to express during the 1956–1957 crisis: a modification of the concept of democratic centralism within parties and within the international movement; an emphasis on the interpretation of Marxism by each individual party in light of the values and traditions of its people; an acceptance of a multiparty political system and democratic procedures. It's ironic that the most fundamental premises of what we now call Eurocommunism were first advocated by American Communists in 1956. But today the European parties support one another in this process of reinterpretation. Many of the greatest Communist leaders throughout the world support these views. At the time we raised them we seemed to be alone in the world Communist movement.

Any chance we had of transforming and reinvigorating the Party (the two were linked in my mind) was crushed in the year following the convention. There were a multitude of problems, but two were especially important. By far the most serious was the continuing erosion of our membership. Some had seen the convention as an acid test to determine how serious their leaders were about changing the Party. Disappointed with the compromises and with the composition of the National Board and sickened by the continuing factionalism, they "voted with their feet." But it was not simply a matter of numbers. Any spirit the membership had seemed to be gone. In the fall of

1957 I headed an effort to save the *Daily Worker* from its ultimate demise. Many of those who would have been most effective in such a drive were gone; the few who were left seemed completely demoralized. In the past they could always feel there was something worth working for, but now they were unsure, defeated. The campaign failed, and the paper eventually collapsed and was replaced by a weekly.

The second major obstacle to accomplishing anything was Foster's faction. At the convention I had taken the view that he and his people had devoted as much to the Party and gone through as much or more than I. If I could change, so could they. The others who shared my political views apparently agreed with this assessment. We were wrong. Foster was still clinging to the shingle "CPUSA—Marxism-Leninism." He and the other tankmen on the new National Board had enough power to subvert the will of the convention. As various representatives of our group dropped off in disgust, the main political resolution that had promised so many changes was just ignored. The new constitution adopted at the convention was scrapped in favor of one with all the old clichés and rhetoric.

I had had serious misgivings at the convention, fears that the Party was already too weak to be resurrected. These doubts were reinforced in the months after the convention as I tried to carry on my work. In Pittsburgh the Party was getting even weaker. People came around to tell me they were going away and to talk one more time. Sometimes they came with an armful of Marxist books, a bad sign. "I want to leave these with you. I can't do any good around here any more. Maybe we'll meet again some day." These were devoted, capable people, but what could they do under the circumstances? Often I felt like crying.

The little things added up. There was a group of young doctors in western Pennsylvania who'd set up a medical center for miners, a wonderful project. They were also great supporters of the Party, and it was important for us to know that they were behind us. Every month or so they sent us a small check that really helped to keep the organization going. I tried to meet them whenever I could to let them know what was going on. Shortly after the convention, we arranged a meeting at the home of one of the doctors. I was supposed to report on the convention, but only one person showed up. Even the doctor who lived there made some excuse and left. The attitude seemed to be, "Who the hell cares about the convention? The Party is finished." I was left sitting alone with an old miner. He had stuck with us through it all, but it was going to take more than one old miner. He looked very sad. "I guess we're going through a real crisis," he said. "We're in trouble, aren't we? But what can we do? My sons all went up to Erie to work in the shops there; they have no interest in the Party. Me and the wife will stay, but there's not much of our old group left."

Around the same time, we offered a course in political economy. The only ones to come were four or five of the oldest Party members in town. These were people who had sat through a dozen similar courses during their lives. No new people were coming into the Party. It was only a matter of time until this kind of situation started to affect those who were still around.

There were the practical problems as well. Since the district could no longer support an organizer, I had to find work, and with my reputation that was practically impossible. An insurance company took me on, even though they knew who I was. I tried it for two months, but finally had to face the fact that I was not an insurance salesman. I told them they were wasting their money. Meanwhile many of my closest friends were talking about leaving the Party. Bill Lawrence lost his position in the New York organization to Foster supporters, so he opened a dry-cleaning establishment. George Charney was retained for a little while, but it became impossible for him to function among people with whom he violently disagreed. Soon he too left.

Though Margaret and I had always had a commitment that helped us through the hard times, now it was fading away. Both of us had always knocked ourselves out, but now we seemed to be just going through the motions. Still, we might have held on if there had been any chance for change. I didn't completely lose hope until I attended a National Committee meeting some time in late 1957. When I came into Party headquarters, I met Max Weiss, who'd been appointed educational director in the New York district. He was in the front of the movement for change, and I deeply respected him. He was sitting in his little office, sifting through mountains of books and pamphlets. As I looked at the literature, it struck me that the official ideology of the movement was really not changing at all in spite of what had happened at the convention.

"Max," I said, "what the hell are we doing. How can we continue under the same Party leadership? When a branch writes for suggestions on literature, what are you going to give them—Foster's books with all the old rhetoric or Stalin's pamphlets?"

"I know," he said. "Everything we have interprets the world through the old view, and this is what we'll be pushing."

"We can't tell people that this is what we believe and ask them to believe it too." I was looking at Max, but I was talking to myself.

He had some pamphlets in his hand. He looked down at them, laid them on the desk, and we walked out of the building together.

The decision to leave had been building since the convention and was founded on months of hopeless work and long discussions with Margaret and others, but the actual break came in the middle of the National Committee meeting. The talk with Max was still fresh in my mind when the meeting turned to interpretation of one of the National Convention resolutions. Despite the clear-cut position adopted by the convention, the tankmen had not given up. One after the other they argued for the old policies, as if the convention had never occurred. The discussion dragged on for almost an hour with Dorothy Healey, Al Richmond, and me arguing for the positions adopted at the convention. But I could tell it was no use. It didn't matter what the majority had voted for. The same group was still in control of the Party, and they were not about to let any real change take place. I recall saying finally, "Damn it! There's no hope for this Party. I can't even tell my own kids to join a Party that holds these views. How can I ask anyone else?" I walked out.

I had worked with some of these people for decades, but it seems that they wrote me off as soon as I made these remarks at the meeting. Of all the National Board members, only Elizabeth Gurley Flynn came at that time to talk to me about my decision. I knew that Dorothy and Al were staying on primarily to carry on the fight for change, and if I was guilty about anything, it was from a sense of abandoning them. Dorothy asked me to stay and come out to California. "Out there," she argued, "things will be different. I'm sure that we could elect you chairman in LA. We still have Schneiderman, Al, Oleta (O'Connor Yates), Louise (Todd), Slim (Connelly), and the others. We still have a lot of the longshoremen with us and links with some of the other unions. Out there we'll do what we think is right." I was tempted for a moment, but I knew she was wrong. "You're kidding yourself," I said. "You can't do what you want. Sooner or later the National Office will pull the rug out from under you." It would also have meant sacrifices for my family, all for something I honestly felt would make little difference in the long run. I told Dorothy I couldn't do it. She, Al, and a few other very good people stayed in, clinging to the hope that things might still work out. Even though I couldn't share their optimism, we remained friends. Within a decade they and others also decided to leave. They had fought the good fight, but in the end they lost.

It would have been foolish to stay around Pittsburgh under the circumstances. Bobby still had to finish high school, and we wanted to give him and Josie a chance in a place where my reputation wouldn't hurt them. We needed to find somewhere to start over. I handed in the membership lists and offered to talk to whomever would take my place. I thought my successor would need to know something about what was happening in various industries and neighborhoods, and about the ins and outs of political work in the area. But the Party never asked about any of this. The National Board seemed only to be interested in the membership list, which by this time didn't amount to much. Margaret stayed to wrap up some business, and I went ahead to New York to look for work and find a place to live.

People left the Party in different ways, depending upon how much the crisis had changed them politically. Some were clearly through with socialism, but I couldn't go this route. My life wasn't wasted, even from a purely selfish point of view. The movement had given me an education, many wonderful friends, and a sense of purpose in my life. I was also proud of much that we had done. In agitating for unemployment insurance and other reforms, in helping to build industrial unions, and in fighting against fascism, we had helped to make the United States a better place for working people to live. The Party itself might only be a shell, but the goal I'd set myself as a young worker in Berk's packinghouse—social and economic equality and an end to wars—was still worth fighting for. My search for some way to make this dream a reality would have to go on outside of the Party now, for I was still not prepared to give it up.

THIRTEEN

Going On: 1957–1980

The twenty-three years since I left the Party have represented a big period of adjustment, rethinking, and searching. Just surviving was a struggle that consumed much of my time and energy, but I also had to try to rebuild my life with the central core missing. That I could not and would not renounce my past, that I was still proud to have been a Communist and still respected many of the people with whom I'd worked over the years—all this made the break more difficult. Part of the struggle was just to live another day, to keep my sanity in a world whose values I couldn't accept, to do whatever little I could. Maybe I wouldn't move the world or even be able to see a change. But I couldn't just sit and do nothing.

We found an apartment in west Manhattan on Eighteenth Street. Josie left the University of Chicago and came back to New York to go to Brooklyn College. Bobby went to high school right across the street. We tried to make theirs the lives of normal teenagers, but we knew that it would be hard. They understood the problems we were facing and tried to be less demanding than "normal" kids, and this helped, as did sharing the experience of estrangement from the Party with a lot of old friends who were going through the same process. Still it was a long haul for Margaret and me.

I was especially hurt that few in the leadership even spoke to us, let alone tried to understand things from our view. Naturally, I didn't expect much from Foster or those closest to him. I think to them I was not a comrade but a threat, and they were probably glad to see me go. But I thought comrades with whom I had had a lot in common over the years, especially those with doubts about Foster's line, would show more concern. For a long time only Elizabeth Gurley Flynn really kept in close touch, though some of the others were at least civil to us.

Eventually a few people showed up. Gus Hall, who later became general secretary of the Party, came by our apartment one night to ask Margaret and me to come back and help rebuild the organization. But since nothing had really changed, the discussions led nowhere. Gil Green, one of the last Smith Act defendants to emerge from prison, visited several times. We have remained friends despite our political disagreements. I also remained close to Sam Brown till the end of his life. Sam set up a meeting with Irving Potash, the fur workers' leader who had been on the National Board for years and had just completed his Smith Act sentence. Potash had left for Poland following his Smith Act conviction but was imprisoned upon his return to the States for a violation of the immigration law. When he came out he insisted that we have a talk; he couldn't believe that an old war-horse like me had left for good. It was a sad experience for both of us. He had not been in on the discussions before the convention, so he was shocked at the sort of fundamental criticisms that some of us had raised: Stalin's crimes and those of the Soviet Party, our sectarian mistakes in the trade union movement, our rejection of the concept of the dictatorship of the proletariat. Although he was visibly shaken, he said he would return. I never saw him again. I think he just felt that I had gone beyond the pale and that we now had little in common, in spite of our years of working together.

Once I heard that Ben Davis was critically ill, so I visited him in the hospital. He said something like, "How can there be an American Party without Steve Nelson?" It was a nice thing to say, and I still respected him as a person. In spite of our frequent clashes over Party policy, he had always been decent toward me and taken an interest in my work. Ben reminded me that it was he who had first nominated me for the National Committee, even before I went to Spain. More than many of the other leaders, he had made a real effort to keep in touch with what was happening in basic industry. I felt terrible watching him die. I had known him as the young lawyer who returned to the Deep South to defend Angelo Herndon, a young black Communist, despite the obvious risks; as the twice-elected Communist councilman for Harlem; and as the witness who stood up for us in our Pittsburgh Smith Act trial even when it meant lengthening his own sentence with citations for contempt of court. Finally, I recalled the day he and Nina Stamler were married in our house in Pittsburgh right after his release from prison. But I still couldn't accept his point of view. And his ideas were those of the Party.

Another time I ran into Bob Thompson on the street. He asked me to stop in somewhere and have a drink with him, but I made some excuse and got away. I couldn't forgive him for the vicious personal attacks he had made on people like Stachel whenever they disagreed with Foster's line. More than anyone else, he was Foster's whip. But I may have made a mistake in not talking to him. People close to him later told me that at the time we met, he was having second thoughts about Foster's position and had said the trouble was that Foster had lived ten years too long. Apparently he was casting about for someone to talk to, and in retrospect I'm sorry that I didn't pay more attention. Soon after this he died.

However strained my relations with the Party leadership had become, I still maintained contacts with many rank and file Party members, especially the Yugoslav waterfront workers in New York City. These were people who had sustained us throughout the trials and prison, and they remained friendly. I think some may have thought I would one day return to the fold. Margaret and I were always invited to their parties and other gatherings. In fact, the Yugoslav Club was right down Eighteenth Street from our apartment building. On my way to work each day I could peek in through the window to see if anyone was around, and I often stopped in for a beer or just to talk.

Here too the past decade had taken its toll. During the war the club had more than two thousand members; now it had trouble attracting a hundred people to its annual affair. On May Day members put on their red buttons and went down to Union Square for the rally, and in the evening they held a dinner. We were always invited. How could we say no? People would talk about how great the rally was, what a wonderful speech had been made. Usually I held my tongue, but sometimes it was too much to see these good, dedicated people living in the past. I would say, "Look, I was on Union Square with you. There was nobody there. We were just going through the motions."

But every May Day they and the other old Party people went down to the square, and every May Day I was with them. People would come up and say, "Steve, it's so good to see you here, to know that you're still around." Many of these people were foreign-born workers to whom May Day really meant something. I felt that I couldn't ignore them, even if the event meant little to most American workers.

The question was, "Where do we go from here? What else is there worth fighting for?" We were never politically paralyzed by the decision to leave. I hoped that somewhere along the line the new movement would develop, perhaps within the next five years or so. It could be a fusion of the ideas that we had put forward at the convention. I talked with many people at the time about this, especially old friends from the anthracite, Philadelphia, and California groups who were sympathetic with the ideas that had won out at the convention. But few people could see any prospect for changing the Party, and everyone seemed to have his or her own idea for what we should do instead. Some argued that we should each join some other socialist or liberal organization or trade union and argue for our ideas there. This would allow us to maintain contacts and win people over to our views. Then, a few years later, we could come together and form a new organization. Others insisted on hanging in there a little longer. After a valiant effort to change the Party from within, most of these ended up leaving it sooner or later.

In New York the situation among those who had left was a little different. Some of these people created a political life of a sort around a little discussion group, but it was nothing with which I could be satisfied. In fact, I had some disagreements with their perspective as well. Some time in 1958 George Charney, Joe Clark, and a few others started meeting, and they invited prominent liberals to speak to them about politics and other matters. Part of my reservation about the groups rose from the question of whether people like Arthur Schlesinger really had anything to offer socialists. In some ways I felt that I had not strayed as far from my earlier political beliefs as many in this group apparently had. At one point, for example, Harrison Salisbury of the *New York Times* addressed the group on the subject of the Soviet Union, which he had recently visited. He had profound disagreements with much of what he found there, of course, but he was impressed by some aspects of Soviet society. Someone who was at the meeting described how he was immediately criticized by several people. He was shocked and said something like, "I am amazed by you people. Up to now, things were turned around. You accepted everything. Now I see some small virtue in what's happening there, and you deny me the right to see things that way."

Most members of the group remained liberals but little more, and I just didn't feel much in common with them politically. Also, many of the people who had been active in promoting the reform movement in New York had spent much of their lives as Party functionaries in the state organization and were simply very tired. Some wanted a more normal life and either started small businesses or went back to school. Others, pessimistic about the chance for a new movement, lost hope and became apolitical.

Obviously I had no illusions about going to college or becoming a businessman. I assumed that I would have to make my living by returning to my trade, but as for politics I was hoping that someone else might take the ball, that I might be able to have a slightly more normal family life. I didn't try in the least to get out of politics; I think I would have rejoined the Party in an instant if there seemed to be any chance for changing it. But there wasn't, so I continued searching for something else. In the meantime I tried to maintain my political sense of balance and to find a job.

Work was the most immediate problem. Margaret transcribed tapes of business meetings, a terrible job for lousy pay, but it was all that she could find. Bobby and Josie found jobs to get some of the money they needed and continued their educations. That took some of the pressure off us.

When I went to look for work, I had some strange experiences. Most of my contacts were of two sorts: people who had been in the Party but had dropped out, and people who were still in. Neither could help me much. Those who had left the Party earlier, say during or even before the McCarthy period, and started up businesses often wouldn't touch me for fear of being red-baited. Most of those who were still in often would not even speak to me. People I knew from the YCL days, friends and comrades for over three decades, would cross the street in order to avoid me. And those who had left recently were usually in the same position as I, looking for some way to get by.

For a long time I found nothing at all, and I got more desperate day by day. I was afraid that carpentry might be out of the question. I was in my mid-fifties and probably too old to be climbing around on scaffolds. Finally I was referred to a former Party member who had already hired several people in my situation, except that they were not quite as notorious. He owned a well-run and profitable print shop. I knew that I couldn't ask him to hire another person; the shop was small, and he had already gone out on a limb by taking on the others. "Look," I said, "I'm not asking you for a job, but just give me some idea of what I could do to get one." He sat down with me and figured out a plan. We worked up an ad to go in the *New York Times*. He even paid for it. It said something like, "Printing salesman—good contacts—willing to work on straight commission." I got twenty-eight letters in response. The reason was obvious. When someone is paying on the basis of straight commission, it's no skin off his back to take you on. If you bring in some business, so much the better. The industry was extremely tight in New York at the time, and the printers were searching for jobs.

It was the only time in my life when I interviewed the bosses. I made appointments with several, and some even took me to lunch. I tried not to' look too hungry. I went back to my friend, the print shop owner, for advice, and he helped me to settle on one, Progressive

Color Lithographers, a good-sized shop with twenty-five or thirty workers.

The day I got the job, I ran into an old friend who was working for a Madison Avenue advertising firm. He looked me over and decided that now that I was a salesman, I needed to look like one, too. He took me out and bought me a suit. I was worried about paying him back, but he told me to forget it. "I make $20,000 a year, and no man is worth that much. If I can't help you, who will?"

The printer made up a little kit for me with samples of the work, prices, and other information. Since I really didn't have any "good contacts," I blundered around for about six months, calling on advertising agencies and other places I thought might need printing. Toward the end I had some luck. I built up a little group of accounts and finally I hit a big one—a $4,000 order. At a 10-percent commission, I stood finally to make a little money. But the success didn't last long. One day the boss called me in to explain that the ad agency with the big account had called. They told him that as long as I was selling for him, he would have to do without their business. I asked him why they were doing this, and he said something about trouble with the government in Pennsylvania. I needed the job badly, so I tried to cover up.

"Oh, that goddamn tax problem."

He said, "Steve, it wasn't a tax problem."

That was it—fired.

It was just as well. I didn't like the work anyway. In selling you have to be a bit of a schemer. You have to pay people off and talk them into things that they really don't want to do. So after visiting a few more printers without much luck, I decided to try something else.

I ran into a fellow who had left the Party and gone into real estate and construction in Westchester County. He had turned into quite an opportunist and was doing well. I asked him for work as a carpenter, and he agreed. I took the bus all the way out to Westchester, but when I got there he said I was too old, that I was finished as a carpenter. He knew how old I was when he agreed to take me on, and he certainly knew who I was, but apparently he got scared. If one of his real estate partners or someone in the bank should learn who he had working as one of his carpenters . . . . I was furious at first, but getting furious didn't get me any closer to finding a job.

Another Spanish vet was working as an independent carpenter in the suburbs. I was reluctant to ask him for work; he seemed to be barely making it on his own. But when I asked, he didn't even hesitate. "Sure, bring your toolbox Monday morning." I could hardly believe it. A job as a carpenter at union wage. It was the most wonderful thing that had happened in a long, long time. Because our jobs were quite a ways outside of town, I stayed with his family four or five days a week and went into the city to be with Margaret and the kids on weekends. A lot of the work was hard for me, especially at the beginning, but eventually I got back into shape, and I enjoyed it.

I continued with my friend for more than a year, until I had a bad accident on the job. A truck loaded with lumber backed into the building site to unload, and it knocked a couple of the braces off our scaffold. Nobody noticed. When I climbed back onto the scaffold, the whole thing collapsed, and I landed on the stairs on my back. I was out of work for about six months, trying to live on state workmen's compensation. Eventually I was paid a small insurance settlement.

While resting after the accident, I visited a friend who was living out on Cape Cod. We walked down to the beach, and I was really struck by the beauty of the spot. He introduced me to a real estate woman who showed me the cheapest lot she had—odd-shaped, wooded, way in on a back road. I thought it was great, and she was asking exactly what I had gotten on the insurance settlement.

Because of the injury and my reputation, I thought at the time that I might never be able to work again. Margaret and I were both getting older, and I had very little social security coming. Also, we found life in a New York apartment stifling. If I built a house on the lot, it could be a place of our own. It was a chance that I had to take.

I called Margaret and told her that I was buying the land. She said, "You're not buying a damn thing." She was being much more rational than I, and Josie took her side. But this brought Bobby in to support me. He knew some of the people up at the Cape from a left-wing summer camp that the kids had gone to during the trials. In the end Bobby and I convinced the other two to go along. We sank the only money we had into the Cape Cod sand. Now I was a landowner without a job.

I often visited Nishino, an old friend from my days of working with the Japanese Bureau in California. He owned a small cabinet shop on Eighteenth Street, a block from our flat. His radical pedigree went back to the Wobblies, who had welcomed him as a young immigrant, and he was an elder statesman among the small group of Japanese Communists.

I came in one day to find him stretched out on the workbench, his shoes off and his feet propped up. He had gout and a heart condition. He couldn't keep up with the shop any more, and he asked me to take it over. I explained that I didn't have any money, but he said I could pay him a little each month. I said I was a poor salesman and didn't know how to run a business. "You've been selling socialism all of your life," he said. "If you can sell that, you can sell cabinets." I talked it over with Margaret, and she agreed that we should give it a try. She understood that I probably couldn't do carpentry anymore, and she knew that we needed the money. So I became a small businessman and a cabinetmaker.

I already had some of the skills I needed. I could handle wood, and I knew some of the tools, but a carpenter is not a cabinetmaker. The cabinetmaker doesn't know how to build for leverage and strength; the carpenter doesn't know how to do the precision cutting. Nishino was good enough to work with me for a couple of weeks to show me the ropes and keep me from wasting material. A teak panel cost $35 at the time. If you made a bad cut, you lost more than a day's pay.

I did custom-built work for apartments, mostly bookcases, benches, and, especially, hi-fi cabinets. I enjoyed the actual woodworking, but there was a lot more to the job than that. The shop was a typical third-floor loft, always stuffy and hot as hell in the summer. In the course of a week, I had to go up and down the stairs dozens of times, either carrying large teak panels up or carrying bookcases and hi-fi cabinets down. The evenings were taken up with making deliveries and taking measurements. The dust in the place was so bad that I developed respiratory problems, and for a while I thought that I had emphysema. After about five years, by which time I'd finished paying Nishino, I'd had enough.

A young fellow, the son of a friend, was working with me to learn the trade. He liked the work and was dying to have the shop. One day I just said, "Here's the key. Pay me what I paid Nishino, bimonthly."

One reason that I wanted to get rid of the shop was so that I could spend a little more time on the Cape. I had built a house over the course of a couple of summers while business was slow and the heat unbearable at the cabinet shop. A friend lent us the money, and Bobby and a group of his college friends agreed to help in exchange for room and board. I rented an old farmhouse for the months of May and June and filled the loft with beds. I went up early and laid the foundation with the help of an old mason in the neighborhood. The boys came up as soon as school let out and helped me frame it in. This meant that we had walls with windows and a roof, but most of the inside work was unfinished. The job took several weeks. Then I had to rush back to work in the cabinet shop, which together with Margaret's wages was paying our rent. I finished the house myself the

Steve Nelson near his home on Cape Cod, 1980.

following summer, and we started spending a few weeks each summer up on the Cape.

At one point I worked a whole season there, building another house for a friend, putting a porch on someone else's, constructing little studios and any other work that I could find. But this sort of work only helped to liquidate the debt on the house we had built. I still had to make my living in the city. I was finally able to get rid of the shop because I found another job that suited my situation well. Again, it was one of the Lincoln Brigade vets who helped. He was an electrician and was able to get me into the union of stage craftsmen who build sets for theaters, movies, and commercials. The work was irregular. You went down to the union hall and waited for the jobs to come in. You might not get anything until the afternoon, or you might not get anything at all. It was usually three or four days work each week, and that was plenty for someone over sixty-five. I told them I was fifty-eight, and no one suspected.

As with the cabinetmaking, I had to pick up some skills, but I already knew most of what I needed. I'd worked from blueprints before, so I knew how to follow the set designs. I found most of the work interesting, though the waste involved, especially in commercials, aggravated me.

For example, a toothpaste company decided to make an extravaganza. We had to build an entire warehouse and fill it with thousands of tubes of toothpaste all stacked just so. Next they needed a bulldozer. They got one that looked pretty much like bulldozers always look, but for them it had to be painted white. Then they took the bulldozer and drove it right through the side of the new warehouse, crushing the tubes of toothpaste. A cameraman was lying on the ground, waiting for the bulldozer to crush the tube right in front of him so that he could get the shot when the colored toothpaste oozed out of the tube. Ridiculous!

It took a lot of lumber and a lot of labor to build that set; and they smashed it to pieces to sell toothpaste. Not all the lumber was broken, and the toothpaste tubes weren't all crushed, so large crowds started forming on the street to pick up toothpaste and boards for bookshelves. Finally they returned the bulldozer to the construction company where they got it, but the company refused to take it back. Who wants a white bulldozer? So the ad agency wrote it off as a loss or passed the $12,000 cost on to the toothpaste company. And who pays for the toothpaste?

I worked as a stage carpenter for about four years. During the summers I built another little house with the help of a friend. Margaret and I lived in the house year round when we retired in 1975. It was probably predictable that politics would follow me out to the Cape. Provincetown had always attracted a number of radical artists and writers from the time in the twenties when Eugene O'Neill was at the Provincetown Playhouse. Then some of these people or their friends retired to live on the Cape, and a small informal network of older radicals began to develop. During the sixties some younger writers, artists, and academics started vacationing in the area, and they blended in with the older crowd. The result is a certain amount of political activity around things like collecting money for civil liberties cases, publishing articles in Cape Cod newspapers on political prisoners, and supporting decent candidates in the local elections.

A lot of my political and social activities since leaving the Party have revolved around the Veterans of the Abraham Lincoln Brigade. I was active in the VALB briefly when I returned from Spain and then for a couple of years in the late forties while I was on the National Board, but until the end of 1957, the Party absorbed most of my time. When I returned to New York in late 1957, the Vets had a secretary but no committee of any kind. We were still on the attorney general's list of subversive organizations, and we decided to involve as few people as possible in the actual leadership, fearing that the whole executive committee might end up in prison. Moe Fishman took the responsibility of guiding the organization, occasionally calling a group together to collect money for Spanish political prisoners, lick stamps, and make collective decisions about the organization's policies.

I felt a close kinship with the other vets, not only because we had fought together, but also because of their continuing loyalty to one another. During the Smith Act trials they were among the first to come to our aid. They set up a committee to defend Irving Weissman, John Gates, Bob Thompson, Saul Wellman, and all the other vets among the defendants.

We had two main activities during the late sixties and early seventies. First, we tried to get the VALB off the list of subversive organizations that the attorney general's office had compiled in the early 1950s. This struggle lasted about twenty years and took the form of a long court battle. We had to raise money for legal expenses and try to publicize the case. It was our efforts to aid Spanish political prisoners, though, that consumed most of our energies. At the time the vets were the only American group helping the Spanish political prisoners. An international prisoners' aid committee was set up in Paris, and they sent us news and lists of those in need. Each year the money we raised at our annual dinner, usually around $20,000, was sent to prisoners or their families. We also protested U.S. recognition and support of the Franco regime by organizing demonstrations and petition campaigns and by visiting individual congressmen, but the cold war still charged the political atmosphere. Most people chose to ignore the fact that the United States supported a fascist dictatorship, and we remained a voice in the wilderness.

It was difficult to carry on much of this sort of work with the handful of vets who were active in the fifties, so we began holding national conventions in an effort to bring more people into the activities. Local posts functioned in San Francisco, Los Angeles, Chicago, Detroit, Cleveland, Philadelphia, and a couple of other cities as well as in New York, where we have our headquarters. In 1963 I was elected national commander of the VALB, a post I have held ever since. Aside from representing the organization at meetings and conferences, I write for our newsletter, help to plan our annual dinner and other affairs, and talk about the Spanish Civil War wherever we're invited to speak. In recent years I have been a little less active because of my health and other practical problems, but the group remains my primary interest aside from my family.

During the sixties the VALB grew and really came alive as a result of the changing political situation in the United States and Spain. Here the growth of the civil rights movement and the struggle against the war in Vietnam drew in a lot of people who had disappeared for one reason or another during the fifties. Often men were reminded of their own pasts and ideals when their children became radicals. Once these comrades became active again, the VALB was a natural focal point for their interest. In Spain the broadening struggle for democratic reforms has rekindled the hope that the goal for which we fought and died in the thirties might yet be achieved.

The civil rights movement probably seemed like a real explosion to most Americans, a giant movement that came from nowhere. That it occurred at all did not surprise me, though I did not envision the size and form of the struggle. The Party had from its earliest days emphasized the fight against racism as one of its most important tasks. This activity was but a part of a larger movement around civil rights that existed long before the sixties. Having lived in a black community for many years and having read the *Pittsburgh Courier* and other black publications, I sensed a real change taking place in black consciousness from the 1940s on. One indication of this came in the struggle to integrate the Highland Park pool. The Pittsburgh District Committee of the Party initiated the action, but the campaign received broad-based support within the black community. The ground-swell of black sympathy suggested a developing militancy. Another indication of an emerging black consciousness was the general failure of McCarthyism to catch on in the black community. Organizations like the NAACP might have had their own little purges, but most Pittsburgh blacks consistently ignored the red-baiting, and this suggested a much keener political awareness than that shown by most whites.

My own involvement in the civil rights movement was minimal. I tried to support it in any way I could and to influence those around me, but I didn't see a role for me beyond that. The wonderful thing about the movement was that it had reached the level where common black people led the fight themselves. They didn't need anyone to tell them they could win or even how to go about it. Civil rights activists advanced the strategy of nonviolent civil disobedience. That and the tremendous spirit at civil rights marches and demonstrations made you feel that this was a movement destined for success.

The movement against the war in Vietnam was comparable to the civil rights movement in this respect. The Communist Party was active, of course, and individual Communists made important contributions within their own communities. But the Party was only one of dozens of groups that helped to mobilize people, and its role was minor.

The Vets were active in the antiwar movement almost from the beginning. The movement was the greatest thing to happen in the United States for a long time because it forced Americans to take another look at the whole system under which they lived. Unfortunately, this reassessment had to come out of a terrible criminal action like the war in Vietnam. Vietnam was like other imperialist wars, but the movement against it reached unprecedented proportions. The government always had a problem in convincing Americans that they had anything at stake in the conflict, and the protracted nature of the war tried the patience of even the most "loyal" Americans. But the most important factor in the disillusionment was simply that Americans saw this war much more clearly than they had seen any other; the whole bloody mess was played out before them on their television screens. Everyone in America saw the little girl running down the road with her clothes burned off by napalm. A constant stream of stories about massacres made people wonder: "Did my son have anything to do with this sort of thing?" With Americans so conscious of what was happening, it was only a matter of time until they turned against the war.

I went with Bill Lawrence, Morry Calow, Moe Fishman, and others to all of the meetings of the New York Peace Council as a delegate from the VALB. It was at these meetings during the late sixties that I came into contact with elements of the New Left. I was heartened by the involvement of thousands of young people in a movement that was not simply a "peace movement," as important as that goal was to all of us, but also a movement against American imperialism. As I watched huge crowds of people fill the streets, marching and chanting, my thoughts often drifted back to the thirties. I sometimes thought that perhaps things *were* changing, and that the spirit of the movement was alive once again.

Robert Colodny, a Spanish vet who teaches history at the University of Pittsburgh, wrote a pamphlet called *Spain and Viet Nam* that linked the antiwar movement to the cause for which we had fought in the thirties. The VALB published the pamphlet and sold more than twenty thousand copies, including some that were smuggled into Spain.

But the generation gap was real enough, even on the Left. The policies that Bill, Morry, and I fought for within the Peace Council were noticeably different from those advanced by some New Left groups.

One problem was Left extremism. One person, for example, collected money to buy guns for the Black Panthers. I thought the idea was crazy. That kind of policy would have wrecked the movement, whittled it down to a few sectarian splinters with little or no influence. The strength of the antiwar movement was that it had a potential for reaching the vast majority of the American people. We argued for policies that would broaden rather than narrow its appeal to common people, not just self-styled revolutionaries. For example, as much as we admired the young people who made up the bulk of the movement, it seemed essential to get labor support. We tried to get the council to build better contacts with the labor movement. Few really opposed the idea, but the attitude seemed to be "O.K., if you think you can do it, go ahead." In fact, we did help to turn out quite a few more trade unionists at demonstrations and meetings.

Another problem came in mixing up issues that were better approached independently. I certainly supported the struggle for Puerto Rican independence, for example, and any one of a dozen other issues of vital concern that were raised at the Peace Council meetings. But I felt it was important to keep attention focused on the war. To bring in a whole range of issues would obscure the central one and might isolate the movement from potential allies.

Ironically, the Vets, who were the original "premature antifascists" and had been branded un-American and persecuted since their return from Spain, were often the only group in antiwar demonstrations who carried the American flag. I still remember a young fellow with flowing hair and a National Liberation Front flag at one of the marches in Washington who came up to ask us which side we were on. We laughed and assured him that we were as much against the war as he was.

All the differences were not political, although they might evolve into political differences. The New Left had a tendency to blend its "counterculture" with its politics, and it sometimes seemed to me that the latter was considered the least important. Their behavior and appearance sometimes turned off people who might otherwise have been sympathetic to their ideas. Often when I saw young people in ragged or dirty clothes, I was bewildered. Whenever I was working in a shop I couldn't stand being covered with all that grease and dirt, but often there was no choice. There was usually no place to clean up, so you had to walk home in your filthy clothes. I still remember the little tub and stove that I installed in my room in Philly so that I could at least go to bed clean. I suppose that the whole hippie trip was in some sense an act of rebellion for young people in the sixties, but it was beyond my comprehension.

In the past few years the New Left and I have both changed. Some people whom I suspected of being frivolous are still around, working hard in the labor movement, the ecology movement, or with some other issue. On the other hand, some of the ultramilitants of the sixties and early seventies have repented and joined the establishment. The fact that a large number of young people who built the antiwar movement remained active, some as socialists, forced me and other older radicals to take their politics more seriously. I still think some of the New Left's tactics are mistaken, but I admire their commitment. And some of the issues they have raised have changed the Left for good.

Some groups are really not of the New Left at all, because they embrace many of the worst aspects of the Old. Within the last few years, a handful of Marxist-Leninist "vanguard" groups has sprung up. Digging through the old Marxist texts for their revolutionary blueprints, they have selected ideas and organizational models reminiscent of the 1920s. But their political programs and day-to-day organizing have little relevance to the American working class or today's political realities. I have spent hours explaining the structure and function of the Party's "shop nuclei" in factories during the twenties to young people from places like Harvard and MIT. I'm happy to do it. But what's the point? The country and the working class have changed enormously since then, and this seems to call for different methods.

But the problem is deeper than a poor choice of strategies. It seems significant that it is the most sectarian period of Communist history and the narrowest aspects of Party policies and practices in which some young radicals are interested. They have picked up the worst of the bookish interpretations of Marxism-Leninism, interpretations that held us back for years from being as effective as we might have been, and they are going ahead without regard to how much things have changed since either Marx or Lenin was around. Apparently unable to see the weaknesses in the past one hundred years of American radicalism, they seem doomed to repeat its mistakes.

I also question whether the idea of "colonizing," sending Party members into a particular neighborhood or industry to organize, is as applicable today as it once was. Many Communists were successful organizers because they were a vital part of the communities in which they lived and worked. Most of these people were recruited and trained in their own communities and then spent most of their lives there, working among their neighbors.

It's true that the Party did sometimes send what it called "professional revolutionaries" into a particular industry or community. This is essentially what Margaret and I were doing during the twenties and thirties. But there was a crucial difference between the way this was done then and the way in which it seems to be done now. Then one was almost always going somewhere to support an existing group of indigenous radicals, not to build a mass movement from scratch. There were always sympathetic people willing to help, and they provided the critical contacts within the community and among rank and file workers. Without such contacts organizing is impossible, regardless of how long one studies Lenin.

Another critical difference between the strategy then and now lies in the social background of the two generations of "colonizers." Nearly all the Communists involved in this sort of work came from working-class backgrounds. They had only to shift from one blue-collar job to another or from one immigrant community to another. Many of the young radicals trying to colonize today come from backgrounds vastly different from those of the workers they seek to organize. Most are from middle-class families and have good educations. This does not mean that is impossible for them to become part of a working-class community, or even that they should not try. But the transition will be much more difficult than it was for people like

Margaret and me. It will require a long-range perspective and all the patience they can muster.

Young, well-educated radicals can make important contributions to a working-class movement inside as well as outside of the factory. If young people go into industry really committed to staying and have long-range and realistic perspectives on what they hope to achieve, they can make a difference. It's not a matter of trying to "take over" a union local but rather of trying to help someone who may be there already. For a long time you may be involved with economic problems and trying to have the union run honestly and democratically. Eventually it might be possible to raise issues of broader political significance, perhaps legislative fights around issues like national health insurance, ecology, or the nationalization of specific industries. Some contact with industrial workers is vital if a socialist movement is to grow, and this is especially important in the United States, where so much of the Left is composed of students and professionals. But the notion of leaving Harvard to make the revolution in a small Boston electronics plant is misguided. Good people are wasting a lot of valuable time.

The main point, however, is that American society has changed so much that this problem of "planting roots" in the factories is not as critical as it was in the old days. In the fifties, while I was still in the Party, I was shocked to discover that there were almost as many white-collar workers in the steel industry as blue collar. White-collar workers are even more important, of course, in many other industries. Even college-educated workers now share many of the grievances of blue-collar workers, and so they have much more in common with them than they once had. Often the line between white collar and blue comes within one generation of the same family. Any socialist movement that wants to develop a broad base of support will have to keep these changes in the structure of the working class in mind.

In spite of some reservations, I have to admire the New Left and its contributions. Perhaps the most important of these is the focus on the issue of women's rights, not just as a problem in capitalist society but within the movement itself. By comparison with most organizations at the time, the Party of the thirties and forties had a good understanding of some of the difficulties facing women. There was a lot of talk and some good demands generated around issues like equal pay for equal work and the need for child care. But there was a minimum done in practice. This includes the relations between men and women in the Party and women's role in the organization. Women were not consistently treated as equals, and there was certainly discrimination in making assignments. Women seldom advanced to the top leadership posts. Photos of the Central Committees of the American and most other parties show only an occasional female face among the crowd of men. Male Communists came out of a male-dominated society, and they carried many of their prejudices into the Party with them. Whatever the reasons, the problem never got the attention it should have.

Young people have made the issue come alive. Part of the explanation, I think, lies in the civil rights movement. In the struggle to achieve equality for blacks, women came to understand better their own inferior status and also saw that the situation could be overcome. The New Left owes a lot to the civil rights movement in general, but I think the connection is particularly close in the case of the women's movement.

Even those aspects of the New Left with which I am a little impatient, like the loose organizational structure of some groups, may turn out to be contributions in the long run. It was in part our mechanical discipline, after all, that allowed us to become uncritical of the Soviet Union and helped to isolate us from other Americans. Tight discipline enabled us to be effective far beyond our numbers and to accomplish all sorts of good work, but it also made us more vulnerable to Stalinism.

Fighting for change in a hostile society, a Marxist movement needs a sense of internal discipline and responsibility as well as strong solidarity. But the ability to evolve, to see the need for change and respond to it, is just as important. The Left in the United States remains weak and fragmented, but the New Left has pushed it to reconsider some of its traditional ideas, and this is good.

After the 1956–1957 crisis, my own political evolution came slowly. For a decade after my decision to leave the Party, I retained some of my admiration for the Soviet Union. It was not an abstract sort of bond but was built on a recognition of the Soviet Union's historic importance in two respects: it was the first country in which an effort was made to replace capitalism with a socialist society, and more than any other nation, it helped to smash fascism, the greatest political evil the world has ever known. No progressive-minded person can underestimate the importance of these two contributions. The revelations of 1956 forced me to see that the American Party had to make a break, but they did not make me lose all faith in the Soviet Party. This final political and emotional break came with the invasion of Czechoslovakia in 1968.

Here there were none of the complications that muddied the picture in Hungary. The movement that was crushed in Czechoslovakia projected a more democratic version of socialism than the Soviet model. In fact, it was the sort of movement that I felt was needed. It was autonomous from the Soviet Union but maintained its support for all socialist countries; it was militant but attempted to broaden its base of support by appealing to the whole population and not just to Party members; and it allowed political and cultural democracy. The Soviets' decision to arbitrarily intervene in the internal life of another socialist country, to crush all semblance of democracy and compel changes in the leadership of a fraternal party by military force, proved that the Soviet Party had not been purged of Stalinism. Stalinism was more than the mentality of one maniac; it was a product of an essentially undemocratic system.

I also object to the treatment of minority and cultural dissidents. I don't agree with some of their ideological views, but their cases demonstrate the continuing repression in Soviet society. The handling of Solzhenitsyn, for example, has created a cultural monster. They delivered him into the arms of American capitalism at the most opportune moment, and he has become the hero of free enterprise. He'll continue to pollute the atmosphere for years to come.

The Czechoslovak crisis had positive as well as negative results. It provided the final break for many Communists in the United States and throughout the world. Perhaps more than any other single event, the invasion encouraged the growth of more autonomous and democratic Communist parties in Western Europe and elsewhere. In the United States, the crisis caused many of the best people who were still in the Party to rethink their positions and lend their support to the democratic socialist movement that is developing in America today.

But on balance it is the credibility of socialism that pays the price for the Soviet actions. For most people, socialism is what happens in China, the Soviet Union, and Eastern Europe, and that includes political and cultural repression. People don't forget things like the Soviet invasions of Czechoslovakia and Afghanistan or China's invasion of Vietnam. For many socialism means totalitarianism and war. One of the main tasks of any American Left movement is to present a much more constructive and democratic image of socialism, to divorce the ideology from the national interests of any one country and to show how the system could function democratically in the United States.

In Spain the political atmosphere also changed over the last two decades. Throughout the forties and for much of the fifties, the Spanish Communist Party (PCE) kept up a guerrilla war against Franco. Small groups of partisans in the mountains and other desolate areas fought engagements with Franco's troops, and even in the cities the cause was kept alive through underground activity. The Spanish Party paid a terrible price for this campaign, especially since it seemed to have little chance of destroying the dictatorship.

Around the time I left the Party and became active with the Vets once again, the PCE changed its strategy from one of direct confrontation to one of "reconciliation." The reconciliation was not with the dictatorship itself; it was with the many Spaniards who had fought with the fascists during the Civil War but now might favor democracy. The PCE declared that the current struggle should be based on contemporary issues rather than old loyalties shaped by the conflicts of the thirties. The new policy freed rank and file Communists to join and organize within the fascist unions and other state-sponsored organizations. Reconciliation brought Communists back into the mainstream of Spanish life and allowed them to forge those alliances that finally led to the downfall of the dictatorship and the introduction of democratic reforms.

At first the change was very hard to take, especially for those of us who had seen comrades die under the fascist guns. But eventually the meaning of the new strategy became clear: this was the only chance to build a mass-based democratic opposition movement. It was essential that the Party be with the workers, even if this meant joining the fascist trade unions.

Within a couple of years, the new policy began to bear fruit. We heard about the *comisiones de obreros* (workers' commissions), loosely organized groups in various industries that pressed employers for concessions and maintained shop floor organizations to fight for better conditions. Soon the government found them extremely difficult to control because they gained the support of the majority of the workers wherever they appeared. The leaders were often not Communists at all but simply militant rank and file unionists.

If a contract was negotiated by the fascist union over the objections of the workers, trouble would start. The union, knowing it had the power of the state behind it, would refuse to budge, but when the employer wanted to start production the next morning, everybody stood with their arms folded. They claimed that they were not violating the law, because they did not walk out. The effect, of course, was the same—no work. Such stoppages often spread, and management was forced to call in stewards from the workers' commission and to make concessions. The strikes greatly increased the power and prestige of the commissions and produced, in effect, an alternative trade union structure that was militant and democratic.

Comparable organizations surfaced in other sectors of Spanish society. In the ten years before Franco's death, more universities were hit by strikes in Spain than in any other European country, with the exception of Italy and France during 1968.

This upsurge in mass activity in Spain, paralleling the emergence of the civil rights and peace movements in the United States, renewed American interest in the struggle for Spanish democracy and reinvigorated the VALB. We stepped up our drive for amnesty for all of Franco's political prisoners and placed pressure on the State Department once again. When I took a young Catalan lawyer to lobby in the early sixties, we found the political atmosphere in Washington was quite different from what it had been a few years earlier. Some congressmen were quite receptive, and gradually the pressure on Franco's regime began to build.

Most of our energies during the sixties went into the antiwar movement here at home, but we continued to follow events in Spain and to help the struggle in every way possible. We worked with the Committee for a Democratic Spain and met in New York with a number of Spaniards, including a journalist and some Spanish airline workers, to discuss the most recent developments.

In 1968 ten leaders of the workers' commissions, the Carabanchel group, were arrested and sentenced to a total of 180 years in prison in an obvious attempt to slow the tremendous growth of the organizations. With the people from the Committee for a Democratic Spain, we helped to set up a number of fund-raising events to help pay for the legal costs of appealing the case and efforts to publicize it internationally. We worked with a young Spanish film maker who was doing a documentary on the American reaction to the Carabanchel case and were able to compile a long list of prominent Americans, including Paul O'Dwyer of the New York City Council and Bishop Daugherty of Newark, who issued statements condemning the frame-up. For me, one of the most gratifying of these statements was the one sent in by Monsignor Charles Owen Rice of Pittsburgh, who had been an important leader in the red-baiting there during the fifties. He attacked the trial as a violation of human rights and admitted the Church had been wrong in its pro-Franco stand during the civil war. With the help of Henry Foner of the Fur and Leather Workers Union, a trade union committee to support the Carabanchel unionists was set up. Two delegations, one headed by Paul O'Dwyer and the other by former Attorney General Ramsey Clark, attended the trial and reported on what they saw. Each delegation included a number of trade unionists. Henry organized a press conference in Madrid at which

Ramsey Clark commented on the legal peculiarities of the trial. The conference was a breakthrough of sorts because meetings of more than nineteen people were outlawed in Spain, and there were nearly thirty people at the conference. The police did nothing. The most important developments, of course, involved the Spanish people themselves and their opposition to the trial, but in a small way we helped to focus international attention on what was happening. This international pressure was at least partly responsible for the release of the Carabanchel group shortly after Franco's death in 1975.

My work with the Committee for a Democratic Spain brought me into contact with several young Spaniards, and it was in discussions with them that I first learned of the changes in the policies and theory of the Spanish Communist Party that have come to be called Eurocommunism. My young Spanish film maker friend told me the story of a meeting between Brezhnev and Santiago Carrillo, general secretary of the PCE. The Spanish Party was in the midst of a fund-raising drive to transform their underground paper, *Mundo obrero,* into a legal daily newspaper as soon as conditions permitted.

"Where will you print it," Brezhnev asked, "Paris?"

"No," Carrillo said, "in Madrid. We're looking for a building now."

Surprised, Brezhnev asked if there was anything he could do to help.

"No, comrade, thank you. We are going to launch the paper with Spanish money and show a receipt for every contribution. This will be a message to the Spanish people that we are going through a major political change and that we want their help."

The story demonstrates the PCE's determination to become a major political force in Spain and chart its own course.

I was elated because the more I heard of developments in Spain, the more I realized that the same ideas which some of us had projected in the American Party in 1956–1957 were now becoming a strong force in the international Communist movement. In Spain the PCE's growing involvement in the new trade unions, its organizational strength, and its evolving critique of orthodox Marxism-Leninism all seemed to reinforce one another.

The political changes in Spain and the growing struggle against Franco made me hope that perhaps one day we could return to a free and democratic Spain. The first breakthrough was when Franco died toward the end of 1975. It's one of the few deaths I can think of that actually made me and a lot of other people happy. I got calls from friends around the country, "Hey, did you hear? The old bastard finally kicked the bucket—isn't it great?" In 1978 my dream came true.

The PCE held its first open convention in Spain since the civil war. Bill Susman, Saul Wellman, and I were invited as visitors representing *Viewpoint,* which is put out by a group predominantly composed of former Party people, some of them Spanish veterans, who are searching for a new democratic movement for socialism in the United States. Margaret and Bill's wife Helene came with us.

In spite of the fact that I was thrilled to be going back to Spain, I had real reservations about the trip. I didn't want the spotlight taken off the convention and put on the returning International Brigade veterans. Also, I didn't realize just how much things had changed already, and I was afraid that our presence would somehow jeopardize the position of the Spanish Left. Happily, my fears were completely unfounded. There was still strong evidence of the Franco rule. The police, army, and many of the old local administrations were still there. But the Franco Right was overwhelmingly defeated in the first free election held in forty years.

Nobody checked our bags or gave us any trouble at the airport, in spite of the fact that they knew we had come for the PCE convention. Police with machine guns could still be seen everywhere, but they did not bother us. We were met by Carlos Torro, who had been the twenty-seven-year-old political commissar of the Thirty-Fifth Division, of which the Lincolns were a part at the time of the battle at Brunete. He had addressed a mass meeting of troops including the Washington and Lincoln battalions on July 4, 1937, the day before the battle began. The fighting was so intense for the next twenty-eight days that I don't think I ever saw him again. After Franco's victory Torro was sentenced to death. Following a heroic effort on the part of his seventeen-year-old wife, his sentence was first commuted to life and later to thirty years, of which he served twenty-four. When he came out of prison, he met his twenty-three-year-old son for the first time. I had the pleasure of meeting the three of them at the first May Day meeting in Madrid in 1978. Carlos showed me sixteen hundred letters that his wife wrote him while he was in prison. He read us a letter he wrote to her at the time he thought he was about to be shot. In it he told her to be brave, to go on living a worthwhile life, to "marry a good man." It ended with love and "Salud, my dear." He called my attention to the fact that "my hand did not shake," which he said in the English he had learned in prison. In the following days we met dozens of Spaniards who'd spent most of their adult lives in jail. They had now emerged to take part in the struggle for Spanish democracy.

The convention drew delegations from around the world. Included

Steve Nelson with former political prisoners in Madrid, May Day, 1978.

were Soviet representatives, who said they had come "to listen and to learn." There were only five parties not represented, among them the American Party. Not a single foreign delegate spoke.

The convention suggested how much the PCE had changed. Throughout the years of the dictatorship, it had continued to function underground. Montero, the head of the Party in Madrid, ran the organization from an apartment building next door to a police station, with two nuns acting as links in the underground network. Stories abound of thousands of leaflets being distributed, seemingly from nowhere. By the time Franco died there were 110,000 Party members. In the two years between his death and the PCE convention, the Party doubled its size and broadly expanded its social base. Most of the delegates I saw at the convention were young (a majority had been born since the civil war), and a good proportion were professionals or intellectuals. My old Spanish comrades told me that because of the rapid growth of the Party, the most critical need now was in the field of political education, and many of the older, more experienced leaders have gone into this work.

What is most impressive about the Spanish Communists is their ability to put the tremendous bitterness and hardship of the civil war and their subsequent imprisonment and torture aside in the broader interests of the fight for democracy. Few objected to the break with the old-style Marxism-Leninism. I asked about the Party's decision to accept the Monarchist flag rather than insist that the Republican flag be adopted. A Communist who had spent more than twenty years in jail described how he had had to argue with his own family to accept the decision. They had kept an old flag folded up, and they unfurled it when he returned home. Now they refused to give it up. "What is it?" he asked. "A piece of cloth. The important thing is to move forward. Will we let a piece of cloth slow down the struggle?"

The revitalization of the PCE and the trade unions has been paralleled by a tremendous growth of the Socialist Party in Spain. It too has emphasized the necessity for unity in the struggle for Spanish democracy.

My return to Spain in the spring of 1978 and what I saw there made me more confident than ever that a strong, democratic Marxist movement is growing throughout the world. The mass movements for social change here in the United States that were built up during the sixties have left a whole generation of radicals searching, as I am, for ways of bringing socialism to America. Many of the ideas that prompted me and other American Communists to leave the Party seem now to have been vindicated as other parties throughout the world adopt them and move into the mainstream of political life. It is the potential for such a movement to develop here in the United States, I believe, that makes my story and the story of the American Communist Party important. Every successful social movement must learn from those that precede it, from their achievements as well as their mistakes. For it is only upon these lessons that a new socialist movement can be built.

Notes

Index

Notes

Introduction

1. Estimates of CPUSA membership vary widely, ranging from Harvey Klehr's conservative 350,000 to Vivian Gornick's "more than a million." Harvey Klehr, *Communist Cadre: The Social Background of the American Communist Party Elite* (Stanford: Hoover Institute Press, 1978), p. 83; Vivian Gornick, *The Romance of American Communism* (New York: Basic Books, 1977), p. 23. See also Joseph Starobin, *American Communism in Crisis, 1943–1957* (Cambridge, Mass.: Harvard University Press, 1972), pp. 21, 247; David Shannon, *The Decline of American Communism: A History of the Communist Party of the United States Since 1945* (Chatham, N.J.: The Chatham Bookseller, 1959), pp. 91–92.

2. Klehr, *Communist Cadre*, pp. 4, 83; Nathan Glazer, *The Social Basis of American Communism* (New York: Harcourt, Brace, 1961), p. 101.

3. In July 1933 the Party was still 70-percent foreign-born (Glazer, *Social Basis of American Communism*, pp. 99, 101). On the overwhelmingly immigrant base of the Party in this period, which its leaders viewed as a serious recruitment problem, see Glazer, ch. 2 and Klehr, *Communist Cadre*, pp. 20–22.

4. Glazer, *Social Basis of American Communism*, pp. 99–100, 174–75; Klehr, *Commmunist Cadre*, pp. 22–23, 57; Nell Irvin Painter, *The Narrative of Hosea Hudson: His Life as a Negro Communist in the Deep South* (Cambridge, Mass.: Harvard University Press, 1978), pp. 13–26; Roy Rosenzweig, "Organizing the Unemployed: The Early Years of the Great Depression, 1929–1933," *Radical America,* 10 (July–August 1976):37–60; Frances Fox Piven and Richard A. Cloward, *Poor People's Movements: Why They Succeed, How They Fail* (New York: Vintage Books, 1979), ch. 2; and Bert Cochran, *Labor and Communism: The Conflict That Shaped American Unions* (Princeton: Princeton University Press, 1977), pp. 43–81.

5. Piven and Cloward, *Poor Peoples' Movements,* pp. 75–76; Albert Prago, "The Organization of the Unemployed and Role of the Radicals, 1929–1935" (Ph.D. diss., Union Graduate School, 1976), pp. 254–59; Cochran, *Labor and Communism,* pp. 96–97; Starobin, *Communism in Crisis,* pp. 35–37; Kenneth Waltzer, "The Party and the Polling Place: American Communism and an American Labor Party in the 1930s," *Radical History Review,* 23 (Spring 1980):104–29.

6. For a thorough analysis of the domestic impact of the cold war, see David Caute, *The Great Fear: The Anti-Communist Purge Under Truman and Eisenhower* (New York: Simon and Schuster, 1978).

7. Maurice Isserman, "The 1956 Generation, An Alternative Approach to the History of American Communism," *Radical America,* 14 (March–April 1980):48–49; Starobin, *Communism in Crisis,* pp. 224–28; Columbia University Russian Institute, *The Anti-Stalin Campaign and International Communism* (New York: Columbia University Press, 1956); Shannon, *Decline of American Communism:* ch. 10; *Proceedings of the 16th National Convention of the Communist Party, U.S.A.* (New York: Century, 1957).

8. Isserman, "The 1956 Generation," pp. 44–45. Irving Howe and Louis Coser, *The American Communist Party, A Critical History, 1919–1957* (New York: Praeger, 1962), from which the "malleable objects" quotation is taken (p. 506), is an example of the totalitarian interpretation, while James Weinstein's treatment of the Party in his *Ambiguous Legacy* (New York: New Viewpoints, 1975) is suggestive of the pick-and-choose approach.

9. These efforts include *The Volunteers* (New York: Masses and Mainstream, 1953), about Spain; *The 13th Juror* (New York: Masses and Mainstream, 1955), about his trial in Pittsburgh; and over one hundred pages of transcribed recollections about the anthracite region. Approximately seventy hours of transcriptions covering Nelson's life have been deposited in the Archives of Industrial Society, Hillman Library, University of Pittsburgh.

10. Isaac Deutscher, *The Prophet Unarmed: Trotsky, 1921–1929* (New York: Oxford University Press, 1959).

11. See Nell Irvin Painter's *Hosea Hudson,* cited above, which contains a bibliographical essay.

12. George Charney, *A Long Journey* (New York: Quadrangle Books, 1968), pp. 123, 126–27, 139, 250; Peggy Dennis, *The Autobiography of an American Communist, A Personal View of a Political Life, 1925–1975* (Westport, Conn.: Lawrence Hill, 1977), pp. 132–37; Nelson Lichtenstein, "Defending the No-Strike Pledge: CIO Politics During World War II," *Radical America,* 9 (July–October 1975):49–76; Ed Jennings, "Wildcat: The Wartime Strike Wave in Auto," ibid.:76–113; and Jeremy Brecher, *Strike!* (Boston: South End Press, 1972), pp. 221–26.

13. We paid for and received a substantial portion of the more than five thousand pages in Nelson's FBI files before deciding that the process of obtaining this material was simply too costly and time-consuming. Jessica Mitford's experience in trying to use the files as a source for her autobiography was equally frustrating: see *A Fine Old Conflict* (New York: Knopf, 1975).

Chapter 1: From Subocka to Pittsburgh

1. On June 28, 1914, a young Serbian nationalist, Gavrillo Princip, acting with other members of the underground Union of Death society, assassinated Archduke Franz Ferdinand in Sarajevo, a Serbian town in the Austro-Hungarian Empire. The assassination set off a chain of events leading to the First World War.

2. Formed just after the dissolution of the First International in 1876, the SLP was a direct descendant of the International Workingmen's Association, the original American Marxist organization. After Daniel DeLeon (1852–1914) assumed intellectual leadership of the organization in the 1890s, the SLP followed an increasingly sectarian course and was badly split by the formation of the Socialist Party of America in 1901. The SLP continued to attract a number of left-wing socialists, however, particularly

among the foreign-born, and many of its members were among the revolutionaries who established the Communist Party in the period between 1919 and 1921.

3. Following the split in the Socialist Party over the issue of the Russian Revolution, two communist parties were formed in the United States in the fall of 1919. The Communist Labor Party drew most of its support from native-born radicals in the Midwest and Far West, while the Communist Party, the larger of the two groups, was based primarily on the foreign language federations of the Socialist Party. The two parties merged in 1921 as the Communist Party of America. An underground organization, the Communist Party launched a legal, public group called the Workers Party later in 1921. With the dissolution of the underground Communist Party of America in 1923, the Workers Party became the sole American Communist Party. During a reorganization in August 1925, this group changed its name to Workers (Communist) party and in 1929 to the Communist Party of the United States of America (CPUSA). For simplicity, we have used the latter name throughout.

4. The Croatian Fraternal Union (CFU), a national fraternal and beneficial organization, traces its origins to the Croatian Association established in 1894. A series of mergers involving this organization and several smaller groups produced the CFU in 1926. The CFU began offering sickness and death benefits as well as other forms of insurance shortly after its foundation. The group has maintained its national headquarters in Pittsburgh since its inception, and during the twenties its office was located in the North Side neighborhood that Nelson describes.

5. A dues checkoff system provided for automatic deduction of union dues from workers' pay envelopes. This arrangement guaranteed financial stability of the organization but also increased the distance between the union leadership and its rank and file. Union officers no longer had to collect dues from individual members, and this frequently meant an end to face-to-face contact.

6. The Slovenian National Benefit Society (SNPJ), formed in Chicago in 1904, was one of many "freethought" fraternal groups that thrived in various ethnic communities during the early twentieth century. Freethinkers generally opposed the pervasive influence of the clergy in immigrant cultures and emphasized the importance of education and other forms of self-improvement. Though primarily a beneficial organization providing death, disability, and other forms of insurance at reasonable rates, the association also advised immigrants in other areas and provided a focus for the cultural life of the Slovenian-American community.

7. 'Wobblies" was a popular name for the Industrial Workers of the World, a federation of revolutionary industrial unions formed by Socialists and other labor activists in Chicago in 1905 as an alternative to the conservative AFL craft unions. Although strongest among western miners and migratory workers of all kinds, the IWW organized in almost every imaginable industry at one time or another. When the organization began disintegrating under government and right-wing repression during and after World War I, some of its members gravitated toward the newly developing Communist Party.

8. The American Federation of Labor, based on a craft union structure, had traditionally been unable to organize the unskilled and semiskilled workers of the mass production industries. Its failure to adopt an industrial union approach (i.e., organizing all the workers in an industry regardless of skill or other considerations) led to the formation of the Committee for Industrial Organization within the AFL. The committee, headed by UMWA president John L. Lewis, promoted industrial unionism and tried to win the AFL to that position. The AFL Executive Council firmly rejected the

concept and in August 1936 expelled the ten international unions that had comprised the committee. These unions formed a rival federation, the Congress of Industrial Organizations (CIO), which led most of the major organizing drives during the 1930s. The rival labor federations merged in December 1955 to form the AFL-CIO. The United Electrical Workers affiliated with the CIO at the union's founding convention in the fall of 1936.

9. The phrase "scientific management" was coined by Frederick Winslow Taylor (1856–1915) to describe his ideas for transforming the character of industrial work, though here the term is meant to describe a wide variety of management reforms including employee welfare measures like sickness and death benefits. The heart of the "Taylor System" was the reorganization of the work process into simpler operations requiring less skill and the application of time and motion studies to find "the one best way to do the job." In addition, Taylor developed piece rate systems that paid workers on the basis of the amount they produced rather than by the hour or the day. Scientific management or the Taylor system was widely used in metalworking shops and particularly in the electrical manufacturing industry throughout the early twentieth century and spread to many other industries in the course of the 1920s.

10. The Brotherhood of Sleeping Car Porters, an all-black union, was launched on August 25, 1925, in Harlem by A. Philip Randolph, an early black socialist, and other radicals and trade unionists. The union was a focal point for labor and political activity in the black community during the 1920s and 1930s when most AFL unions followed rigid policies of segregation and exclusion.

11. Jimmy Higgens was a mythical character meant to symbolize the thousands of rank and file activists who carried on the day-to-day work of the Socialist Party. Though the name was later used for a character in one of Upton Sinclair's novels, it was coined by Ben Hanford, the Party's vice-presidential candidate in the 1904 election.

12. William Z. Foster (1881–1961) was a brilliant labor organizer in his early years but spent most of his life as a top Communist Party functionary. He began work at the age of ten after only three years of schooling and worked at a variety of jobs including steam engineer, steamfitter, railroad brakeman, fireman, and car inspector, salesman, streetcar motorman, and longshoreman. After being expelled from the Socialist Party in 1909 as a syndicalist, he joined the IWW, which he left two years later to found the Syndicalist League of North America. The latter organization and another, the International Trade Union Educational League, formed in 1917, were both short-lived but had considerable influence locally, particularly in Chicago.

From 1917 to 1919, Foster was the prime mover behind successful national drives to organize packinghouse and steelworkers. He led the unsuccessful national steelworkers' strike in 1919 and the following year established the Trade Union Educational League (TUEL), an independent organization of left-wing trade unionists, which he served as national secretary. He brought the TUEL under Communist influence when he joined the Party in 1921, following a trip to the first international congress of the Comintern and the Red International of Labor Unions (RILU). Foster ran as the presidential candidate on the CPUSA ticket in 1924, 1928, and 1932 and served as the Party's chairman from 1932 to 1957, at which point he retired.

Ella Reeve ("Mother") Bloor (1862–1951) became associated with the labor movement when she joined a local of the Knights of Labor. Active in the Women's Christian Temperance Union, then the Social Democracy of America and the Socialist Labor Party, Bloor joined the Socialist Party in 1902. A tireless organizer, she worked with striking miners from Pennsylvania to Colorado. She joined the Communist Party at its foundation in 1919 and served it as an organizer and spokeswoman for several decades.

Chapter 2: On the Line

1. His wife was Malvina Reynolds, the popular radical song writer and singer.

2. The TUEL was set up in late 1920 by William Z. Foster and other left-wing labor activists to organize radical pressure groups within the existing trade unions. The TUUL was its successor and operated as a national federation of revolutionary industrial unions founded under Communist leadership in September 1929. TUUL unions were formed in mining, steel, auto, and textiles where the AFL had given up on organizing, and in the needle trades and restaurant work, where the Party actually had a following among the rank and file. The TUUL unions reflected the Party's "class against class" line of the early 1930s. The TUUL was dissolved in March 1935 and many of those Communist workers who had helped to build it became active in the CIO organizing drives.

3. The United Automobile Workers (UAW) was in the forefront of the CIO movement of the late 1930s and had organized the auto industry by the end of the Second World War.

4. Shortly after the introduction of its assembly line system in 1914, the Ford Motor Company established its own Sociology Department with a staff of one hundred investigators. These "sociologists" went to workers' homes to determine whether family values and behavior were consistent with the company's goals of efficient production. Thus, Ford actively promoted individualistic values.

5. The Lenin School was founded in Moscow in 1926 as a training school for cadres from Communist parties throughout the world.

6. Although the Bolsheviks seized control of the Russian government in October 1917, they continued to face stiff internal resistance from various anti-Communist forces. This civil war lasted into the early 1920s.

7. For a description of the Save the Union movement, see pages 87–88.

8. Jay Lovestone (1898–   ) was born in Lithuania and educated at the City College of New York, New York University, and Columbia. Having worked as a social worker and a statistician, Lovestone was one of the Party's few intellectuals in its early years. After helping to establish the Communist Party of America in 1919, he was elected to its Central Committee and in 1927 succeeded Charles Ruthenberg as general secretary. He carried out an elaborate reorganization of branches in an effort to Americanize the Party and increase its effectiveness, particularly in industry, but he was denounced at the 1928 Comintern congress, removed from office, and in 1929 expelled from the Party. After trying to build up an opposition party in the 1930s, he turned his attention to fighting labor radicals, first as an adviser to various trade union officials and later, in the fifties and sixties, as chairman of the AFL-CIO's International Affairs Department. Here he worked closely with the Central Intelligence Agency (CIA) to undermine left-wing labor movements throughout the world.

9. A year-long textile workers' strike broke out in Passaic, New Jersey, over wage cuts in January 1926. The strikers were organized and led by a group called the United Front Committee of Textile Workers in which the TUEL was prominent. After the workers had been reorganized under the AFL's United Textile Workers, the employers restored the old wage, rehired all strikers, and agreed to recognize grievance committees. The strike was significant not only because it was successful but also because it was the first mass strike led independently by Communist trade union activists.

10. May 1, 1886, was designated by trade unions and labor reform organizations as the day on which workers would strike to win the eight-hour day. Although this was a

nationwide effort, the strikes were most successful in Chicago where eighty thousand workers took part.

11. Brookwood Labor College was founded at Katonah, New York, in 1921 by A. J. Muste, a minister, and other labor radicals as a training school for rank and file workers and trade union organizers.

12. The TUEL had its strongest base among garment and fur workers in New York City. After a series of bitter factional conflicts between Socialists and Communists in the International Ladies Garment Workers Union (ILGWU), the left wing, under TUEL leadership, won control of the key New York Joint Board in 1925. The following year the Communists led a disastrous strike that greatly weakened the union and reduced their own influence within it. Among the fur workers, however, a left-led 1926 strike was enormously successful, establishing the first forty-hour week in the industry and winning a 10 percent wage increase. This victory helped to ensure Party influence among fur workers for a generation to come.

13. In 1926 Augusto César Sandino launched a revolutionary movement against the presence of United States Marines and the elite-backed government that the Marines had been sent in to protect. Sandino was assassinated by a group of high-ranking National Guard officers with the tacit approval of their commander-in-chief, Anastasio Somoza García. With the support of the United States, Somoza became president-for-life in Nicaragua. His sons took over the position after his assassination. The Frente Sandanista de Liberación Nacional took both its name and its anti-imperialist, pro-peasant politics from Sandino and overthrew Anastasio Somoza Debayle in the summer of 1979.

14. The Conference for Progressive Political Action, a coalition of farmer and labor groups, met in July 1924 to establish the Progressive Party, which received the endorsements of the Farmer-Labor Party, the Socialist Party, and the AFL. The Progressives called for nationalization of railroads and hydroelectricity, an end to the use of the labor injunction, legal recognition of the right of farmers and workers to organize and bargain collectively, and other reforms. The Progressive Party did not field candidates, but Senator Robert M. LaFollette (1855–1925) ran independently with a similar program and finished third in the election with 4,822,856 votes, while Foster received only 33,361 running on the Workers (Communist) Party ticket. LaFollette had served as a congressman and governor of Wisconsin before being elected senator. He built his reputation on his advocacy of progressive measures such as direct primary elections, regulation of the railroads, and equal taxation of corporate property.

15. Earl Browder (1891–1973), general secretary of the CPUSA from 1934 to 1945, is best known for his emphasis on peaceful coexistence between the United States and the Soviet Union and his efforts to Americanize the image of the Party during the popular front era. Browder worked as a telegrapher from 1913 to 1917, when he was imprisoned for draft evasion. He served as a delegate to the first congress of the Red International of Labor Unions in 1921 and then as editor of the TUEL's *Labor Herald*. During the late 1920s, he worked for the Comintern, particularly in the Far East, and was elected to the Central Committee of the CPUSA in 1930. In 1936 Browder ran on the Communist ticket against Roosevelt. Worsening relations between the United States and the Soviet Union in late 1945 weakened Browder's position, and his policies were blasted by the Comintern. He was removed from leadership at the end of 1945 and expelled from the Party the following year. He lived out the remainder of his life in political obscurity.

16. Joe and Rose Jursak are fictitious names. Joe Jursak went on to organize miners in Harlan County, Kentucky, and later became an organizer for the CIO.

17. A plenum was an expanded meeting of the Party's National Committee to which trade union and district-level Party organizers were invited.

Chapter 3: Chicago and the Southern Illinois Coalfields

1. On May 4, 1886, in the wake of the great eight-hour strike, a bomb exploded in the midst of a large workers' rally at Haymarket Square in Chicago, killing seven policemen and wounding several others. The police then opened fire, and some of the people in the crowd shot back. In all, ten men were killed and fifty injured. Although the eight men charged with the bombing represented diverse political viewpoints, they were all labeled "anarchists." August Spies, Albert Parsons, Adolph Fischer, and George Engel were executed at the Cook County Jail on November 11, 1887. Oscar Neebe was sentenced to fifteen years in prison, while Michael Schwab and Samuel Fielden appealed to the governor and had their sentences changed to life imprisonment. An eighth defendant, Louis Lingg, became despondent and committed suicide during the trial. As a result of numerous irregularities and a general lack of evidence, Governor John Peter Altgeld unconditionally pardoned the survivors on June 26, 1893.

Eugene Victor Debs (1855–1926) was probably the most famous Socialist the United States has ever produced. He left school at the age of fifteen to work in a railroad enginehouse and later was a locomotive fireman. In 1880 Debs was elected grand secretary and treasurer of the Brotherhood of Locomotive Firemen (BLF) and also became editor of *Fireman's Magazine*. He resigned from these positions to begin organizing the American Railway Union (ARU), an industrial union that aimed to include every railroad worker in the country regardless of occupation or skill. In the summer of 1894, Debs led a national railroad strike in support of the workers at George Pullman's car works just south of Chicago. Federal troops were called in to help break the strike and with it the ARU, which declined quickly in the wake of the defeat.

Debs was instrumental in forming the Social Democracy of America (1897), the Socialist Party of America (1901), and the IWW (1905). He was sentenced to ten years in prison in 1918 for his antiwar speeches but was pardoned by President Harding three years later. A brilliant orator, Debs served as presidential candidate for the Socialists in 1904, 1908, 1912, and 1920, when he received more than a million votes while confined to Atlanta Penitentiary.

2. The Chicago Federation of Labor (CFL) established the Cook County Labor Party, one of the largest of the postwar local labor parties, in 1919 and was a leading force behind the formation of a national Farmer-Labor Party in the early twenties.

3. The Steel and Metal Workers Industrial Union (S&MWIU) was the dual revolutionary union for machinists and other metalworkers and an affiliate of the TUUL. Based largely on skilled workers in the electrical manufacturing industry, the union also led at least two important strikes in the steel industry, at Sparrow's Point, Maryland, and Ambridge, Pennsylvania, in the early thirties. After the formation of the CIO in 1936, many S&MWIU activists became organizers for both the United Electrical Workers (UE) and the Steel Workers Organizing Committee (SWOC-CIO). The Journeyman Tailors Union of America (JTUA) was established as an organization for custom tailors in August 1883, and it affiliated with the AFL four years later. By the early twentieth century, the JTUA was in decline as a result of the rise of ready-made clothing and competition from the United Garment Workers (UGW), the International Ladies Garment Workers Union (ILGWU), and the Amalgamated Clothing Workers of America (ACWA). In 1930 the JTUA, which maintained its headquarters in Chicago,

had only a few thousand members, and the organization had disappeared by the end of the decade.

4. At its Fifth Congress in February 1928, the Comintern declared that international capitalism had entered a third period in which its collapse was imminent. Within this context of heightened revolutionary expectations, Communists veered sharply to the left, distancing themselves from social-democratic movements, which they deemed "social fascist," as well as from the established trade unions. The shift to the new line included the creation of dual revolutionary unions linked internationally through the Trade Union Unity League (TUUL) to the Red International of Labor Unions (RILU). This sectarian line was not officially reversed until the Comintern's declaration of a Popular Front in 1936.

5. John Brophy (1883–1963) was born into a family of miners in Lancashire, England, and migrated to central Pennsylvania at the age of ten. At twelve years of age he was already in the mines, and by fifteen he was a member of the UMWA. He was president of the union's central Pennsylvania district and a leader in the opposition to John L. Lewis in the twenties. In the thirties, following a reconciliation with Lewis, Brophy was appointed director of organization for the CIO.

6. William D. "Big Bill" Haywood (1869–1928) was a leader of the Western Federation of Miners, the IWW, and the Socialist Party. He was expelled from the last organization in 1913 on charges of anarcho-syndicalism and then devoted all of his energies to the Wobblies. He was indicted along with other IWW leaders during the First World War and fled to the Soviet Union in the midst of the 1920 Red Scare. He died in Moscow.

7. The Progressive Miners of America (PMA) was established as an independent union by rank and file UMWA dissidents on September 1, 1939, at Gillespie, Illinois. Although confined to the Illinois coalfields, the PMA is the only one of numerous UMWA breakaways that continues to exist.

Chapter 4: The People of the Anthracite

1. The Women's International League for Peace and Freedom (WILPF), with sections in twenty-two countries and an international headquarters in Geneva, Switzerland, has existed since the early twentieth century. Through lobbying and educational work, it has campaigned for freedom and economic security. One example of the WILPF's work in the United States was its opposition to the presence of American troops in Nicaragua during the 1920s.

2. During the depression of the 1870s, anthracite miners suffered a series of wage cuts following the unsuccessful 1875 strike of the Miners National Association against the Philadelphia and Reading Iron and Coal Company. In the face of continued opposition to these cuts among Irish immigrant miners, the company hired a Pinkerton detective to act as a spy and agent provocateur within the Ancient Order of Hibernians, an Irish-American fraternal group suspected of labor agitation. In 1877, on the strength of highly contradictory testimony, twenty-four men, all acknowledged leaders among the miners, were charged with destroying company property and murdering mine foremen and company officials. All the men were convicted, and between 1877 and 1879, ten were hung. Although the prosecutor claimed the existence of a secret terrorist organization called the Molly Maguires, modeled on a similar group in Ireland, the defendants denied this charge to the end. The effect of the trial and executions was to break the resistance of the miners and temporarily end union organization in the anthracite fields.

3. Charles Edward Coughlin (1891–1979) was pastor of the Roman Catholic Shrine of the Little Flower in Royal Oak Michigan and became famous for his radio addresses during the 1930s. He used his radio show and magazine, *Social Justice,* to attack the nation's financial leaders for causing the Depression. His other targets included Franklin D. Roosevelt and the Jews. By World War II he was openly exhibiting sympathies for the Nazis that eventually led church and government authorities to silence him.

Huey Long (1893–1935) won wide support from workers and farmers in his campaign against vested interests. He built a powerful political organization in Louisiana where he was elected governor and then U.S. senator. An early FDR backer, he broke with the New Deal and offered his own "Share the Wealth" program as a prelude to the 1936 election, in which he planned to run as a third-party candidate. He was shot to death in September 1935, however, by the son-in-law of a political enemy.

4. The American Liberty League was set up in Washington, D.C., in August 1934 by a group of businessmen, notably DuPont Corporation and General Motors executives, hostile to Roosevelt and his New Deal policies. William Randolph Hearst, a pioneer in the "yellow journalism" of the 1890s and the early twentieth century, controlled thirty newspapers, two wire services, and six magazines by 1934. Between them the Liberty League and the Hearst chain of publications provided the main conservative bulwark against New Deal liberalism.

5. Rosa Luxemburg (1871–1919), Polish-born revolutionary Socialist, was a leader in first the Polish and then the German revolutionary movements. In the era of the First World War, she was one of the leading theoreticians in the German Social Democratic Party (SPD). She headed a faction within the Party that opposed its support for the German war effort and helped to form the Spartacus League as a revolutionary alternative. The League launched an ill-fated revolution in January 1919 in the wake of which Luxemburg and other Sparticist leaders were murdered by German soldiers.

6. Montenegro, a former kingdom north of Albania, is now a federated republic of Yugoslavia.

7. These are pseudonyms for individuals who might wish to remain anonymous.

Chapter 5: Two Years Abroad: 1931—1933

1. A majority of the SPD deputies in the Reichstag voted in favor of armaments bills and generally supported the German war effort. Most of the other national parties represented in the Second International also supported their governments during the First World War. This and the question of support for the new Bolshevik government in Russia helped to split most of the major parties into right and left wings, the former remaining in the Second International and the latter breaking away to join the new Communist Third International after the end of the war.

2. John Reed, radical journalist and a founder of the Communist Labor Party, wrote *Ten Days That Shook the World,* a vivid account of the Bolshevik seizure of power in October 1917, and *Insurgent Mexico,* a personal memoir of his days riding with Pancho Villa during the Mexican Revolution.

3. During the civil war that followed the Russian Revolution, the White Guards were military units that fought against the Red Army and people's militia for control of the country. By the early 1930s however, the term was used much more loosely to discredit any "antigovernment" elements.

4. Karlov is a fictitious name.

5. A soviet is the classic form of communist government based on elected councils

of workers, peasants, and soldiers. In 1931 a Chinese Soviet Republic was proclaimed in the Kiangsi-Hunan region with Mao Tse-tung as its chairman.

6. Chiang Kai-shek (1887–1975) was a Chinese military leader and the first constitutional president of the Republic of China (Taiwan). He joined the revolutionary Kuomintang, Sun Yat-sen's nationalist party, in 1918 and later gained total control of the organization. The Kuomintang worked with the Chinese Communists against the Japanese but also fought them both before and after the Chinese-Japanese War (1937–1945). Chiang was defeated by the Communists in the civil war of the late 1940s and fled to Taiwan where he ruled through an authoritarian government until his death.

7. Russians who opposed the Revolution and either fled or fought against it were commonly known as White Russians.

8. In late fall 1934, the Eighth Route Army, the Chinese Communist Party's main fighting force, set out on a six-thousand-mile journey from Kiangsi across the mountains and wastelands of western China to a new base camp at Shensi. Of the 130,000 who set out on the strategic retreat, fewer than 30,000 made it to Shensi. This epic Long March saved the Chinese Communist movement and provided inspiration for its cadres over the next generation of war and revolution.

Chapter 6: The Struggle of the Unemployed in the Anthracite

1. The Civil Works Emergency Relief Act, signed into law on February 15, 1934, authorized the allocation of $950 million in federal funds through the end of 1935 for direct relief grants and civil works grants to the states. The Works Progress Administration (WPA) was established to coordinate the public works projects, and by March 1936, 3.4 million unemployed were on its rolls. On August 14, 1935, the Social Security Act became law, providing for a cooperative federal-state system of unemployment compensation, federal grants for old-age and survivors' pensions, and state relief programs for the destitute, handicapped, homeless, crippled and dependent, and for delinquent children.

2. Louis Adamic, *My America, 1928–1938* (New York: Harper, 1938), p. 323.

3. Ibid.

4. With the end of the Jacksonville Agreement in early 1927, a strike broke out in the central bituminous coalfields. Though ostensibly over wage cuts, it was in effect a fight to save union recognition in the region. The heart of the movement was in eastern Ohio, western Pennsylvania, and northern West Virginia, and the Communist Party was particularly active in relief work and mass picketing in western Pennsylvania. In some areas the miners held out for more than a year, but the strike was eventually broken, its remnants providing a base for the Communist National Miners Union.

5. The Workers' Alliance, a nonpartisan national federation of unemployed organizations, was set up at Washington, D.C., in January 1935 by delegates from five hundred groups representing more than one hundred thousand members. David Lasser, a Socialist, was named chairman and Herbert Benjamin, the Communist national secretary of the unemployed councils, organizational secretary. Later the national unemployed councils merged with the Workers' Alliance. By 1937 the Alliance had sixteen hundred locals in forty-three states and represented a paying membership of about three hundred thousand. Pennsylvania's was one of the largest state organizations.

6. The National Labor Relations or Wagner Act (NLRA) was signed by President Roosevelt on July 5, 1936. It recognized the right of all employees to join labor organizations and bargain collectively through representatives of their own choosing, i.e., it provided legal sanction for the mass organizing drives of the 1930s. The act also

established the National Labor Relations Board to supervise collective bargaining elections, take testimony about unfair labor practices, and order recalcitrant employers to comply with the NLRA.

7. The Noble and Holy Order of the Knights of Labor was a labor reform organization founded by a small group of garment cutters in Philadelphia on December 28, 1869. The organization rejected the idea of wage labor and advocated producers' cooperatives, education, and labor politics as strategies for doing away with the wage system. The order grew quickly during the 1880s, reaching a high point of seven hundred thousand members during the agitation for the eight-hour day in 1886. By the end of the century, however, the Knights had shrunk to only a few thousand members as a result of depression conditions, internal conflicts, and competition from the new American Federation of Labor.

8. Georgi Dimitrov (1882–1949) joined the Bulgarian Social Democratic Party when he was twenty and became a leader of the Bulgarian Communist Party when it was formed in 1919. He gained worldwide attention when he was arrested in 1933 in connection with the burning of the German Reichstag. The trial was part of a Nazi attempt to discredit the German Communist Party (KPD). He defended himself at the trial and was acquitted. Dimitrov was active in the Comintern, an organizer of the Bulgarian resistance during World War II, and later head of the Bulgarian government.

9. Elizabeth Gurley Flynn (1890–1964) was the daughter of Irish republican revolutionaries and left high school at the age of sixteen to become a lecturer and organizer for the IWW from 1906 to 1916. She was active in the Wobblies' West Coast free speech fights from 1906 to 1909 and in the Lawrence, Massachusetts, and Paterson, New Jersey, textile workers' strikes in 1912 and 1913. She was indicted in 1917 in Chicago and later imprisoned along with other IWW leaders for her agitation against the First World War. In 1920 she was a founding member of the National Committee of the American Civil Liberties Union and was chairman of the ILD between 1927 and 1930. She joined the Communist Party in 1937 and was expelled from the ACLU for this membership in 1940. Imprisoned from 1955 to 1959 for her conviction under the Smith Act, she emerged from jail to become the first woman to be elected chairman of the Party's National Committee in 1961.

10. In 1931 nine young black men were tried in Scottsboro, Alabama, on charges of having raped two white women who had been riding with them on a freight train. Eight of the nine were sentenced to death and one to life imprisonment in a jury trial characterized by blatant racism. It took twenty years and a series of trials and appeals before all the defendants were freed. The "Scottsboro Boys" became a symbol for racial oppression in the South, and the Communist Party was instrumental in raising funds, providing legal help, and building public sentiment against the convictions.

Chapter 7: Civil War in Spain: 1937–1938

1. The beginnings of fascist rule in Italy date to 1922, when Benito Mussolini became the head of the government, and in Germany to 1933, when Adolf Hitler assumed power.

2. The Paris Commune, a government set up by radical workers and liberal reformers in the spring of 1871, proposed a democratization of the political system and sweeping social reform. The Commune was suppressed by the French armed forces in May 1871.

3. The Asturian and Basque provinces in the northwest of Spain were largely cut off from the central government of the Republic early in the civil war.

4. The Partido Obrero de Unificación Marxista (POUM) was formed in September 1935 when the Bloc Obrer i Camperol (BOC) fused with the Izquierda Comunista (IC). The IC was a Trotskyist split from the Spanish Communist Party (PCE), while the BOC was a dissident Communist party based in Catalonia.

5. The literature of the civil war in Spain is extensive and often quite partisan. A good deal of it concerns charges and countercharges about the personal activities of various people. In Jason Gurney's *Crusade in Spain* (London: Faber and Faber, 1974), the following is said about Steve Nelson:

> Steve Nelson, a big tough shipyard worker from Philadelphia, became Battalion Political Commissar.... He did not bunk with Marty and myself at the Battalion HQ dug-out but preferred to live up with No. 1 Company, so we saw comparatively little of him.... He never seemed to be very active and was frequently absent for several days at a time. However, looking back on it I think he must have been responsible for the mysterious disappearances of a number of people from among our ranks and for the secret trials, for real or imagined offences, which caused so much fear and suspicion within the Battalion. (P. 137)

If Mr. Gurney saw little of Nelson during his stay in Spain, it was because Gurney had left Spain before Nelson ever arrived. There were no political trials or executions of any kind during Nelson's tenure as commissar. Why Gurney made these charges is difficult to say. He offers no evidence other than personal observations that could not have occurred. When legal action was threatened against Faber and Faber, Gurney's publishers, they replied that references to Nelson were "highly defamatory" and that the book contained "two inaccurate and prejudicial statements" relating to his part in Spain (Charles Monteith, Chairman, Faber and Faber, to Steve Nelson, July 8, 1980).

Chapter 8: The West Coast: 1939–1945

1. Robert M. LaFollette, Jr., finished his father's unexpired Senate term upon his death in 1925. He was a progressive voice in the U.S. Senate until his defeat by Joseph McCarthy in 1946. In 1933 he headed a Senate subcommittee to investigate antilabor techniques used by employers to fight union organizing. The committee's report, published in December 1937, documented systematic blacklisting, espionage, vigilante terrorism, professional strikebreaking services, and private armies.

The ACLU, an organization devoted to defending the constitutional rights of American citizens, was established at New York City in 1920 with Roger Baldwin as its national chairman.

2. On the morning of October 1, 1910, the *Los Angeles Times* building was bombed and twenty people killed in the explosion. Two leaders of the Iron Workers Union, John and James McNamara, were charged and convicted in the case. Their trial drew national attention, with Clarence Darrow defending the brothers who, at the last minute, confessed they had planted the bomb in retaliation for the viciously antiunion policies of Harrison Gray Otis, the owner of the *Times*.

3. The ILWU traces its origins to the San Francisco general strike of July 1934. Dissatisfied by the conservative policies of the AFL's International Longshoremen's Association (ILA) and its failure to support the general strike as well as by a contract dispute at the end of 1936, the West Coast longshoremen's leadership led its members into the CIO in August 1937. Throughout its history the ILWU has had a left-wing leadership.

4. After a series of longshoremen's strikes in the spring and summer of 1934, followed by sympathy strikes by other workers and a violent reaction by city authorities, over 130,000 workers went out in a general strike in July 1934. Although the strike was finally defeated, control of the city hung in the balance for several days, and the strike had a radicalizing effect on the working-class population of San Franscisco.

Chapter 9: On the National Board, New York City: 1945–1948

1. The American Slav Congress was set up under the leadership of Louis Adamic, the Slovenian-American writer, as an umbrella group for Slavic-American fraternal organizations who wished to support the American war effort. Though a united front representing a broad spectrum of nationality groups and political views, the congress had its greatest support among South Slavs, and left-wing influence was strong.

The National Negro Congress (NNC) was organized in 1936 and consisted of more than three hundred organizations representing all segments of the black community. The congress was formed to present a unified activist response to racism. In 1940 many groups withdrew from the organization because of charges of Communist domination.

The National Citizens' Political Action Committee (NCPAC) grew out of the CIO's Political Action Committee (PAC) and was designed to mobilize middle-class support for labor and progressive causes.

2. In June 1945 Secretary of State George C. Marshall proposed that U.S. policy be directed toward rebuilding the shattered economies of Western Europe following the Second World War. In December President Truman submitted the $17-billion European Recovery Program to Congress which was enacted the following year. The Soviet Union contended that the Marshall Plan was primarily designed to ensure U.S. political hegemony and refused to take part in the program. In March 1947 President Truman called for the containment of Communist influence and pledged U.S. economic and military aid to right-wing forces in Greece and Turkey. The Senate formally endorsed this doctrine in April when it appropriated funds for the aid. The Truman Doctrine is generally acknowledged to be the cornerstone of America's cold war foreign policy.

3. The Taft-Hartley Act of 1947 was drawn up largely on the recommendations of the National Association of Manufacturers and was designed to severely curtail the power of labor unions. By defining a whole range of unfair labor practices, the act restricted the organizing and political activities of the labor movement. By requiring every union official to sign a non-Communist affidavit, the act also provided a legal basis for the purge of left-wing unions and individual labor leaders over the next several years.

4. Eugene Dennis (Francis Eugene Waldron, 1905–1961) joined the IWW at the age of fourteen and took part in the Seattle general strike of 1919. After working as an electrician, teamster, carpenter, lumberjack, and longshoreman, he joined the Communist Party in 1926, traveled to Russia at the end of 1930 where he attended the Lenin School, and worked for several years for the Comintern. Elected to the Party's National Committee in 1939, he rose to a position on the Central Committee in 1945 and was elected national chairman in 1959. Dennis served a total of more than five years in prison, first for contempt of Congress (HUAC) in 1947 and then from 1951 to 1955 for his conviction under the Smith Act.

5. Keynesian economics (from the British economic theorist John Maynard Keynes, 1883–1946) is a set of fiscal practices, such as government spending to revive purchas-

ing power, which has been used by the federal government to fight economic recession from the period of the New Deal on.

6. Largely as a result of the CPUSA's failure to recruit blacks during the 1920s, the Comintern's Sixth Congress in 1928 proposed a theory of national self-determination for American blacks. The theory was based on the Soviet Party's own policies toward national minorities and on the writings of Joseph Stalin. The CPUSA argued that in many areas of the South where they constituted a majority of the population, blacks were in fact an oppressed nation that should have the right to determine its future, including, if necessary, separation from the United States. In practice the theory had little appeal, and most blacks who joined the Party in the 1930s did so because of the Communists' militant struggle for civil rights and relief for the unemployed.

7. HUAC was formed in 1938 during a period of conservative domination of Congress. Under its chairman, Texas Democrat Martin Dies, it held hearings about the "international Communist conspiracy." Dies permitted witnesses to make charges against individuals and organizations without substantiating evidence and often refused to allow the accused a chance to reply. HUAC hearings frequently degenerated into a kind of witch-hunt, but the committee continued to hold them over the next three decades.

8. HUAC, "Hearings Regarding Communist Infiltration of the Radiation Laboratory and Atomic Bomb Project at the University of California, Berkeley," in *Hearings Before Committee on Un-American Activities,* House of Representatives, 81st Congress, 1st sess. (Washington, D.C.: U.S. Government Printing Office, 1949), April 22, 26; May 25; June 10, 14, 1949, and the foreword to this volume.

9. The American-Soviet Friendship Council grew out of the Friends of Soviet Russia, an organization set up in the early twenties to foster good will between the American and Soviet peoples.

10. In 1953 Julius and Ethel Rosenberg were executed for conspiring to commit espionage for the Soviet Union. They were alleged to have passed top-secret information about the atomic bomb to a Soviet agent in 1944–1945. The evidence and methods used by the prosecution have aroused a great deal of controversy. The judge was subsequently criticized for his partisan role in the case, and many reviews of the court record have concluded that the evidence was flimsy. The trial took place at the height of cold war hysteria and generated a worldwide effort, first to free the Rosenbergs, and later to save their lives. The case continues to stir debate.

11. Cedric Belfrage, *The American Inquisition, 1945–1960* (Indianapolis: Bobbs-Merrill, 1973).

Chapter 10: Pittsburgh: Under Attack

1. David Caute, *The Great Fear: The Anti-communist Purge Under Truman and Eisenhower* (New York: Simon and Schuster, 1978), p. 216.

2. The Joint Anti-Fascist Refugee Committee chairman, Dr. Edward K. Barksy, and several of the committee's board members were charged with and convicted of contempt of Congress for refusing to turn over the names of their contributors and the Spanish Republican refugees with whom they had contact. The Hollywood Ten were screenwriters and directors who refused to cooperate with HUAC investigations of the motion picture industry.

3. The two defendants who did not receive the maximum five-year sentence were Robert Thompson, who had been awarded the Distinguished Service Cross for his valor

in World War II and who was given three years, and William Z. Foster, who was severed from the trial because of his poor health.

4. The Association of Catholic Trade Unionists (ACTU), formed in 1937, promoted trade unionism but also acted as a conservative force within the labor movement, particularly the CIO, and militantly opposed all left-wing influence.

5. *Pittsburgh Press*, April 3, 4, 1949.

6. Americans Battling Communism (ABC) was a local anti-Communist organization formed by some of Pittsburgh's most prominent citizens, including a judge, in 1949. By identifying individuals it considered to be Communists or Communist sympathizers, the ABC became an important instrument of political repression in the city during the McCarthy years.

7. The Office of Strategic Services (OSS) was formed in 1942 and placed under the jurisdiction of the Joint Chiefs of Staff to engage in intelligence operations abroad and to analyze strategic information.

8. *Pittsburgh Press*, Sept. 29, 1949, p. 14.

9. When workers opposed wage cuts at Carnegie Steel Company's Homestead, Pennsylvania, plant in 1892, a lockout was the result. In the confrontation that ensued, strikers fought a pitched battle with an army of Pinkerton detectives, and martial law was declared. The state militia intervened to crush the workers' resistance, and few of the men were able to get their jobs back. The Amalgamated Association suffered a terrible defeat from which it never really recovered.

An excellent fictional account of three generations of steelworkers in the Monongahela River Valley near Pittsburgh is Thomas Bell's *Out of This Furnace* (Pittsburgh, Pa.: University of Pittsburgh Press, 1976).

10. Under Pennsylvania law between 1886 and 1931, coal operators and steel mill management were allowed to employ their own police forces, which were used largely to disrupt union organizations and protect strikebreakers. This "coal and iron police" became notorious in mining and steel mill towns because they were directly responsible for beatings and even deaths in both industries during the late nineteenth and early twentieth centuries.

11. The Civil Rights Congress (CRC) was founded in 1946 as a successor to the International Labor Defense. It provided both legal aid and publicity in order to mobilize public opinion around cases primarily involving Party members and sympathizers. The CRC was directed by William Patterson and Aubrey Grossman and counted singer Paul Robeson, Congressman Vito Marcantonio of New York City, CIO legal counsel Lee Pressman, and the Reverend Harry F. Ward as sponsors. During the early fifties, the CRC's bail fund trustees, its national executive secretary, and other members of the organization were all jailed for refusing to turn over to the government its list of contributors. The CRC was dissolved under government pressure in 1956.

12. Michael Musmanno, *Across the Street from the Courthouse* (Philadelphia: Dorrance, 1954), p. 53. Concerning Musmanno, later a state supreme court judge, William O. Douglas wrote: "State judges, elected to office, were often mere mouthpieces of the most intolerant members of the community. Michael A. Musmanno of the Pennsylvania Supreme Court was a notorious example of this kind of official." (*The Court Years, 1939–1975* [New York: Random House, 1980], pp. 92–93).

13. Quoted trial dialogue in the following section is from: Volume 1 and 2, Transcript of the Record, Supreme Court of the United States, October Term, 1956, No. 10. *Commonwealth of Pennsylvania* v. *Steve Nelson*, On Writ of Certiorari to the Supreme Court of the Commonwealth of Pennsylvania, Western District (Washington, D.C.: Judd and Detweiler, Printers, June 14, 1956).

14. *Saturday Evening Post*, 223, Nos. 3, 4, 5, July 15, 22, 29, 1950.

Chapter 11: In the Hole

1. The VALB was formed toward the end of the Spanish Civil War with the purpose of continuing the fight against fascism in Spain.

2. This name is fictitious.

3. In the 1920s and 1930s, Chancellor John G. Bowman fired, caused to resign, or failed to renew contracts of several professors for engaging in what he considered to be controversial outside activites. The Pennsylvania General Assembly held public hearings on the University. The University was also placed on the American Association of University Professors' list of institutions that had violated the principles of academic freedom.

4. Under the Internal Security (McCarran) Act in 1950, the U.S. attorney general could petition the Subversive Activities Control Board (SACB) to order an organization to register as Communist-infiltrated. SACB hearings, like those of the House Committee on Un-American activities, tended to degenerate into witch-hunts designed to identify individuals who might be guilty of harboring subversive ideas. The SACB was not abolished until March 27, 1973.

Chapter 12: The Crisis: 1956–1957

1. The term "reform group" was not used at the time. It is used here simply to identify those people who urged a complete reevaluation of the Party's policies and does not suggest a specific political positon or group.

2. Nelson's thinking at this time is reflected in his article, "On a New Party of Socialism," *Political Affairs* (October 1956), pp. 57–65.

Index

PITTSBURGH SERIES IN SOCIAL AND LABOR HISTORY

Maurine Weiner Greenwald, Editor

And the Wolf Finally Came: The Decline of the American Steel Industry
John P. Hoerr

The Battle for Homestead, 1880-1892: Politics, Culture, and Steel
Paul Krause

City at the Point: Essays on the Social History of Pittsburgh
Samuel P. Hays, Editor

The Correspondence of Mother Jones
Edward M. Steel, Editor

Distribution of Wealth and Income in the United States in 1798
Lee Soltow

Don't Call Me Boss: David L. Lawrence, Pittsburgh's Renaissance Mayor
Michael P. Weber

The Inside History of the Carnegie Steel Company
James Howard Bridge

The Shadow of the Mills: Working-Class Families in Pittsburgh, 1870-1907
S. J. Kleinberg

The Speeches and Writings of Mother Jones
Edward M. Steel, Editor

The Steel Workers
John A. Fitch

Trade Unions and the New Industrialisation of the Third World
Roger Southall, Editor

The Transformation of Western Pennsylvania, 1770-1880
R. Eugene Harper

What's a Coal Miner to Do? The Mechanization of Coal Mining
Keith Dix

Women and the Trades
Elizabeth Beardsley Butler

Other titles in the series

The Emergence of a UAW Local, 1936-1939: A Study in Class and Culture
Peter Friedlander

Homestead: The Households of a Mill Town
Margaret F. Byington

The Homestead Strike of 1892
Arthur G. Burgoyne

Steelton: Immigration and Industrialization, 1870-1940
John Bodnar